THE SWISS

WALTER SORELL

THE SWISS

A

CULTURAL PANORAMA

OF

SWITZERLAND

THE BOBBS-MERRILL COMPANY, INC.

NEW YORK   INDIANAPOLIS

The Bobbs-Merrill Company, Inc.
Indianapolis   New York

For
Gaby and André
Ruth and Jean-Pierre

ACKNOWLEDGMENTS

I wish to acknowledge my indebtedness to the many publishers and their authors from whose works I have quoted, to the many librarians and curators of Swiss museums for their advice and assistance, and, above all, to Dr. Max Schäppi, secretary of Pro Helvetia, who made it possible for me to meet many Swiss luminaries and who patiently called my attention to a series of books which might otherwise have eluded me. Both, people and printed material, afforded me new and renewed insight into Swiss cultural accomplishments.

My deep-felt thanks go to all those persons who have spent many hours with me discussing the specific field of their activities and whose very personal feelings for and thoughts about many issues gave me a greater understanding of how they see themselves, their past and present problems. I am particularly grateful that a feeling of friendship has developed from such an interview in one or another case.

I deem it only fair to mention alphabetically some of those who, through their active interest in this book as much as through casual remarks, have greatly furthered and facilitated my work: Professor Max Bill, Dr. Erika Billeter, Professor Dr. Elisabeth Brock-Sulzer, Alexander Chasen, Max Frisch, Heiner Hesse, Samuel Hirschi, Dr. Jolande Jacobi, Dr. Paul Kamer, Dr. Hugo Lötscher, Hans Neuburg, Professor Dr. Kurt Pahlen, Professor Alfred Roth, Dr. Daniel Roth, Peter Schifferli, Dr. Edmund Stadler, Dr. Werner Weber, Irene Wydler-Roth.

My thanks also go to some of my good friends, including my wife, whose encouragements were meaningful, and especially to Ruth and Jean-Pierre Vuilleumier for their help in researching this book and to Penny West for her indefatigable energy, criticism, and advice. Last but not least, I gratefully think of those many people who must remain unnamed but who gave me a great deal of food for thought. Glimpses of their attitudes and ideas have helped form a total image which, I hope, is reflected in this book.

CONTENTS

GENESIS AND SOME REVELATIONS xi

PART ONE

THE CREATIVE SPIRIT OF THE SWISS

RELIGION: FROM ZWINGLI TO BARTH 3 HUMANISM AND THE
REFORMATION 3 CALVINISM AND THE CONSEQUENCES 9 THE
CATHOLIC IMAGE 13 NEW ROADS 17 MAN, THE FREE PART-
NER OF GOD 19 **EDUCATION, OR THE BELIEF IN LOVE** 23
NOTHING IS LOST THAT IS DONE WITH LOVE 23 THE REVOLU-
TION THAT WAS ROUSSEAU 28 FROM BURCKHARDT TO BURCK-
HARDT 31 A DREAM FULFILLED 47 **SCIENCE + A FEW RAN-
DOM REMARKS** 49 THE DREAM OF THE MIND 49 INDUSTRY,
INGENUITY, AND POLITICS 54 THE ADVENTURE OF HEALING
AND EXPLORING 58 MAN AND THE SECRETS OF HIS SUBCON-
SCIOUS 66 **THE LITERARY LINGUAE OF THE SWISS** 79
FRENCH 79 ITALIAN 93 GERMAN 99 **THE VISUAL IMAGE
BEYOND HODLER** 127 **MUSIC TO SWISS EARS** 150 **THE THEA-
TRE'S THE THING** 165 **DANCE: INFLUENCES AND EFFECTS** 181
ARCHITECTURE AND LANDSCAPE 196

PART TWO

THE CREATIVE ATMOSPHERE OF SWITZERLAND

SOME CAME TO STAY 205 NECROPOLIS 205 CASTALIA 220
SANCTUARY 236 **SOME CAME TO SEE** 246 FROM CELLINI TO
KLEIST 246 A ROMANTIC VICTORIAN TREND 252 STRINDBERG
AND TOLSTOY 259 **CODA** 265

BIBLIOGRAPHY

INDEX

GENESIS AND SOME REVELATIONS

THERE are many motivations for writing a book. But whatever they may be, a great part of the writer's inspiration should be provoked by a desire to accept a challenge. Through his work should speak a good measure of intoxication, that kind of enthusiasm that creates a sense of excitement without which the *Gestalt* of verbal images falls flat. By the same token, the writer's enthusiasm should neither color nor discolor his intent and message.

Probably many latent desires and one strange incident have made me write about the cultural achievements of the Swiss, a people of six million unevenly divided souls, tongues, minds, backgrounds, and idiosyncrasies. One can say very little about the hidden powers prompting us into doing something which, in the light of its sudden existence, seems to be the result of a thousand and one coincidences. One of them is certainly connected with my travels through Switzerland at that youthful and dangerous age when falling-in-love is obligatory and one's impressions gain an almost physical intensity.

The statement with which Herbert Lüthy (1918–   ), Swiss essayist and philosopher-historian, opened his little book, *Switzerland as Antithesis*, intrigued me: "Striking family portraits are rarely the work of members of the family. Perhaps someone not being Swiss should be able to draw a good likeness of Switzerland." This remark insinuates that the aesthetic distance badly needed for the creation of any work is, if not paramount, of great advantage to the observer of a scene to be described. Obviously, one gets a better view and perspective looking in on something from outside than from being within, even though such a vantage point does not necessarily assure a more objective observation, reaction, and presentation.

The choice of any subjective matter is self-revealing and an act of subjective determination. Also, the incident propelling this writer's decision to create a panoramic image of Switzerland's cultural contribution to Western civilization speaks for itself.

It was on one of my lecture tours in America that a faculty mem-

ber of a university invited me to come to his home in order to meet
with the dean and other colleagues. We sat around the fireplace, and
our conversation covered much slightly elevated cocktail ground.
In discussing the accomplishments of nations that have gone
through great challenges and upheavals, wars and revolutions,
someone compared the achievements of Italy—which certainly has
had a great deal of triumphs and tribulations—with those of Switzerland.

"Look," said my host, an erudite man and brilliant physicist,
"how invaluable are Italy's cultural treasures and humanistic
achievements in comparison with those of Switzerland, which has
but suffered from peace and prosperity for the last four hundred
years. And what did the Swiss produce? Holes in the cheese and
watches to tell us the precise time!"

I felt challenged, as I would watching somebody being wronged
who cannot defend himself. "Six millions of Swiss people, herdsmen
who have gradually become urbanized, are compared with fifty
millions of Italians, or with forty millions of Frenchmen, or sixty
millions of Germans. Are you not falsifying facts in your mind?"

"We must not slight them," another voice was heard. "They produced more than holes in the cheese and clocks. They are fabulous
hotelkeepers and bankers."

I loathe hearing generalizations and clichés playing pingpong in
livingrooms in order to keep the conversation going. "I love to
straighten historic facts, if you don't mind . . ."

"Not at all," my host said quickly in a jovial tone. "Why don't
you have another drink?"

"Or would you prefer a cup of coffee?" his wife seconded. "With
a drop of milk—?"

"That reminds me of a story I must have read or heard somewhere," a theologian said, laughing away half his joke. "When our
Lord created the world the Swiss asked for the biggest mountains,
loveliest valleys, lakes, and pastures. When, on the seventh day, the
Lord wanted to rest and asked the Swiss for a glass of milk, they
quickly brought it to Him. He thanked them. 'Oh, that's all right,'
they said. 'That makes one franc fifty without service.' "

My sense of humor was engaged, and I joined the laughers. But
I could not help thinking that, since the days the Phoenicians invented money, rarely have individuals or nations been blind to its
value. "I thought the Americans invented the worship of the golden
calf," said my hostess, who was apparently eager to come to my
rescue. At that point an academic bore and expert in economics

monopolized the conversation for some time, and little Switzerland was forgotten.

That day I decided to write this book.

The characteristics and complexities of Switzerland are not easily categorized because one cannot force the Swiss into the configuration of a nation with *one* distinct profile. The idea of the melting pot has at closer examination never stood the test in America, a country of immigrants, and would be altogether wrong when applied to the Swiss, whose major distinction is having kept their four separate linguistic, ethnographic, topographic, economic, cultural, religious, and folkloric qualities fully alive through more than 350 years while living together in a federal republic.

It must remain an object of wonder that such splendid manifoldness is kept strongly unified, that the Swiss feel oriented towards living together in a "native" land, while within this land separatist movements are going on all the time (particularly in the Jura, which, being a part of the canton Berne and essentially French, desires autonomic rule). The German, French, and Italian Swiss people are, first and last, Swiss before they are anything else. They may be fully aware of their linguistic and ethnic links, but they also greatly appreciate the borders which separate them from their neighbors. Moreover, one only has to cross the frontiers on all three sides into Switzerland in order to be struck by the difference between the Swiss and their neighborly brothers. The Swiss, as a generic totality, would never think in terms of giving up or losing their Swiss identity. They have a proverb that says, "When one shuts one eye, one does not hear everything." It is only too true that they have learned to keep an observant and watchful eye open, so that they do not have to hear everything.

In dealing with the humanistic aspects and cultural accomplishments of the Swiss, we find many surprising and contradictory facts. They have achieved a far-reaching splendid isolation as a national and geographic unity within the center of Europe. Through the centuries the Swiss have cultivated a sacred conservatism while bringing forth some of the most revolutionary minds and most fervent religious reformers. Their conservative attitudes have deeply-lying roots in their being a people of peasant stock, although their peasants are dying out more rapidly than is the peasantry in any other European region.

They have acquired an unsophisticated sophistication. When in

1967 the city of Basle had to decide whether to buy two Picasso paintings, the majority of voters asked their city fathers to spend six million francs for the Picassos. Another interesting fact is the exceptional paucity of light-entertainment literature written by the Swiss; their writers show a strong predilection towards purposefulness, social awareness, and civic-mindedness.

The Swiss have aggravated their quadrilingual problem by keeping alive their German dialect as *the* colloquial idiom in all social stratifications. Moreover, the variety of local versions of Switzerdütsch is as confusing as it is surprising. Most writers using German as their expressive idiom preserve—partly purposely, partly unconsciously—a distinct Swiss flavor by interweaving words and phrases common in their colloquial usage.

To the puzzling and problematic question of why Switzerland has for so long attracted artists from all over the world to stay for a short while or forever within its boundaries, Max Frisch was quick in pointing out to me that it is a country of refuge because it offers an atmosphere of political and social noninvolvement, briefly, because of Switzerland's *Geschichtslosigkeit* (lack of history). In some cases financial advantages may have been inviting, but essentially Switzerland has been a refuge for radicals and for those who wanted to retire to an atmosphere conducive to creativity, as much as to an atmosphere of peacefulness and security safeguarded by traditional neutrality.

The Swiss are a literary people; in relation to their population, Zürich, Basle, Berne, Lausanne, and Geneva have more bookstores than any other big cities in the world. One of the reasons humanism played such a great role in Switzerland was that Roman culture and, in its wake, Christianity, had a strong and lasting influence on Swiss territory.

The Romans were preceded by the Helvetians, who were related to the culturally advanced Gauls. Next came the Rhaetians with their Romansh, the Rhaeto-Romanic language, presumably an Illyrian tribe and now a small group of about 50,000 inhabitants living in the Grisons. In the days of the *Völkerwanderung* two Germanic tribes came to, and settled in, what is now Swiss territory: The Alemannians and the Burgundians. The latter soon became latinized, but the Alemannic people kept certain Teutonic characteristics alive. They have contributed a great deal to the seventy per cent of the Swiss population now living in German-speaking cantons and have not readily and totally absorbed the culture of their conquered country. Due to their Nordic temperament, they displayed an ambivalent attitude towards the remnants of the Roman conquerors and their culture for some time. Some vestiges of this culture are still extant, such as Aventicum, Vindonissa, or Augusta Rauracorum, Roman settlements that had amphitheatres in which were applauded not only gladiatorial fights but also performances of the famous Roman mimes, dancers, and musicians.

Being a composite of parts of Germany, France, and Italy, Switzerland could never develop a unified culture with a single and central core from which its arts could unfold and grow. It has a variety of folkloric backgrounds and a threefold verbal resonance from cultures neighboring its borders. In this way, Switzerland's limitations have also become its great potentialities. It has always felt free and independent, but it could never help being constantly fructified by the semen that the winds carried across its borders, nor could it help spilling its amazing abundance of creativity across the very same borders into the lands of its neighbors and across the seas. In other words, through the very gates and with the same speed and intensity with which so many strangers came, many of Switzerland's great creative minds left. The Swiss artists have often felt frustrated by the smallness of everything Swiss and narrowed-in by the overt and latent narrow-mindedness of their compatriots, an aspect about which more will be said in the concluding chapter.

Those who came to Switzerland found what they searched for, a place of visual inspiration and retreat, the last imaginary ivory tower, a fictitious West of Eden. For those artists who have a need for a vacuous freedom and an isolated mindscape of peaceful beauty, Switzerland has remained a sanctuary. Nowhere but on this figurative island can one be so removed from the world's ills and exultations. And nowhere else can one be close enough to all that is happening in the world to enjoy or to bear it, whatever it may be, in condensed, hygienically wrapped, small doses.

The shelves of the bookstores and libraries all over the world contain innumerable books on Switzerland, describing its scenic wonders, outlining its history and ethnic background, praising and prizing the comforts of its commercialized hospitality, discussing its industrial and economic accomplishments. Over the years books have appeared on the international literary scene, books which dealt with certain Swiss personalities and aspects of cultural life. No publication has as yet made the attempt to paint an all-embracing canvas of Switzerland's cultural achievements.

Man is accustomed to believing mainly in figures and statistics, in what he can weigh and measure. There are treasures in print, color, shape, and sound which never show up on any financial balance sheet. This book is concerned with these real and yet intangible aspects of Switzerland. Without intending to be encyclopaedic, this book is interested in recording the cultural contribution of about six million Central Europeans to Western civilization, in the main originally peasants and herdsmen who have now become strongly urbanized. In brief, I have attempted to write a very personal, however imperfect, cultural Baedeker through Switzerland.

PART ONE

THE CREATIVE SPIRIT OF THE SWISS

RELIGION:
FROM ZWINGLI TO BARTH

HUMANISM AND THE REFORMATION

AN interesting aspect of the concurrencies of life and religion, of the arts and humanism in Switzerland is that so many of this country's great sons have emerged from the background of the church, were sons of pastors, and have wrestled in one way or another with God and with doubt.

It is not mere coincidence that Pestalozzi studied theology but was forced to abandon the thought of an ecclesiastical career because of his political activities. Nor need we wonder about Friedrich Dürrenmatt, who, as the son of the Pastor of Konolfingen, studied theology and philosophy in Berne before turning to the graphic and literary arts. He once called himself a "grim-doggedly writing Protestant" and realized that "The difficulties a Protestant has with the art of the drama are exactly those of his faith." Or how about Jacob Burckhardt, who began his studies in Basle as a student of theology to fulfill his father's wish to have his son follow him in the clergy?

In the beginning it was Burckhardt's desire to accept the task of a pastor, but he was soon to give up this idea when his teacher de Wette interpreted the Bible with the critical approach of a raging rationalist. It undermined his faith in orthodox beliefs. Under the spell of his teacher, Burckhardt wrote to a friend: ". . . every day there disappears under his hands a fragment of the traditional teaching of the Church. Today I have finally discovered that he regards the birth of Christ a myth—and I with him. . . ."

In man's everlasting struggle with himself and that of his soul with God, the Swiss were in the forefront, fighting orthodoxy as reformers of the dogma or as restorers of the dogma seen in the light of truth and in its significance in time and eternity. No one can doubt the bravery of a Zwingli or a Bullinger, who, in the tumultuous days of the Renaissance, dared to break away from certain Catholic tenets in order to establish a religious and personal freedom which seemed to them dictated by the persuasion of their inner faith. Nor can we question the peaceful reformation accompanying our own tumultuous days in which men like Karl Barth have called vociferously for a "change of direction in the thinking of evangelical theology."

3

The geographic and historic crossroads of Europe having their virtual center in Switzerland may have contributed in more than one way to this country's key position in spiritual aspects. More than anywhere else can we find here an actual, practical, and never clearly defined amalgamation of deep-rooted conservatism with revolutionary concepts. The reason for it must be found in the enclosure and penetration of Switzerland by her three formidable neighbors, the papal power from the south confronted by the revolutionary spirit of Gallic hot-headedness and Teutonic stubbornness.

This contrasting combination resulting in an ambivalent tendency may also explain Basle's attraction for Desiderius Erasmus (c. 1466–1536), who considered this town's atmosphere just right for the spirit of his revolutionary conservatism. It certainly was in Basle that he wrote his finest works, and where, after many years spent as a wandering scholar, he settled in November 1521 and found the most satisfactory humanistic congeniality of the many places he had lived in. At that time Basle was a focal point of scholastic knowledge, a university city famous for its publishing houses and its rich men with their intellectual interests, attracting such divergent talents as painters and preachers.

Among the latter was John Oecolampadius (1482–1531), a native of Weinsberg in Württemberg, who came to Basle as a printer, lecturer, professor of theology, and preacher. He lectured to large audiences in three languages. He had befriended Erasmus, which did not preclude his being a loyal friend and ally of Huldrich Zwingli. Oecolampadius' reputation grew when, in 1526, he acquitted himself successfully at a disputation in Baden where he had almost alone to defend the cause of the Reformation against a redoubtable Roman Catholic team. Two years later in Berne the disputation was packed with reformers, and it was characteristic of Oecolampadius that he preached "On the Love of Christ for the Church." He was mainly responsible for effecting the most bloodless reformation in Basle.

For many years Erasmus played the role of an editor for the Basle publisher Froben. After the triumph of the Reformation he left the city for Freiburg in Breisgau, from which, however, he returned seven years later, aging and sick. It was as if he wanted to die in Basle, and his fate willed it so. That very year of his return he died without benefit of the sacraments, which shocked Luther. But Boniface Amerbach (1496–1564), his heir and executor, a great humanist in his own right, said that Erasmus "in a most holy manner left us with his entire hope for Christ, the Saviour, whose name was on his lips to the very end." We have it from Amerbach that the last words of Erasmus were "dear God," uttered in his native Dutch as *Lieve God*, after having murmured in Latin: "O Jesu misericordia. Domine libera me. Domine face finem. Domine miserere mei."*

If we wish to imagine a humanist of intellectual elegance and wit, then this description fits Erasmus best. The range of his knowledge and his brilliant style, with a flair for Lucianic satire, characterize his fame. In the beginning Erasmus' criticism of the church gave Luther hope of having found an ally, and the Italian cardinal, Aleandro Girolano, who was sent to lead the opposition against Luther at the Diet of Worms, rightly denounced Erasmus as the real author of schism. ("Everything that Luther demands," Erasmus wrote Zwingli, "I myself have thought, but not so violent and without that language going to extremes.")

Erasmus and Luther soon became involved in disputes, attacks, and counterattacks. As the great humanist he was, Erasmus dreamt of a "reflorescentia," a rejuvenation of the Christian idea in returning to its once Nazarene purity, not of a rebellion against the church. When Luther reproached Erasmus for his "peace-loving theology, you don't care about the truth," Erasmus replied: "What happens to truth when men are embroiled in a war of religion? Concordia! concordia! concordia!" Erasmus had a deep concern for freedom and peace. The hypersensitive aesthete in him was repelled by the violent and vulgar aspects of the Reformation, always a by-product of any revolutionary movement.

Erasmus had fervent admirers among the Reformers even through the periods in which he alienated them. Among them was Huldrych Zwingli (1484–1531), the most impressive and strongest personality of the Swiss ecclesiastic revolution and an influential force in the Reformation movement. But before speaking about him, I must say a few words about Thomas Lüber (1524–1583), born in the Aargau, who became an important adherent of the Zürich theological school. A devout Zwinglian, he was closely associated with the introduction of Reformed Protestantism in Germany and turned into an avowed opponent of the Calvinist system of

* O Jesus, have mercy. Lord, deliver me. Lord, bring the end. Lord, have mercy upon me.

church discipline. He was a humanist and physician, known under the name of Thomas Erastus. His major work is a treatise on excommunication, arguing that it is unscriptural to excommunicate and deny someone the sacraments who wishes to receive them. Although the doctrine of the supremacy of the state in ecclesiastical affairs is now known as "Erastianism," Erastus nowhere expressed the thought of the magistrate being responsible for the government of the church. However, he felt that in a Christian society the punishment of sin was a matter for the magistrate.

Zwingli studied in Basle and then in Berne, where his teacher Heinrich Wölflin instilled in him lasting enthusiasm for the classics and such a deep love for music that theology might almost have lost him. He was an impressionable man with a great desire for knowledge, with insight into the tangible powers and intangible beauties of life, with a sensuous but also sensual feeling for all fibres of existence. What probably was the propelling force in Zwingli was his being very human and ambitious.

When he was ordained and appointed Pastor of Glarus in 1506, he not only wanted to be a good shepherd to each soul, but he also believed it to be his pastoral duty to guide his congregation in political as well as moral matters. When he served as chaplain with the Swiss forces, he became vehemently opposed to the mercenary system. The stern attitude he took—anything he approached became a significant issue and challenge—soon involved him in hostilities in Glarus, and, though not forced to resign, he deemed it wise to move to Einsiedeln. There he had the opportunity to preach to the many pilgrims, to study at a convent whose abbot was a humanist, and to meditate. It was an important period of transition in his life in which he came closer to the evangelical understanding of the Scriptures, to the significance of worldly and civic matters as they relate to man's conscience, and to the problem of sensuality.

Before he was appointed people's priest at the Grossmünster in Zürich, he had begun to preach his new convictions—this was in the same year in which Luther refused to recant—and emerged from an indulgence crisis, which had involved the Franciscan Bernhard Samson, as a sharp-witted castigator of social evils and ecclesiastic abuses. In Zürich he sought approval of the city's council to preach what he referred to as the "true divine Scriptures," and it was through his sermons against fasting and clerical celibacy that the Swiss people were aroused and put into a frame of rebellious spirit. His Oetenbach addresses about *The Clarity and Certainty of the Word of God* were crucial for the beginning and for the final victory of the Zürich Reformation. His great challenge to

Rome was neatly packed into *Sixty-Seven Articles*, in the consequences of which his rebellious contentions were, in the main, adopted and gradually put into effect.

He publicly celebrated his marriage to Anna Reinhard a year later, and the liturgical reforms were begun. Zwingli opposed the Lenten observances, had images and pictures removed, the Mass replaced by a simple service, and the baptismal office reformed. He successfully argued for acceptance of the Holy Word as the only basis of truth; he dared thunder the denial of all authority invested in the Pope and the Church. In his eyes, the Church could only be born of the Word of God and Christ alone was its head. Zwingli challenged the greatest powers on earth, but he succeeded because the governing council in Zürich approved his dissenting positions, and Zwingli never forgot who helped him to succeed.

Since there has never been any movement protesting the *status quo* and trying to change conditions without creating in its wake a radical wing dissatisfied with the scope and tactics employed, we observe the same during the struggle of the Reformation: groups came into being which would not give allegiance to any form of reformed Christianity. Such a strong and troublesome movement was the one of the Anabaptists, which had its origins in Zürich. It is fascinating to read today—and it almost sounds like a twentieth-century report—that a group of young intellectuals crystallized among the "Swiss brethren," humanistically inspired youths very close to Zwingli, and rebelled against his seeming subservience to the magistrates, against his hesitancy and then unwillingness to inaugurate swiftly thoroughgoing reforms.

As in the late sixties of the twentieth century the rebellious youths emerged from a well-to-do middle class. Moreover, those rebellious leaders of the early sixteenth century were such sons of the old patrician families as Conrad Grebel, Felix Manz, and Georg Blaurock, all highly educated humanists. They broke with Zwingli on the issue of establishing a free church separated from the state. Their emphasis was on a voluntary believers' church, and they rejected all forms of warfare and aimed at high ethics of love and a form of holy living. The sacrament of baptism became a focal point of their fight, a conspicuous symptom rather than the real basis of their viewpoint. The first adult baptism took place at Zollikon, then outside of Zürich, early in 1525. This movement had a hypnotic effect on the masses. A particularly strong group existed in Sankt Gallen.

Their intransigent defiance had revolutionary implications which their teachings did not conceal. The establishment recognized the explosive danger in this radical movement. Very soon a forceful reaction was put into motion. First, they were expulsed from one city after another, a fact which, of course, promoted the missionary aspect of their nonviolent religious fervor. The next step led to imprisonment of the early Anabaptist leaders, many of whom died in prison or were executed. In order to save the movement, a more conservative wing of the Anabaptists, under the leadership of Michael Sattler, drew up a public confession in Schleitheim which was a kind of apologia, in part only, concentrating rather on the repudiation of the extreme elements within the Anabaptist camp.

Zwingli felt compelled to act against the demands of these extremists and radical rebels since his conception of a Christian commonwealth saw life as something indivisible as to private and public morality, and as a sounding board for the Gospel. What he visualized was a noble image of his city as a prophetic community in which the Church could rely on the magistracy, and the worldly powers in turn on the ecclesiastics. Of course Zwingli was not only a dreamer; he was also a rationalist who saw the victory of his doctrines assured by the support of the civil powers. In principle, Zwingli envisioned a Church founded upon the republican basis of the congregation, and he was convinced that only through political reform could Protestantism become established in Europe.

As a Swiss patriot he saw the outside pressures against the fortress of his ideals menacingly growing, and he became intoxicated with a local patriotism which was identical with Zürich imperialism, most manifest in the determined way in which he dealt with Sankt Gallen and Waldshut. He persuaded Berne and Basle to follow Zürich's example in its revolt against Rome. In order to fortify his own position he strove to build the "Christian Civic League," particularly in view of the obstinacy of the five forest cantons—Lucerne, Zug, Schwyz, Uri, and Unterwalden—which, remaining faithful to the Pope, resisted the Reformation. After a short-lived truce, Zürich imposed a trade embargo on those cantons which, unwilling to bow to force in good old Swiss fashion, used force to fight back. During the battle of Kappel, Zwingli was killed and his body mutilated as if he had been a traitor, which in the eyes of the southern Catholics he was. Thus he paid for an ill-fated adventure into high politics.

Heinrich Bullinger (1504–1575) succeeded Zwingli at the Grossmünster to Zürich, where he had worked with the great reformer, and continued to solidify the Zwinglian doctrine in the immediate years to follow. A less ambitious figure than his predecessor, and cleverly staying away from any political involvements, he made it possible for Zürich to remain a significant center of the movement without exerting any dominating influence on the Reformation in the south.

Bullinger, married to the former nun Anna Adlischweiler, was a great scholar who had his hand in the First Helvetic Confession (1536). However, unable to reach an agreement with Luther on the Eucharist, he deepened the Zwinglian conception. Also, having kept closely in touch with the men exiled by Mary Tudor, Bullinger was able to exert his influence on the English settlement under Elizabeth I, a fact which can be readily deduced from his *Zürich Letters* and a series of sermons, *The Decades*.

Bullinger lived long enough to witness the rise of Calvinism and—unwittingly, or being of a far more conciliatory nature than the strong-willed Zwingli—finally helped the Swiss Reformation depart from Zwinglian to Calvinist doctrine. This was mainly brought about when Bullinger came to terms with Calvin on the question of the Lord's Supper, as laid down in the *Consensus Tigurinus* (1549). Zwingli had maintained that the Holy Scripture does not teach Christ's corporeal presence in the bread and wine at the Lord's Supper, whereas for Calvin, the Lord's Supper was a sacred communication of Christ's flesh and blood, transfusing His life into believers and thus uniting by the Spirit "things which are separated in space," while truly presenting his body and blood through the symbols of bread and wine.

However much or little John Calvin's doctrines may vary from those of Zwingli, the fact remains that Zwingli laid down the groundwork on which Calvin built a far more comprehensive theological system. But in eschatological terms, Zwingli, as much as Calvin or Luther, felt engaged in a struggle with Antichrist for the purification of the Church. Without accepting a quietist or pacifist attitude, these reformers lived with the apocalyptic image deeply impressed upon them, nurtured as it was by the turbulence of the time and by the return to Ur-Christianity or the Scripture.

CALVINISM AND THE CONSEQUENCES

IN the final analysis it is Martin Luther and John Calvin (1509–1564) who are most strongly associated with the Reformation, and no one can be more German than Luther, just as no one can be more Swiss than Calvin—even though he was a native of France.

Calvin, destined by his father for an ecclesiastical career, only briefly deviated from it towards the study of law. Very early his genius was noticeable in the unusual brilliance with which he discharged himself in college disputations. As a master of the classics and armed with a strong feeling for medieval thought, he sharpened his agility and gift for articulation with his ever-widening humanistic curiosity.

The minds of certain geniuses are destined to deepen and broaden the flow of existent thoughts; others cannot help but break through established boundaries into new realms of experience, groping towards symbols, forms, and thoughts that create a new world of awareness. Calvin soon forsook the formal logic of scholasticism, which he referred to as a "science of wind." The environmental influences to which he became exposed helped in his development. Among his early friends were Nicholas and Michel Cop, the sons of the king's Swiss physician, a leading humanist scholar of medicine.

Calvin mentioned his "sudden conversion" in the Preface to his *Commentary on the Psalms*. This conversion took place in his early twenties. When he had reached his twenty-third year, he by-passed being ordained and traveled to Paris, Orléans, and Poitiers. More and more he was drawn into the circles of Protestants whose intellectual leadership fell upon him with an almost decreed inescapability. In 1534 he sensed danger to his physical being—the militant Protestant Étienne de la Forge, in whose house he had lived while working on Seneca, was later martyred—and fled to Basle. There Calvin was welcomed by the leaders of the Reformation among whom he lived, studying and writing, under the assumed name of Martianus Lucanius. He gave full account of Protestant belief in a work entitled *Institutes of the Christian Religion*. It contained all his basic precepts, which, in the course of the years, he was to reorganize and develop, to solidify and elaborate.

Calvinism was born and spelled out at that time in Basle where the book was printed and published. His thoughts went beyond such obvious notions as the rejection of papal authority and the acceptance of justification by faith alone. Foreshadowed by other reformers, the fundamental doctrine of predestination and grace was presented in the *Institutes*, generally considered to be one of the finest theological works of all time.

The city far more than Basle to be identified with Calvin is Geneva, which at that point of history was not yet a member of the Swiss confederation but had already entered into a contract of joint citizenship with Berne, if for no reason other than to protect itself against Savoy. While Calvin's *Institutes* went to press in Basle, he left for Northern Italy intending to return and continue his studies in that city of learning. But, caught by the war between Francis I and Charles V, he was forced to make a detour, which brought him to Geneva.

Guillaume Farel, another French iconoclast, had found refuge in Geneva. Farel's story somewhat parallels Calvin's. On Swiss soil Farel received permission to spread the reformed gospel throughout the canton of Berne. The powerful bishop of Geneva expelled Farel, who, after a public disputation, won the favor of the citizens. In 1535 the town council adopted formally the Reformation. However, Farel's position in Geneva was not quite secure. This was mainly due to the fact that this fiery reformer was a poor thinker and organizer.

When Calvin arrived in Geneva, Farel entreated him to assist in the organization of the new Protestant republic. Calvin reluctantly accepted this bid for help and inconspicuously began to lecture on Paul's epistles in the church of St. Pierre in the autumn of 1536. He was later made a pastor there. Officially, Farel remained the leading figure in Geneva although Calvin's influence became increasingly noticeable as the devising spirit of compulsory education and close moral supervision of Geneva's gay-living citizens. Long before the Reformation the Genevan laws were known for their inclusion of severe moral restrictions, but their strict enforcement was now controlled by the church rather than by the magistrate —an unpleasant novelty for many citizens who cherished their independence. These ill-feelings became particularly obvious when the citizens were forced under threat of expulsion to make public avowal of a confession of faith written by Farel. A far more important and controversial document emerged from this period with Calvin's impressive *Instruction in Faith*, composed in support of his conception of public education.

The Genevans first supported the Farel-Calvin policies, but within a year the opposition gained control. It was not an anti-Reformation party, but it seems that Calvin went too far too fast, and the new leaders veered towards Berne, which enjoyed a more relaxed liturgical and moral pattern of reform. In consequence of these events, Calvin and Farel had to leave Geneva. With devotion and gratitude Farel worked unceasingly for Calvin's return to Geneva from his new headquarters in Basle and Neuchâtel.

Calvin lived in Basle and Strasbourg for three years, preaching and writing. In 1540 he married Idelette de Bure, whom he had converted from Anabaptism, and found in her "the precious help" he often needed in his struggles and many illnesses, referring to her as "the excellent companion of my life." During this time Roman Catholicism tried to fight its way back in Geneva, an attempt which was frustrated mainly by a letter Calvin wrote, one of the strongest apologies and appeals for the Reformation. He was entreated by the council to return to Geneva. Again, he agreed reluctantly, and arrived in September 1541.

More than ever he was determined to enforce all the reforms which, meanwhile, had matured in his mind. Essentially, he constructed a government based on the subordination of the state to the Church. The Bible had to be accepted as the sole source of God's laws—similar to Zwingli's concept—which had to be obeyed according to ecclesiastical interpretation, and their obeyance had to be enforced by the magistrate. Calvin's concept of life was a total one, the function of state and Church clearly defined, with his ethic beliefs extended to all areas of existence.

All his life Calvin was involved in theological controversies of which those with Michael Servetus, a brilliant scholar and eccentric fanatic, blacken Calvin's record. Servetus' denial of the prime doctrine of Catholic *and* Protestant orthodoxy, the Trinity, aroused the fury of both denominations. Moreover, he believed in the celestial flesh of Christ, in Anabaptism, and in psychopannychism, which assumes that the human soul sleeps or dies with the human body. There can be no doubt that Servetus was a serious scholar of the Bible, honestly and passionately devoted to Christ.

Servetus was naïve enough to have opened a correspondence with Calvin, in whom he may have seen a related iconoclastic soul searching, as did he, for the truth. He sent many letters to Calvin and a manuscript in which he expounded his ideas. In some of his letters Servetus expressed his desire to meet and debate with the reformer in Geneva. After a while Calvin left Servetus' letters unanswered, although he kept the manuscript. Servetus eventually rewrote it and had an edition of 1,000 copies printed in Vienne. He was condemned to die at the stake by the Catholics, but miraculously escaped during the trial. Whether it was his belief in Calvin's assistance, as a co-dissenting voice, or just quixotic stupidity, Servetus escaped to Geneva where he was recognized and arrested.

Before his capture Calvin had assured Farel that if Servetus should ever be caught in Geneva, he would personally see to it that this heretic would not leave alive. He did not. His trial lasted more than two months. The other Reformed Swiss churches were invited to give their theological and judicial counsel. On theological grounds they found Servetus guilty and recommended punishment, but there is no evidence that these spokesmen asked for the death penalty. Calvin pressed for execution by beheading. True to the spirit of the Inquisition, Servetus was burnt alive at Champel on October 27, 1553. The only positive result from this public display of successful rebels burning rebels, in the name of their newly established power, was a Protestant controversy on the death penalty for heresy. The pros were as vociferous as the cons.

Calvinism went through several forms and reinterpretations, but it spread throughout the Western world and achieved its purest forms through the Scottish reformer John Knox and the Puritans in England, many of whom settled in New England in the Western hemisphere. The reformation in which the Swiss were most significantly involved took place at a decisive change in history, the rebirth of antiquity coinciding with the birth of modern man. The world was shifting from a medieval agrarian economy to a commercial and, later, industrial era. Money and the growing acquisitiveness of man became manifest in everyday existence.

The forces unleashed during the Renaissance, of which the Reformation was only one aspect, the intellectual energy and daring vitality, the expansive search for man's identity and the meaning of life—all have become the trademark of modern man. While Luther did not fully realize these significant changes, desiring a return to a primitive simplicity which he associated with the Ur-image of Christianity, Calvin's concepts took the newborn capitalism into account by stressing and stimulating trade and production, although not forgetting to point to the dangers of self-indulgence and exploitation. The virtues of sobriety, thrift, and diligence were not only essential for the achievement of the reign of God on earth, they were also prescribed as the pillars on which a successful community and industrial economy must rest. This may have placed the Swiss one step ahead of other nations in a world of constantly growing commercialism.*

THE CATHOLIC IMAGE

THE Catholics, of course, were here first. They are strongest in the so-called Ur-cantons. About twenty per cent of the Swiss population is Catholic. The nerve center and carrier of Catholic culture

---

* In his editorial, "On the Nobility of Old Age," in *The New York Times* of September 23, 1970, James Reston has his mother say that "the trouble now is that people expect so much and deserve so little. The great thing about Calvinism . . . is that you expect so little that you are always ahead of the game."

from the days of the early Roman settlements have always been the monasteries, of which a few gained international fame.

One of them is St. Gallen. The name itself goes back to the Irish monk Gallus who came to this region as a missionary at the beginning of the seventh century. Gallus was a man with charisma, and among the many legends connected with him is the one of the bear who took a fancy to the monk, shared his meals with him, and is said to have prayed with him. The animal was immortalized for all that in the coat of arms of the city of St. Gallen. The mission there soon began to flourish as a Benedictine monastery.

As early as 830 the monastery was alive with scholastic activity and soon after became famous as a seat of learning in theology as well as in the natural sciences. In spite of many entanglements in wars over the centuries, the monastery's library remained intact. It is today one of the most priceless treasures of the country, having over 100,000 volumes, 2,000 of them handwritten from the Irish and Carolingian times. The library also has a rare collection of early printed works and manuscript B of the Old High German *Nibelungen* saga. As in most of these monasteries the monks translated Latin texts into German, thereby furthering a consistent development of the written language. Some of the monks with artistic inclinations did pioneer work in music and rhetoric.

St. Gallen went through some quite troubled times, particularly in 1403 when it was defeated by its neighboring Appenzellers. The town around the monastery grew to a considerable size and there were frictions between the populace and the abbot in the middle of the fifteenth century, a condition which worsened during the height of the Reformation. Mayor Joachim Vadian, a humanist and medical man of great potentiality, joined the reformers, who occupied the monastery and destroyed all "graven images." After Zwingli's death the monastery was re-established and, as a symbol of past frictions, was separated from the town by a thick wall still visible today. And visible, indeed, is its baroque cathedral with its impressive eighteenth-century dome.

There are two more important monasteries of the Benedictine Order. The abbey in Engelberg was founded in the early twelfth century and experienced, after many difficult periods, a rise to considerable importance. Its library offers the works of the so-called Engelberg *Schreibschule* of the twelfth century and handwritten manuscripts of some mystics. The abbey runs a Gymnasium and Lyceum, but its greatest fame rests with its rich tradition as a place where good music has been furthered.

The third Benedictine cloister is Einsiedeln in the heart of the Ur-cantons, Schwyz. It was originally a hermitage where the hermit Meinrad was murdered in 861. He was later canonized. The Bishop of Metz built a monastery there which achieved its reputation for its many learned abbots as much as for its century-old horse-breeding. It was in Einsiedeln, as we said, where Zwingli found a haven of freedom and a place for meditation. Also Einsiedeln has a beautiful baroque cathedral with a huge square leading to its gates. Every five years Calderon's *The Great World Theatre* is performed on this square by lay actors recruited from the townspeople.

Chur was the first Christian center with the oldest church north of the Alps under the Romans. It had a turbulent history without losing anything of its importance. Emperor Diocletian made Chur his administrative center of the north. In the tenth century the emperors of the European north became interested in what is known as the Holy Roman Empire of the German Nation, and because of Chur's strategic situation this bishopry profited from it.

By the twelfth century Chur was the powerful seat of a rich bishop. His difficulties with the population began in 1422, when it rebelled. Chur became reformed in 1523 under the leadership of Pastor Commander, Zwingli's friend. Then the break between bishopry and population was complete. Only the fortresslike ring around the church enabled the continuation of the bishopry. A long period of political disorders followed. The great powers, Austria, France, and Spain, played their incessant games of intrigue and staged wars. The fourth power, death, resulting from the plague, added more misery to the political troubles. The fascinating figure of Jörg Jenatsch arose in Chur. He played off successfully one great power against the other before he was murdered during Carnival festivities. Chur saw better days in the seventeenth century and achieved a vital position within the Swiss Federation in the days of Napoleon.

Two Catholic writers of world renown must be mentioned. Hans von Balthasar (1905–   ) emerged from the Gymnasium Engelberg to become a great scholar, writer, and humanist. He is one of the more important theologians of powerful articulation and one of the rare men of the Church who shows a deep-seated congeniality for the arts and literature. He rendered into German the French

Catholic poets Paul Claudel, Charles Péguy, and Georges Bernanos. Like Karl Barth, his Protestant counterpart about whom he wrote an illuminating book, he has made known his lifelong love for Mozart.

He joined the Jesuit Order in his youth and left it later, probably to remain even truer to the ideas of Ignatius Loyola. He saw new possibilities in the worldly community. The result was the foundation of a publishing house where Balthasar has edited not less than nine different series of books, besides translating many Church Fathers. He still has found time to write more than ten thousand pages of his philosophical and theological thoughts, and his talks with Martin Buber led to his *Lonesome Dialogue.*

Balthasar's *Cosmic Liturgy,* in which he turned to Greek Christianity, is an attempt to bring the notion closer to us: "One can only love what one knows." But his main work to this very day is his most difficult and penetrating study which is supposed to grow to seven volumes, *Magnificence,* with the daring subtitle, "A Theological Aesthetics," treating the eternal beauty in all timeless forms of truth and the good on earth. The tenor of Balthasar's life's work is to make love credible again and to demolish the artificial walls of fear and distrust that separate the Church from man and man from the Church.

The controversial Swiss scholar Hans Küng is feared and respected for his courage in having written *Infallible? An Inquiry,* in which he takes issue with one of the crucial dogmas of the Roman Catholic Church. He argues that no one in the Church hierarchy—neither Pope nor ecumenical council—can proclaim dogmas that are not fallible. He claims that there is simply no basis in Scripture and in Christian tradition for such claims.

In the beginning he took the official Roman theology very seriously until one day he discovered that he could not preach it. Theology for him is not a private ecclesiastical game to keep some theologians happy and out of trouble, but serves the Church's primary task of reaching the "sheep" and preaching the Gospel. And Küng's theology reaches the person right in front of him in the pew. His book about infallibility was preceded by one called *Truthfulness,* and his direct approach to fundamental questions of belief are uncommon.

Küng is a humble man, but one with a burning passion for simplicity and truth. He dreamt of becoming a parish priest, but found himself summoned to the university chair in Tübingen at a rather young age. To spread the Gospel is one thing, but to understand one's faith more deeply and to be able to live it profoundly seems to be more important to him.

Küng's opponents maintain that it is hard to treat him as a Catholic any longer. "Under the circumstances," one of them declared, "one can only carry on a discussion with Küng as one would with a liberal Protestant." Perhaps. Perhaps a modern-day Zwingli emerged from among the Swiss brethren.

NEW ROADS

AS an aside I must also mention a small group of religious men whose ethos forced them to take the social realities into account and who have attempted to re-evaluate the meaning of what is Christian. The second half of the nineteenth century, with its first serious consequences of the Industrial Revolution, created a more acute awareness of the discrepancies between dogma and reality. Among the more progressive thinkers was the Swiss Catholic sociologist, Caspar Decurtins (1855–1916), a renowned sociopolitician, who, as adviser to Pope Leo XIII, had a great share in devising the Pope's epochal encyclic *Rerum novarum.*

In his own country Decurtins left his imprint as a politician and man of letters. He was one of the most active co-founders of the Christian-Socialist movement in Switzerland; he edited the Rhaeto-Romanic *Chresthomatie,* one of the important literary documents of the country; and he was vitally interested in widening the ground of higher education and helped to bring the University of Freiburg into existence.

His activities coincided with those of Leonhard Ragaz (1868–1945), who held the offices of pastor and professor of theology in Zürich. One of the first pioneers of an anti-war movement, he became the editor of a very courageous magazine, *Neue Wege* (*New Roads*), in which he fought for a progressive re-orientation of man's political and social attitudes within the Church. His concepts and guidelines were vehemently attacked by his contemporaries, but he continued to stand by his principles. In order to devote all his time and energy to spreading his gospel of religious socialism, which should have given Protestantism a new image, he withdrew from his chair at the University of Zürich. The reasons for his withdrawal were more than the mere need for a consolidation of his own strength; they included his deep-founded convictions and his need to be his own free agent, independent from curricula, set formats, and rules. Ragaz wrote a great deal, and one of his most impressive works was a unique interpretation of the Bible.

Particularly since World War II, religion and its representatives have tried in various ways to come closer to the problems created by our age of anxiety and confusion. From the religious drama and sacred dance performed on the steps of the altar to a handful of priests who have devoted their lives to the working people in an active manner—thus becoming a new breed of missionary with a touch of the revolutionary—religion has attempted to keep in step with the needs of the time. These attempts, however, seem loosely organized, only sporadically flaming up, and, wherever they appear, rather isolated from the huge ecclesiastic machinery.

A noticeable trend wedding marxism and its consequences with the very essence of Christianity has of necessity become more manifest in the East European than in the nonsocialist countries. Although the Church and bourgeois society in Switzerland may frown on any such fusion, one of the important representatives of this movement is Konrad Farner, a Swiss art historian and born iconoclast. He encountered difficulties not only within the Communist Party but also with his fellow citizens. In 1956, caught in a vortex of anti-communist hysteria, they could not restrain themselves from making Dr. Farner the victim of a miniature "witch-hunt," as Pastor Kurt Marti referred to this outbreak of "defense-neurosis." (The young Swiss writer, Walter Matthias Diggelmann, pictured these events in the chapter "Pogroms in T." of his novel *Die Hinterlassenschaft [The Legacy]*.)

"If the Church of Christ is a Church of pilgrimage," Farner wrote, "then the road so far has not led to the God-altar of love and a new Christian human being, but to an idol-altar of the Golden Calf and the old, un-Christian man. If faith is essentially nothing else but 'the participation in the creative freedom of God,' to use Jürgen Moltmann's words, then this freedom has more and more been misunderstood in the course of bourgeois history as a human freedom of egoism and not of altruism." Konrad Farner comes to the conclusion "that the materialistic-economic as much as the spiritual-ethic liberation of man must be realized simultaneously and with equal intensity: neither the one nor the other is really revolution. In other words: marxist revisionism of the right and

left as well as Christian revisionism must be challenged—the re-
vision of revisionism must ensue."

MAN, THE FREE PARTNER OF GOD

TWENTIETH-CENTURY man is Renaissance man's fulfilled dream
image, writing his own *mene, mene, tekel, upharsin* into the sky.
The cataclysmic events of the century have toppled all old values,
and religion has had to adjust to an age in which man's self-made
madness has tried to demystify myth and has seen in metaphysics
a parlor game of an intelligentsia, bored and desperate while losing
its bearing. For man, living in a mass culture and being daily fed by
the mass media, the meaning of traditional religion has become
lost in his secular concerns, so formidable and crucial that they
take his breath of faith away. Perhaps much truth lies in Dietrich
Bonhoeffer's tortured voice, warning us that we must learn to
speak of God in a secular fashion and find a nonreligious interpretation of Biblical concepts.

The circumstances are as turbulent now as they were in the
sixteenth century, but the contemporary interpreters of the Bible
and Christ have a more difficult task to perform than the Renaissance heretics. It was easy to rebel against the abuses of the
Church in comparison to bringing God back to man, who says,
with a shrug of his shoulders, "Don't you know that He is dead?"

Swiss theologians are in the forefront of the struggle to bring
man and God together again. Gerhard Ebeling (1912–   ) comes
from an historic Protestant heritage, reaching from Martin Luther
and Friedrich Schleiermacher to the critical methodology of the
seventeenth and eighteenth centuries. His thoughts have an existentialist flavor, seeing, as he does, God, man, and world as a
single interrelated reality. He feels that the questions of faith
strongly involve the *me*, and if asked we are challenged to answer,
which in turn involves man's responsibility. As he also expresses
in his work, *The Nature of Faith*, God can be known only in terms
of what He does in relation to man. On the other hand, real knowledge of man is not revealed by what man is in himself, but as he
is in relation to God, the true reality which concerns him.

Basically, Ebeling's theology—not too far removed from Karl
Barth's—could be called a theology of the Word of God, and in
this respect his most important work is *Word and Faith*. In it he

tries to elucidate the meaning of *word* in general and God's Word in particular, maintaining that the word must go beyond its self-expressing value as the communicative means of a human being; the word is man's existence, man himself. Translated into more obvious terms: when a man gives you his word, he has given a share of himself. The church is basic to the summons of faith and thus carries forward the word-event that originated with Jesus.

Ebeling's concept is one of dynamic relationship between God and man, and his stress on the word creates a God who is constantly seeking to speak and reveal himself to man.

In his *Theology of Crisis*, Emil Brunner (1889–   ) attacked theological liberalism and also turned against a humanistic picture of Jesus Christ as much as against the rose-colored view of man's essential goodness. He simply tries to declare the *Word* of the Bible to the *World*. In coming into contact with the world, the word of God is broken because of the inherent limitations of man's mind, and the resulting crisis can only be solved by each individual, by affirming or denying God in faith or revolt.

Of the Swiss theologians, Karl Barth (1886–1969) was probably the greatest; one of the greats of the world in our century. He never gave up searching for an answer. He realized that to be a Christian today one must be tough-minded. Born in Basle, the son of a pastor and professor of theology, he was strongly influenced by the liberal theologians Wilhelm Herrmann and Friedrich Schleiermacher. Barth hesitated to enter the ministry but served as Reformed Church pastor in Geneva and Safenwil between 1909 and 1921. The preacher then turned into teacher. Barth tried "to grasp the nettle of modern man's secularity and to bring the message of the Bible to him . . . Barth has done it by trying to penetrate the layers of idealism and ideology . . . and find again the timeless Word of God," Harvey Cox said in *The Secular City*.

There were, of course, two different Barths, or rather two different theologians in Karl Barth: the radical one, who in 1918 came out with his *Commentary on Romans*, and the august and conservative Barth, who since the late 1920's had written twelve volumes of his *Church Dogmatics*. The theologian as a young man still saw in World War I some hope for a total reassessment of values—a possible reconstruction of society, liberated from the blinding snares of an industrial capitalism which so far had nurtured militarism and selfishness. He did not accept the notion that the interpretation of external events could be left to secular investigations only. He, as a preacher, daily faced people puzzled and disturbed by life, and it was his task to interpret to them the message of the Bible, dealing, as it does, with all questions of human values and certainties, with the obvious and ultimate.

Sören Kierkegaard's influence on Barth is noticeable in his radical theories which speak of revelation by faith, not by reason. Man's rather passive role must be understood in the light of Barth's belief that the Gospel had to be separated from religion, God from man, heaven from earth. God as He is manifest in Christ is the creative source of all being and knowing from which man remains separated and alienated. We must submit to the distance of faith from Him; the way to know Him is to be known by Him. From its origin to its limitation, causing crises after crises, this death-destined universe is nevertheless a vital part of the transcendent source of all life. This relation—mysterious, inexplicable, and paradoxical as it may be, symbol and consummation at the same time—is inherent in the death and resurrection of Christ in its constantly timely timelessness. We must see a timeless significance in the movement from God to man as manifested in the Christ figure, and visualize a decisive deed in His life, death and resurrection, to which Barth referred as "the great disturbance."

The second edition of his *Commentary on Romans* shows a change in Barth from the disturbed interpreter to the great believer. In his Preface to this edition, he said: "If I have a system it consists in the fact that I keep before me . . . what Kierkegaard has called the 'infinite qualitative distinction between time and eternity.' "

From the late twenties on, Barth built a dogmatic edifice in which all finite being and knowing, all concrete reality, is based on the Word of God. With this belief in the Scripture and the belief in man's predestination as an act of divine graciousness taking place in Jesus of Nazareth, the circle is closed in a reversion to Calvinism, with the connotations of our time being fully accounted for.

For many years Barth emphasized the total freedom of God and the concrete reality as solely and wholly united in the figure of Christ, the "God-for-us." Barth felt the urgent need to stress, ever more strongly, that the most important thing to visualize is that the yawning gap between God and man has been bridged, that God has crossed the chasm in Jesus Christ.

The danger embedded in such thinking, as many of Barth's critics have pointed out, is a false identification of Christ with all reality. But Barth's turnabout from his earlier negative to an all-embracing affirmative approach set the stage for the understanding of God and man as two entities, fully differentiated from one another. Thus, God—not needing man—can let man live and work out his responsibilities and the meaningfulness of his life. In other words, God can come near to man without limiting his freedom in exploring, shaping, and mastering his creative potentialities. Despite or because of Barth's utter belief in the Word of God, man plays an important part in his theological edifice, although "We cannot say and demand and expect too much or too great things from man. . . ."

> It is apparent that the formula, "God is everything and man nothing" . . . is not merely a shocking simplification but complete nonsense . . . By the grace of God man is not nothing. He is God's man . . . He is recognized as himself a free subject, a subject who has been made free once and for all by his restoration as the free covenant partner of God. . . .

Barth was teaching in Germany when the Nazis came to power, and he was one of the first to resist strongly the Nazification of the Church. Based on theological reasons, he then rejected Nazism as a political system. In 1935 he was asked to leave his position in Bonn, and he returned to Basle. After the war Barth rejected the necessity for a similar theological decision against communism, even though he rejected it as a political system.

Pope John XXIII compared Karl Barth's accomplishment to that of Aquinas and the *Summa Theologica*. This is a rare honor bestowed by the Pope upon a Protestant theologian. In striving valiantly to bring God to the understanding of twentieth-century man, Barth realized that, owing to man's limitations, he can only formulate concepts that are not identical with God. This thought, recurring in his work and stressed in his *Church Dogmatics*, led Barth to the conclusion that there can be no adequacy between God and man's concepts of God.

EDUCATION, OR THE BELIEF IN LOVE

NOTHING IS LOST THAT IS DONE WITH LOVE

IT has often and rightly been claimed that most Swiss writers cannot deny the didactic touch of the pedagogue in their writings, which may be one of the major reasons for the Swiss to have become master essayists. This has often been recognized and discussed. A good pedagogue, as a serious writer, must also be carried by the wish to share with his world—be it a classroom or a stage (and they are identical)—his beliefs and visions. His words and actions must be propelled by a desire to go beyond the dissemination of knowledge. He can teach and reach his audience only when he is concerned and when his concern and love for man demand that he improve and better man's lot.* This does not necessarily make him a revolutionary. Two of the world's greatest educators were Swiss: Jean Jacques Rousseau and Heinrich J. Pestalozzi. And, however different their concerns, visions, and aims may have been, both were revolutionaries in their thoughts and deeds. Their influence has been felt all over the civilized world.

I doubt it is fair to say that the search for knowledge and its dissemination are more intense in Switzerland than anywhere else, but both have helped to create Switzerland's reputation as a land of schools and education. The world as a classroom or a library room is a very distinct world, in its spatial dimensions small and narrow, in its spiritual dimensions worldwide and all-embracing. The smallness and narrowness of Switzerland as a country, with its built-in sheltered feeling, so important for the scholar, may have played a decisive role in creating the country's reputation in educational leadership. Also, the great number of important European educators, historians, psychologists, and philosophers which Switzerland has brought forth goes far beyond any normal ratio to the size of its population. Characteristic of the innate need for knowledge and the impetus with which it is approached is the remark made by the Swiss historian Jacob Burckhardt in the early 1840's:

> We may all perish, but at least I want to discover the interest
> for which I am to perish—namely the old culture of Europe.

* One can easily trace the didactic trend in the Swiss men of letters from Jeremias Gotthelf and Gottfried Keller to Max Frisch and Friedrich Dürrenmatt.

Many of the well-to-do in Europe, America, and Asia have traditionally sent their children to Swiss schools—in the main, to private schools. There is more than snob appeal to it. Beyond the assurance of finding good and probably the best schoolmates—who may become helpful friends or at least good references later in life—there is the certainty of receiving a well-founded humanistic education with particular stress on the mastering of languages.

No illiterate person can be found anywhere in the twenty-five cantons, and for six million inhabitants there are no fewer than ten institutions of higher learning, seven universities, two institutes of technology, and a graduate school of economics and social sciences as well as a number of other institutions of university status. The German-speaking cantons have five schools and the French-speaking four schools on the university level. Strangely enough, there is no school in the Italian-speaking canton having the rank of a university.

The school system more or less varies from canton to canton, but, whether a given canton demands that its children attend school for seven, eight, or nine years, primary education is compulsory. Local and regional conditions play their part in the schools' curricula, which also vary with the intelligence of the pupils and their aim in continuing their education. It may seem bewildering that such a small state has twenty-five different school systems, but, just as everything else is decentralized and decided upon on a local level by a population that differs from its neighbors in culture, religion, and language, so is education. Switzerland has no national ministry of education, but great efforts are being made by the Federal Government towards a rather unified school system to find more common denominators in most areas without depriving the populace of its right of self-determination on whatever issue.

Although the aims of education are not laid down in the Federal Constitution, century-old traditions have created basic approaches defined by the various school regulations. Their preambles are worded differently, but the tenor is the same. For example, for the canton of Berne we read:

> The school gives support to the family in educating its children. Its task is to help to train the characters and minds of the young people entrusted to it, to impart knowledge and further their abilities and physical development. School education should help

to awaken reverence for God and, in the Christian sense, the will to act towards one's fellow-men in accordance with the demands of conscience.

For the canton of Zürich the preamble says:

> In conjunction with the home, the primary school aims at the harmonious development of the child's physical and mental powers so that the result may be a balanced, vital personality.

The stress on the family as the bedrock of all education is not coincidental. It is the pivotal thought of Switzerland's and the world's greatest educator, Johann Heinrich Pestalozzi (1746–1827), an autodidact who taught mankind its most important lesson. A political revolutionary in his youth, he turned away from theology in order to bring to man the simple message of love, of the sanctuary of man's home, and of the right of man to be man before being a citizen.

Pestalozzi wrote several books. He wrote well because he wrote with the ink of his blood. His prose has the pathos of his ethos:

> Will of man! I adore you. I am only a human being because I am able to will.

Or:

> God is for man only through man the God of man. Man knows God only inasmuch as he knows man, that is, himself, and honors God only inasmuch as he honors himself, that is, inasmuch as he acts towards himself and his fellowmen according to his purest and best instincts.

To this very day Pestalozzi's words sound like incantations imploring man to rise above himself, to grow through education away from the rights of the animal towards those of society and ethics, away from sinister views towards the awareness of his self. A frightful fear about man lies in his words: his concern colors his language darkly, its content makes it appear heavy. In his despair his voice rises sometimes to a Cassandra cry:

> Who dares say it be against God if man is worried about man? And it be against authority if he speaks for the poor and miserable and uncared-for in the country with fire that burns? Oh, you people, the fire of the zealot who is driven to speak the language

of despair in view of the neglect of our kind is a holy fire and his
language is like a shadow of the heavenly truth and like a faded
seal of divinity of our nature.

Pestalozzi was a dreamer who dreamt with sad, wide-open eyes
in a world of reality. His life was beset by ill-fortune and a chain of
failures. "But in his long life," as the Swiss essayist Fritz Ernst said,
"never thinking of his own dire needs, he followed only one aim:
to save the human being in man, to help the fool back to his reason
and the criminal to morality, to strengthen the weak and to enable
the poor to act. . . ."

From his early days as a student, spent in the Zürich Carolinum,
he was guided by the principle that "man is something precious and
his life is grace." Pestalozzi first tried to establish himself as an
agriculturist and merchant. But his heart was not in it. He established a poor-house at the farm of Neuhof near Zürich where he
attempted to give neglected and underprivileged children self-
reliance and a trade by teaching them agriculture and simple crafts.
His lack of organization turned this experiment into a failure after
a few years, and in moments of despair he wrote a series of reflections and aphorisms which were collected in a book under the title
of *The Evening Hour of a Hermit*. In those years he also wrote his
popular story of *Leonard and Gertrude*, a novel of social reform
through education.

In 1798 the French invaded Switzerland. When the village of
Stans was destroyed and most of its inhabitants massacred by their
army, Pestalozzi cared for all destitute children in the orphanage
there for several months under the most trying conditions. Some
time later he opened a school in Burgdorf which he had to give up
due to the political changes. In 1805 Pestalozzi founded his famous
institute in Yverdon which flourished for ten years as one of the
greatest experiments in education, only to be dissolved in 1825 after
years of difficulties caused by quarreling disciples. But for a short
period Pestalozzi realized his visions, and his New Year's speech,
one of the world's great speeches, in Yverdon in 1808 reflected
his triumphant feelings wrapped in the mantle of honest modesty:

> My work is transitory, it is at this very moment already de-
> stroyed; only what is beyond the personal in it will go on living
> as the work of God . . .
>
> It is a miracle that I am still with you, that I am still active. I
> was poor and tried what the rich not only do not do, I tried what
> the rich never thought possible . . . Being powerless I asked

powerlessness, being ignorant I asked ignorance, being humble I asked humility, being imperfect I asked imperfection for help in my work which should rest on the eternal pillars of wisdom and strength, of dignity and the growing maturity of human nature as its sole, unshakable groundwork. The world considered it as an act of foolishness, but the hand of God sheltered me. My work succeeded. I found friends for my heart and work. I did not know what I was doing. I hardly knew what I wanted. But it worked. It emerged like the Creation out of nothing. It is the work of God.

Pestalozzi never tired of wrestling with the adversities of life, and even though many of his plans and schemes did not work out, the inner strength of the man with a mission did not leave him. He had laid the cornerstone of his beliefs early in life and was unfalteringly working on the edifice of his dreams. Looking back at his long struggle with life, he described his feelings of it with the words: "It was as if the people would call at me: Step down from the cross, then we will believe you."

He thought that only a healthy family life could make a morally healthy society possible. The process of education must begin in the home, which remains the sanctuary for the building of community and state. ("The livingroom of the people is somehow the center where everything divine lying in the formative powers of human nature is united.") Pestalozzi strongly believed that the home came before classroom education because only the security of well-rooted home life gives a human being the ability to love. And "love is for man the only true holy service. Where there is no love there is death and destruction on earth. The best powers of man die if he does not love his brother."

On the other hand, he did not underrate formal instruction. He devoted his entire life to finding the best method for primary school education, which he visualized as the best training ground for democracy. As much as the state needs humanizing and not worshiping, as he said, so the teaching needs to be humanized, to be brought closer to the requirements of the growing child. The contemporary Swiss educator Paul Häberlin pointed out the ideal for which Pestalozzi lived, when he wrote: "Education is based on the trust that nothing can be lost that is done with love. To use Pestalozzi's words, it is certain that there is no salvation for man other than the education of the human to true humanity."

Pestalozzi's educational principles, as elaborated in his book, *How Gertrude Teaches Her Children*, were derived from the process of nature to which he adjusted the basic elements of education. The awareness of exactitude, clearness, and distinctness is created in the child through sense impressions. Accurate thinking is dependent upon accurate observations of actual objects. Numbers and forms, language and ideas can gain meaning in the child's mind only when related to concrete things. The Yverdon curriculum stressed the point of concrete experiences in the natural development of the individual, making allowance for individual differences and for grouping children according to their abilities.

Educators from two continents came to Yverdon to study Pestalozzi's method and his teacher training efforts. Robert Owen, one of the earliest founders of English socialism, journeyed to Yverdon to meet Pestalozzi, to whom the world began to look as to a patriarchal reformer. This most humble man was towards the end of his life often referred to as "Father Pestalozzi" by his contemporaries, a man who could write in his last book, *Swan Song:* "I wish nothing more than to see myself repudiated in all someone else understands better than I do and with which mankind can be helped better than I was able to do it."

The American naturalist William McLure was much impressed by his educational method and spread the Pestalozzian message in the New World. Scores of schools based on his principles were gradually established in Europe, particularly in Germany, and in America. The resurgent nationalism in Germany at that time embraced the Pestalozzi concept for the wrong reasons. Fichte visualized a superior Germany, its youth being educated along Pestalozzian lines, and the white-bearded German god of gymnastics, Father Jahn, twisted Pestalozzi's concepts to serve nationalistic strength and military preparedness. During the 1830's and 40's the foundations were laid for primary schools all over Switzerland in which rich and poor children alike could benefit from a system stressing individual needs, and educating free and independent human beings whose humanity could be of loving use to their community and mankind.

THE REVOLUTION THAT WAS ROUSSEAU

WHEN Pestalozzi was sixteen years old, Jean Jacques Rousseau (1712–1778) published his famous educational story, *Émile*, which depicts the bringing up of a boy according to the principles of nature. Émile is an ordinary child who is educated to feel morally and intellectually self-assured and thus free as much as well-balanced. Pestalozzi makes the child's home the nucleus of education; Rousseau admits that education begins with birth, but he does not make the home life a focal point of his approach. Rousseau was far less realistic in his visualization of the growth of a child than Pestalozzi. He underlined the importance of maternal affection and advocated mothers nursing their own children. These facets of early childhood and Rousseau's inclination towards what we would call today permissive freedoms for children are by-products of a romantic concept celebrating nature and the natural man. The revolutionizing ideas in *Émile* which correspond with those of Pestalozzi in a tangential manner are Rousseau's stress on manual training and physical exercise as well as pre-eminently on learning by doing.

Rousseau was mainly interested in showing the evils of society ensnaring the basic innocence of the child in man—man, who is neither good nor evil before he becomes the victim of circumstances. As a product of the Age of Enlightenment, Rousseau, without turning against it, precipitated the era of Romanticism. His ideas were still acceptable to the philosophers, but he was far ahead of their concepts and vision. When Victor Hugo said, "To name Voltaire is to characterize the entire eighteenth century," then we can say that to name Rousseau is to foreshadow the nineteenth century. He recognized the struggle between nature and reason, whereby the instinctual life of man becomes suppressed by civilization as the outgrowth of reason. His influence was of a far-reaching nature—we may not yet have grown out of it— changing decisively man's outlook on life. Therefore, he was revolutionary, even though he did not approve of violence and radical changes; he passionately believed that corruption is caused by the dominating drive of reason over instinct and identified the image of man as being his own helpless victim, with the establishment playing the role of evil, thriving on the evil it breeds.

The simplified summarization of his basic concept as "back to nature" is deceptive and may be descriptive of his very beginning as a writer on social themes. But his more important works, such as his *Social Contract*, make it quite clear that Rousseau was a thinker of great stature who had the good fortune of being able to express his thoughts with passion and panache. He was an impressive phrasemaker which seemed to give the power of his convictions a compelling sound: "The voice of the people is the voice of God." Or: "Man is born free, and everywhere he is in chains."

When Rousseau stressed that man is unhappy, full of anxieties, feeble and frustrated, he saw man's entrapment in the complexities of his social environment like that of an animal in a self-styled cage. To him the structure of society has great bearing on the moral and psychological state of man. ("God makes all things good; man meddles with them and they become evil.") The inequalities of wealth and the growth of society with its mushrooming intricacies are beyond man's mastery. His contention was that man can be happy and free only in a community small and simple enough to be within his grasp. What Rousseau visualized was exactly what has been happening to twentieth-century man: he no longer lives his life, but is lived. We must understand his message in this contemporary sense: There is no emotional security possible without social-economic security. We must be able to understand and love ourselves in order to understand and love our neighbors.

Rousseau's ideal was an egalitarian, small state. This alone would type him as the man who saw in a federation of small communities the only possibility to overcome the difficulties inherent in a complex state machinery. (He could not foresee, of course, that even small states would not be able to escape the consequences of power invested in power or of the inequalities forced upon a consumer world by the Industrial and Technological Revolution.)

Rousseau was born as a fifth-generation child in Geneva. His ancestor, Didier Rousseau, a convert to Calvinism, came to Geneva as a refugee in the middle of the sixteenth century. Rousseau was proud of having been a "citoyen d'un état libre," and when Corsica and Poland asked him to delineate an appropriate new constitution, his ideas for it were based on the Swiss model.

He called himself citizen of Geneva, but in fact his father, a watchmaker by trade and musician by avocation, did not belong to the privileged class. The circumstances in which Rousseau grew up were rather proletarian, and his experiences as an apprentice engraver, before he ran away to try his luck in France, were bitter enough to have influenced his outlook on society. That his mother died giving birth to him deeply affected his great sensitivity as well as his relationship to his father. ("He believed that he saw his wife again in me, without being able to forget that it was I who had robbed him of her.")

All this, of course, must have been on his mind when writing *Émile.* Also, his formative years, which he spent in Switzerland as a teacher of music in Lausanne and Neuchâtel, found their reflection in this educational romance containing sections offensive to authority. After an order was issued for his arrest, he fled to Neuchâtel, from there to Bernese territory and, finally, with the help of David Hume, to England. His last years were spent in a psychotic condition in France.

Rousseau was a great moral force in the development of mankind, a writer of social conscience, with political vision. In him were embedded the characteristics of the romantic of all times: passionate individualism; excessive sensibility; rebellion against the established social order; the glorification of instinct, introspection, imagination; the idealization of simplicity, primitivism, sentiment, sensual and platonic love; escape from reality and return to nature. Romanticism in literature and life started with Rousseau. It started with a man who loved nature, and man as a virtual part of nature. It started in the landscape of a country famous for its scenic wonders.

FROM BURCKHARDT TO BURCKHARDT

BASLE brought forth one of Europe's most important savants and historians whose influence on the cultural conception of modern man has been profound: Jacob Burckhardt (1818–1897).

It can safely be said that with Burckhardt begins a new epoch in criticism, embracing art and man's cultural achievements in their totality. Nobody before him described the development of modern man as he did, and no one recognized so penetratingly the ramifications of modern man's accomplishments.

With a power of urgency he pictured the emergence of man in our time and the menaces he himself had created. The description of the age of Constantine, of the downfall of antiquity, shows the reflection of Burckhardt's own time. With merciless clarity he criticized his bourgeois environment, and he indefatigably held the mirror up to the dangers of an approaching civilization dominated by the masses, a beginning tyranny. He visualized with the historian's perspicacity how, in brief time, the liberalism of 1848 would imprison man in his own concepts. He pictured the inevitable consequences towards which the materialistic and mindless man of the nineteenth century moved, to a time which would be little more than "a certain well-controlled measure of misery with some progress. . . ." The question of human freedom, the question of freedom in general was put to the test by Burckhardt.

Burckhardt became skeptical of Prussia's aims and wrote on

September 27, 1870, to his friend Friedrich von Preen: "Oh, how will the poor German nation be mistaken in thinking they can put their rifles into a corner and dedicate themselves to the arts and happiness of peace. Then they will be told: you have to carry on with your military training! And after some time no one will be able to say what meaning there is still to life." Some time later, on April 26, 1872, he wrote again to Preen: "The strangest lot will befall the workers; I have a premonition which, at the moment, still sounds like a foolish idea, but of which I cannot rid myself: the military state must become a large-scale industrialist. Those masses in the huge factories cannot be left forever to their poverty and greed; logically there must come into being a certain well-controlled measure of misery with some progress and in uniforms, and everything will start and conclude daily with a roll of drums."

Burckhardt anticipated in almost Orwellian visions what would befall a thoroughly mechanized world order (or rather, disorder). But as a young man of 21, when Burckhardt left Basle and the study of theology in order to plunge himself into history and the history of the arts in Germany, he was still full of romantic enthusiasm. His first love belonged to Germany; only later did his feeling shift gradually to Italy. There can be no doubt that this aristocratic aesthete became the great classical humanist he was through the influence of these two countries, through Germany's scholarship and Italy as a living museum.

In the period between 1839 and 1848, the young Burckhardt loathed the liberal-democratic trends in Switzerland and strongly advocated a Swiss union with the "great German nation." ("Often I would like to kneel down on the sacred German soil and to thank God that I speak the German language," he wrote to his sister Louise on April 5, 1841.) The revolutionary, radical trends then far more articulate in Switzerland than in any other country were opposed by Burckhardt, whose emotions had developed in the conservative atmosphere of patrician life in Basle. In 1846 he was still afraid of seeing political liberty in the hands of the people, who "easily can turn into a barbaric mob." Three years later, at the age of thirty-one, he wrote: "I know too much of history to expect from this despotism of the masses anything but a future tyranny."

At that time his Germanophile leanings gave way to his enthusiasm for Italy. He was too clever not to see the frightening growth of German nationalism under Bismarck. Moreover, Switzerland's constitution of 1848 turned out to be less radical in its liberalism than Burckhardt had feared. But what he foresaw and dreaded was

the twofold process of a sterile capitalism on the one hand and
the rise of the mass of man on the other. His shifting enthusiasm
from Germany to Italy is characterized by an exclamation in one
of his letters to his German friend Gottfried Kinkel, written on
September 11, 1846: "Basle . . . looks at me with boring and philis-
tine eyes that I would be very grateful to God even for a winter in
Berlin. No, no real human being can stand it here among those
rich show-offs. Rome! Rome! Rome! capisce?" This was written
during his first Italian trip, a period which was often referred to
as the "journey of his becoming humanized" (*die Menschwerdungs-
reise*).

Only one third of his works were written and published during the
earlier part of his life; two thirds of them were issued posthu-
mously. He accumulated a huge knowledge of the arts, which he
penetrated with an original and visionary look. What is so important about his enthusiastic re-experience of the past was that he
saw the artist's wrestling with his genius and with God as a highly
individual and ecstatic growth, out of his time, out of the historic
setting of his era, from which he liberated the meaning for his own
contemporaries.

In his introduction to *Reflections on History*, he said: "We, however, shall start out from the one point accessible to us, the one
eternal center of all things—man suffering, striving, doing, as he
is and was and ever shall be." In 1860 Burckhardt, who was called
by the Dutch historian Johann Huizinga the "wisest man of the
nineteenth century," and by Friedrich Nietzsche "our greatest
sage," published *Die Kultur der Renaissance in Italien* which,
strangely, was translated as *The Civilization of the Renaissance in
Italy*. Burckhardt chose to add to his title: *Ein Versuch* ("An Attempt"). But it has become the basic work to give the necessary
foundation to our insight into our past and the so often puzzling
knowledge of what we are, and why we are what we are.

Burckhardt realized in all modesty that such a work could not be
foolproof for all scholarly studies and interpretations of those coming after him. This is why he called it *An Attempt*. And he wrote:
"In the wide ocean upon which we venture, the possible ways and
directions are many; and the same studies which have served for
this work might easily, in other hands, not only receive a wholly
different treatment and application, but lead also to essentially
different conclusions. Such, indeed, is the importance of the subject that it still calls for fresh investigation and may be studied with
advantage from the most varied points of view." As in all great

works of history which have meaning beyond the moment, this cultural history was written with personal fervor and intensity, displaying the opinion of one man only, but one whose insight and vision opened new vistas into man's creative will and interior landscape.

Burckhardt was more interested in the totality of the Renaissance image than in any part of it. As a historian, he was well aware of the slow waning of the Middle Ages. He realized that a revival of antiquity, the study of classical literature, and the philosophy of its arts and architecture do not themselves create a new age or culture, but that only their fusion with the elements of the new era—in this case the physical and cultural awakening of the late Middle Ages—could bring about a new culture. For Burckhardt there was no doubt that Greek culture and Roman civilization exerted great influence on medieval Europe and was particularly strong in certain centuries and at certain places. (Only the Florence of the Renaissance can measure up to the Athens of the Golden Age, he once said.) His chief aim was to re-create the charismatic minds and the underlying motivational patterns of the Italian people during the fourteenth, fifteenth, and sixteenth centuries.

Medieval men were individuals, but it never reached their consciousness or self-consciousness as was the case with Renaissance man: "Man became a spiritual *individual* and recognized himself as such." Burckhardt explained the outburst of creativity in Italy and the very distinct artistic-humanistic atmosphere as shaped by the political situation at that time, through a need created by despots:

> The illegitimacy of his rule isolated the tyrant and surrounded him with constant danger; the most honorable alliance which he could form was with intellectual merit, without regard to its origin. The liberality of the northern princes of the thirteenth century was confined to the knights, to the nobility which served and sang. It was otherwise with the Italian despot. With his thirst for fame and his passion for monumental works, it was talent not birth which he needed. In the company of the poet and the scholar he felt himself in a new position—almost, indeed, in possession of a new legitimacy.

The self-styled dukes, princes, and even popes needed the stamp of their glory which they found in the monumental works of those artists they patronized. It was a ready-made atmosphere for individual greatness, nurtured by the unceasing competition between the political rivals. It was because and not in spite of the incessant struggles, fights, and wars between these rulers that individual creativity was in great demand. But also, in such great republics as Florence and Venice, the beginning evolution of "capitalism," the growing economic enterprise by prominent individual merchants and bankers, contributed its share to the renaissance of the arts.

Burckhardt realized that it was first necessary for noblemen and wealthy burghers to learn "to dwell together on equal terms." Only then, as it happened in the fourteenth century, could a social world come into being which "felt the want of culture, and had the leisure and the means to obtain it." No era and no nation has ever managed to create its specific culture by starting from scratch. Also, the Italians of the fourteenth century "needed a guide, and found one in the ancient civilization, with its wealth of truth and knowledge in every spiritual interest." Both the form and substance of this civilization were adopted with admiring gratitude; it became the chief part of the culture of the age.

What Burckhardt was most interested in was the entirely new attitude which emerged from the relationship between the creative mind and the patron needing its unfolding for his own glory, "the natural alliance between the despot and the scholar, each relying solely on his personal talent."

Burckhardt's beginning as a student of theology and his entire patrician background played their part in his realization that the much admired individualism of the scholar and artist, whose position "was almost incompatible with a fixed home," had more than a touch of paganism. In a period of unchecked subjectivity and unbridled egotism, of the desperate attempt to reconcile Christianity and the pagan world of the classics, humanism became, in Burckhardt's eyes, pagan, particularly with the humanist's and artist's predominant role in the fifteenth century, when individualism was at a premium. Burckhardt visualized that the circumstances of existence, which were often precarious and most of the time dangerous, created certain "principal features in the Italian character of that time. . . ." But he conceded that "The fundamental vice of this character was at the same time a condition of its greatness, namely excessive individualism."

With such and similar references, Burckhardt hinted at the grave dangers of an amorality going hand in hand with the greatness of individual accomplishments characterizing the dominating Renaissance spirit. Thus, Burckhardt feared that the legacy of the Renaissance, fraught with contrasting extremes, was full of ambiguities. Would man understand the need for exerting the utmost measure of responsibility, or would he indulge in the Renaissance man's release from restraints? He saw the growing danger in the weakness of man to tend towards the latter attitude. He saw the first signs of how the unfettered drive which we so proudly inherited from Renaissance man can reach proportions of doom when the civilization gives way to the pressures of the mass of men in a dynamic age of technology. Burckhardt realized that the drive of man's ego is the halo of his accomplishment, but also his sign of Cain. And Burckhardt saw only the very modest beginnings of the Industrial Revolution which catapulted itself into the tremendous power and frightening puzzle of the technological era.

We can add a few more facets to Burckhardt's personality with the help of one of his foremost students, Heinrich Wölfflin (1864–1945), destined to become one of the great art historians of the twentieth century. Born in Winterthur near Zürich, Wölfflin studied with Burckhardt in Basle and was often fortified in his progress by Burckhardt's advice and admonitions.

One late evening after the seminar, Burckhardt asked Wölfflin to accompany him on his way home and, walking up and down under the trees on Münster Square, the professor talked about many things to his student. Wölfflin recorded some of his remarks: "Whatever you want to study, above all, take care of an all-round education. Use half your reading time for the ancient writers. Never read a book without making notes. Go always back to the real sources, there is a great blessing on it. The main thing in life is to get some satisfaction from one's daily work done. You have to get your work done day after day to be satisfied."

Wölfflin explained what Burckhardt meant when he spoke of a universal education. His definition was: "Universal does not mean to read as much as possible but to love as much as possible." We have it from Wölfflin's mouth that Burckhardt was one of the most industrious persons he knew: "He never pushed hard, but he was always active. Burckhardt himself referred to his even-paced, pleasant diligence." Wölfflin was strongly impressed by Burckhardt as a lecturer, particularly about the old professor's awe for works of great magnitude. Less sensitive people than Wölfflin could not help coming under his spell, even though Burckhardt did not use an extensive vocabulary. What concerned Burckhardt so very much was to awaken the belief that art was one of the great forces in the history of man and that there was much reward in being constantly occupied with it—not as an art expert but simply as a human being.

Wölfflin's remarks about Burckhardt are quoted here because they also shed light on Wölfflin and his work as an art historian who, in many ways, continued where Burckhardt stopped. He, of course, had the advantage over his teacher of being a twentieth-century man, a century marked and stigmatized, among other things, by its heightened psychological awareness. His doctoral thesis, entitled *Prolegomena to a Psychology of Architecture* (1886), foreshadowed his interest in the psychological aspect of the creative processes and the interrelation of style and period changes. He was endowed with the ability to see with a sharp and discerning eye, to which was added his capacity for precise and descriptive verbalization. He pursued and refined his method from his student days and the publication of his first book, *Renaissance and Baroque*, in 1888, to his crowning achievement, *Principles of Art History* (1915), with which he established a new terminology and an aesthetic system that has become basic to the study of art history.

Burckhardt as much as Ruskin still used the term "baroque" in a rather derogatory way, seeing in the Renaissance the ideal, and in what followed it, a deterioration into odd and overdone decoration. Wölfflin separated the Baroque from the Renaissance as a period and style, so that the word "baroque" came to define essentially a historic entity rather than a form of creative expression (even though it is still used as an epithet of approval or disparagement). He proceeded from Burckhardt's concept of "equivalents" in art, which show the interrelation between the value of a work and the ideal of life, or how interchangeable visual and ideal values are. Wölfflin investigated the idea of intuitive forms as related to a particular period and, especially, the differences in the development from the Renaissance to the Baroque.

He believed that throughout the various layers of culture, the objectivity and formal strictness of a classical period are always followed by a trend towards subjectivity, sensualism, and freedom of form. Thus, Renaissance dissolving into Baroque is a logical polarity to him and applicable as a basic formula in art history. Wölfflin's concept accepts the change of style as a *psychological* consequence, due only to purely internal reasons. (Later critics, such as Arnold Hauser in *The Social History of Art*, have pointed out that Wölfflin's ideas omit the socio-cultural forces at work in regard to changes in style and taste.)

Wölfflin's system, nevertheless, has had a decisive influence on art evaluation and criticism. Taking a characteristic of the Renaissance and opposing it to one of the Baroque period, he evolved a concept of antinomies which more or less show a trend from a formal towards a freer artistic ideology. He summarized his principles in stipulating his famous five pairs of categories. (1) The *linear* Renaissance art with its clear lines and contours is opposed to what he called the *painterly* (the German *malerisch* is a more descriptive expression). Painterly refers to blurred outlines, merging colors and images, as indicative of Baroque art. (2) *Plane* and *recessional* refer to self-containment and the logical horizontal planes of the Renaissance, to baroque composition in depth, with the illusion of distance. (3) *Closed* and *open* forms show the contrast between a balanced space, limiting the vision of the spectator, and an indefinite space, giving the eye the freedom to wander beyond any limitation. (4) *Multiplicity* and *unity* indicate a transformation of a seemingly harmonious group, in which the parts remain independent, into a functional unity, in which all parts have a single motivating rhythm; in other words, the contrast between a static being and a meaningful becoming. (5) *Clearness* and *unclearness*, a juxtaposition in which absolute clarity exists in its clearly defined forms, while in relative clarity, each part and each form contribute to the dramatic structure of the whole.

To the degree that Burckhardt's interest was focused on the Renaissance, Wölfflin's sympathies were with the Baroque, of which he wrote in his *Principles of Art History:* "In the final analysis, the tendency is to make a picture seem not a self-contained piece of reality, but a passing show in which the beholder has the good luck to participate just for a moment. . . . The whole intention is to make the totality of the picture seem unintentional."

Wölfflin held chairs at several universities in Munich and Berlin, and for eighteen years he was professor at the universities in Basle and Zürich. He was the second great art historian Switzerland produced, but in his own advancement towards a better understanding of the arts he was second to none. And yet he probably was a less colorful personality than Burckhardt. He had the good fortune to have a great master and the misfortune to have had to take his place. Jacob Burckhardt's influence as a human being and thinker was of such a penetrating power that it went far beyond a circle of artists, art historians, and critics. I have only to cite the example of Hermann Hesse who, in delineating the three strong and lifelong educational influences on him, said: "It was the Christian and almost totally un-nationalistic spirit in my parental home, it was my reading of the great Chinese and, last but not least, the influence of the only historian to whom I felt attached with confidence, awe, and grateful following: Jacob Burckhardt."

It seems that the atmosphere of Basle is conducive to speculative thinking. Erasmus felt a magic attraction to this city, and so did one of the greatest philosophers of our time, Karl Jaspers (1883–1969), as well as Rudolf Steiner (1861–1925) a few decades before him.

Together with Martin Heidegger, Jaspers gave existentialist philosophy its basic foundation. He began his career as psychopathologist. His *Psychologie der Weltanschauungen*, published in 1919, is still considered one of the most important documents of existentialist philosophy, which he further substantiated with his *Existenzphilosophie* in 1938. But even before this book was issued, the Nazis dismissed him. He had been professor of philosophy at the University of Heidelberg from 1920 to 1937. In the year 1945 he was reinstated, but three years later he accepted an invitation from Basle, whose university offered him the chair of philosophy. He became Professor Emeritus in 1961 and died in Basle in 1969.

Switzerland can hardly claim Jaspers as one of its philosophers; Jaspers wrote in German, even though his thought was international, and his ties with the German Kultur were very strong. But he had to hibernate during the many years of the Hitlerean holocaust. This was a long winter of his discontent, and we may assume that the disappointment in his countrymen must have weighed heavily on his mind. Moreover, he enjoyed the intellectual atmosphere of Basle, where he spent the last twenty-one years of his life. During this period he laid the foundation to a new philosophy which he simply defined as world philosophy.

In 1966 he asked to be made a citizen of Basle, and a year later he held the citizenship paper in his hands. It has been said that his reasons for not returning to Germany were twofold: his growing mistrust of the political wisdom of the land of his birth and, even more, his strong belief in his adopted country. He often and proudly referred to the fact that for the first time in his life he was a citizen of a state whose principles he could affirm as a totality.

Jaspers succeeded Paul Häberlin (1878–1960), who, as a philosopher and psychologist, was most interested in education. Besides treating the basic principles of philosophy and philosophy in relation to science, he wrote a series of books dealing with the problems of education. Some of the titles initially reveal that he was seriously occupied with the meaning of education from the viewpoint of the higher destiny of man. Taking the individual's psychophysical duality and his motivations into account, he explores the right roads and wrong ways to education in *The Aim of Education* (1917), *Parents and Children* (1922), and *Body and Soul* (1923), to name only three.

Häberlin proceeded from the highest ideals, which he did not visualize as utopian. To him, culture is the realization of that human ideal which fulfills the *optimum* of man's possible spiritualization; culture can be seen only in the light of truth which we cannot "have," but for which we must search. "Ethical culture in particular," he wrote, "demands the recognition of the absolute value of all existence. This is the idea of true love. Love is the principle of ethic culture."

In accepting love—not the love of subjective and sentimental sympathies, but the will to do justice to all existence according to its true meaning—as a pivotal point of departure towards education, Häberlin continued on the way of Pestalozzi's spiritual legacy. The true image of a cultured, i.e., educated, man cannot be equated with knowledge, but only with the dominance of the spirit over non-spirit. Häberlin says that the principle of love demands from each human being the furthering of his fellowman's inner refinement, that this alone is education, which, in his words, "means assisting in one's partner's inner growth." He refutes all dogmatic methods of education and echoes Pestalozzi most when he maintains that "the only constant in all methods is the *love* for the student, love which affirms him in his existence and destiny and, because of doing this, approaches him as the particular human being he is."

Of the didactic minds which Switzerland brought forth there was never any want of those whose curiosity and restlessness were evenly matched by a predilection for the meticulous recording of their findings. Aegidius Tschudy (1505–1572) and Johannes von Müller (1752–1809)—to mention only two—are probably outstanding examples of historians who have helped with their chronicles of the Swiss to create an educational mirror image of their native country. Müller—a boy from Schaffhausen, knighted by the Austrian Emperor Leopold II—often gave uncertain events the glamour of certainty in his burning eagerness to embrace all details of history. The best parts of his five huge volumes are those dealing with the Middle Ages which, in his vision, escape their proverbial darkness and reveal quite a few endearing touches of romanticism. Müller, whose writings cannot belie that he was caught by the romantic fever of his time, was a spiritual descendant of Tschudy, a Renaissance figure for whom action was as important as meditation, a predisposition which made him the famous chronicler of events he was. Tschudy's chronicles are masterly drawn historic pictures of a heroic age, and certain inexactitudes are easily outweighed by his penetrating power of insight into the happenings he describes. His two major works, *Gallia comata* and *Chronicon Helveticum* (which were published in the eighteenth century only), justify his reputation as Switzerland's first great historian, often referred to as the "Father of Swiss Historia."

Even though the concepts of Rudolf Steiner's (1861–1925) anthroposophy reach far beyond educational purposes, a great many educational activities derive from his work. This may be mainly due to the fact that his school of "spiritual science," which essentially is concerned with the explanation of the world in terms of the nature of man and with the creation of a higher cosmic awareness, establishes a very specific philosophy of life.

His philosophy assumes that there are spiritual processes in the world in which we have originally participated through a dreamlike consciousness, from which our present consciousness has emerged as the part of a totality. Man can comprehend the existing spiritual world through pure thinking, but he can penetrate and fully embrace it only through the higher faculties of knowing, which are latent in every human being. Steiner's philosophic edifice creates space for man in which to find a heightened consciousness of himself and an awareness of spiritual worlds.

Rudolf Steiner was an Austrian scientist and artist. While still studying, he worked on an edition of Goethe's scientific writings and continued his work in Weimar, assisting in the issue of a standard edition of Goethe's works. This took several years, during which Steiner wrote several books: *Truth and Science* as his Ph.D. paper; one of his most important books, *The Philosophy of Spiritual Activity* (1894); and *Goethe's Conception of the World* (1897). Goethe remained a focal point of interest with Rudolf Steiner throughout his life.

At the turn of the century he discovered a faculty for spiritual perception, independent of the senses. His research in this area resulted in a philosophic theory which he called anthroposophy, in contrast to theosophy, and which he characterized as "knowledge produced by the higher self in man."

I am speaking of Rudolf Steiner and the emanations of his work because, in 1913, we find him building his first school in Dornach, near Basle. It is significant for his philosophy of inner freedom and becoming that he called his school "Goetheanum." When it burned down in 1922, he immediately designed a new building of molded concrete. It has remained the school and center of the Anthroposophical Society ever since.

Steiner's movement had its impact particularly in Europe and America. Based on his educational principles, about 60 Waldorf Schools sprang up, caring for more than 25,000 children. At Arlesheim, also near Basle, a special therapeutic clinic was opened, and, inspired by the Rudolf Steiner movement, homes and schools for maladjusted and defective children can be found in many lands. Centers for scientific research, mainly in mathematics, for the development of the biodynamic method of farming and gardening have scored success. The Goetheanum in Dornach is best known for its eurhythmic studies, in which the art of physical movement to spoken poetry and music is taught. Furthermore, there are schools carrying the stamp of Anthroposophical Society in many disciplines of the arts, from drama to architecture, from painting to music.

That the nerve center of this world-wide movement should be in Switzerland seems fitting, since its philosophy has been applied there in most practical terms. One man's visionary dream was pushed to the very edge of its full realization.

Three philosophers and exceptional men of letters shall close this wide circle of personalities.

In his many-sidedness, but, above all, in his mental agility and philosophy of life, Ignaz Paul Vital Troxler (1780–1866) is a spiritual relative of Goethe, whom he greatly admired. Also, Paracelsus's unbridled imagination appealed to the medical man in him.

Troxler's restless, uncompromising spirit got him into trouble with the partly aristocratic, partly conservative-clerical Lucerne when he pointed out the poor medical and sanitary conditions he discovered there. To avoid arrest he escaped to Vienna where, for many years, his medical practice flourished. He married there and counted Beethoven among his best friends. His mother called him back home to Beromünster. Clandestinely he went from there to Lucerne in the hope that he would be able to settle his old differences, but he was put into prison and forced to recant and beg for his pardon.

Meanwhile, his fame as a physician had spread abroad, and the medical faculty in Berlin asked him to join it. Not wanting to leave his home, he rejected the offer. He gave up medical practice and accepted a professorship in philosophy and history at the Lyceum in Lucerne in 1819. But again he did not get along with the generally conservative trend in city and school. As a radical idealist, Pestalozzi's spirit hovered over him ("Instruction is only a part of education"). It almost sounds contemporary, but it was Troxler who said: "Only the revolution in the schools will fortify and complete the one in church and state." He had to leave Lucerne, but later in Basle he met with similar difficulties as professor of philosophy and dean at the University. In the 1830's he played a major political role among the Radicals and contributed greatly to the draft of a new constitution.

Troxler's thinking was always close to the realities of life in spite of his love for metaphysics. But "philosophy," he once said, "has always been my beloved, science my wife, medicine only my concubine." He always valued humaneness highest. This is why he could write: "More and more I am falling in love with a philosophy which absorbs the heart's feelings into the mind's ideas. It is the only true philosophy." He saw the seat of the emotions as the center of the human being and, like in nature, he hoped for divine intelligence combining both light and warmth so that he could find traces of this entity in every emanation and manifestation.

The titles of two of his major books, *On Life and Its Problem* and *Glances into the Being of Man*, reveal his basic interest in wanting to heal and help, his interest in a total philosophy of life that can be practically applied. In this, and in more than this respect, he was a forerunner of Rudolf Steiner's anthroposophic ideas.

His philosophic thoughts had a romantic bent to which he remained true all his life. A higher perception depends on a deeper awareness of our mind: "We do not think the most secret thoughts, they think us." More and more a mystic belief permeated his thought-feelings. But he never lost his viewpoint on the positive aspects of reality, and so he could say: "We do not move from the real Something to Nothing, but from seeming Nothingness we approach Something." There was nothing static about his mind; he never gave up believing in the total consciousness of man and in the necessary growth of individuality. "Every human being has his mission," he said, and "the more individual he is, the more exemplary his mission." One cannot imagine any person more individualistic and many-sided or who lived his life more consciously than Troxler.

"I begin to believe that the historians of the twentieth century will have to treat America and Russia only. The old world of Europe lies on its deathbed." This prophetic sentence was written in 1869 by a great anthropologist and mythologist of the Romantic period, Johann Jakob Bachofen (1815–1887). Though Europe is still on its feet, and very much so, this visionary foresaw the crystallization of the two superpowers which have dominated the political world of our century.

Bachofen's work has been important in many ways, but he became most famous for his book, *The Maternal Right*, which exerted great influence upon ethnological research and theory. He challenged the prevailing patriarchal theory of evolution when he found evidence of matrilineal descent in the beginnings of human society. In this culture the mother was the head of the family, and only its female members had the right of succession. Sons who married received a dowry from their sisters, who also had to take care of their parents when they were old. This condition, Bachofen theorized, was preceded by promiscuity, and, as a logical consequence, the females finally established their rights. Only gradually men gained ascendency, and the state of patriarchy was permanently established.

Bachofen saw in these sequences the universal stages of social evolution. In his evaluation and perception of this early stage of society, he was helped by recreating its myth, in which not only religious conceptions are reflected, but also the historic experiences of a people. Thus, myth becomes "a true image of the oldest epochs."

For many years, this historic empiricist was preoccupied with the myth of the Orient and Occident. He created with his then revolutionary sociological and mythological concepts a huge system of historic philosophy. As one of his basic notions, he visualized the story of mankind as a struggle between spirit and matter, ending with the triumph of the former. Bachofen equated matter with womanhood and saw the mastery of the spirit in the potentialities of patriarchy.

In the background of Bachofen's historic thinking is the "gradual process of overcoming the animalistic aspects of our nature." He saw in Rome's conquest of the world of antiquity a victory over the "Mosaic Orientalism" and "Asiatic passivity." But he also realized "how difficult it was for man—at all times and under the dominion of the most different religions—to overcome the pressures of material nature and to reach the highest goal of man's destiny, the rise from worldly existence to the purity of the divine paternal principle." On the surface, Bachofen's great dream for mankind, namely to find its way from the animalistic below to a "heavenly-spiritual principle" above, has only partly found realization. It is questionable whether the Romans have shown us the right way to overcome "the night of matter" and how to find the light. But however it may turn out, Bachofen's principal thoughts have shed some light on our cumbersome way. Great dreams, even those of visionaries, can of course—through unforeseen pressures of history—turn into nightmares.

The name Burckhardt lights up again in Carl Jacob Burckhardt (1891–   ), historian, writer, and diplomat. Time and again he felt that however clearly he could capture the secrets of the past and return, richly rewarded for his insight, from the wells of historic existence, he had to leave his desk and pen to become an active part of contemporary events. This dichotomy between the writer and doer in him has never led to conflicts and has only enriched the moments of contemplation. Rilke, referring to Burckhardt's *Journey in Minor Asia*, precisely circumscribed this positive dichotomy when he described the book as the record of one who acts and experiences. What he experiences, he does with discernment and power, reaching beyond the momentous past and confusing present into the puzzling tomorrow. Burckhardt, a young

man in his early thirties, wrote from a corner of the Asiatic continent that an Asiatic movement had begun "whose effect will be
felt throughout the entire century."

When, in 1937, Burckhardt was sent as High Commissioner of
the League of Nations to Danzig and unfolded his diplomatic skill
in a politically delicate situation, he recorded his two-year experience in an enlightening book on his peaceful mission. Over the
years he held many public offices, was President of the Red Cross,
taught at the universities in Zürich and Geneva, and fulfilled several diplomatic tasks.

In the course of his active life he met a number of great personalities. The writer in him could not help putting his impressions
and thoughts on paper, recalling pictures of past memories, drawing
portraits of people whose images fascinated him, and recapturing
his own life in the strangely flickering light of time. As a diplomat
in Vienna immediately after the collapse of the Habsburg Mon-
archy, he met Hugo von Hofmannsthal. The result was a close
friendship between the young man and the older poet, a friendship which brought consolation to Hofmannsthal and enrichment
to Burckhardt, and finally great gain for the literary world when
Burckhardt published his memories of Hofmannsthal and the exchange of their letters. ("It was difficult for his nature to extinguish
the light of hope which ennobles everything tragic, and to stop
in front of a fully gloomy finale. The deepest tragic movements
were always in himself only the last steps before walking out into
freedom, into light.")

Carl J. Burckhardt is by profession a man of the world, by
avocation a historian, by nature a storytelling poet. His three-
volume study of *Richelieu* is not only a penetrating profile of one
of the most influential shapers of Europe's history, it unfolds as a
study of political power within the socio-cultural scene in France
at her most glorious epoch. Yet Burckhardt's greatest merit as a
writer and philosopher lies in his collected speeches and his *Contacts* with some of those who were instrumental in having given
our time its political stamp and cultural expression.

I would like to close these few paragraphs on an immensely
rich and active life with Carl Zuckmayer's words about Carl J.
Burckhardt. He spoke about his "clear and pensive eyes in which
live scepticism and mourning next to courage and self-assurance,
and always something of that secret dream of truth which lit up
and burdened his youth. . . . He gives us of his most beautiful
when he can draw from the living well. . . . when he speaks of

Johann Peter Hebel, of his visit with Rilke at the Paris book-
seller. . . . of the geniuses who crossed his path, of those he met
on the way and which accompanied him. . . . the stories. . . . which
he carries along with him, and whose contents circumscribe his
best: the work of art which is his life."

A DREAM FULFILLED

THE Children's Village Pestalozzi in Trogen, a village in the Appenzell mountains, is one of Pestalozzi's dreams turned into reality.
Walking through this village—with its view of massive mountains
towards the south and the Lake of Constance in the north—one
sees a cluster of houses which, at first sight, seem in no way different from other Appenzell houses. But a closer look reveals that
each house is characterized by a name, and a strange-sounding
name at that: Pinocchio, Les Cigales, Thames, Jukola, Kukoricza
Jancsi, Yambhu Lagang, or Al-Amal. The names of these buildings
indicate the nationality of the fifteen or twenty children who live
there together under the guardianship of couples who, of the same
nationality as the children, take the place of their parents. First,
war orphans were given a new home. Then refugee children and
those who no longer have a home, for whatever reason, were
brought here.

Within their own four walls the children speak the tongue of
their home country and create the image of a national family,
with its native customs and habits. On their national holidays the
flag of their country is hoisted on their building. Everything inside
reminds the children of their homeland—books, pictures, wall
decorations. In the morning hours the children are taught the subjects of the first six years of primary schooling in their native
language. The afternoons are reserved for international courses
which range from sports to the arts and handicrafts in workshops.
According to their talents and inclinations, the children choose
the groups they wish to join. In the afternoon courses a common
language is spoken by all—by the Koreans and Tibetans, the Fin-
nish, Austrian, French, Hungarian, Greek, and English children,
and those coming from North Africa. Since the Pestalozzi Village
lies in the German-speaking part of Switzerland, the first common
language is German, to which a second, chosen language is added
when the secondary schooling begins.

In August 1944 an article was published by the magazine *Du* in which the Swiss philosopher Walter Robert Corti submitted the suggestion to Switzerland, one of the few countries that had escaped the horrors of World War II, to create an international model village of education for those children who had lost their homes or parents or both. Two years later, on April 28, 1946, the cornerstone for the *Kinderdorf* Pestalozzi was laid.

The children live together and grow up there in an ideal atmosphere of international spirit; they work and play together, they have their common interests; the older children have regular meetings of the "young village citizens" and make their own decisions. They are instrumental in keeping the village life in a democratic working order.

When the youngsters are ready to enter life in a world rather remote from this utopian village, they receive what is called a "Bürgerbrief," a document which is a kind of miniature citizenship of the Children's Village. With such a letter and the wishes of the entire village is tied the hope that this young person will try to live up to the principles taught him at the Pestalozzi Village. The Children's Village in Trogen inspired other international settlements with the same or similar aims, of which those in Sedlescombe in England and Wahlwies in Germany are closely associated with Trogen.

The Children's Village could not have conjured up a more appropriate spirit then that of Pestalozzi. It was inspired by his love for the orphans in Stans and by his concept of the *Wohnstube* ("livingroom") as a point of departure for all genuine education— for the harmonious shaping of a young person's head, heart, and hand. Pestalozzi cannot be identified with a clearly devised pedagogic system and method, but rather with the forging of the human character, with conviction, with a basic educational attitude towards the higher values of life. It is as if Pestalozzi himself had written, in 1804, the motto for the children's village in Trogen:

A model school does not change the world in the first hours of its existence. But the means of change can render the human spirit gay and the human heart tender and smooth the way from afar for what the human spirit has ever set as aim for its nobler aspirations.

SCIENCE + A FEW RANDOM REMARKS

THE DREAM OF THE MIND

IN discussing science from the vantage point of the twentieth century, one can hardly go wrong in beginning with Albert Einstein (1879–1955). Robert Whitehead said, "philosophy starts with wonder," and wonder may consequently lead to the resolution of mysteries or new discoveries which again may provoke wonder. Einstein was no *Wunderkind*, but he began to wonder and question when still a small boy. All his life he was a daydreamer, a lone wolf or outsider, little concerned with the realities of life. Somehow he was attuned to the music of the spheres, an Orphic personality who, throughout his life, could not be separated from his violin. His entire being seemed destined to live on the plane of a higher reality. Holding the key to new concepts of universal significance, he had a Spinoza-like belief in a cosmic religious force while rejecting all organized religions. ("This deep intuitive conviction of the existence of a higher power of thought which manifests itself in the inscrutable universe represents the content of my definition of God.")

As with Newton, whom Einstein unseated, there were no early signs of genius in the boy. Unobservant people may have thought him even dull or, at best, withdrawn. But there were notable moments early in his youth as, for example, at the age of five, when he inquired about the mystery of the compass needle. If one looks for indications and signs in the lives of geniuses, then the incident of the compass needle which intrigued the little boy points the way to Einstein's later interest and involvement in scientific speculations.

No trace remains of the house in Ulm, Southern Germany, where Einstein was born—another sign of the darkness of our age. In 1945 bombs destroyed the birthplace of the man whose work was so instrumental in the development of nuclear fission and who implored President Truman not to drop the atom bomb without first demonstrating its power to the world by public tests.

Much had been made of Einstein's flunking his entrance exam at the Zürich Polytechnic Institute. Even though he excelled in mathematics, he had to first obtain his diploma at the Gymnasium in Aarau before they would accept him at the Polytechnic Institute. He was then seventeen and more inclined to pursue theoretical

49

physics than mathematics. Einstein acquired far more knowledge from reading than from attending lectures. From early school days in Munich he adjusted only with difficulty to a routine curriculum and conventional teaching.

At the *Hochschule* in Zürich he found inspiring friends—friends were often used by him as a sounding board for his ideas—rather than stimulating teachers who could sufficiently satisfy his curiosity. His professor Heinrich Weber took a great dislike to Einstein and later prevented him from becoming an assistant. His only strong professorial influence from those days was from the famous mathematician Hermann Minkowski, whose lectures on analytical mechanics enriched him. Minkowski's concepts of space and time gave Einstein much food for thought, although the student does not seem to have made a favorable impression on the lecturer. When Einstein published his sensational theory of relativity in 1905, Minkowski, who remembered that "in his student days Einstein had been a lazy dog," was greatly surprised.

After his graduation he had little means of support and eked out a meager existence by doing odd jobs such as calculations for the director of the Federal Observatory, and several months of replacement teaching in Winterthur. Meanwhile, Einstein had applied for Swiss citizenship and was made a Swiss citizen of Zürich, an honor not readily bestowed upon foreigners. He wanted to go through the training of the *Miliz*, as any other young Swiss, and was very unhappy when the authorities rejected him because of his varicose veins and flat feet.

He searched in vain for an academic position and, though trained as a physics and mathematics teacher, finally accepted a post as a staff member at the Swiss Patent Office in Berne. There he was a technical editor, rewriting patent applications to clarify the basic concepts and to give them the necessary scientific precision. This was good training and also gave him ample time to ponder and speculate on mass-energy equivalence, the velocity of light, statistical mechanics, and radiation. The epoch-making theory of relativity was born during these three years (1902–1905) which Einstein spent at the Patent Office in Berne. 1905 was Einstein's *annus mirabilis*. Volume 17 of the *Annalen der Physik* featured three essays by Albert Einstein, each one a masterpiece.

The world of science at that time was startled by Einstein's advanced work and prophetic equations, but the University of Berne was not and refused to give him a teaching post in theoretical physics on the grounds of mere technicalities. Three years later, however, he was made a full-time associate professor at the University of Zürich, but at such a low salary that he left to teach at the University of Prague for a year and a half. After that, he accepted a chair in the Federal Institute of Technology, where he once had been a student.

He soon became a world-famous pioneer in theoretical physics. Universities everywhere tried to persuade him to join their faculties, and Einstein accepted a chair at the University of Berlin in 1913 which he held until Hitler forced him to emigrate to America.

After Einstein's death, three countries claimed him as their "son": Germany, because he was born there; the United States, for having made him a citizen through a special *lex Einstein,* and Switzerland, because he expressly applied for citizenship there. Nazi Germany had deprived him of the right to call himself a German. Although anyone becoming a United States citizen must renounce any other citizenship, Einstein never repudiated his Swiss citizenship. The only diploma he kept hanging on the wall of his Princeton office was the one that cited him as an honorary member of the Berne Society of Sciences, and this despite the slowness and hesitation of his Berne colleagues to recognize his genius. He must have kept this one diploma demonstratively visible from sheer sentiment. After all, it was in Berne that the thought of all relativity was born.

The first accomplishments in the abstract sciences were achieved in Basle, where the family Bernoulli brought forth an entire dynasty of mathematicians in the Age of Enlightenment. They were remarkable talents and teachers in abstract thinking and theoretical speculation, but the genius they brought forth was Jean Bernoulli's student, Leonhard Euler (1707–1783), who was born in Basle and, having been acclaimed internationally, was also active in Germany and Russia. Euler made some of the greatest contributions to modern mathematical analysis.

From his early beginnings Euler's interests were not limited and embraced physics, astronomy, and philosophy, even though his decisive contributions lay in the field of pure mathematics. He was a man of astounding talent and energy. Next to his French disciple, J. L. Lagrange, Euler is considered the great pioneering mathematician of the eighteenth century, who excelled in the skillful and imaginative use of algorithmic devices. Euler was far more than a weighty textbook writer. His restless and inventive mind roamed into far-reaching fields of speculation. He enriched the world of mathematics with astounding results and attempted to replace synthetic by analytic methods. It can be said of him that he prepared the basic material in this field for the systematic exploitations during the nineteenth century.

Euler proved that most geniuses are also prolific, that their productive curiosity is matched by industry. In his time he was most popular for his *Lettres à une Princesse d'Allemagne,* an easy exposition of principles in physics and astronomy to which he added some penetrating thoughts on religion and philosophy. This work had great influence on his contemporaries. But within his complete oeuvre, comprising about eighty quarto volumes, these letters now play a rather modest part. His major contribution was his *Introductio in analysin infinitorum,* which did for modern analysis what the *Elements of Euclid* had once done for ancient geometry. It was Euler who started the tendency to arithmetize mathematics and physics. His concepts served as guidelines down to the twentieth century. This can particularly be said about his important textbooks in the calculus, *Institutiones calculi differentialis* and *Institutiones calculi integralis.* From elementary geometry, with the Eulerian line determining a triangle, to advanced calculus, where the Eulerian integrals define the beta and gamma functions, his name has remained familiar to the student of higher mathematics.

I can telescope only a few more accomplishments of this genius: he proved the addition theorem for elliptic integrals; in the theory of numbers he found the law of quadratic reciprocity; he propounded the analytic treatment of the trigonometric functions as numerical ratios, relating them through the Euler identities, with imaginary exponentials; moreover, differentive geometry had its first real start in his studies of lines of curvature; and it was Euler who discovered the achromatic lens which became indispensable in the production of telescopes and microscopes. Just as Leonardo once lacked only the technical know-how to get the flying machine off the ground, so Euler discovered and theorized about the modern turbine in the mid-eighteenth century. We could continue to list his accomplishments for quite a while.

Even those readers who have as scant a knowledge of these matters as I have must sense the weightiness of these achievements that have built significant theoretical bridges into our time. Euler certainly must have impressed his contemporaries. At the age of twenty he followed an invitation of Catherine I, who made him an associate of the Academy of Sciences at St. Petersburg. There he became a colleague of Daniel and Nicolas Bernoulli, the two sons of Jean Bernoulli, who was Euler's teacher. Seven years later he became professor of physics and, shortly after, succeeded Daniel Bernoulli in the chair of mathematics.

Euler's career had a much easier start than Einstein's, but both careers followed a parallel pattern when, at the peak of his fame, each accepted a most tempting offer from Berlin. In 1741, Frederick the Great invited Euler to accept membership in the Academy of Sciences at Berlin where, for the following twenty-five years, he made known his discoveries and notations in a constant stream of publications.

Another parallel between the two careers was less tragic for Euler than was the Nazis' coming into power to Einstein. At one point Frederick's attitude towards Euler cooled off noticeably, and in 1766 this great scientist gladly accepted a renewed invitation from St. Petersburg. There he remained to the day of his death. More than thirty years previously he had lost his sight in one eye. Soon after his arrival at the Russian capital a cataract formed in the other eye, and Euler was condemned to spend the remaining years of his life in blindness. This could have crushed any man but Euler, whose energy and productive urge overcame all his physical handicaps. Supported by an unusual memory and an exemplary facility of speculative thinking, he continued to give creative expression to the bright world of his mind, however dark his external world had become.

It was often pointed out that, through the universality of his mind, Euler was the scientific conscience of his time. He crowned the work of his teacher Jean Bernoulli who, together with his brother Jakob, laid the groundwork to Euler's accomplishments. History, in its often nonchalant injustice, has the habit of minimizing the importance of teachers blessed by destiny with disciples whose works go beyond or overshadow those of their masters. But even the great Leibnitz admitted that mathematical analysis is as much indebted to the Brothers Bernoulli as to him.

The Bernoullis were not the first mathematicians Switzerland produced, for they were preceded by Joost Bürgi (1552–1632), a Renaissance figure of quite some interest. His discovery of the logarithmic principle is one of his great achievements. Unfortunately, his "Progress Tabulen" was published in Prague a few years after his Scottish contemporary Neper had come out with the same discovery. But no one less than Johannes Kepler, the great astronomer, whom Bürgi had befriended while working at the court of Rudolf II in Prague, tells us that Bürgi had made his discovery many years earlier and, in mock modesty, thinking little of it, neglected to publicize it immediately.

Bürgi must be mentioned here because he was a watchmaker before becoming an astronomer and mathematician. He entered the service of Count Wilhelm IV von Hessen (who was in love with astronomy) as a *Hofuhrmacher* (court watchmaker) in 1597 and continued after Wilhelm's death in 1592 to run his planetarium alone. Bürgi's fame as a watchmaker and astronomer made Emperor Rudolf II entreat him to come to Prague, then an important cultural center, in 1604. Bürgi's two great virtues were practicality and exactitude. He produced clocks that not only gave the most exact time, but also showed each second, something unheard-of in those days. He loved to construct new mathematical instruments, and above all he became famous for his celestial globe with an artistically built-in clock mechanism.

INDUSTRY, INGENUITY, AND POLITICS

INDUSTRY cannot easily be divorced from science and its technological applications. That Switzerland has become a highly industrialized country today has many reasons. For a country to flourish, it needs not only an industrious population—it can be said without exaggeration that the average Swiss works harder and longer hours than workers in many other countries—but also God-given means. If all roads lead to Rome, then all roads lead across Switzerland, situated in the heart of Europe. Nowadays it takes merely an hour or two to reach every European metropolis from Switzerland by air. Without transport communications, no industry can properly develop.

The country is known for its smallness. Intellectually, its people may suffer from a claustrophobic feeling; psychologically, from a feeling of inferiority. But industrially, the fact of its smallness has worked to the country's advantage even though its size is further reduced by its topography. Only three-quarters of Swiss territory can be cultivated without great difficulty. Add to it the space taken up by the concrete, stone, and asphalt of the roads, cities, and towns. Since the soil fed fewer and fewer of its growing population, more and more people were concentrated in trade and industry, in commerce and transport.

The regions which can be little, or not at all, cultivated, the mighty mountains, lovely lakes, and impressive waterfalls of which this country has more than it needs—except for its electrification of industry and transport—have become exploited by what is known as tourism. On all mountain slopes and on the edges of its lakes hotels have grown overnight like mushrooms. Moreover, with the democratization of a world which is shrinking rapidly through the means of modern transportation, tourism has become the twentieth-century plague which the Swiss treat with cashocratic efficiency and commercial heroism.

Successful industry means export. Swiss products vary from chemical and pharmaceutical articles to a sophisticated variety of cheeses and chocolates, from the tiniest watches to the most powerful machines that can be found anywhere in the world. But the least publicized export article is the Swiss himself. Even in medieval days, overpopulation led to emigration. The earliest and most famous product in human shape was the mercenary soldier who, later, was replaced by the skilled worker and specialist. Five per cent of today's population lives abroad, close to 200,000 in European countries, and more than 80,000 in America alone.

Since 1515, when Swiss policy turned to perpetual neutrality, guaranteed by all great powers again in 1815, its neutrality has been —figuratively speaking—its hottest export item. In a war-torn world, Switzerland became a storehouse for treasure and fortunes. By the grace of neutrality and the greed of the wealthy of the world, the vaults of the Swiss banks grew to mighty money mountains. It has already become difficult for smaller investors to leave their money there, and I can foresee the day when Swiss banks will pay interest to those who will refrain from hiding their gold behind the altar of Switzerland's neutrality.

In order to accomplish what this country has achieved industrially, one needs more than individual industriousness, ingenuity, and will power. Above all, one needs manpower. This word, with its English sound of intensity and strength, is used everywhere in Switzerland. There is no unemployment. On the contrary there are many vacant positions begging to be filled. Advertisements coax the people with all possible promises, offering certain advantages. It is only a seeming contradiction that five per cent of its citizenry lives and works in other countries, while Switzerland has to import many hundreds of thousands of workers. They are mainly seasonal workers or those employed in hotels and hospitals, for the construction of roads, tunnels, and buildings. Laborers and menial workers, they do not compete with what the Swiss are looking for, but are badly needed to keep the ship afloat. All branches of industry have become overdeveloped and overexpanded. Men are needed on board and at the machines.

These workers, however, have come from impoverished parts and families in Italy and Spain mainly, with some from Greece and Yugoslavia. They are Mediterranean types, and their way of being, their background, and their often lacking education are different from the reactions and habits of the rather staid and less hot-tempered Swiss. One day the Swiss woke up to the realization that almost twenty per cent of those living with and among them were foreigners. "A small nation of masters feels endangered; it asked for laborers, but human beings arrived," were Max Frisch's words with which he characterized the sudden fear of his contemporaries that their country could be *überfremdet*, overwhelmed, penetrated, influenced by foreigners. The Swiss Firsters raised their voices and fists and, forced by one of their leaders, James Schwarzenbach, the Swiss were asked to vote on whether at least 300,000 of the 930,000-odd foreigners should not be expelled from the country. This move was voted down, but with an uncomfortably small margin, in the spring of 1970. No one can claim that the Swiss are not human and may not lose their nerve or, translated into political terms, that the cries of their conservative stock cannot have a convincing sound to many Swiss ears.

Liberalism and tolerance have always been strong forces in this country. But it is very likely that many who voted against Schwarzenbach's proposal realized that keeping Switzerland clean and safe from Mediterranean infection, morally and physically, could be achieved only at the expense of a reduction in industrial output. Swiss crafts and industry were at stake, and both have come a long way. By the late Middle Ages the craftsmen, organized into guilds, proved the industriousness of the people. The textile industry flourished in Fribourg as early as the thirteenth to the fifteenth centuries, while St. Gallen was famous not only for its cloister, but also for the manufacturing of linen, which in the seventeenth and eighteenth centuries was replaced by cotton.

In the days of the late Renaissance, Zürich became a center of silk manufacturing, a position which it maintained into the nineteenth century. This carried diplomatic overtones for some time at the end of the sixteenth and the beginning of the seventeenth centuries, when Protestant refugees from Locarno contributed a great deal to the intensification of this industry and carried it to Basle. We now think of Venice as a city for honeymooners and other travelers who want to imbibe the champagne image of this city's beauty. But in those early days Venice was an important point of commerce with the East, importing raw silk to Zürich which Venice then tried to sell again in its manufactured state. But it was also a bulwark against the Turks and required soldiers. It fought, so it claimed, to save Christendom from the Turks. Ideals have never been separated from the question of economics. Swiss soldiery, at that time famous and feared all over the world, was the earliest export article of Switzerland. To keep its silk industry going, Zürich delivered mercenaries to Venice which, additionally, kept a depot of harnesses, muskets, and other armors in Zürich (in Gassen 18). The Venetian government paid 4,000 ducats annually to Zürich, which was allied with Berne in this deal.

Although Switzerland now moves in the forefront of heavy industry, of tool and machine factories, of chemical and pharmaceutical manufacturers of world renown, it has always been associated with clockmaking, introduced to Geneva by the Huguenot refugees from France. The adjoining French-speaking Jura became the home of the watch and clock industry which, in 1679, was actually founded in Le Locle by a locksmith's apprentice named Daniel Jean Richard who is said to have repaired the first clock.

Switzerland has never lacked men of ingenuity to further its industry. Among the many who could be named, Johann Georg Bodmer (1786–1864) was the most interesting one. Many of his inventions were far ahead of his time. As a matter of fact, it can be said that certain of his inventions were re-invented by later generations. In the early days of the steam engine, England was the Mecca for engineers and inventors. In 1824, when the first locomotive ran from Manchester to Liverpool at the unheard-of speed of twenty miles an hour, Bodmer was in England where, in Bolton and Manchester, he had his own workshops, financed by other people, for twenty-four years.

Bodmer was more appreciated abroad than in his home country. The list of his inventions is endless, from textile machines and mountain locomotives to a variety of tools and corridor cars which greatly improved the railways. Although born in Zürich as the son of a merchant, there was little that was mercantile about him. The money he made with one invention was used for the solution of another problem. He was neither practical nor realistic, obsessed only with his ideas. But what was certainly Swiss about him was his endurance and ability to keep a fifteen-hour working day for seven days a week.

Due to its central position and privileged status of neutrality, Switzerland was destined to play a special role in the nuclear world, too. Beyond housing many international organizations which try to cure the ills of mankind in a peaceful way, Geneva was chosen as the seat of a laboratory in which physicists of all lands try to unriddle miracles by creating new ones. At Meyrin, a few miles from Geneva, a pan-European research institute for high-energy physics was opened in 1959, the twenty-eight-billion-electron-volt accelerator (proton synchrotron) constructed at CERN (Conseil Européen pour la Recherche Nucléaire). In June 1953 the citizens of the Canton of Geneva were asked to vote on whether they would permit an international physics laboratory near their city, and they approved of the project. The construction of the "big machine" for all kinds of experiments cost the member states, of which there are thirteen now, twenty-eight million dollars.

All the experiments undertaken (a single one may take more than a year and may easily cost a million dollars) are no longer the work of one scientist, but of a team of a dozen or more physicists from various countries. Only future generations will be able to determine the value of these experiments, but there can be no doubt that high-energy physics is at the ultimate frontier of our understanding of nature and perhaps of man's role in the universe. However enlightening or revolutionary the findings of these scientists may be, it stands to reason in our nuclear age that mankind's fate may not be decided so much in Washington, Moscow, or Peking as it will be in Meyrin, Switzerland.

THE ADVENTURE OF HEALING AND EXPLORING

IF one looks through the chronicles written about life at the various European courts from the early Renaissance to the late eighteenth century, one cannot help stumbling over many Swiss physicians in the service of royalty. The Swiss medical school has an old tradition, but most of the Swiss medical men were searchers for new truths, from Paracelsus (c. 1490–1541) to Theodor Kocher (1841–1917). Kocher was a Berne surgeon whose work and writings on surgery were pioneering in the days of antisepsis, asepsis, and anesthetics, and who was one of the first to receive the Nobel prize in medicine. Medical men realized that the ills of man are as much psychic as they are social and often expanded their activities into psychology, as Carl Gustav Jung (1875–1961) did. Paul

Usteri (1768–1831) was active in socio-political spheres and became President of the Helvetic Republic in 1798. He was an intrepid representative of political freedom and freedom of the press and the actual bearer of all revolutionary thinking in Zürich at his time. To give another example, Robert Steiger (1801–1862), a member of the National Council and its president from 1848 to 1849, was a zealot who published a good deal about medicine, politics, and botany. He played a great part in the irregular partisan movement, was sentenced to death in a State trial, but was then set free.

This trend began with Valerius Anshelm who settled in Berne in 1505. He was first a schoolmaster before he was installed as chief medical adviser to the city. In his cycle of Dance of Death, the painter-poet Niklaus Manuel used him as his model for Death calling on the healer of man. His contemporaries knew and revered Anshelm for what he did for them as a medical man, but they also recognized him as a great humanist and trusted him with the writing of the *Berner Chronik*. It was as chronicler of the dramatic events of his time that he became most important, creating a work of lasting historic value.

Johann Conrad Brunner (1653–1727), born in Diessenhofen, was a physician of world renown, best exemplified by the fact that his medical advice was sought by the Emperor in Vienna, the kings of Denmark, England, Prussia, and Sweden, and almost all princes, dukes, and counts. It is not difficult to see that he was the most fashionable doctor of his time. But it was also said of him that he never neglected his duties towards the common man. In the annals of medicine we may come across the term "Brunner glands," which goes back to his investigation published under the title of *De glandulis in duodeno intestino hominis detectis* in 1687. Brunner's motto was, "Truth be above everything," and he tried to base his art of healing on reason and experience. He strongly believed that there must be a specific medication for each disease, and he was one of the first to discover the curing effect of the cinchona bark against fever. (In extracted form, it later became the well-known quinine.) But Brunner still administered bloodletting, as did all his contemporaries either as a panacea or as a final act of desperation.

A number of multitalented men in the eighteenth century were professors of anatomy, surgery, and botany. Such a genius was Johann Jakob Scheuchzer (1672–1733). He was a medical man, mathematician, paleontologist, historian, theologist, philologist, and an Helvetian patriot whose *Natural History of Switzerland* is one of the fundamental works of the country.

Almost a century earlier, Conrad Gessner (1516–1565), born in Zürich, was a little Renaissance giant. As a philologist, he edited the writers of antiquity. He must be considered the father of bibliography. At the age of twenty-nine, he issued his *Bibliotheca universalis,* in which he listed alphabetically on 1,264 folio pages about 3,000 authors, their works and brief biographies, from the earliest times. As a physician he experimented on himself and on animals, and his book on the preparation of medications achieved thirty editions and was translated into many languages, one of the first best-sellers in the field of science. There was nothing that he was not interested in and his explorations and findings were systematized and re-created with telling words and pictures. He published four volumes on the animal world and a similar work about plants. He was the first to recognize that plant life could be classified naturally by families (genera) and species. Linnaeus took up the same idea two hundred years later, in 1735. Another work, registering and classifying stones and fossils, was published in the year of his death. Gessner was not really a pioneer, but he certainly was an unusual genius.

No one can contest that Paracelsus was an unusual person, although many of his contemporaries claimed that he was a charlatan hiding behind a mask of genius. Undoubtedly, he was one of the most fascinating figures of the early sixteenth century. He probably did not open the gate of modern medical science, but he certainly stood on its threshold and hammered at it with both fists, not quite knowing what vast horizons lay behind it.

Theophrastus Bombastus von Hohenheim, physician and alchemist, was born near Einsiedeln in the canton Schwyz. He wanted to be known as Paracelsus, an epithet he chose to prove his superiority to Celsus (an eclectic Platonist who lived in Alexandria or Rome in the second century, A.D., one of the first iconoclasts, representing the most powerful pagan reaction against Christianity). He saw a challenge in medicine as practiced at his time and tried to find new solutions to old questions. He was a fantast who throve on challenge, which he often invented.

With medieval concepts and riddles torturing his mind, he constantly dreamt of having come upon the wonder of tomorrow. But he still believed in yesterday's images, even though they had the touch of Renaissance man's daring. Thus he believed in elemental beings of the air, which he perceived as mortal but soulless, and gave them the name of *sylphs*. On the other hand, when lecturing at the University of Basle, he burned publicly and solemnly the works of Galen and Avicenna, setting forth new theories and methods of treating disease. He often diagnosed certain phenomena correctly, but in prescribing the cure he lapsed into the primitive and obvious. For example, he recognized dansomania, also known as St. Vitus' dance in the North and tarantella in Italy, for the hysteria it was and rejected the then customary use of charms. He also distinguished between three aspects of the disease: *chorea imaginativa*, the result of self-hypnosis; *chorea naturalis*, uncontrollable hysterical laughter; and *chorea lasciva*, or sexual excitement, for which latter aspect he recommended throwing its victims into cold water.

When he went to the mines in the Tyrol, he became interested in the mechanical difficulties in mining and in the nature of minerals, but especially in the miners' diseases. In his time lectures on medicine were delivered in Latin, but Paracelsus lectured in German. Although he had studied at the University of Basle and later with J. Trithemius, abbot of Sponheim, his opponents accused him of having no degree (which probably was true) and pointed out that his system was riddled with defects. Theophrastus Bombastus' way of being invited controversy, and eventually led to a crisis through a dispute about fees. Disgusted by the diatribes of colleagues he considered his inferiors, he resumed his wanderings in 1529. In 1541, invited by the Archbishop Ernst of Salzburg—who took a liking to this fantast with the touch of magic—to stay and work in this city under his protection, Paracelsus' wanderings came to an end. Soon after he settled in Salzburg he died and was buried in the churchyard of St. Sebastian. The cause of his death remains shrouded in darkness. Did he die due to drunkenness and debauchery, or did a couple of thugs hired by jealous physicians and apothecaries throw him down a steep precipice? We shall never know. But we do know that it was 211 years before a monument was erected to his memory.

In order to treat all kinds of diseases, Paracelsus popularized tinctures and alcoholic extracts, prescribed mineral baths and, being ahead of his time, prepared medications out of opium, mercury, lead, sulfur, iron, arsenic, and copper sulfate. Paracelsus believed that a physician's requirements were threefold: above all, he must know the physical sciences and alchemy, because man contains all elements and requires them to cure his diseases; secondly, he must know astronomy, because the stars influence and guide man's fate, penetrating him with astral spirits, and can be the direct cause and cure for diseases; thirdly, the physician must be a theologist of sorts and realize that man has not only a body and spirit, but also a soul created by God, and that his soul lives in man's spirit, equal to the body in matters of disease.

As a genuine child of his age he believed in the Neo-Platonic philosophy which saw the life of man as something inseparable from the universe. He thought that the human as a product of the scriptural *limus terrae* is actually an extract of all beings previously alive. Man is compounded primarily of salt, sulfur, and mercury —mystic elements—and their separation in man unbalances the human system and causes sickness. When this separation occurs, a vital occult force located in the pit of the stomach fails to perform its function in separating the useful from the poisonous.

Paracelsus stood between two ages—the medieval one full of superstitions, and the modern one in which medicine had begun to unfold its usefulness with medications composed of extracts and mixtures of salts, minerals, and metallic elements. Was he a quack or a genius? From the vantage point of the late twentieth century, this question can easily be answered: in all likelihood he was both.

_____

Speaking to young or old in Switzerland, I was often struck by their adventurous spirit. To express it most simply, quite a few of them feel the urge to leave their country and explore the world. It is as if they were driven to look for bigger challenges than their geographically limited home country can offer. They are also often obsessed by a missionary idea—to prove to themselves and to the world that they can be of use to mankind. It is difficult to say how much of the missionary mania is influenced by their historic role of mediation and how much is an unconscious self-sacrifice to repay the gods for having bestowed upon them more than their fair share.

If the feeling of narrowness, as so often claimed, can drive the Swiss artist into self-imposed exile, then it can certainly nourish a man's curiosity and make him search for the unknown in faraway countries, particularly when his latent soldierly instincts can be channeled into the courage needed by the explorer. The best example is John Augustus Sutter, probably more an adventurer than explorer. In history he became identified as one of the famous pioneer settlers in California on whose land, unfortunately for him, gold was discovered in 1848.

His story reads like fiction. In 1834, abandoning wife and children, he fled from bankruptcy to America, where he became a captain in the service of the Mexican government. Only he knew how he became known as "General Sutter." He had the desire to go to the Pacific coast, went to Oregon and, while failing as a trader, as far as the Hawaiian islands. His audacity and charm induced the Mexican governor to grant him lands in the Sacramento valley, where he established a fortified, large, and rich colony which he called—proud of his ancestry—New Helvetia, now the city of Sacramento, the capital of California. He was then a powerful man and well known as the General who would help newcomers to California in a lavish way. He was always in debt because he was utterly unrealistic in his enterprises, with no business sense whatsoever. He was a dreamer. But he would not have been a Swiss dreamer had he not founded frontier industries, cultivated land, and raised cattle.

When Mexico was at war with the United States, the Sutter Fort became strategically important. Sutter asked for American citizenship, but General John C. Frémont, the commanding officer of the United States forces, thought little of Sutter and was unappreciative of what he had done for the early Californian settlers. With peace restored, Sutter's fortune began to look brighter. While a sawmill was being built on his grounds, fifty miles off New Helvetia, gold was discovered on his land. Although he tried to keep it a secret, foreseeing its corrupting influence, news about it leaked out. His own people deserted him, and swarms of adventurers came from everywhere, hunting for gold, digging and searching, overrunning his lands, stealing his property, and slaughtering his cattle. His fight against them was as valiant as it was vain.

Sutter left for Pennsylvania, a bankrupt man, failing to convince the United States government that his claims as to land and past service were justified. He died in Washington, a broken man of 77 years. The family had joined him after sixteen years of separation, at a time when his grandeur had turned into frustration and his seeming luck into misfortune. There are Sutter streets in several American cities, and Sutter County in California keeps his name alive. The Sutter Fort in Sacramento was repaired and can be visited.

It is quite natural that the Swiss were destined to become great mountaineers and, in the course of such pursuits, would make sensational discoveries in geology and mineralogy. Accom-

panied by the guide Jacques Balmat and a certain Dr. Paccard from
Chamonix, Horace-Bénédict de Saussure (1740–1799), a native
of Geneva and professor of philosophy, reached the summit of
Mont Blanc for the first time on August 8, 1786. On later expedi-
tions, including the exploration of the region of the Monte Rosa,
Saussure was accompanied by his son Nicolas-Theodore (1767–
1845). Primarily interested in an investigation of plants, he published an impressive work which he called *Recherches chimiques
sur la végétation.*

The name Burckhardt is one of the best known in the history
of Basle, and if we can speak of an intellectual aristocracy, the
Burckhardts would have to be considered one of the important
Swiss dynasties. Johann Ludwig Burckhardt (1784–1817), one of
the descendants of the Basle family, was born in Lausanne. Fascinated by the Orient and Africa, he became one of the great ex-
plorers of the early nineteenth century, a well-known Orientalist
and most notable traveler who was employed by the African
Society in England during the pioneer age of the dark continent's
exploration between 1788 and 1830.

Burckhardt spent about three years in Syria, mainly to learn
the language, habits, and customs of some of the Oriental people.
He hoped it would help him to be able to live among various tribes
in Central Africa as an "Oriental." On his journeys from Syria to
Egypt he made many discoveries, among them the Greco-Roman
ruins of Djerash and the famous rock-city Petra which, in the days
of Christ, was an important trading post on the road leading from
Babylon and Syria into Egypt.

When Burckhardt arrived in Cairo in 1812, he had to resign
himself to the fact that he could not get to the heart of Africa. No
reliable caravan would dare the journey since too much fighting
between the various tribes was going on. He decided instead to
travel along the Nile and undertook the pilgrimage to Mecca from
where he returned to Cairo by way of Medina. He made his journeys under the assumed name of Sheikh Ibrahim ibn Abdullah,
wearing Muslim dress in order to participate in holy ceremonies to
which no "infidel" would be permitted. Due to his deep sympathy
for the Islam, he achieved profound knowledge of Moslem laws and
customs, as reflected in his five travel books. When everything
could finally be arranged for his journey into the heart of Africa,
a journey which should have crowned his explorations, he was so

weakened from his arduous travels that he had not enough resistance to overcome an attack of dysentery.

The Helvetian flag is a simple white cross on a red background.
Flags have always been considered as symbols and regarded with
fanaticism and near-religious awe. The holy wars in the Middle
Ages were conducted in the name of the Prince of Peace, and the
warriors felt their bloody deeds sanctioned when they wore a white
cross on their banner. The red flag has always symbolized the
fighting spirit of a people, ready to give their proverbial last drop
of blood for country or cause. The men of Schwyz had such a banner from the middle of the thirteenth century. They were born
fighters and proud of their red flag. When they took the chestnuts
out of the fire for the Austrian army fighting Burgundy in 1291,
King Rudolph von Habsburg rewarded them with what came
cheapest to him but was considered a signal honor at that time: a
small white cross in the upper right corner on their red flag. Later,
the cross, enlarged and moved into the center of the red background, became the flag of Switzerland.

When in 1863 the idea of the International Red Cross (originated
by a Swiss and constituted on Swiss soil) became a reality, it was
logical to use a red cross on a white background as its symbol, the
white standing for peace and surrender to sanity, the red for man's
blood. The Red Cross has become such a worldwide organization—
the cross was changed into the crescent in the Middle East—that
hardly anyone associates its humanitarian activities any longer with
the Swiss people.

Jean Henry Dunant (1828–1910), born in Geneva, an eyewitness
to the horror and suffering during and after the battle of Solferino
in June 1859, made it his life's purpose and mission to create an
organization that would aid the unfortunate victims of war and
would bring voluntary relief to all kinds of suffering. Dunant immediately organized an emergency service to aid the 40,000 French
and Austrian casualties.

Three years later he published his book, *Un Souvenir de Solférino*, in which he implored the world to create a voluntary relief
society in all countries, to prevent and alleviate man's suffering in
war and peace regardless of color or creed. In 1863 a committee
convened in Geneva and the basic principles of the Red Cross were
formulated. The following year the first Geneva convention came
into being, and its statutes were revised and adjusted in later

decades to the growing penalty man paid for the growing menace of civilization. Dunant continued to fight for a better treatment of war prisoners, for the abolition of slavery, disarmament, international arbitration of serious conflicts between states, and, as a non-Jew, for a Jewish homeland.

Occasionally it is lightly said of a man that he gave his all for the welfare of other people; Dunant is a prime example of such a man. He neglected his private business for the realization of his mission in life. The result was bankruptcy. In 1867 Dunant left Geneva. Poverty and obscurity were his immediate rewards for what he had done for mankind. He lived in the small town of Heiden in Switzerland, where a journalist rediscovered him. He then received many honors and annuities, among them the first Nobel Peace Prize in 1901. He continued to live in Heiden, where he died with the comforting realization that his missionary urge had brought about the first peaceful victory over a war-mad world.

MAN AND THE SECRETS OF HIS SUBCONSCIOUS

OUR century will be remembered for many astounding events and experiences which will have the aftertaste of the unbelievable, and among those many things will be the attempt to know and bare the inner mechanism of man which the ancient, pre-nuclear people vaguely referred to as the human soul. No one will dispute that the first half of this century could be called a psychological era, and the phrase "Freudian Age" has often been heard. It could just as well be called the "Age of Jung."

> I am convinced that exploration of the psyche is the science of the future . . . This is the science we need most of all, for it is gradually becoming more and more obvious that neither famine nor earthquakes nor microbes nor carcinoma, but man himself is the greatest peril to man, just because there is no adequate defense against psychic epidemics, which cause infinitely more devastation than the greatest natural catastrophes.

So wrote Jung in 1944. Carl Gustav Jung became the founder of analytical psychology. Like so many great Swiss, he, too, was the son of a clergyman. Born in Kesswil, a small town on Lake Constance, he came to Basle at the age of four and always regarded this city of humanism as his home town. In his early youth he developed a great enthusiasm for biology, zoology, and paleontology. It was later that he returned to medicine, a study, however, which did not fulfill him. Of logical phases in his development, the study of philosophy and religion began to overshadow his interest in medicine. This extended to mythology which he enthusiastically embraced and through which he slipped into occultism and mysticism. All three occupied him to the end of his life. Even for his doctorate in medicine, conferred upon him by the University of Zürich in 1902, he wrote a dissertation entitled *On the Psychology and Pathology of So-called Occult Phenomena.* His basic concept of a "totality of the psyche" was already formulated in his first paper.

Since the phenomenon of heritage played a major part in Jung's thought processes, it is important to point out what constituted the essential impetus to his own psychic developmental process. Medical and theological interests were predominant among his ancestors, with several Protestant theologians on his mother's side. His paternal forefathers were Germans, and many of them were physicians. His great-grandfather was a leading member of the Catholic community in Mainz. His grandfather was converted to Protestantism in his early youth and was described as a minor poet and aesthete who had to leave Metternich's Germany because of his revolutionary leanings. No one less than Alexander von Humboldt made it possible for Jung's grandfather to settle in Basle and take over the chair of surgery at the university of this city. It must be underlined that he took great interest in mentally disturbed people and founded the first insane asylum in Basle and a home for mentally retarded children.

In the development of his concepts Jung was able to combine and unify such contradictory aspects as occultism and mysticism with medicine and pathology, and the lucidity of the natural sciences with studies of a purely speculative nature. In his opinion this was the only possible approach to the multifaceted psychic make-up of man. Moreover, he thought of practical medicine as an art and of the creative process as something outside and beyond all theories. Jung's advice to the beginning analyst was to put his theories aside as soon as he has to deal with the wonder of the living soul because the analyst's creative potentialities will always be more decisive than his theories.

In 1900 Jung began to work with Eugen Bleuler at the psychiatric clinic of the University of Zürich and continued his studies in Paris under Pierre Janet. In those early years he published *Studies in*

Word-Association, through which significant groups of ideas in the unconscious can be revealed. The term "complexes" was then created by Jung and has since become a household word. Word-association as a method of testing is still used for personality diagnosis and vocational guidance. This aspect of Jung's work brought him to Sigmund Freud in 1907.

A great deal has been made of Jung's relationship with Freud. His attitude towards his "Master," whom he once called "the first important man I've met," has been considered ambivalent by many; as a matter of fact, Jung has been typecast in the role of the unfaithful disciple. Undoubtedly, Jung worked closely with Freud for six years, was with him on a joint lecture in the United States, and was editor of the Bleuler-Freud *Jahrbuch für psychologische und psychopathologische Forschungen*. During all that time he accepted most of Freud's ideas. But for Jung it was like going through the school of a master many years his senior whose concepts he studied and whose methods he probed. It was not Jung's fault that he was considered Freud's foremost disciple, or that, at the time when he joined him, he had already envisioned a certain, although yet inconclusive, image of the mechanism of man's soul and that he had to grope his way in order to give that image its final features.

During those years Jung gradually built his own theories of the libido and the unconscious, essentially rejecting Freud's ideas of infantile sexuality and wish fulfillment as set forth in Jung's book *Wandlungen and Symbole der Libido (Symbols of Transformation)*. This was published in 1912 and finally led to his break with Freud. Jung resigned his post as President of the International Psychoanalytic Society and founded a new school with A. Maeder in Zürich, calling his own theory "analytical psychology" from then on in order to make the differences among his own, Freud's, and Alfred Adler's doctrines unmistakably clear.

To fully understand his split with Freud, as well as his constant probing and correlating of the unconscious manifestations of modern Western man with those of primitive peoples, of medical and mythical facts, we must visualize Jung as a man driven by an unconscious urge "to penetrate the secret of personality," to create the most revealing realization of a higher awareness. "All my writings," he said, "were so to speak assignments from deep within; they emerged from under a compulsion dictated by destiny (*als schicksalhafter Zwang*)."

It has been claimed by Jungian disciples that the difference between their master and Freud lay deeply anchored in two irreconcilable *Weltanschauungen,* with Freud being still closely tied to concepts of the nineteenth century while Jung's ideas were those of a man who understood and was keyed to the problems of the twentieth century with its many revolutionary innovations and its restless search for the meaning of man. Dr. Jolande Jacobi phrased it succinctly: "If it was Freud's attempt to release those people who came to him from their past, it was Jung's concern to connect them with their past as much as to open the way to their future so that in this way the timely human being can meet again the timeless being in his soul."

Beyond the term *complexes,* Jung enriched the imagery of our vocabulary with the descriptive words *introvert* and *extrovert,* a ready-made classification of man as two distinctive types. Furthermore, he propounded the idea that in each person one or more of the four primary functions of the mind predominate, namely, thinking, feeling, sensation, and intuition. In contrast to Freudian analysis, Jung stressed the need to analyze man's immediate conflicts as more significant and useful than the uncovering of the traumas and conflicts of childhood. He changed the image of the libido by enlarging its concept from mere sexuality to man's will to live, to the whole of vital energy comparable to the pulsebeat of the psyche which, with its ups and downs, furnishes us with a lead to psychic processes.

Another most important contribution to the understanding of the inner mechanism of man is his distinction between the personal and collective unconscious. The former includes all the highly individual factors; the latter refers to the disposition inherited from ancestors, to behavior patterns, actions, and reactions of the psyche that reach far back into the history and conflicting matters of the entire race. Jung introduced for these rather speculative potentialities which appear in the form of symbols in man's dreams, fantasies, and visions, the term *archetypes.* He stressed the intimate relationship between archetype and instinct in man. He also gave the archetypal patterns and processes a significance leading beyond all individual psychic revelations, into the sphere of creative expression, as manifested in the myths, sagas, and legends, in religious concepts and fairy tales, in most works of art of all times and cultures.

After his marriage in 1903 to Emma Rauschenbach of Schaffhausen, who was also his scientific collaborator, Jung moved to a house with a large garden in Küsnacht on Lake Zürich. It is characteristic of Jung the psychologist, and even more of Jung the Swiss, that he was nature-bound and felt that one of modern man's greatest needs was to hold on to a piece of land he could call his own. Man's bond with his soil (to which he often referred in his conversations) had, of course, psychological implications for him. "Everyone should possess a piece of his own soil, then his old instinct will re-emerge," he once said to Hans Carol. "One's own soil is psychologically important, and there is no substitute for it." There are primitive layers in our soul which reveal that we are still primates. The peasant is the least uprooted although he cannot derive full satisfaction from his work, his reward being no longer real but abstract—in the form of money. Life in a small city is still preferable to life in a metropolis, as Jung pointed out. Big cities are responsible for our being uprooted. "With all my heart and mind I am for man having roots in the soil," he reiterated. In this context Jung also referred to the Swiss, whom he thought of as mentally better balanced and less neurotic than many other people. "It is of great advantage that we live in many small cities. If I don't have what I need for my soul, I become dangerous."

Particularly in our rapidly growing mechanization, the Swiss are undoubtedly better off than other nations because the structure and natural growth of their country has called for a small city-state. It is, of course, too much of a generalization to see the Swiss as less neurotic than contemporaries in other lands. True, they are involved in fewer social frictions than other people. For instance, for quite some time there have been no strikes to create unrest and ill-feelings or to shake the economic-industrial edifice—not since the Trade Unions gave up the right to strike and accepted the duty to submit their grievances to arbitration. On the other hand, the Swiss people cannot escape being neurotic. They are much too intent on success and the acquisition of fortunes, even if they try never to flaunt their bank accounts. It is also questionable whether the Swiss is the most balanced person—a fact borne out by the high suicide rate, the second highest of all nations. He is well-known to incline to heaviness and melancholy, and such climatic influences as the warm wind called *Föhn* can throw some Swiss off balance. But Jung was on safer ground when he told his interviewer Hans Carol, a city planner, on the occasion of discussing man and his environment: "Since we do not derive direct help from the government in our country, everything that is nevertheless achieved, is more genuine and of greater value."

In spite of his incontestable greatness Jung suffered a psychological derailment (was he trapped by his own concept of the collective unconscious?) when he wrote in the *Zentralblatt für Psychotherapie* (Nazi-Berlin, 1934) about the "precious secret of the German being," whose "spiritual basis with its anticipatory feeling of creativity" (*schoepferischer ahnungsvoller Seelengrund*) Sigmund Freud held in suspicion as "childish banal mire." Jung explained: "He [Freud] did not know the Germanic soul as little as his Germanic sycophant disciples (*Nachbeter*) knew it. Has the powerful appearance of National-Socialism to which the entire world looks up with amazed eyes taught them differently?"

Attacked for his attitude in the *Neue Zürcher Zeitung,* Jung tried to justify his viewpoint with rather weak arguments, such as with a myth-styled history at the basis of which was a new missionary consciousness and, above all, with the idea of "a holy center of all peoples." At that early stage of National-Socialism, when Hitler began to build his Reich of a thousand years, not only Jung but also a great many other mainly German-speaking Swiss were stunned and fascinated by the sham myth of racism.

Such writers as Max Eduard Liehburg, forgotten today, extolled similar concepts and visualized Switzerland as having a historic mission as *The Guardian of the Center*—this was the title of Liehburg's new Wilhelm Tell drama—due to the country's geopolitical position. Myths are seemingly contagious, and the question of whether "it could ever happen here" may be answered in the negative with a fair amount of certainty, but also with some caution. The first half of the thirties, with the cataclysmic depression in the United States, the raging inflation and unemployment in Europe, was a period of confusion in which many people all over the globe saw in fascism a panacea. In Switzerland many saw in it at least a smaller evil, and a bulwark against communism. Blinded by the immediate success of Nazism, some did not look beyond their today and forgot that their country's trademark had always been freedom and tolerance.

It was not the first time that doubts about the fundamental question of Swiss nationhood came up. When Germany overran Belgium and invaded France in 1914, the French-speaking Swiss were outraged, while a great number of the German-speaking Swiss admired Germany and believed in her invincibility. With passions rising and loyalties confused, the liberal and more responsible forces saw a need to act. People remembered how once the poet and novelist Gottfried Keller had influenced the Swiss when he raised his voice in favor of liberalism during the times of trial in the nineteenth century. The poet Carl Spitteler, at the age of seventy, leaving his Olympian heights, stood in front of a Zürich audience in December 1914, entreating his countrymen to understand the danger they were facing when they believed themselves more closely attached to the people of another nation than to one another: "We must realize that our political brother is closer to us than the best neighbor and racial kinsman. To strengthen this realization is our patriotic duty. It is not an easy duty. We must feel united without being similar."

Soon afterwards Switzerland was at its most neutral behavior, which was welcomed by all warring nations, doing humanitarian work during the entire war years. It cared for sick prisoners, helped others get in touch with their families, took care of close to 70,000 internees, and gave thousands of students a chance to continue their studies at Swiss universities. The Red Cross worked day and night. Switzerland was also host to deserters, spies, and famous pacifists. Lenin spent the three years prior to his return to Russia in Berne and Zürich. Moreover, conservative Switzerland did not prevent the socialist congress from taking place at the Bernese villages of Zimmerwald and Kiental in 1915–16, the very same congress which laid the foundations for the Third International, the Comintern, and the beginning of international communism. Switzerland never lacked the color of contrasts.

Spitteler's words were forgotten in the thirties, and the dangers which little Switzerland faced, surrounded as it was by Hitler and Mussolini, became a thousand times magnified. The magic of the race of supermen went so far that attempts were made to undermine the Confederation. While the country opened its gates for many refugees, notably for well-known intellectuals and artists, a Fifth Column was established, and the *Nationale Bewegung der Schweiz* was ready to join the German Reich.

Readiness for compromise and defeatism were rampant in those early days of World War II. There was no poet of Spitteler's stature who could have overcome the demoralizing fear by which the Swiss, like any other European nation, were gripped. It is doubtful that a poet could have done the trick. Before Hitler unleashed the *Blitzkrieg*, the Federal Council declared a state of active service all over the country. The popular Henri Guisan of Vaud was elected leading general of the mobilized army.

The summer of 1940 was one of the most crucial moments in modern Switzerland's history. With Germany triumphant on all fronts and with the swift collapse of countries stronger than Switzerland, the morale of the people was at its lowest. A declaration of the Federal Council that "Switzerland will resist to the utmost with all means at its command" was of little avail when shortly afterwards, on June 25, 1940, Swiss government officials made surprising remarks in a broadcast urging the people to "discard the old attitudes." About a month later General Guisan gathered his senior officers to the Rütli meadow, the place where Switzerland's history began. It was not a poet but a general who then turned the tide. To the officers and the people his words to stand firm and to defend their freedom as well as their unity came "like a mysterious call of the past." The danger of subversion was neither immediately nor totally eliminated, although the Nazi Front and Communist Party were banned. But the courage of one man and the determination of the majority of the people saved Switzerland from voluntary destruction in 1940.

In other words, Carl Gustav Jung was no exception; he was only a sad example, one of many, and one who had lost his better judgment over his own theories. Dr. Jolande Jacobi, one of the intellectuals from Vienna who found refuge in Switzerland in the late thirties, worked with Jung and was greatly instrumental in the founding of the Jung Institute in Zürich. She was one of Jung's close collaborators and intimated in our conversation that Jung later regretted having written those incriminating lines in praise of Nazism. But besides being *weltfremd* ("little attuned to the realities of the world"), as she pointed out, Jung strongly believed that human greatness and the purification of the species can only emerge from chaos. Also believing in the inner strength of races, he welcomed Nazism as a powerful ferment in mankind's development. At a later stage Jung tried somewhat to dissociate himself from his previously held viewpoint and attitude towards Hitlerism.

To understand Jung's actions and reactions better, we must turn to what Dr. Jacobi once wrote about Jung, the man. She referred to him as "an extraordinary personality, combining the keenest contradictions. Contemplativeness and childlike cheerfulness, delicate sensibility and robust simplicity, cold reserve and true devotion, rigor and tolerance, humor and severity, aloofness and love for mankind were equally prominent traits in his make-up." Although this enumeration of traits seems to come straight out of a book of synonyms and antonyms, it nevertheless characterizes the man who all his life was aware of the complexities (*Zwienatur*) of his own being.

The rational, conscious man in him who had to cope with the

realities of life was a mortal, time-conditioned "ephemeral appear-ance." He stood in opposition to another timeless and primeval man in him who belonged to the world of the irrationalities, of myth, of nocturnal visions and those emerging during the day. These men lived together, even though in different departments and at different times. Dr. Jacobi stressed that Jung's work con-sisted of his lifelong attempt to reconcile and unite these two basically different beings in him. "I was a sum total of emotions, and something else in me was the timeless 'stone,' " Jung admitted in his autobiography *Erinnerungen, Traeume und Gedanken* (*Memories, Dreams and Reflections*). This timeless stone could have meant to him a related, indestructible substantiality, or a philo-sophic stone, as the end product of all alchemistic attempts.

Written in his autobiography, this sounds almost like a Kierke-gaardian thought: "As a child I felt lonesome, and I still do to this very day because I know and must intimate things of which others apparently know nothing and also most often do not want to know anything. Lonesomeness does not exist because one is not sur-rounded by any human being, but rather because one cannot tell anyone those things which seem important or because one con-siders thoughts as valid which appear improbable to others." Jung never lost the feeling "of being expelled or chosen, cursed or blessed." It is a feeling which may be symbolic of the Swiss, sur-rounded and narrowed-in, as they are, by their towering moun-tains, cursed and blessed, as they feel, to stand at the crossroads of Europe, compelled to play the part of the mediator and missionary.

At the very end of his autobiography Jung admits: "The older I became, the less I understood or recognized or knew myself . . . I can pass no judgment on myself and my life." In deference to the monument he set himself, with his great and lasting work encom-passing about two hundred books and shorter essays, we ought to join him in passing no judgment on him and his life.

Jung may represent a climactic moment in the development of psychology in Switzerland, but he is not the only Swiss psycholo-gist of world reputation. One of the first to have worked with Freud and Jung was the above-mentioned Eugen Bleuler (1857–1959), a son of Zürich, who, after completing his studies, became director of a hospital in Zürich and professor of psychiatry at the university. He was still strongly influenced by Wilhelm Wundt's rather old-fashioned approach to psychology, whose concepts were diametrically opposed to those of Freud. Standing on a bridge between two worlds, Bleuler tried somehow to reconcile Wundt's laboratory approach with the rather philosophical approach of Freud in studying the problems of mental disorder. As a consequence he vacillated between the ideas that mental disorders could best he explained as an organic or as a psychogenic disease.

Bleuler was most interested in dementia praecox, that form of insanity which develops mostly in late adolescence and is characterized by loss of interest in people and things and by a certain incoherence of thought and action. He intensely studied this type of psychosis and tried to learn to communicate with those sick people who had lost contact with their environment. It was Bleuler who introduced the term *schizophrenia* as a more descriptive term for dementia praecox. He dealt with the regressive behavior of the schizophrenic and thought that the conflict caused by the individual's inability to cope with his desires and aspirations sets the stage for the development of delusions.

A great deal of experimental work towards the testing of personality has been done in Switzerland, and the name that comes immediately to mind is that of Hermann Rorschach (1884–1922), whose inkblot test, known as the Rorschach test, has been used all over the world. Rorschach thought of his work as an experiment in perception, attempting to explore an individual's personality in depth, as well as the range of his intellectual ability. Rorschach's test seeks to reach into man's emotional make-up and the unconscious, reflecting man's psychopathological conditions.

He devised ten symmetrical inkblots which, first limited to the study of the thematic content, have widely and perhaps too indiscriminately been used as stimuli for free association. The patient's attention is focused on the entire image or on certain details of the blot figures, their color and shading, the apparent movement resulting in the perception of human forms, and other factors. Various patterns were correlated with certain clinical pictures. In his interpretative analysis Rorschach proceeded to find, through the patient's reactions, the dynamics of psychological processes or the structure of the personality.

In these tests a good deal depends on the analyst's interpretative skill, leaving a rather wide margin of speculative error. Because of the obvious difficulty of keeping its variables under strict laboratory control, Rorschach and his test were criticized and attacked. But his method has been used in hospitals and in institutions of vocational guidance. Used as one of several aids towards diagnosis in psychopathology, it has proved itself quite valuable. But the Rorschach test is not as fashionable today as it was earlier in the century.

Probably less important and reliable is the Szondi test, designed by the Swiss-Hungarian Leopold Szondi, who relies totally on heredity and man's predispositions in his analyses, based on the patient's sympathetic or antipathetic reactions to images of eight different diseases.

There are at least two renowned psychologists who have added to the many existing schools and their off-shoots another trend which runs parallel to existentialism as a philosophy and is known as existential psychology or analysis. Ludwig Binswanger (1881–1969) and Medard Boss (1903–   ) must be mentioned in this context. Binswanger created the very foundation of this branch of analytical psychology which had great influence on the so-called *Daseinanalyse* and which, rejecting the preponderous value attributed to the unconscious, has taken most of its guidelines from Heidegger's philosophy.

There are other schools and men denying the unconscious its due, and among them is one of the great psychologists who has become the world's foremost authority in child psychology, the Swiss Jean Piaget (1896–   ), born in Neuchâtel. He is a pragmatist who explores and explains how the consciousness of the child develops. He has done wonders with his investigations of *The Child's Conception of Time and The Mechanisms of Perception.*

Between 1923 and 1932 he published five books which deal with language and the thought processes, with the world image and moral judgment of the child. These books reflect the way children see the world and the change of the world conditioned by their own growth. Three later books, written between 1936 and 1945, treat the preschool period of the child and are based mainly on observations of his own three children. Piaget progressively made studies of *The Psychology of Intelligence* (1947), summing up his experiences with children up to twelve years, before he wrote *From the Logic of the Child to the Logic of the Adolescent* (1955). These are only some of his many books and essays in a series of experimental studies on perception, some of them written with his colleagues B. Inhelder and A. Szeminska. If a prolific outpour of works is characteristic of genius, then Jean Piaget is certainly a genius. In his field, in the developmental approach to experimental psychology, he undoubtedly is.

His entire life has been devoted to the progressive study of the child. In order to gain insight into the various processes of man's growth, Piaget has shown an admirable patience and willingness to observe children, virtually to relive their lives with them, to keep learning from the way they learn about the world. As the painstaking investigator he is, he has concentrated on all cognitive functions, that is, those providing knowledge of the external world, since he believes that most affective or emotional functions are closely bound up with these. He studied the development of perception and intelligence in the child with the purpose in mind not only to use his findings for practical pedagogical means but also, and probably in the main, to throw light on the miracle of how the human being develops psychologically.

Jean Piaget was a child prodigy. An article he wrote at the age of ten on an albino sparrow called attention to his clear thinking and interest in the sciences, and five years later his writing on mollusks carried his reputation beyond the Swiss borders. He obtained his doctorate at the University of Neuchâtel at the age of eighteen. His biological training and his interest in epistemology and logic led to his studies in psychology. He has held chairs at the universities of Neuchâtel, Lausanne, and Paris since he was appointed director of studies at the Institut J. J. Rousseau of Geneva in 1921 and received a professorship at the University of Geneva in 1929.

In his discussion of the development of logical structures in children, he made the distinction between two complementary aspects of thought, the figurative and the operative. The former, always subordinated to the latter,

> is an imitation of states taken as momentary and static. In the cognitive area the figurative functions are, above all, perception, imitation, and mental imagery, which is interiorized imitation. The operative aspect deals not with states but with transformations from one state to another. It includes actions themselves, which transform objects or states, and intellectual operations . . . Any state can be understood only as the result of certain transformations, or as the point of departure for other transformations. To me, therefore, the essential aspect of thought is its operative aspect. I think that human knowledge is essentially active. To know is to assimilate reality into system of transformation. To know is to transform reality in order to understand how a certain state is brought about.

I am quoting this passage from his study of genetic epistemology —the study of the development of the notions and processes that subserve knowledge in the individual and society—at such length because it is characteristic of Jean Piaget's sober and lucid thinking and style, his remarkably restrained presentation of his ideas and deductions. It shows a bit of the man himself, who is probably not a born essayist as Freud and Jung were, but who knows how to give his thoughts and the results of his elaborate investigations memorable form and imagery. Sometimes a humorous remark slips into his writings, as, for example, when he says, "Unfortunately for psychology, everybody thinks of himself as a psychologist."

Piaget's genius, with a touch of the human, strives towards a more thorough and intelligent adaptation to the environment, enabling the individual to achieve a more complete equilibrium between psychological processes. I wonder whether Jean Piaget will not one day be referred to as the Pestalozzi of psychology.

THE LITERARY LINGUAE OF THE SWISS

FRENCH

OUR story of Mme. de Staël and Benjamin Constant, two Swiss writers of strong ties with France, must begin with Mme. de Staël's mother, Suzanne Curchod, and the English historian, Edward Gibbon (1737–1794), the famous author of *The Decline and Fall of the Roman Empire*.

Suzanne, a pastor's daughter from the Canton de Vaud, fell in love with the future historian when both were very young. At the age of sixteen, Gibbon had been sent to Switzerland by his father to be saved from his follies and fascination with the Roman Catholic Church. The Gibbons were financially independent. His father had a seat in Parliament, and, as a rich and important man, he did not want to see his only son disqualified under the existing laws from taking any public office or service. The next best thing to do was to send the boy to Lausanne in order to reconvert him to Protestantism, which, under the clever surveillance of the Calvinist minister Rev. Daniel Pavillard, succeeded very well indeed. After about a year, Edward Gibbon was readmitted to the Protestant communion at Christmas 1754.

More important than his reconversion, however, were Gibbon's intense studies of the Latin classics and French contemporary literature at an age in which his mind was molded. He also found during these formative years a lifelong friend in the Swiss Georges Deyverdun, whose emotional influence and intellectual stimulation on Gibbon were significant. Gibbon's father called him back to England when the boy reached his twenty-first year, rewarding him with a handsome annuity.

After the Seven Years' War he returned to the continent, spending some time in Paris, but he soon went back to Lausanne for his studies and a very gay time. A trip to Rome cemented his conviction that he would rather be a writer on history than anything else. While studying in Rome, he was vaguely inspired to write of the decline and fall of that city. He was still uncertain about what subject he would find most rewarding when he returned to England. His emotional ties with Switzerland made him start with a book, written in French, on the liberty of the Swiss, but he was easily dissuaded from finishing it and instead wrote with Deyverdun the two volumes, *Grande Bretagne*.

Shortly thereafter he began to work on the book for which he is best known, *The History of the Decline and Fall of the Roman Empire*. In it Gibbon covered a tremendous span of history from the first to the fifteenth century, the periods from the reign of the Emperor Trajan to the capture of Constantinople by the Turks. He was attacked for his objectively agnostic and often hostile attitude towards Christianity, maintaining that religions must be treated as phenomena of human experience. He described the triumph of barbarism and religion, he said, while tracing the causes of decay leading to the downfall of the Greco-Roman world. His was one of the first great contributions to historical knowledge. In a sophisticated way he made it quite clear that history consists mainly of crime and folly.

Gibbon wrote the various volumes of this work at different periods of his life. He completed the last three of the six volumes in Lausanne where he lived with Deyverdun, whose death in 1789 was soon followed by the French Revolution. Fearing that Switzerland would be invaded, Gibbon left for England, a lonely, unhappy, obese man. This was in 1793. A year later he was dead.

In many ways Gibbon's life would have taken a different turn had he not broken off his engagement with Suzanne Curchod, who later married Jacques Necker and gave birth to the future Mme. de Staël. Suzanne must have been a fascinating creature, even without the flair and raging impetuosity which characterized her daughter. Gibbon confessed that when he met her, "I saw and loved," but when his father did not want to hear of "this strange alliance," he realized that "without his consent, I was myself destitute and helpless." The historian "sighed as a lover," but "obeyed as a son. My wound was insensibly healed by time, absence, and the habits of a new life. . . ."

Suzanne took his rejection less lightly and, through friends, she turned to Jean Jacques Rousseau, who had a few comforting words for her: "The coldness of Mr. Gibbon gives me a bad idea of his character. I have read his book again [*L'Essai sur l'étude de la littérature*]. He wants to be clever; it is a mistake. Gibbon is not my sort of man. I can't believe that he's the sort who would suit Mademoiselle Curchod."

Mademoiselle went to Paris as a governess and met in the house of her employer an interesting and intelligent young banker whose name was Jacques Necker, a native of Geneva and *the* financial wizard of his time. He was engaged to Suzanne's employer, but in her admiration for him, Suzanne made him marry her instead.

Necker became Minister of Geneva in Paris and later was in control of French finances during three ministries and France's most turbulent period before the Revolution. Suzanne's salon in Paris was important for his career (careers were mostly made in salons at that time) and was one of the best known meeting places of the greatest minds of France and Europe in general. Whenever Necker's political star paled, he retired to his Swiss retreat, "Coppet," an estate at the Lake of Geneva, which his daughter made famous.

Suzanne was a minor writer on moral and literary subjects. Her greatest work was her daughter Germaine, who went into literary history as Mme. de Staël (1766–1817). She was not beautiful, but she was irresistible. She was not a genius of letters, but certainly a genius of life. Germaine was well known for her insatiable intellectual curiosity and sparkling wit. Using all literary forms, she succeeded in putting the stamp of her personality on the culture of her time. She mingled Montesquieu's rationalistic philosophy with Rousseau's philosophic enthusiasm. But she was not satisfied with reflecting history, she wanted to make it. She was one of the first French Swiss writers of stature to accept wholeheartedly Paris as the cultural center of the world (which, at that time, it undoubtedly was) while reviling Switzerland with such outbursts as, "I loathe everything Swiss. These great mountains shut us off from the world as completely as convent gates. We lead the most dreadfully peaceful existence. We might as well be dead in this void."

Mme. de Staël flirted with liberalism and espoused Jacobinism while thinking little of the lower classes whose lack of refinement she despised. Sympathizing with the French Revolution in the fashion of a drawing-room communist, she fled Paris in 1792 to open much later her Parisian salon under the rule of the Directory. She made it a far more powerful political and intellectual center than her mother's salon ever was. But "Coppet" near Geneva remained her lifelong headquarters where she was always surrounded by a more intimate but just as brilliant circle of men.

Her books were best-sellers at her time, and her enthusiasm for German romanticism, put into print as *De L'Allemagne,* enraged Napoleon but strongly influenced European thought and literature. Her two novels must be considered poor from a literary viewpoint, in spite of their popularity in the nineteenth century. *Delphine* shows a preoccupation with the sociological background of her story, and *Corrine,* written after a journey through Italy, stresses the differences between Nordic and southern mentalities. She was intrigued by the polarities of Nordic and classical ideas and ideals;

she felt mysteriously drawn to the former, even though her own upbringing and personal taste could not deny the latter.

With German literature and German romanticism making history during her era, her ambivalent attitude between the classics and a new *Kultur* expressed properly the ambivalence of the *Zeitgeist*. If she was often reproached for not having realized the concomitant spirit of nationalism in the development of German literature, such criticism was dictated by too much hindsight. Her essayistic writings prove her great understanding of the decisive changes in the socio-cultural scene from the turn of the eighteenth into the nineteenth century. She was the last glamorous figure of a century that saw some of man's most traumatic events in history and embodied, at the same time, the spirit of a new era.

With her health beginning to fail, her winter of discontent reached her in 1815 during Napoleon's Hundred Days. After a short journey through Italy she returned to "Coppet" to wait out this period of uncertainties. There she had a visitor, another refugee from himself, Lord Byron, in flight from England and his unhappy matrimonial adventure. Mme. de Staël and Byron developed a great understanding and feeling of friendship for each other. We would have gained immeasurably had a tape recorder accompanied their thoughts and conversations during those few months at "Coppet."

It must be mentioned that William Pitt was first considered a suitable choice for Germaine Necker when she was still in her teens. But the young girl loathed the idea of having to live in England and wrote in her diary: "Why did this wretched England have to turn my own mother against me?" When not yet twenty she was married to the Swedish Ambassador in Paris, Baron Eric de Staël-Holstein. This marriage went the way of most marriages of convenience. The two separated amicably eleven years later. Mme. de Staël remarried in 1812, a Swiss officer of no particular distinction, after her much publicized love affair with Benjamin Constant had run its passionate and torturous course.

Those who believe in the stars could easily claim that one day Mme. de Staël and Benjamin Constant (1767–1830) could not help meeting, uniting while colliding, colliding while uniting. There has never been a more heated love-hate relationship on a mutually inspiring, highly intellectual level than theirs. They probably would have met one day, and not only because Lausanne, where he was born and lived, was not too far from "Coppet."

On a September day in 1794 when she was driving from "Coppet" to Mézery, a young man of twenty-seven years of age, on horseback, stopped her carriage to tell her that he had just been at her house since he felt he had to see her and was told in which direction she had gone. She invited him to enter her carriage and ride with her. They went together in the same direction on an emotionally bumpy road for about fourteen years. At that moment of his life he could look back on many love affairs. He seemed to have been a restless, compulsive Don Juan, a man who had not yet found himself. She, however, with several books and plays to her credit, was self-assured, sunning in her early fame and dominating her environment with relentless fury and disarming charm.

"I met this evening a very clever man whose name is Benjamin Constant," Mme. de Staël wrote to another of her lovers. "He isn't very handsome, but he is terribly clever." Benjamin Constant noted in his diary: "No one will ever appreciate my mind as completely as she does. No one will ever set me farther apart from the rest of humanity. But how busy she is! How absorbed she is! She has a man's mind and wants to be loved like a woman . . . Germaine has the makings in her for ten or twelve exceptional men . . . but she sets all her friends' teeth on edge . . . She's the best creature on earth, but she is so restless and subject to fits of melancholy that I can never lead a happy life in her shadow."

In another letter Mme. de Staël explained more of her relationship with Benjamin: ". . . there are very few other people I so much enjoy talking to, especially about literature. So much for his accomplishments. As far as his character is concerned, he has devoted himself to me, under the conditions I have laid down, more faithfully than anyone I could imagine. . . ."

After four months of their acquaintance Germaine and Benjamin signed a solemn agreement which has all the earmarks of youthful romanticism and fatal love: "We promise to devote our lives to each other, we swear that we are bound to each other for life, that we can never be divided, that we will never contract any other attachment, and that we will strengthen the ties that bind us as soon as we are able to do so."

Shortly thereafter she wrote to a friend: "He's so passionately in love with me that I feel sorry for him; I do all I can to make him travel. . . ." And some time later we find the following entry in Constant's diary: "She has a real need for the language of love, a language I find it more and more difficult to speak with each day that passes. We'll be bound to quarrel; we'll be bound to go on our own ways. The longer our liaison lasts, the older we'll be; we'll be isolated, discontented, and we'll have forgotten how to take our pleasures elsewhere." Such realization did not prevent him from offering her his hand in marriage at least twice: when her husband died and later, after the death of Jacques Necker, the only man to whom she was sincerely devoted. When she rejected him twice, she took his offer as the nice gesture it was meant to be. They had loved and tormented each other fervently, and she was too clever not to see the end of their relationship waiting for them at the next turn. For him the turn came when he fell in love with Madame Récamier, with whom Mme. de Staël had to share Constant's devotion and the fame of being the most illustrious women of their time.

Germaine and Benjamin influenced each other's lives and careers. Her influence on him was on a more worldly and political plane, his on a literary level. Her interest in German romanticism was vastly nourished by his interest in it, and her book *De L'Allemagne* would never have been written without his inspiration. When they finally parted in 1806, her influence on his work lingered on and some of it is reflected in his most profound work *De la religion considérée dans sa source, ses formes et ses dévelopements* (*History of Religion*), which grew to five volumes. It is a serious investigation of religious feelings in all its forms, a long argument, positive in its skepticism, towards the threat of death. The afterthoughts of his very private relationship with Mme. de Staël are even more strongly felt in the book *Adolphe*, for which Benjamin Constant is best known and which he wrote immediately after their parting.

His novel *Adolphe* was published in 1816. This work and his *Journal intime* are now reading material for the literary connoisseur who is particularly interested in the very beginning of the probing of the psyche, the literary self-revelations in fiction, at his time gently referred to as "the history of the human heart." Greater general interest in Constant's novel may be revived again when our mass media, our electronic and technological madness, will drive the naked human being into the last corner of his self. The importance of *Adolphe* lies in the fact that it was the first modern account of brutal self-revelation (still in the form of fiction), an assault on the central mystery of the self, which may have come to a self-defeating climax in Philip Roth's *Portnoy's Complaint*. *Adolphe* was written at a time when Amiel was not yet born, and Stendhal was still doing hackwork as a critic on music and the arts and was still a long way from becoming a master of self-analysis.

From Benjamin's self-analysis it becomes clear that he, or

Adolphe, is not a sympathetic character—intelligent, no doubt, but highly unattractive as a human being. When we assume that self-love is basic to the ability to love another person, then Adolphe's loves are empty, passionate gestures to glorify his own ego, to give his life meaning beyond the meaning it has. Constant confessed in his diary, "I possess excellent qualities such as pride, generosity, and devotion, but I am not quite a real person." Such self-condemnation has the overtones of romantic exaggeration. His dualism enabled him to penetrate his own ego and lay bare the simultaneous existence of his appalling weakness and frightening strength, his ruthlessness and vanity. Constant is one of the most fascinating Don Juan types: he suffered incredibly from being able to inflict terrible pain on others, or rather from being unable not to act from sheer vanity and weakness. He suffered because his gift of self-observation and detachment from his own actions was remarkable. As the actor of his own life he must have watched himself playing another character in true Brechtian fashion. The result was *Adolphe*, the first unashamed fictional account of the soul's mechanism. Auguste Maurice Barrès visualized him as the "Great Saint" of the *culte de moi*, as the intellectual who becomes the victim of his overcleverness, as the human being who never really matures and cannot help playing with his own sensations.

It is an understatement to say that sex played a predominant part in the life of Mme. de Staël and Benjamin Constant. It undoubtedly had certain destructive connotations, but in the main was a part of their life force, and as such it contained and renewed the impulses without which the spark of creativity cannot catch fire. However torturous their lives may have been, exuberance and the most ecstatic feelings obviously counterbalanced rather well their mostly self-inflicted dramas and traumas.

Henri-Frédéric Amiel (1821–1881) is a far more interesting case for the psychoanaylst than for the literary historian. He went to the other extreme of not daring to be himself or to let the natural forces play their natural part in balancing and stimulating the psyche through physical, purely animalistic, impulses. Sex, or rather the fear of it, interfered with his giving himself a chance to be himself. If he had been ugly or crippled we could understand much better his reaction to his very self, to accepting sex as a major concern, as the torturing monster it was to him. But he was a man of far better looks than Benjamin Constant; he had the appearance of a distinguished personality and seemed to have attracted many women.

At the age of forty he confessed in his *Journal intime* that sex utterly confused and tormented him: "Sexuality has been my Nemesis, my torture ever since childhood. My extraordinary timidity, my violent desires, my ardent imagination, my pernicious readings in adolescence . . . the fatal attraction which I exerted later on delicate and tender women: all this proceeds from a false notion of sexuality. This error has poisoned my life."

At about forty Amiel reacted like a schoolboy in his climactic years of puberty, perplexed by his biological needs and the fear "to take the plunge," as he expressed it, when in October 1860 he forced himself to approach a thirty-year-old widow, Marie Faure, who is pictured as young and pretty. But it was a platonic relationship which continued as such for ten years. His passionless pursuit vexed and perplexed Philine, as he referred to her in his diaries, who, not understanding his nonaction, fell only more and more in love with him. He tried to marry a clergyman's daughter and made the first steps in 1867 by becoming engaged to her. But his self-delusion was of very short duration. Another platonic friend of his, Fanny Mercier, headmistress of a private high school for girls, was rewarded for enduring his continent friendship with the manuscript of his journal, the tremendous task of reading this mammoth manuscript, and preparing a selection for publication. It was a heroic task for that woman, who read about herself in his diary: "Is there anybody better made for heroism than this poor little Calvinist without any looks, but whose inner being is a flame?"

Amiel cast himself in a role all his life. Essentially, he lived like a medieval monk in his cell, left alone with God and himself or the puzzle of his being. His Victorian prudity covered his fear with the mask of the highest moral principles, as his many descriptions of the ideal woman prove. In playing the role of the monk repressing the lustful language of his body, he seemed to have enjoyed the game he played with himself without knowing it. There was an unnatural delight in having conquered himself when he wrote in 1860:

> The invisible mind has changed its direction, the sensual miasmas have been blown away like the emanations of a swamp. I had to prepare a lecture for tonight, and work has restored my spirituality. From nature I return to morality, from appetites to

conscience. I climb up the mountain and find again the healthy
air and the high spirits which I had missed for several days.

He played his roles in full consciousness of playing a fantastic,
weird, macabre, romantic game with himself, escaping from his
well-ordered, rather uneventful reality into a world of relentless
metamorphoses. He exclaimed that he was "no longer his own
self" and felt he might surprise himself the following day by being
a Japanese, a woman, a madman, child, camel, the man from the
moon, or from Jupiter. He sensed total "sympathy with the universe," and tried to submerge in the mystery of being until he
broke out into an anarchic cry, into the negation of his self, searching for his own identity, asking his friends who he was. He lived
his life as though walking by himself as a stranger. In his macabre
romanticism were a great deal of the negating connotations of a
mid-twentieth-century existentialist.

Locked in a world of his own, he had a pathological need to pour
out the tormenting images of his soul. He functioned on the
periphery of his being as a professor at the University of Geneva
but never distinguished himself as a teacher. ("I have as little hope,
energy, faith, and determination as ever, yet I read, I speak, I
teach, I write. But it is as a sleepwalker.") When he returns to his
cell, he bends over his journal which becomes a substitute for an
analyst's couch. ("It is my dialogue, my society, my companion,
my confidant. It is also my consolation, my memory, my victim,
my echo, the repository of my experience, my psychological itinerary, my protection against intellectual rust, my pretext to live, almost
the only useful thing that I can leave behind.")

There were 175 *Cahiers* of this journal. Fanny Mercier sent a
few samples to Edmond Schérer (1815–1889), a born Genevan,
who spent most of his life as a critic in Paris writing influential
articles for *Le Temps.** Schérer knew Amiel from their home town
and at first refused to look at the manuscript: "I have known Amiel:
he never succeeded in anything he did." But on the insistence of

* The *Goncourt Journals* mention Schérer, and this little incident may
shed some light on the man who wrote ten volumes of literary essays,
Études sur la littérature contemporains. In 1863 he was in the company
of Gautier, Sainte-Beuve, the Brothers Goncourt, and others. Schérer remained silent throughout their heated, self-revealing conversation: "As
we rose to go, Gautier went over to Schérer, the silent member of the
company, and said to him: 'As for you, I hope that the next time you
come, you will compromise yourself. We all compromise ourselves here,
and it is not fair that you sit by dispassionately observing us.'"

Fanny Mercier and her intermediary in Paris, Schérer finally read parts of the *Journal*. It was the beginning of the collaboration between her and the renowned critic.

As an ironic aside, it should be mentioned that this most introspective writer, and a bad poet to boot, wrote in a moment of national danger one of Switzerland's most popular patriotic songs, *Roulez Tambours!*, the only lines for which he was known during his lifetime.

In his essay on Amiel, Matthew Arnold hesitated to acknowledge Amiel's "speculative intuition" and doubted "his beatific vision of absolute knowledge." He considered Amiel's revelation of "his sublime malady . . . a study of morbid pathology." On the other hand, he pointed out that the "real power, originality, and value" could be found in Amiel, the literary and social critic.

Are we not justified in visualizing Amiel as a rather "ordinary" case from the vantage point of our psychological age? Amiel's awareness of having different egos, his feeble attempts at approaching women, his demand of rare moral qualities in women, and his vision of sex as a tormenting demon may very well indicate homosexual leanings which his environment and upbringing prevented him from recognizing and accepting. This may explain his feeling of total frustration, of fear and fundamental disharmony between the man in him and the world around him. He probed his psyche as best as he could, but by not coming to grips with his real self, his real problem, he could not function properly nor write the books for which he undoubtedly had the abilities. This was what Matthew Arnold alluded to when he visualized the lost opportunities of a great writer, locked within himself.

Leo Tolstoi was deeply impressed by Amiel's *Journal*. Of course, we must not forget that Tolstoi kept a diary most of his life, and in *A Confession*, he tells us of his incessant probing into the purpose and meaning of life, and pictures his suffering while searching for an answer. At one point Tolstoi even thought of committing suicide. In reading Amiel's *Journal* he must have had the impression of a man who, in cross-examining his ego, pictured life as a process of nonexistence, of waiting for death in a state of numb terror. Tolstoi wrote about the *Journal intime:* "Throughout the thirty years of his diary he felt what we are so eager to forget, namely that we are sentenced to die and that these verdicts are only delayed. This is why this book is so honest, so serious and so important."

Amiel continued Benjamin Constant's soul-searching and brought this form of self-analysis to the point of a clinical investigation, thus foreshadowing the scientific onslaught on man's soul at the end of the nineteenth century. This inclination displayed by Constant and Amiel seems to be far more indicative of the sickly aspect of the romantic *Zeitgeist* than of the "esprit Suisse," with its emphasis on a literature dealing with civic and political questions, with moral or ethical problems. On the other hand, to feel pent up, unable to communicate easily, to be thrown into a brooding mood, into the very private need to confide, into a lifelong monologue is not atypically Swiss at all, and not limited to those writing in French. Max Frisch is the most outstanding example of a German-writing Swiss for whom the diary is still a most intense necessity, to address his readers while speaking with himself.

Amiel said that French-speaking Switzerland was "a body in search of a soul." It seems to me that many writers coming from this area have naturally gravitated towards the center of French culture, Paris. There were many who left some imprint of their thought-feelings between the two proverbial covers, such as Blaise Cendrars (1887–   ), Charles-Albert Cingria (1883–1954), and Edmond Gilliard (1875–1969). These are only a few who were gifted above all averages but who never achieved international recognition.

Gilliard, a poet at heart, wrote esoteric prose which he referred to as *La dramatique du moi*; the writings of Cendrars and Cingria reflect the restlessness by which their lives were marked, the adventurous instinct that drove them around the world. Cendrars said: "I do not dip my pen into a ink-well, but into life itself," and this holds true for Cingria in a far more traumatic way. Cingria, who wrote several books of essays dealing with Switzerland from a historic and artistic viewpoint, denied himself by denying his ties with his native country ("I loathe being called a Swiss and above all a 'Swiss figure of whimsy' "). Claudel called him "an elusive goblin" and Cocteau, "a luminescent dancing elf." His restlessness drove him from place to place, and his search for himself gave his writing an unsteady, elusive feeling. His character seemed to have defeated his talent.

At the other pole we find one of the most serious novelists and poets of French-speaking Switzerland: Charles Ferdinand Ramuz (1878–1947). He found the soul of which Amiel spoke. Even though he went to Paris for a few years, in his mind and on the written pages he never left the mountains and valleys, the peasants and people of the Valais and the Vaud.

The soil and the people of the land were his sources of inspiration. He wrote about them as a painter wields his brush, and the landscapes of Cézanne come to mind when we read how *Aimé Pache, peintre vaudois* (1911) finds himself within the world of his landscape:

> Evening strode uphill from the hollows and on the Jura the sun was coming down, nearly touching the mountain tops: it was that time of day when the shadows reach their maximum length. They could be seen lengthening still, from the foot of the trees, a black line with a black ball at the end of it: the trunk and crown: but the broadest and swiftest shadow of all was that of the mountain, with the sun diving behind it, and darkness spreading like a tide across the vast landscape, all of vales and hills, with a foam of forests topping the hills. Darkness was growing eastward, and the more it grew the lower the sun sank; the shadows came upon Aimé, and it came upon the village, and then the sun was no more. Whereupon a new peace stretched over the world, a coolness in the air, a surrender, an overwhelming peace: and Aimé could feel that peace flow into him.

The simplicity of most of Ramuz's descriptions have the power, the flow and cadence of the Bible. When he speaks of human beings springing from the roots of the soil, stepping out of the landscape into a life of their own, their life cannot be visualized but as a part of the land becoming the mindscape of their existence. We can open his books at random to find this proved. Here is a paragraph from his novel *When the Mountain Fell* (1934):

> That evening Therese was sitting in front of her house, where a board nailed on four stakes made a bench close to the stone foundation. She sat there in her full brown dress, cut to show the rough linen sleeves of her blouse. She sat leaning forward with her arms loosely on her knees, looking aimlessly below her over the low trees of the orchard to the valley at the bottom of the great slope which plunged away from her gaze in its deep descent; to the valley and the plain—the great paper-smooth plain far below, through which flowed the Rhône.

Ramuz is an allegorical writer who gives his metaphors deeper meaning and who seeks revelation through mystery. His many novels are permeated with man facing a fathomless loneliness which has to be accepted, as the flower, the tree, and the rock accept their loneliness. He tried to find the human symbols in the vaguely concealed manifestations of nature, in its seemingly obvious laws and many frightening secrets and surprises. Beyond man's confrontation with nature and God, Ramuz depicts man's rising conflict with the complex artifices of a society, full of follies, often fatal in their consequences.

A Biblical and Greek feeling of the inescapability of fate runs through his stories, Job and Oedipus rolled into one. His peasants are symbols of simplicity, free from modern man's complexities or overcleverness. And yet in their being naked, they easily become the prey of a higher power, the victim of their hubris. Ramuz does not believe in evil per se, as he demonstrated in *The Reign of the Evil One*, nor in evil as ever-triumphant over the good in men, but he pictures time and again how evil corrupts and contaminates, paralyzes and destroys their lives.

Ramuz was suspicious of overcleverness, which Cocteau, who was guilty of it himself, considered the great danger of our time. Ramuz instinctively visualized excessive sophistication and refinement as a complete severance from the creative mind's sources. He believed in everything "primitive, noble, unadorned, devoid of complexities" and despised "the conventions mediocrity wallows in." There is a touching allusion illustrative of Ramuz's basic beliefs in his *Souvenirs sur Igor Stravinsky* (1929): "We became friends through the good offices of objects, of things. I don't remember at all what we talked about. What I do recall vividly is this complete and immediate agreement on the importance of bread and wine. Thus I saw right away, Stravinsky, that like myself, you liked bread when bread was good, and wine when wine was good, bread and wine together, one meant for the other."

Life is reduced to the symbolic and religious simplicity of bread and wine. Ramuz said of Stravinsky, who exerted great influence on such men as Cocteau and Balanchine and on a host of painters and musicians, that he reminded him of the need of his people, the Romands, to liberate themselves from a feeling of oppressive, "mountainous" self-confrontation:

> You have freed me of my doubts and scruples; by being yourself, you taught me how to become myself. You showed me how to be spontaneous, what we Romands need above all . . . in a country where the individual is so tempted to pass judgment on himself, to confront himself, thus ceasing to act or even to react.

However searching and introspective Ramuz's work may appear, however often he was "accused of loving what is inert," he nevertheless could not detach himself from "objects that live. For a living being nothing is ever deprived of life." In this reality of life and in its anti-poetry, he found the key to the living poetry that permeates his work. He was among the first to say that "Only from anti-poetry is a true poem fashioned."

We can learn more about Ramuz and the part of Switzerland he comes from when we read what he has to say about Stravinsky's music to the ballet *Les Noces:*

> You probably don't like *Noces* much any more, Stravinsky . . .
> Perhaps you now somewhat regret its impulsiveness, its apparent lack of control—its picturesqueness. Perhaps, having placed yourself, in the course of events, under the sign of Apollo, you reproach yourself today for what your music owed to Dionysus. It is . . . your privilege. But I, who have remained more naturalistic than you—or more a disciple of nature—have the privilege of continuing to admire, in memory, the splendid storm that *Noces* created all one long afternoon, above the little square where the pigeons in their pretty plumage strutted in measured steps. And where the women, who raised their heads, ended by saying, indulgently of course, "It is the Russian gentleman," and did not interfere because many things are permitted foreigners that are forbidden to residents.
>
> To them you were a stranger. May I say that to me you were just the opposite? To me you were the exact counterpart of my country. Not perhaps what it was, but what I should have wished it to be. I believe many things were permitted you there, not because you were a stranger but because, on the contrary, you could never in the slightest degree be a stranger anywhere on earth, never lack a connection with things, with men, with life, could never be apart from beings and from *being*. And this is the greatest of gifts. That is why it is written: to him that hath shall be given.

Ramuz did not have the greatest of gifts, but much was given to him that had the makings, the poetry and integrity of a memorable writer. The world, in its haste towards nowhere and in its abundance of talent, quickly likes to categorize its creative minds. Ramuz fell into the category of the "poet of the *terroir*," where his works stand next to those of Jean Giono, neglected for the wrong reasons, accumulating dust.

ITALIAN

ONE of the strangest phenomena of Swiss literature is the relatively small accomplishment of the Ticinese writers. Undoubtedly, this must have deep psychological and socio-cultural reasons. The Ticino and Italian-speaking Grisons were for too long a political appendix to the Swiss in the north and west, and they seem emotionally more strongly tied to their maternal culture than any other part of Switzerland. In comparison to the small linguistic entity of the Romansh-speaking Swiss, who have shown an astounding vitality of locally focused poetic works, the Ticinese literature has brought forth only sporadically a few good writers, most of them in the twentieth century. We find such extremes as the elegant, highly imaginative and somewhat cynically decadent stylist Angelo Nessi (1873–1932), who lived most of the time in Italy, and Fellici Filippini (1917–   ), one of the younger writers, bursting with energy and artistic activities ranging from poetry and novels to radio plays, from fresco painting to composing music. The Ticinese can also point with pride to Piero Bianconi (1899–   ) who, in his stories, "elevates the simple things of his Ticinese environment into a magic world of stylistically sophisticated nuances and shades," as Alice Vollenweider pointed out in her introduction to *New Story-Tellers from the Ticino*.

The Ticinese people brought a very specific, italianate culture with them when they became the third important part of the Swiss Federation. The disarming charm of these people lies in their playfulness and spontaneity, mostly pursued with a touch of seriousness. As Max Wermelinger explains in his book, *Italian Switzerland Today*, "there is never any lack of convincing ideas, plans and early starts, but when it comes to the real execution of things, discouragement sets in; instead of assuring continuity and further development, one is rather inclined to begin something new."

This *dolce far niente* mentality finds an emotional vent in parades, open-air concerts, and festivities. The people's predilection for joyful playfulness can be seen in villages of the Blenio valley where the people annually celebrate their forefathers' participation in Napoleon's ill-fated campaign against Russia in 1812. The parade of the old Napoleon guards is as colorful as the Easter processions in Mendrisio.

More than in any other Swiss canton the urge and capacity for creativity has led to the emigration of its ablest sons and, in consequence, to a weakening of the spiritual potentiality on native soil. But considering the people's vivaciousness and lighthearted temperament, it is truly amazing how much of their cultural heritage has been somehow preserved and furthered. Without a university, a conservatory, or an academy of the arts, and despite the constant rivalry between its three urban centers—Lugano, Locarno, and Bellinzona—the Ticinese have nevertheless brought forth outstanding architects and sculptors as well as a few men of letters who mirror the ambience of their country and the joy of living of its people. Furthermore, they have never lost a flair for brilliant improvisation, one of their more outstanding characteristics.

Of their six daily newspapers, three regularly run feuilletons and literary commentaries, and a great many volumes of poetry and prose are issued by several smaller publishers in the Ticino. Perhaps because of their cultural isolation—if we overlook the cultural gate into Italy—the publications stress historic monographs and, in general, *Ticinensia* material. Guilio Topi, a publisher with a rare love for the beautiful book in limited edition, has specialized in and greatly contributed to the cultural history of Switzerland's south. On a much broader basis, the Instituto Editoriale Ticinese in Bellinzona has constantly helped to further the struggling native writers.

One must point out the obvious—and many students of the Ticino have done so—namely, that this canton badly needs a focal point of learning, such as a university or academy, where analysis and criticism, discussion and stimulation could help realize far greater incentives and awaken a quickening, creative impulse. However many artists and writers from foreign lands have found inspiration on the Swiss-Italian soil, the native genius has profited little from it, left to grow and wilt, to be recognized too quickly, or driven to Milan or Turin, to Florence or Rome.

The one Ticinese writer of great stature is Francesco Chiesa (1871–   ), who never left his native soil and whose vast imaginative skill produced a rich oeuvre over many decades. He is basically a poet, and his lyricism, which is close to the soil and landscape of his native land, permeates his prose. In his entire work he demonstrates that poetry is the most essential part of life, whether he tries to probe its complexities or re-creates the simple beauty of existence. He has never lost touch with the soil, and even though he was a schoolmaster most of his life, he always regarded the simple work of the peasant the only comfort and counterbalance to his literary pursuits. Similarly, in his work he found his way from the abstract and remote to the simplicity of what moves man, to the unaffectedness of spontaneous experience. By the same token, his stories show his contemplative nature, a philosophy of life presented with poetic insight into the secret of all existence.

Without ever losing contact with what is specifically Ticinese, Chiesa explored contemporaneous life and timeless allegories with admirable sensibility, giving his work the stamp of local originality and universal meaning.

"Francesco Chiesa was the first to set up standards in the Ticino," wrote Max Wermelinger in the *Neue Zürcher Zeitung* on the occasion of the poet's hundredth birthday, "and established the writing of good Italian, a sure awareness of style which never was an end in itself. He was the founder of the proper Ticinese literature. Before him there were mainly politicians, pedagogues and scientists who were also active as writers. There were—above all, in the seventeenth century—poets who came from the upper educational layer of society and poetized on occasion, and, in the nineteenth century, there were a few *poeti* whose literary radiation, however, remained rather limited. All those who came after Chiesa were his disciples and followers in one way or another, often painfully feeling confined by a paragon difficult to overcome. A gradual detachment is only now, among the youngest generation of writers, noticeable."

Guiseppe Zoppi (1896–1952) and the Bernese Adolfo Jenni (1911–   ) are both interesting writers. The former's work is characterized by a delight in the sunnier side of life and a poetic freshness which has, more often than not, an enchanting melodic rhythm; the latter has achieved a strange blend of criticism and inventive fiction, and his many volumes of poetry and *prose di romanzo* show a very personal, introspective attitude and remoteness from the hustle and bustle of life and literature.

I mention both these writers first by way of illustrating a specific dilemma. It seems difficult for these writers to unfold fully and to become known beyond a small circle of Swiss readers and a somewhat wider one in Italy. It is unjustified to stamp them as regional writers. As much as creative work is essentially autobiographical, it is, in most cases, also regional. What gives one regional work more universal power than another often has less to do with quality than with a thousand and one coincidences. The one coincidence intensely counteracting general acceptance of the Ticinese writers may lie in the cultural trauma of this region.

Some of the younger writers try to liberate themselves from it. After World War II they made themselves heard by completely breaking with the past as did their confrères in the north and west, and they created in terms of contemporary life with its neo-romantic *Sachlichkeit* characterized by a cool, unemotional approach to reality. The astute literary critic Werner Weber once pointed out that to have broken with the idyll was one of the most significant steps of the new generation of Swiss writers. Weber may have thought mainly of those writing in German. But the same holds true of the Ticinese for whom the landscape and the rustic idyll—in which even poverty had a picturesque touch—were dominating motives until recently. To have turned away from it gave the new writers of the Ticino their first chance to enter the international literary scene.

In their new spiritual freedom most of these writers still grope to find themselves. Some of their products prove the presence of individual talents, but in their totality the trend towards the "nouveau story" is obvious and more important. The already mentioned Adolfo Jenni contributed to this trend with his report about a salesman and the banality of his death which is matched only by the banality of the hero's existence. True, as a young man this salesman had dreamt of success and adventures. But then marriage and job undermined his life, and its futility and emptiness finally engulfed him. One day—at 2:24 P.M. to be as precise as the story's author—this existentialist hero stepped too close to the edge of the sidewalk and was knocked down by a little truck going a bit too fast. In order to avoid a tram the driver could not avoid killing the salesman. *Doom* is the title of the story. The classical hubris is the hero's desire to attract the attention of a girl whose legs have caught his fancy. One step aside, half a step too far. The inevitable fate dictated by the gods is turned into an accident provoked by the machine. This is a variation to a favorite theme of Friedrich Dürrenmatt, and Jenni almost echoes him when he writes:

> Carlo Mainardi: there are still thirty seconds left, still twenty. One lives only once. Now you are about to disappear. Perhaps God observes what is happening to you. But he must not intervene.

Even more matter-of-fact and full of colorless anonymity as well as futility are the stories of Carlo Castelli (1909–   ), who treats the smallest everyday events in a philosophically nonchalant manner. "Since some time it happens to me that I undertake something, that I plan an excursion, that I try to solve a problem and then notice how superfluous everything is," remains the undercurrent running through his thoughts. However, he knows how to plant a coincidental experience in his stories, in itself meaningless and yet mysterious, creating an often tantalizing, disturbing feeling.

There is hardly any narrative in the traditional sense and only a vague situation in Castelli's stories, or in those of Martino della Valle (1922–   ), who likes to depict the valleys of the Ticino. But della Valle's tales are devoid of any idyllic description. His valleys are haunted by the ruthlessness of progress, by the artificialities of our time. He writes in architecturally monolithic blocks, not paragraphs; he shapes long sections in a pointillistic manner; he carries together incidental thoughts and experiences in tiny different shades without rhyme or reason but in a breathless rhythm.

Most of the contemporary writers are poets whose lyricism can be felt in their prose. This is particularly true of Giorgio Orelli (1921–   ) and Plinio Martini (1923–   ). By virtue of being poets, and Ticinese poets, nature and the remembrance of things past are uppermost on their minds and hearts, even if they no longer indulge in folkloric dreams and Arcadian escapes. As Alice Vollenweider pointed out, the self-denial of seeing themselves as the focal point "within the frame of folk literature" has opened for these writers "new impulses, but without giving them in their own environment the contemporary problematic issues and the living space which they would need for their literary work." Moreover, when we speak of the young generation of Ticinese writers, we find most of them between forty and fifty years of age, which proves, if nothing else, the many difficulties and the few opportunities they find to practice their craft and art. In spite of having found a new approach and language they still feel lost in a world of television and rockets, or as Plinio Martini expressed it, "we look around like people who have gone astray."

The youngest among the so-called young writers is Enrico Filippini, whose work is most promising and unconventional. He is a translator (who rendered Günter Grass, Uwe Johnson, and Max Frisch into Italian), essayist, and novelist. Whatever he has done so far is characterized by an intellectual brilliancy, a witty sophistication, and a penetrating philosophy. All of this is tele-scoped in his long short story *September*, which is a novelistic essay or an essayistic novella. In it Filippini tells us of a novel he plans to write, detailing some characters, evoking a landscape (which seems to be the one around Ascona), but, above all, creating the totality of a microcosmic world out of joint—and he does it with bizarre bravura.

Speaking of his hero, Filippini says:

> . . . the best way of not recognizing yourself is to contradict yourself. This is why he continues in the third person after hav-ing begun to speak in the first: the third person opposes, contra-dicts him: it denies him and announces other possibilities (of his self): those that cannot be, but ought to be (and this compul-sion to overcome oneself is repulsive: for him who does it).
>
> This is his affair, not mine. I have another problem: the world does not consist of thoughts: the most difficult thing is to recre-ate the flow of life's immediacy (and this lies in the first person: it is everything: is nothing: and is overcome): the most insig-nificant perceptions: the immediate sensations: the realistic pres-ence (do not forget the tree). . . . there is a letter, a sun, there are trees, a room, and then a series of events happen of which one knows that they happen but which one does not see (and perhaps those count a great deal). Our point of departure is also tiny: someone stands in front of a tree (in front of the world), with a letter in his pocket. We could add: that a window is opened in the yard where a ray of light is caught: that it is quiet in the yard, only someone coughs from time to time, and a win-dow is closed. . . .

A loose sequence of impressions and thoughts are being reeled off. Enrico Filippini records them with minute precision. He cele-brates the holy services of the *Non Sequitur* with the dignified seriousness of a priest-poet-philosopher who was ordained by Albert Camus. (Or was it Jean-Paul Sartre?) And at the beginning of the novel's conclusion, Filippini says:

> Try to understand me, please, because: you will tell me that actually nothing has happened: that the matter is not explained, and you are certainly not wrong in saying so: never has any-thing happened. . . . —as far as the new circumstances are con-

cerned which he should have embodied: it is something else to translate a conversation into a deed. Apart from this: nothing; but this nothing is everything: as the absent space is so real it never exists: and besides he became guilty: and it says so in the letter. . . .

Nota bene: Enrico Filippini was born in Locarno in 1934: He left the Ticino and now lives in Milan as an editor: He belongs with the leading experimental revolutionary writers of Italy: was co-founder of the Group 63.

This sunny part of Switzerland has the greatest inspirational potentialities, as it has proved time and again with some world-known writers and artists who have been attracted by its intoxicating ambience. Is it possible that those born in this paradise feel compelled to flee it either by going into self-imposed exile or by denying its idyll, while others coming with a great dream from somewhere and with a preconceived notion of the best of all paradises find it right there in the Ticino? It only goes to show how ambiguous life's cornucopia can be and how inscrutable are the ways of God and creativity which, after all, means borrowing or filching a spark from His greatness.

GERMAN

SUPERFICIAL associations reign supreme in the world, and it is therefore understandable that the average person would think of *Heidi* first when thinking of any book that is characteristically Swiss. This does not speak against Heidi's author, Johanna Spyri (1827–1901), born at the Lake Zürich, who knew how to captivate a young person's mind with a story that has all the necessary ingredients: a burning love for the child's homeland, for tradition and constancy symbolized by Heidi's longing to return to her native mountains and grandfather; a sincere feeling for nature; a sense of humor matched by an even dose of sentimentality and piety.

Johanna Spyri's insight into the mind of the child, mingled with restrained gaiety and cheerful wisdom, gave most of her stories their attraction. True, *Heidi*, her best work, does not have the symbolic depth and many-faceted meaningfulness of Lewis Carroll's *Alice in Wonderland*, nor has it the literary value and substance of Hans Christian Andersen's stories. But *Heidi* has disarming naïveté and endearing charm in common with its memorable fictional companions.

———————————

It has been said before that one can see the entire world from one's own window. Some writers are born with the universe in their hearts, visible and palpable in their own four walls, in the valley in which they live, in the street of their little town. Many Swiss writers whose native tongue is German show a creative power that grew out of their specific Swissness, but also far beyond it. They succeed in formulating their experiences and visions in a universally legible and identifiable manner. Characters grounded in the narrowness of their country grow wings, and the *Gestalt* of their lives, their dreams and hopes, their frustrations and failures are generally meaningful. From Gotthelf and Keller to Dürrenmatt and Frisch—the literary world recognizes the valid image they create, the human pulsebeat, and the moral in the message of these writers.

They never deny their heritage, and the reader can easily detect their Swiss background, which reveals itself in many ways. Since Switzerdütsch is used as the vernacular on all social levels, its idioms phrase and color the writer's language. His civic-mindedness and social conscience are blended with his tendency to explain himself while teaching a lesson, but, most of all, to gratify the innate need for self-realization. The German-Swiss writer is prompted by a didactic purpose to chastise evil, to defend the higher values in life. There are many reasons for this, but the roots for it can be found in the religious background of most of the writers, who have never completely freed themselves from the sermon.

———————————

The two contemporary writers, Friedrich Dürrenmatt and Max Frisch, of whom I speak in more detail in the chapter on theatre, answer to most points of this description. Our century is characterized by man's desperate search for his identity, and Frisch is one of the best chroniclers of this search. It may be Stiller who denies being himself in order to retain his inner freedom to choose the being he wants to be, to preserve the uniqueness of his existence; or it may be Bin in one of Frisch's early stories, the alter ego of a young man (Frisch himself) who finds himself in a tender and tantalizing conversation with Bin on an imaginary journey to Peking; or *Let My Name Be Gantenbein*, in which pretended blindness only proves that we cannot escape the life forced upon us by our environment. Frisch loves to pose questions and expects his reader or spectator to find his own answers "which they can only give through their own lives." But he suspects that "we do not really want answers, we merely want to forget the question. So as not to become responsible." Responsibility and concern are the major themes running throughout his work.

Max Frisch cries out to be heard. Friedrich Dürrenmatt's laughter of scorn and derision is just as loud. "The tyrants on this planet are not moved by the poet's works, they yawn when they hear their lamentations, they take their heroic songs for stupid fairy tales, they fall asleep while listening to their religious poems, they fear one thing only: their mockery." Dürrenmatt's tyrants are not only despots, generals, and judges; essentially, they are the little burghers, the philistines who do evil in many variations on the same theme but go to bed with a good conscience since they cannot help doing what they do if they want to stay on top and live. So many of his characters are murderers, attorneys, and hangmen. All three play a game with the scapegoat of society, the victim. Tragedy is fulfilled through an accident, the failure of an engine. Dürrenmatt thinks that the classic *Moira* is now replaced by a mishap.

Dürrenmatt's fiction has the same dramatic impulse and desperate laughter as his plays. As Elisabeth Brock-Sulzer pointed out, for instance, in Dürrenmatt's play *The Meteor* can be found the metaphor and visual image of death which Dürrenmatt pictured thirteen years previously in his story, *Tunnel:* "Death racing towards us like a locomotive, eternity whistles around our ears, worlds howl and collapse, the whole thing, a huge accident . . ." The difference between his prose and plays lies more or less in the locale he chooses. The action in his prose occurs in Switzerland, that of his plays anywhere. His fiction is more autobiographic than any character in his plays, with the exception of the writer Schwitter in *The Meteor*.

The prose work closest to his plays is *Die Panne*, translated as *Traps* after the name of the hero, Alfredo Traps, traveling salesman. The story was dramatized as a radio play and for the stage. The coincidental accident with his car is for Traps what the predestined meeting with his father was for Oedipus: the inevitable road to crime and punishment. Or as Dürrenmatt sees Traps facing his judges and confessing his guilt in terms of how hard luck unintentionally widens, creating another dimension of universal validity. I consider *Die Panne* a masterpiece in which the absurd grotesqueries of our time are shown in their full tragic light.

Perhaps to amuse himself, to make some money, and to escape the literary critics, Dürrenmatt has also written a few mystery stories in which the Bernese commissar Bärlach figures prominently and in which Dürrenmatt, moreover, succeeds in writing parodies on the mystery story. He cannot write any story without showing his wit ("Otherwise, he had little sympathy for the city of Zürich, he thought it was pure exaggeration to find 400,000 Swiss together on one spot"), and he cannot help creating dramatic scenes marked by black humor whether he turns to prose or to drama.

Obsessed with the idea that chance and accident play the role of predestined fate in our time, he rejects the pattern of the traditional mystery story in which the detective is aware of having to act in the framework of certain rules in which justice is done. In *Das Versprechen (The Promise)*, chance is given a decisive part and rules are thrown overboard; at the end of the story we read of the murderer's wife: ". . . it really was as if she had told the two children a fairy tale in which the evil and the absurd happen as something that is just as wonderful as the good . . ." The theme of this "requiem on the mystery story," as the subtitle says, is justice, as it is in almost anything he writes, the justice of our fate dictated by chance.

When Frisch's work has accents of pathos, Dürrenmatt's has accents of sardonic laughter. Whether they cry or laugh, hiding behind their tears or mockery, they are both moralists.

Dürrenmatt once called himself a product of village life, and as such he closes the circle that began with Jeremias Gotthelf. Not all of the writers before and after Gotthelf came from small communities, but the nerve center of Swiss life lies in the countryside. Swiss life and landscape are unthinkable without each other, a fact reflected in the earliest literary accomplishments. The Bernese Albrecht von Haller (1708–1777), a spiritual descendant of the Renaissance polyhistorians, started this trend with his famous poem, *Die Alpen,* which, when published in 1732, gave the creation of German poetry a strong impetus.

German literature was then in its infancy, and the literary taste in German lands was dominated by the French, who accepted

Haller's poems with some interest. Initiative and encouragement to overthrow the literary domination of French pseudo-classicism came from the Zürich school of criticism and its two most articulate spokesmen, J. J. Bodmer (1698–1783) and J. J. Breitinger (1701–1776). Through their endeavor, the influence shifted from French to English literature. The immediate impact on such poets as Klopstock and Wieland was quite noticeable. But, more important, the two Swiss critics prepared the ground for the renaissance of German literature that reached its heights with Lessing, Goethe, and Schiller a generation later.

Throughout the eighteenth century and certainly until the coming of these three German giants in the latter half of the century, Swiss literary accomplishments were rated highly in all of Europe. For instance, Salomon Gessner (1730–1788) enjoyed international fame which can hardly be fathomed today. His revival of the idyll and his short bucolic stories, which he illustrated, were characteristic products of the artificial rococo atmosphere, with a touch of the sentimental and the romantic yearning for man's return to nature:

> . . . Oh, how beautiful you are, Nature! In your littlest ornament, how beautiful! He who passes your beauties carelessly misses the purest joys; he whose mind is spoiled by raging passions and false delights is incapable of the purest joys. Blissful is the man whose soul—darkened by no dim thoughts, persecuted by no self-reproaches—can sense each impression of your beauty . . . all his senses always find endless sources of joy on every path he walks, in the shade he rests; gentle delights bubble from each well, exhale fragrances from each flower, sound and whisper out of each bush . . .

Posterity has sometimes a strange way of treating those who were favorites of their own time. Salomon Gessner was famous from Paris to St. Petersburg (then Leningrad), from Stockholm to Rome. The intellectuals of his age paid homage to his image, a duchess invited him to settle in Paris, his head was used as imprint on a Russian medal, and no one less than Rousseau bowed to his "moving and ancient simplicity which touches one's heart."

Jeremias Gotthelf was the pseudonym for Albert Bitzius, who lived from 1797 to 1854. He lived at several places in Switzerland, but basic to his work is the Bernese environment as it is powerfully reflected in his many stories. Northeast of Berne in the Emme valley, at the country parish of Lützelflüh (there could be no other place sounding more Swiss than Lützelflüh), the thirty-three-year-old Bitzius arrived, and there he stayed for the rest of his life.

While working on his *Doctor Faustus*, Thomas Mann read one of Gotthelf's stories, *Uli der Knecht (Uli the Farmhand)*, "in order to keep in touch with great narrative literature," as he admitted in his Genesis of *Doctor Faustus*. Gotthelf was not a skilled nor a sophisticated teller of tales. On the contrary, his stories lack structure and tightness. He easily loses patience with his narrative when he comes across an idea or finds fault with one of his characters. Then, in scorn and a didactic tone, he says his piece or ruminates and reflects. But these interruptions of the narrative flow are presented with such vigor and intense linguistic power that the reader is caught by the writer's sincerity and ethos. Arising from a down-to-earth scene or character, his vociferous denunciations of his time and the people by whom he was surrounded have the ring of something very real. His chastising sermons are as convincing as his characters in their realistic setting. He forces the reader to accept the totality of his world which he attacks because it needed to be reformed and which he defends because he loved it, being the only world he knew, that is, the world of peasants and country tradesmen whom he christened and wedded and accompanied to the grave as their pastor. He was conservative while defending the traditional Christian way of life and he was a prophetic liberal in fighting the materialistic attitude of the many. He loathed progressive radicalism and preached belief in Good and Evil in a world that is "God's immense temple."

Gotthelf wrote with astounding ease and profound purpose. He began most of his stories in flawless *Schriftdeutsch* but could not help allowing his characters to drift into their Bernese dialect. (". . . I feel compelled to do so whether I want it or not; and certainly many things can truly be expressed in dialect only. Furthermore, our dialect is to the point and forceful, and many expressions would deserve to be incorporated in the general German vocabulary.") The mingling of dialect in no way detracts from his epic power; it only adds spice to his deep understanding of human nature—of course, a fair knowledge of Bernese helps a great deal.

In a brief autobiography which Gotthelf wrote in 1848, he tells us how and why he became a writer:

> After the death of Herr Fasnacht (the pastor of Lützelflüh) I was
> elected pastor of the parish . . . At that period the canton of

Berne was the scene of various struggles, none of which was
fought out with more bitterness than the educational one . . .
This, and the character of my parish (the Emmental farmers
were proud and reserved, and viewed their pastor, an 'outsider,'
with suspicion), which condemned me to a slow wait, to a kind
of passivity, awoke in me more and more the urge to express
myself in writing on matters concerning the people, although
nothing was more contrary to my nature than sitting down to
write. My nature had to submit; in July 1836 the continually in-
creasing need broke out in the 'Bauernspiegel.' Since then there
is no end to it, so that I am constantly amazed how a boy who
could not keep his feet still could develop into a man who spends
so much time sitting and writing.

In many ways Gottfried Keller (1819–1890), who is generally
considered the most representative writer among the German
Swiss, is on the opposite fence from Jeremias Gotthelf. Politically, he
stood on the side of those who wanted to usher in a new era, a
new order, and who liberalized the constitution. In his twenties
he was inspired by the political poets of Germany, writing revolutionaries such as Ferdinand Freiligrath and Georg Herwegh. Even
though Keller began as a political poet, the best verses he produced extolled nature. He wrote moving paeans to the beauty of
creation, to the ever-comforting and all-embracing feeling he derived from nature.

His nature poems reflected Keller's first great dream, to become
a landscape painter. After a couple of years of relentless attempts
with pencil, brush, and colors in Munich, he returned to Zürich
with a sense of utter frustration and failure. It was only then
that he turned to writing. Recognized as a poet by his native
canton, he received a public grant that enabled him to study in
Heidelberg. There he fell under the spell of the atheistic philosopher Ludwig Feuerbach, whose ideas shook the foundation of his
belief. He had then moved far away from Gotthelf's principles.

Keller left Heidelberg for Berlin, where he studied the theatre
with the thought of writing for it. The stage dream never came
close to fulfillment. After a few drafts of some plays, he seemingly
gave up and saved himself the agonies of frustration to which
Henry James exposed himself. Like James he was a born novelist,
and the large canvas of epic narrative was his forte. As the
frustrated painter in him had once discovered the poet, the frustrated dramatist found a great novelist waiting for his opportunity.

At that time in Berlin he began to work on the novel which was to establish his reputation as a writer: *Der grüne Heinrich* (*Green Henry*).

An autobiographical novel in four volumes, it depicts Heinrich's rise from innocence to awareness and artistic expression. It is considered one of the finest *Bildungsromane* in German literature. Like all such educational novels, it offers the reader an opportunity to observe the growing pains of a human being, but essentially to see the man as he sees himself. As in most such novels, *Green Henry* has passages that are overemphasized and others whose fictionalized treatment is overdone. But Keller was a serious draftsman. Twenty-five years after the first version had impressed its readers, he rewrote it, pruning from it extraneous incidents and giving it a chronological sequence.

While still in Berlin he wrote the first volume of longer short stories, *Die Leute von Seldwyla* (*The People of Seldwyla*), followed by a second volume almost twenty years later while working as a conscientious city clerk for his canton. Probably the most touching story he ever wrote, *Romeo und Julia auf dem Dorfe* (*Romeo and Juliet in the Village*), appeared in the first book and transposed the innocent beauty and tragedy of love into a rural setting. The quarrel between two peasant families forces their children to drown themselves. The famous Renaissance balcony scene turns into a ladder leading to a hay barge in which, hidden from the world, they taste of the joys of love before committing suicide. The stories of the second volume are somewhat more critical of the social scene in Seldwyla, which Keller introduces in the very beginning:

> According to the older language Seldwyla means a blissful and sunny place, and so indeed is the little town of this name situated somewhere in Switzerland. It is still confined within the same old town walls and towers as it was three hundred years ago, and also remained the same tiny place . . .

Even if the locale is imaginary, it is very much a part of Switzerland. Keller depicted historic figures in his *Züricher Novellen*, but he saw them with the eyes of a nineteenth-century Swiss writer. The moralist in him tells us that only a person true to himself and of wholesome character can succeed. One of the stories, *Hadlaub*, goes back to the period of the Minnesingers, of whom a great many lived in what is now Swiss territory. Hadlaub was the son of a Swiss peasant, but exceptionally gifted. His aristocratic patron, Rüdiger Manesse (1224–1304), assigned him to collect and preserve all poems of *Minnesang* in a volume before they could get lost. Keller made use of the factual background of the so-called Codex Manesse, the famous manuscript of *Minnesang* which originated in Zürich and is proof of some of the earliest Swiss literary creations.

Gottfried Keller's rather pleasant stories in *Sieben Legenden (Seven Legends)* preceded the *Züricher Novellen,* and other stories and novels followed. His collected works comprise ten volumes. They are representative of a Swiss writer who rose above all regional confinements to international stature, and this despite having been thoroughly Swiss and never leaving his landscape. He had the poetic power to give his characters the touch of mystery through which they reveal themselves to whoever can see and hear and feel.

Whenever Gotthelf and Keller are mentioned, the name of Conrad Ferdinand Meyer (1825–1898) is usually added. But Meyer has very little in common with them. His life, work, and, above all, his personality are very much remote from everything that has to do with the popular notion of what is Swiss.

He was the offspring of a patrician Zürich family and endowed with independent means which permitted him to pursue a life to his own liking. In his early youth and towards the end of his life he spent some time in a mental home. This only goes to show how different this high-strung, oversensitive, depressive person was from the robust Keller. The only thing the two had in common was the realization of their potential talents rather late in life. Keller despised this neurotic man of the world, this "aloof human being with his patronizing manners." Meyer considered Keller a boorish person who lacked "education," and both were probably right to some extent in their estimation of each other.

What must be pointed out is the variety of personalities Switzerland produced, and Meyer is of the plutocratic variety which, in many cases, added a passionate love of the arts to patrician dignity. Meyer's creativity emerged only after he had immersed himself in Latin culture in France and Italy while journeying through these countries. It was at about the same time that he also liberated himself from his early anxieties brought about by the zealous religiousness of his mother, which may account for the anti-clerical attitude in many of his writings.

"The comic leaves me with a bitter aftertaste" and only "the tragic elevates and inspires me." This explains his dwarfed sense of humor. He loved to escape into the big gesture, related in his mind with the monumental figures of the Renaissance. Meyer disliked the German poetasters of romanticism and, through the years, put the great men of the quattrocento on the highest pedestals. Michelangelo's vision became his vision of statuesque greatness. His verbal images have something plastic about them; they are rich in color, but at the same time terse and tense. Meyer avoided, particularly in his lyrics, any direct personal statement revealing emotion. Symbolism became the underlying and propelling force of his motifs. He was a symbolist long before the symbolist manifesto was published by Jean Moréas in *Le Figaro* in 1886.

In most of his novellas he used idealized figures of history, but the drama of history was always secondary, little more than a setting, to the drama of the human problem, the meaning of destiny and death, guilt and atonement, humility and resignation. His heroes are either strong or pathological. He adored the strong ones and understood those divided within themselves. Because of his own psychological difficulties, he could easily project himself into inner torment. He was one of the nineteenth-century personalities who foreshadowed the trend of the psychological school of writing in our century.

Armed with insight into man's psyche, he started the rising interest of the Swiss in psychological explorations at the end of the last century. Meyer was never interested in realism per se, only in the symbolic meanings and values of reality. This is how we must understand the remark he made in a letter addressed to Carl Spitteler, saying that he did not desire "to make the poetic real," but "to make the real poetic."

Romain Rolland called Carl Spitteler (1845–1924) "the greatest German poet since Goethe." Rolland's enthusiasm for Spitteler resulted in the highest international award, the Nobel Prize for Literature (1919), for the Swiss poet. Psychoanalysis also honored him. Sigmund Freud borrowed the title of one of Spitteler's novels, *Imago*, for the name of a "Periodical for the Application of Psychoanalysis to the Humanities," the most important organ of psychoanalysis from 1912 on. Dr. Hanns Sachs, one of its editors, praised the novel, published in 1906, as a primary example of the phenomenon of the Oedipus-complex.

Spitteler said that *Imago* was "not just a work of art, but . . . life-blood," a confessional novel which re-created personal problems of his past, aggravated by wounds which probably never healed.

This experience went back to the year 1880, when Spitteler wrote his first mythical epic, *Prometheus and Epimetheus*. The hero of the novel is a kind of Prometheus finding himself pitted against the narrow, selfish world of the bourgeois. This Prometheus walking "among the democrats" reflects the poet's inner conflict, his visionary gift and inability to come to terms with middle-class values.

Prometheus and Epimetheus, characterized by an elevated rhythmic prose style which Nietzsche mastered to perfection in his *Thus Spake Zarathustra*, and *Der Olympische Frühling* (*Olympian Spring*) were created at the beginning of his career. At its very end Spitteler returned to the topic of his youth in *Prometheus der Dulder*. Picturing Prometheus as more enduring and suffering, the second version attains a greater maturity; the hero's defiance becomes an act of inner necessity. It is symbolically the more interesting work.

In his middle period he seemingly tried to be down to earth as best he could, and a wide variety of fiction, verse, and essays testify to a rather realistic approach. In his novel *Conrad der Leutnant*, he intended to outdo all naturalists and came close to satirizing their method. One of Meyer's best stories is *Die Mädchenfeinde* (*Enemies of Girls*), written in 1907, a year after *Imago*, which depicts with deep insight and poetic power the awakening of a boy's soul.

Spitteler's forte, however, was lofty language in epic form. He lacked the touch of human warmth, which accounts, too for his rather less musical and more intellectual lyricism rarely being nourished by everyday occurrences. What Keller said about Spitteler seems to be to the point: "If only the poor man would use his talent and his strong imagination to create some really human poetry, he would be one of the best."

In the beginning Spitteler found little or no appreciation of his work. Later he was catapulted into fame. And now, after his death, his name evokes mere silence or an embarrassed rejection by his own compatriots (as by Werner Günther, essayist from Neuchâtel). But Spitteler will always remain one of the grand names of Swiss literature. Grand names have the habit of fading, some forever, and if some blossom again it is not necessarily because of their own merit but because of the desperate needs of another generation.

Robert Walser (1877–1943) was Spitteler's contemporary, but in many ways our own generation of Swiss writers begins with him.

Walser was neglected, but lately he has been remembered and appreciated by many people, both within and outside Switzerland. When his novel, *Jakob von Gunten*, was published, Franz Kafka admired it for the similarity to his own world, in which the individual faces an undefined and, in its indefiniteness, frightening environment. Published in 1909, it foreshadowed the eerie quality of the works Kafka was later to write.

When the hero of his novel, Jakob, felt that "sometimes my whole stay here seems to me like an incomprehensible dream," then he expressed also the forlornness of its author. Walser was a poet stranded in a world that has less and less patience with such dreamers. His strength lies in the poetic description of things, places, and people in a most casual way which, however, is highly deceptive. His tender prose is a beautiful veneer covering a depth of feelings, thoughts, moods. He has a way of writing a con-sordino-style, but at the corner of turning a phrase there is always some light shining through. And yet we can feel how easily these burning lights can be extinguished by tears.

Walser lived some time in Berlin where he was close to his brother Karl, a well-known painter in his day. But most of Robert Walser's life was spent in Switzerland. Later, looking back to his lost opportunities, he criticized himself too harshly:

> If I could worm myself back to the age of thirty, I would not write again without purpose and aim like a romantic will-o'-the-wisp, eccentric and uncaring. It is wrong to deny society. We must live in it, and fight either for or against it. That is the fault of my novels. They are too odd and reflective, often too slack in structure. Escaping all artistic laws, I simply wrote what came to my mind.

But he was aware of the Dionysian power forcing him to write, and of the act of creating, which is finally all that matters: the exhilarating experience of giving visions and feelings a verbal life of their own, of giving *Gestalt* to thoughts. He once described this rhapsodic feeling:

> The poet must roam and boldly lose himself, he must always dare and dare again, must hope, nay, may only hope . . . The better thought and with it the courage to create appeared slowly only, but just because of it even more mysteriously, from the abyss of self-denial and frivolous disbelief. It was like the morn-

ing sun coming up. Evening and morning, past and future and the enticing present lay as if at my feet, and I thought I could grasp with my hands all human activities, the human existence, because it looked so much alive to me.—One image followed the other and the ideas played with one another like happy, lovely, good children. Full of rapture I clung to the cheerful basic thought, and in continuing to write busily, things fell into place.

Perhaps in Walser's poem, *Zu Philosophisch* (*Too Philosophical*), he described his destiny as a man and artist most precisely when he spoke of how unreal his life was in its rise and fall, how he could see himself beckoning to his self and always escaping the beckoning hand, how he saw himself as pure laughter and then again as an image of sadness, or as unbridled orator. But all this disappeared. He came to the almost existentialist conclusion in the last stanza: probably all this has never really existed at any time, "I have been chosen to wander through forgotten distances."

Another notable writer whose major activities fell between the two wars was Albin Zollinger (1895–1941). Like Walser, he had a very personal, inimitable way of lighting up images in his evocative prose in which he tried to come to terms with himself and his time, trying to reach beyond man's limitations. We must not wonder that so many Swiss writers, being as close to nature as they are, have mastered landscape description. So did Zollinger, who brought to it a delightful, lyrical feeling, a sensuous quality which gives his writing a special lustre.

But there were many more writers at work between the two cataclysmic events, writers like Meinrad Inglin with his *Swiss Mirror*, the novelist Traugott Vogel, and some great essayists whose writings reflect their realization of and anxiety over the fateful changes in the German-speaking world as well as the growing awareness of their Swiss heritage. In 1918 Eduard Korrodi said in his *Swiss Literary Letters* that the Swiss writers ought to put down "a creative word of hope and belief in a change of the world." And eleven years later Korrodi told them in his *Spiritual Heritage of Switzerland* that they will never be able to exist without that heritage and that "an irrational attachment will always call them back to their own origin."

There was Max Rychner, a poet of great verbal subtleties, who for many years combined the task of a creative editor with the ability of a discerning essayist. Werner Weber, as the literary critic and editor of the *Neue Zürcher Zeitung*, defined his own

role when he wrote in the *Diary of a Reader:* "In criticism it is
not a question of being right or wrong. The critic owes himself
only one thing and only this can his followers demand from him:
to say clearly what he means from case to case—determined by
politeness of passion." Weber has also a word of exhortation for
his readers, a word we find in his book *Challenges:* "We experience
something in the encounter with a poetic work of art, something
that we are. . . ." Above all, during this encounter "we learn
what it means: to see and to listen."

There are many more impressive names which cannot be cata-
logued here, from the tradition-bound Emil Staiger to Walter
Muschg. The latter impressed me with his *Tragic History of
Literature* in which he no longer approaches the creative work of
the poet from a purely aesthetic or historic viewpoint but sees
the tragic aspects of the poet's humanness as the crucial criteria.
("What makes Orpheus mainly memorable is the fact that he is not
a triumphant magician, but a suffering human being." Or: "The
poet's tragedy not only consists of poverty and persecution, af-
flictions that press upon him from outside. It is also part of his
own doing that he is rarely happy. He must suffer in order to be a
poet. All great writing is the fruit of suffering.")

The essayist most significant for the theme of this book is
Karl Schmid, who has published several volumes of speeches and
essays. In one of them, treating the *Difficulties with the Arts,*
he addresses himself to the problem of the "concerned" writer and
finds that the new Germany needs more second-rate writers who
are truly concerned rather than "one new Rilke or Benn." It is
indicative of the ethic postulate basic to his attitude towards all
problems that he visualizes the great danger for any concerned
writer in the tempting and easy formula, in a catching and bluffing
phrase (". . . endlessly more frequent than high treason is the
treason of truth which he commits when he lets himself to be
taken in by a formulation").

Schmid hit the nerve center of the Swiss intellectuals with
his book, *Discomfort in a Small State,* in which he investigates
how the problematic magic of "greatness" influenced the thought
processes and lives of five significant Swiss writers; how the fear
of being nameless between world-dominating cultures, of being
reduced to a total lack of destiny, of having to live outside the
crossroads of decision has had a decisive influence on these writers.
They all sought roads of escape and refuge in lands of their own
imagination or of a fictitious reality.

Conrad Ferdinand Meyer succeeded in translating the fascination for greatness into a magnificent pathos of history and its reflection in poetry; Schmid visualizes Meyer as the image of a lifelong "nocturnal swimmer who keeps himself from drowning with noiseless strokes." We spoke here before of Amiel who escaped into the ivory tower of his *Journal intime*. Max Frisch is characterized by Schmid as the man who sees his country as "a model of uncreative pharisaism," as a prison from which he cannot flee because he feels compelled to deny it. But in Schmid's opinion "the case Frisch" seems to lead beyond Swiss frontiers. It is "the drama of an individual to whom parallels are to be found far less in Switzerland than in the European generation to which he belongs: with Camus, Malraux, Saint-Exupéry, for example."

Jakob Schaffner (1875–1944) is a special case, a gifted Swiss writer tainted with the stamp of a traitor. He succumbed to the fascination of the German Reich in the worst way; it was to him a "symbol of the great totality." He was a man of remarkable sensibilities, and Karl Schmid ranks his novel *Johannes* next to Keller's *Green Henry*. Schaffner's decision to emigrate to Germany and embrace wholeheartedly Hitler's mythology of the Third Reich is reminiscent of Ezra Pound. Schmid maintains, "Ezra Pound could be declared sick, but not Schaffner," who interpreted his early struggles as "humiliations suffered from Switzerland." Excessive ambition mingled with traumatic memories of a poor childhood —a comparison with Hitler's personal problems is painfully obvious—led Schaffner to his political and, with it, human derailment.

Even the great Jacob Burckhardt (as indicated in the essay devoted to him) was not immune to the fascination of "greatness" which he thought to have discovered in Germany first and then in Italy during his youth. However, as Schmid points out, Burckhardt's saving grace was finally the "energy with which he came to terms with all the uncertain fascinations radiating fanfarelike words like *Reich* and Renaissance, life, beauty, happiness and greatness." Owing to his strong self-criticism and self-awareness, Burckhardt was able to withstand those "insinuations of greatness" and to come to the realization—in the process of being cured from his feverish longing for Italy—that to wherever one escapes "only he can find happiness who brings it along."

How about those writers born in the late twenties and thirties, who are today's new voices? They have something meaningful to say, something expressing their deep concern. I would have to mention at least twenty-five names of those who are articulate and who may be tomorrow's Max Frisch and Friedrich Dürrenmatt. But only a few examples can be singled out. Do they have anything in common, except their obvious impatience with the complacency of their immediate environment, the materialism of their time, their commitment to change the world they inherited? Yes, there is one surprising element which may prove that the new generation of Swiss writers is outgrowing the "narrowness" of their existence, against which they rebel. It is amazing that Switzerland, geographically and spiritually, no longer plays an important part in their stories and plays. The experiences of these writers and their characters are universal and have risen above and beyond all boundaries. And whenever Switzerland serves as a background, the setting is no longer an essential part of events and characters. The specific Swissness has lost its significance for the new generation. With man walking on the moon, the world is frightfully shrinking to the size of a global Switzerland. The Swiss writer of today has taken notice of it.

Some writers will always belong to the youngest generation, even though their birthdates betray them. Such a writer is Ludwig Hohl (1904–   ). He is timeless because he does not care about being a part of the literary world, of movements and isms. He is a poet apart. He lives the aloneness of life, unperturbed by tides and tidings. He stands there in his splendid isolation like the Swiss mountains. If they rage, they send men to death. If Ludwig Hohl rages, he does not mind condemning men. From time to time he is forgotten. But from time to time he is rediscovered. He acts and writes like a man who knows that his time is now and ever.

If our era (particularly in the Anglo-Saxon world) had not sold its reading soul to the devil of bigness and the documentary novel, it would have embraced Ludwig Hohl a long time ago. For he simply cannot say on a hundred pages what he can say on ten with the weight of depth and the lightness of vision. He believes in the aphorism which he extends to the scope of the narrative without giving up the allegoric image, the deeper meaning living in a gesture, the huge reflection of a seemingly unimportant event thrown against the wall like mankind's *mene tekel upharsin*.

It is not the story, not the narrative that matters, but the imagery with which he captivates. He is a writer who makes you stop and think here and there. He makes you stop and dream now and then. He creates microcosmic images and means the world. Here are one or two examples. A leaf falls from a tree upon a man, no, into the life of a man, who reveals himself and his environment through his reaction to the leaf. Or: A tired workhorse collapses on a street as if half dead. Policemen and passersby are caught tragically in this seemingly unimportant event. And Ludwig Hohl, the observer and narrator, closes this story with the words:

> I did not give the horse any sugar, I did not touch it, I did not speak to it. Too unknowing, too alien was I to its body. I alone loved it. I did not touch it. I alone followed it from afar. Until it reached the square . . .
> . . . which I, too, then crossed quite alone.

Or, in his almost classical story of *The Three Old Women in a Mountain Village,* we find three realistically drawn portraits growing to symbols of the primary phases of man, three beings who are perhaps little more than extensions of the landscape: a monumental shape like stone without growth or movement; the silence of existence, a being so silent that one can "only perceive it when the world around it turns to silence"; and the third one, a frightening being with the power and fury of a bull, endowed with "utmost fear and utmost violence," with a "penetrating" voice that can grow into a hurricane. These three old women are creatures of nature, helplessly caught in their individualities. As Hohl maintains in his introduction, he remembers them "as if they had been the only old women of the village . . . or of all mountain villages or even of the world."

Everything in his work is *Reflections and Nuances,* the title of one of his books. Everything has poetic power. Had he believed in the epic flow of a story, he might have become a Swiss Knut Hamsun. But he believes in the epigram; he loves to paint the *Sketch of a Sketch of the World,* as he calls one of his verbal miniatures, on a page and a half.

Perhaps Ludwig Hohl is a bridge to the post-World War II generation of Swiss writers who master the essayistic feuilleton, the minor theme which they know how to turn into a major subject. The incidental event becomes isolated and magnified through its isolation. The themes picked up at random are those of the ordinary lives of ordinary people. Life is often presented in its banal nakedness. The reader is charged with giving the literary product the meaning he sees in it.

All this goes back to Jean Cocteau, who, already in 1917, in his highly intellectualized playfulness was fascinated by the idea of elevating the banality of reality onto a higher poetic level. The idea was taken up again by different artists in different media in the 1950's and helped influence the creation of such divergent artistic forms as the *nouveau roman* and concrete poetry, and it may have played godfather to pop art. This trend, moving on a broad front against the last remnants of traditional art, coincided with a deeply rooted predilection in Swiss writing towards the essayistic feuilleton.

Peter Bichsel (1935–   ) and his stories, particularly *Frau Blum Wants to Meet the Milkman*, come to mind. He records "the inventory of his environment," as he once said. He can put a word, a sentence on paper and is interested in what it evokes: images, human beings, more words. Language is important because words help create human beings—for him, the two are inseparable—and create situations.

I imagine Peter Bichsel taking a train. He waits on the platform near the station restaurant. There he sees a girl sitting at a table. It is evening. "In the evening," he thinks, "they are waiting for Monika." The name occurred to him while looking at her, and this sentence follows him now wherever he goes. It becomes the beginning of a story. Who is Monika? "She works in the city," he thinks. But why should she be sitting there? "The train connections are bad." We have the first three sentences of a story.

One word leads to another and to a situation which leads to an idea—a tableau, as a matter of fact—to a snapshot of the banality of life. But when we read those few pages we know Monika, her parents, her office, the cliché of her existence. We knew her before we read the story because we also take trains and while waiting must have seen a girl sitting in a restaurant. Peter Bichsel admits that he has no "ideas" at all, that he "only discovers what actually had been there before." But what he has done to us is to heighten our awareness of the many girls existing on the margin of their own realities.

He wrote other books, and a longer one called *The Seasons*. He said it consists of many little stories, and that the last stories could be read first or one could start in the middle, or could shuffle the stories around at will. He is a short-short-story writer who can capture the totality of the ordinariness of life on two pages.

Kurt Marti (1921–   ), who combines theology and poetry—he gave the Bernese dialect a new poetic license—the essay and short story, is when writing fictional prose a distant cousin of Bichsel. *Marti's Stories from the Village* prove it. They were evoked by real experience or shreds of memories converted into imaginary life. For instance, a young man sitting in the compartment of a train watches the people around him and imagines their lives. Marti is a strongly motivated writer and leaves nothing to the whims of linguistic and accidental improvisation. As in this case, the lives of these people are determined by the sad ambience of a suburban train.

He came late to writing, in his mid-thirties, from the sermon to literature. But there is nothing unctuous about his writing. He is utterly human and provoked by ethic considerations. As a progressive pastor he believes in the possibilities of a paradise on earth. This makes him, by necessity, into a social critic, a fighter for justice and social changes. Kafka, Joyce, and Robert Walser were great influences on him and, among other things, helped to shape his belief in the purity and power of the language. He does not feel frustrated by the proverbial narrowness of his country. The greatest themes, he thinks, can emerge from the smallest place ("The narrowness of the country should compel us to think beyond its borders"). But he has not yet written a novel. Does he not trust the sweep of his pen? Perhaps. But he is mainly afraid he would too much be absorbed by his characters at the expense of the real people in his community who need his concern. And concern is the key word for what Kurt Marti writes, be they poems, essays, or stories.

Perhaps not more concerned but more radically engaged in trying to say his say and to fight for his beliefs is Walter M. Diggelmann (1927–   ). He has authored a number of novels and stories as well as plays for stage, radio, and television. For Diggelmann, writing is one way of coming to terms with society and himself. As an illegitimate child he spent his formative years in constant uproar; his early experiences were a string of fights and flights, of being wronged and doing wrong in defending himself. One day he was told that there was a writer in him. This born outsider of society settled down and became a writer.

He is more than a brilliant journalist—which he is, as his many polemics prove. But he stands at the opposite end of *l'art pour l'art*. He does not understand how anyone can desire to become a writer's writer, or why he shouldn't use a cliché if it fits the occasion. He is best at writing the documentary story (for instance, *The Pleasure Journey* or *The Legacy*) even though many critics maintain his most perfect, because poetic, book is *The Trial of Harry Wind*. (Fortunately for him, he could not care less what his critics say. Or does he?)

For Diggelmann, writing is one of many forms of expressing an opinion about conditions and people. This is why, in almost all his works, he conducts a private trial of man which is constantly in session and over which he presides while simultaneously being prosecutor and attorney for the defense. This is why he can see the many faces in man ("A human being is an enormous multiplicity of human beings").

Among the young writers are a few stylists of great verbal power who, standing at the beginning of their literary career, may still write the great novel which every writer carries along with him. Paul Nizon (1929–   ), novelist, essayist, and art historian, seems to find a most subjective gratification of his ego through the subtleties of expressive sounds. His train of thought runs simultaneously on the two tracks of surrealism and expressionism. The music of the words is essential to him; it carries him like a ship out into the ocean without destination, and in a state of intoxication he listens to the waves of words and their rhythm. What is then on paper may sound like spoken language, somewhat elevated, but meticulously scanned. Evocative and provocative contents and messages count less than the symphony of verbal sounds rising to an image, to the pitch of a situation or a relationship. One example chosen at random can convey the self-willed intricacies of Nizon's style. In his sketch for his *Canto*, which was the result of a journey to Rome, he writes:

> I can't name you, yet I can travel you.
> To travel.
> There is only the green leather sweated through sour from smoke, the narrow four-seat compartment, underneath the hard racing wheels. Highest speed towards destination, to have no and all the time and nothing to do. Landscapes caress you, hamlets, villages, also towns, day and night are given away and wasted. There is little luggage with you and over your head in the net, your clothes stick on you, all the sweat permeates your skin, only you are still there, hot and cold and steaming with things . . . evening is evening, cold is cold, sun is sun, hunger is hunger and not Ravioli or Sauce Béarnaise. That is no longer boredom or impatience. It becomes a condition, light and serious, while the wheels race on steel after steel. . . . There you are outside,

you possess the world and are not its slave. Perhaps your brother sits down next to you, now finally you can sit opposite yourself, you can't help it, something rises there, undisguised and without make-up, there you can carry yourself off. There is something added to you. The limbs tied, the senses entangled in movement and rolling land, you've got it and can't reach it, there remains and comes what you really have, rises, enters the flying room, sits down, hello, eye to eye, you've had it. You can forget it, it is. In a landscape near Port-Bou? Can't remember. . . .

In *Canto*, published in 1963, the writer's ego running verbally amuck tries to free himself from the spectre of his past, his youth, and in Paul Nizon's *Novel*, written seven years later, this prose-poet attempts to investigate the devouring, killing circumstances of adult existence with the innocent eyes of a child. The author seems to be escaping constantly the established conditions, his past which is his today as much as it was his yesterday. He is a revolutionary disguised in the verbal clothes of an aesthete.

The concept of flight as a result of the feeling of isolation and narrowness occupies many Swiss writers who approach this theme and depict it in a variety of forms, shades, and nuances. Jörg Steiner (1930–   ), who, compared with Nizon, must be considered a cool realist, treats this problem in some of his novels. He, too, realizes the feeling of isolation, but behind the inability to integrate towers the need for building a new society in which human isolation can be eradicated.

In many devious forms and on all levels of existence we search for and try out possibilities of flight; this seems to be one of Steiner's dominating thoughts, only some of us reject it as an acceptable norm. He varies this theme in *Punitive Work* and *A Knife for the Honest Finder*. These are probably some major questions of our time: Can we overcome our isolation by fleeing into a group and accepting its norms? How long can we put up with isolation and thus function in a group as if we were a part of it? Are we not all outsiders within the established society, isolated from the mainstream whose components are just as isolated? Perhaps this is why Jörg Steiner may have come to the conclusion that running away is never a solution.

There are many variants of the themes of these mentioned writers, but they generally agree in their critical attitudes towards society and the time in which they live. Herbert Meier (1928–   ), a writer of plays, novels, and poems, published a manifest whose title defines his viewpoint: "The new human being stands neither right nor left—he moves on." The Platonian idea of the talent which should lead is visualized as the ultimate potential of man, the total man. To fructify life through the talent should not be an utopian idea but self-realization of a state in which profit and aggression are eliminated. This idea finds its echo in most of Meier's works, in which the old theme of evil against good is varied by man's greed or lust for power undermining the positive work of the talent.

The younger generation of Swiss writers reflect the dangers of a constantly growing industrialization in one way or another. They realize that one cannot stop the march of time with a novel or play, as Diggelmann said, but they also know one must not stop holding up the mirror to man's foolish nature. A new type of writer may emerge from this situation, one who tries to domesticate the industrial beast by accepting it, by creeping under its skin and working from within its greater potentialities and/or undermining its uglier aspects. Some literary critics have pointed out this growing symbiosis, and the names of Markus Kutter (1925–   ) and Hugo Loetscher (1929–   ) have been mentioned as best examples.

Kutter, historian and advertising agent, leaning towards concrete art, feels as a passionate activist and doer that literature has to promote ideas and new concepts of existence. ("One should expect help or a guide-post from literature, quite simply from the written word. . . .") Together with Lucius Burckhardt and Max Frisch he was co-author of *Attention: Switzerland* in 1955, in which the notion of a model town was promoted (in connection with the international exposition of 1964), a town that should have shown the way towards reasonable urban planning and be kept standing and alive—not for the duration of an exhibition (what a waste of money and effort!) but for all the world to see at all times. To be such a small state as Switzerland not only brings with it a great deal of happiness, he thinks, but also the responsibility to utilize it as a model with which one can experiment.

Markus Kutter has always been preoccupied with social questions, mainly with those arising from industrialization as his book, *Matters and Private Matters—Notes from the Viewpoint of Switzerland*, reveals. He realizes that in our era a model state must remain flexible to quickly adjust to changing conditions, and industry and state must work hand in glove and constantly promote new concepts by educating the people. Kutter seems to be a born teacher ("The world is not too intellectual, it is not enough so") with the passion of an artist and the knowing and yet playful gesture of an advertising agent.

Hugo Loetscher is a highly intellectual writer who clearly separates his journalistic from his novelistic work, even though he adheres to precision, clarity in formulating his thoughts, and to well-founded evidence in whatever he writes. Each theme demands its own form and creates for itself its own artistic, linguistic, and aesthetic rules. But since he is a socially motivated writer, his literary themes are never remote from the actualities of life and its political connotations.

As we cannot escape the system (or system within many systems), Hugo Loetscher sees the writer's great task as trying to humanize it. Because no system can ever be perfect, it carries the semen for its own changes along with it, and all we have to do is to create a higher awareness and to strengthen the will to act. This is what Loetscher's work does. He tries to present a balance sheet of reality in which the evil flowers, the seamy and seedy side of life count as well. He comes neither to praise nor to bury the dirty aspects of existence. In recognizing them and their role in society, he faces their challenge. Admittedly, he is somewhat fascinated by the darker side in man and life. When a fulfilled society tries to deny or silence it, he feels the need to defend it. He once proudly mentioned in an interview that a character of his gives "insight into the bowels of society."

Noah, a novel about economic boom, is a subtle analysis of the constructive and destructive elements at work in a capitalistic society. His social criticism is quite direct when he tells us that a society living for and on profit is lost. How more ironic could any judgment about Noah be than the one in the final, crowning sentence of the book: "Now only the deluge can still save him." But however painfully his satiric arrow hits the target, the situation is clear: By the skin of our teeth, as Thornton Wilder said, man goes on living, and Loetscher also strongly believes that through the ages man has always proved his desperate will and fitness to survive.

His figures are tragic but strong. They grow beyond their own reality. In his first novel, *Waste Water*, the inspector of drainage is a man of minor importance and major stature. Suspended during a revolution which is a pivotal point of the story, he asks to be reinstated. While doing so he unfolds through shreds of memory and the account of incidental but relevant events a pan-

orama of the undercurrent in the life of a city. Hidden behind
a language of correct technical terms and a feigned matter-of-fact
approach are the sinister images of sewer existence. The inspector
who makes his living on the fact that "man is not a clean human
being" rises to the figure of an ironic moralist, pointing his finger
at our wounds while trying to help man get rid of the remnants
of his conflicts, of his everyday dirt. Not everything in the story is
sad and serious; there are always reconciling moments of gaiety
and tenderness. But the river of waste goes on day and night; it
must be filtered, canalized, and disposed of. We learn how much
of life takes place in hidden depths.

The Wreath Winder, who is on intimate terms with death, has,
in her symbolic meaningfulness, almost the appearance of a Greek
heroine. She is a very simple woman who goes through her daily
experience with tremendous tenacity. The intensity with which
she functions in society, how she masters a miserable life, and
how many destinies are mirrored in her own fate elevate her to a
major figure of fiction. There is a bit of *Mother Courage* in her,
and the Brechtian intent of relating the fate of one person to the
fate of a city and epoch is not too remote in this novel.

Loetscher loves brevity, the event clipped of its ornament, the
telescoped view. He wrote a play before he wrote novels. But all
his books are constructed like plays, and they are well constructed. As a dramatist of life, he chooses carefully his point of
departure. He visualizes climax and denouement well in advance.
Episode is piled upon episode. The result is a kaleidoscope of
stories within the story, tales which in their totality make the
theme transparent, focus on its quintessence, give the novel its
artistic shape.

He is a dramatist at heart, for he sees in dramatic contrasts.
He once pointed out that certain sections in his novels, such as
the psychiatrist scene in *Noah,* are ready-made scenes for the
stage. When *The Wreath Winder* met her brother again, I could
well imagine her reminiscing words to be part of a dialogue spoken
on stage. This isolated passage has a Pinteresque touch:

> . . . . you see, I go to the movies. How I was getting around
> in the movies for hours, an entire evening I dragged myself
> through the desert, and I know how a ship sinks. Here quite in
> front is the lake, there I went on a steamer. No, one cannot al-
> ways remain at the same spot. How did I move around in the
> same bed, from lodger to lodger. Markus, there I travelled from

the pillow to the footend of the bed, and when I arrived, I prepared breakfast. Why travel through countries if one knew the
Steinacherfranz. . . .

A sense of theatre is present in his novels even if there are
no spoken words. There is never description for the sake of description, but to create a new dimension, to open a new vista on
the theme. There is never philosophy for philosophy's sake. It
is not Hugo Loetscher who then thinks (although he does); it is
always his character. This is how *The Wreath Winder* philosophizes
about people's deaths in democracies and dictatorships:

> "It is not right. . . . to wind a wreath for so many millions.
> Everyone should get his wreath. Oh, politics, and dictatorship to
> boot, as if democracy wouldn't be bad enough. . . . Why exe-
> cute them in masses? They don't stay alive where we are either,
> they die all right, only at greater intervals, and one can keep up
> with the wreaths." Anna thought of the equality before death
> and of the fraternity of all cemeteries and dreamt: Mortals of all
> countries unite.

A few words must be said about two diametrically opposed
poets: Erika Burkart (1922–   ), who is in many ways quite
typically Swiss; and Eugen Gomringer (1925–   ), whose work
could grow on the asphalt of any metropolis in the twentieth-
century world.

"He who writes books speaks to many," Erika Burkart wrote in
her novel, *Moraine,* and "They are the words that change the
world" we can read in one of her eight volumes of poetry published
between 1952 and 1967. She strongly believes in the power of the
word. "If one day it should get lost," she said in an interview,
"mankind would waste away . . . Together with music, language
is the most moving expression of the human soul."

The meaning of the word, its substance and not only its singing lilt, weighs heavily with her, as some of her poems prove:

> To remain silent in the ear of stillness.
> Thought playing again at the well:
> Trust in that which I do not know,
> adventure, to live
> at the opening of a huge cave,

To sow where tomorrow
others will harvest,
scars which slowly
become capable of bearing.

Her prose is full of poetic imagery. One can open her novel,
Moraine, at random: "It was senseless to go to Lilith now, to scrape
the gravel in front of her bolted house and to stare at the tightly
pulled curtains. The intoxication brightened all windows of his
life." What is her novel all about? The title signifies a geological
reality, but it also symbolizes the eruptive deposit after a glacial
erosion of the soul. The division of the book into three major sections—The Wells, The River, The River's Mouth—indicates the
author's involvement with life's ultimate questions. Moreover, nature plays as great a part in her prose as in her poetry—"The
evening . . . . was oppressively sultry. A large hand swept along
the sky, moved slowly down and remained lying across the dry
soil. Already for some time the white sun rested between the two
similar branches. The cleared foliage created the feeling of a swarm
of butterflies. . . ."

In her novel she investigates psychologically and celebrates
poetically the relationship between two children, the proximity of
sister and stepbrother, the mystery of their love. The novel touches
upon essential experiences in life: the realization of closeness
(which is closest when the partner is not present); the totality of
man (who becomes total only when he accepts the shadows of his
darker side); the picture of our memory (which can pale and die
as events and people die if our own thoughts do not give them
new life).

For Erika Burkart, realities have more than one level. In order to
capture their essence, to deepen their meaning, she can see and
shape them only in surrealistic terms. The novel has a strange ending which is illogically realistic and logically surrealistic. One early
morning the brother returns home, tired and irritated. He shoots
an arrow at the peacock which is fed by the teacher at the same
spot in the garden daily at the same time. "In deep absence as if
they knew nothing of one another and did not know to whom they
belonged, the hands executed the shot. Laurin thought of the
teacher and shot at the peacock whom he did not intend to kill.
The arrow hurtled through the hedge and split the plumage of the
bird which flew into a tree with a shrill cry." The arrow killed his

sister, who was picking flowers behind the hedge. It is only seemingly an accident, the physical death mere symbol for spiritual death, for feelings falling apart, for the inevitable finality.

Erika Burkart and Eugen Gomringer are contemporaries. She lives in Althäusern near Muri, he in Frauenfeld. One would think they are only about forty miles from one another, but in reality they are light-years apart. He is to literature what Max Bill is to painting. He was, in fact, secretary to Bill for a few years. Gomringer is the designer of concrete poetry.

With the publication of *Constellations* in 1953, Gomringer became a pioneer of a synthetic and rationalistically structured form of poetic expression. Structure—perhaps at the expense of depth— is the key word. The more complicated our life becomes, the more simplified must we construct the roads on which it moves. Overpasses, underpasses, and one-way streets are the result of a traffic threatening in its density. Gomringer reacted to the complexities of modern life with a streamlined, concrete order of poetic lines on which the images, reduced to their bold nakedness, run with thoughtbreaking speed. He may be a Swiss writing poetry. He is no longer a Swiss poet. His train of thought runs on international tracks.

He admits he uses the rational working methods of industry. He designs his poetry visually. There is nothing new about it. Apollinaire and the Dadaists were the first to practice it. Josef Albers loves to write his poems that way. Gomringer believes that any meditative concentration must find its visual precision in "concreteness." For instance, he writes:

> from the edge
> inward
>
> within
> toward the centre
>
> through the centre
> of the middle
>
> outward
> to the edge

The use of punctuation in poetry or capital letters in principle must be overcome. Like the futurists early in this century, the writer of concrete poetry believes in the visual function of the factual. Gomringer—speaking of *Poetry as a Means in Shaping the Environment*—says:

> The many-sided technological, machine-made, economic, aesthetic, psychological and generally human aspects which converge in the industrial design demand in the case of verbal presentation clarity, functionalism, easy legibility—a seemingly simple, yet precise, language inasmuch as we deal at all with a kind of representation.

Language is the music of the soul, Erika Burkart says. In *from the diary*, Gomringer feels challenged by the word and writing:

> and to begin. and to put a period after each sentence. and to begin again with a word and another word and another and to have written a sentence again. and to reread both sentences and the new sentence and to think of other sentences. and perhaps also to write them down. and write them in another sequence and to put a period after each sentence. and to begin again and now the whole. and now to reread the whole. and now to reread and think it through. and perhaps to find it right and to leave it. and to go on writing. and to put a period after each sentence. and time and again to start anew and to carry along everything written. and time and again to add something and nevertheless to put a period time and again, and to feel that suddenly everything is said. and to stop, exactly to stop. and to put the last period after everything. uncertain and yet sure.

Nobody can maintain that the experiences of our time are not traumatic. And what a difference in the expression of our traumas lies between Althäusern near Muri and Frauenfeld. As to sheer space, Switzerland may be crossed from one end to the other within a few hours. Spiritually, however, the distance between Althäusern and Frauenfeld cannot be measured in time and metres, if measured it can be at all.

THE VISUAL IMAGE BEYOND HODLER

I am not sure one can maintain that the Swiss as a people are more visual-minded than other peoples. But if nothing else, their innate relation to nature has always been the first and foremost object lesson for them. Indeed, nature plays a very specific role in the works of the visual artists of Switzerland.

Ferdinand Hodler (1853–1918) is for Switzerland what Johann Strauss is for Austria, or Goethe for Germany. He is most representative for the nation whose people can easily identify with significant and immediately recognizable features of his work. I am not necessarily thinking of Hodler's *Wilhelm Tell* painting, which retains the idealized expression of the simple peasant, the glorified fighter for his rights. This is one of the many historic pictures he liked to paint. At the age of forty-four he was commissioned to create the monumental murals for the Schweizerische Landesmuseum. With this work he changed conventional historical painting.

Influenced by the Jugendstil at the turn of the century, Hodler strove for a decorative but lucid simplification and heightened symbolic meaning; he stressed the linear concept and developed a geometric style of composition. His favorite term for it was "parallelism." There is a repetition of lines and colors, of people and trees in many of his designs. This parallelism which Hodler saw in nature everywhere—in forests and flowers, in the formation of rocks and fields, in human features and gestures—gives his canvases a feeling of intensity. It was decisive for Hodler's career that in 1905 he had an entire room to himself at the exhibition of the Berlin Secessionists, an honor also bestowed only on Gustav Klimt. But this period in Hodler's life was far more important for the Swiss than for the artist himself. It is an undeniable fact that at that time art consciousness penetrated the people. Hodler must be credited for it.

Hodler descended from peasant stock and never tried to deny it. When he came to Paris the sophisticated French took him for what he was, a robust realist with a strong temperament, a simple peasant from the Bernese Alps, a true man of nature as Rousseau imagined him to be. Hodler was eager to learn, to acquire knowledge in different disciplines, and with the same intensity he wanted to teach, to explain and justify his art. He had a strong feeling for the monumental, larger than life scene and loathed the anecdotal motives in genre painting in which the storytelling reveals inner emptiness (to use his words). He looked for content and form as the true expression of a simple sensation and singular perception.

His canvases show that he experimented a great deal and that he went through many styles while remaining true to himself. He painted many female figures, was fond of motion as the expression of a state of agitation. He made not less than forty-one portraits of himself, but figure painting never quite satisfied him. He began as a landscape painter and ended his life as a sick man, sitting at his window for many years and painting the panorama of Mont Blanc. Hodler deserves the epithet of being the world's greatest mountain painter.

The landscape of the Bernese Alps inspired him first. He said that "The wonderful beauty of the city of Berne alone, as I saw it in my childhood, awakened in me and nourished my artistry." The sharply etched contour in Ferdinand Hodler's paintings were also compared by Rainer Maria Rilke with the hard and clean-cut contours of the landscape around Berne. Rilke thought that Hodler's early impressions remained ever decisive for his work. That may be true, but it was Hodler's blessing to see the mountains in the way that only he could see them.

He was one of three Swiss painters of the nineteenth century who achieved international reputation. I could have said four painters, if we wish to consider Giovanni Segantini (1858–1899), an Italian born in the Tyrol, as a Swiss. He, who spent his mature life in Switzerland, is often named beside Hodler as the most important landscape painter. He discovered himself when discovering the mountains of the Engadin. Segantini settled there among the farmers and shepherds when he was about twenty-eight. A museum in St. Moritz, solely devoted to his work, reminds us that he truly became the painter of that Alpine world: "My soul is overwhelmed with happiness here; my eyes enchanted by the blue sky, the sap green of the pastures and splendid mountains, observe all this magnificence with a conqueror's look eager for plundering."

In the beginning Segantini indulged in genre paintings, strongly influenced by Millet, in the very same sentimental and chatty manner which Hodler detested. Basically, Segantini remained a painter of the simple country life. Being in the open air, surrounded by clearly delineated mountains, he had to find a technique with which to re-create the airiness and contrasting drama of distant mountains appearing close to the eye. What he called "divisionism," more or less unbroken color strokes side by side, approximated the concept of the impressionistic plein-air painters.

That Segantini so often courted sentimentalism, and probably against his conscious will, had much to do with his meditative as well as ecstatic inclinations, and with his need to express himself through symbolic and allegoric imagery. Hodler created outside the ambience of human existence, whereas Segantini was concerned about life itself, the human element within a landscape. His greatest work, *Triptychon*, had to remain unfinished. But its design reveals the man and his work fully: *la vita*, the growing, is indicated by an early spring landscape with mother and child; *la natura*, the being, with a man and woman walking on a small path and a blue-gray mountain in the background; *la morte*, the dying, with a coffin being carried from a lonely house on a snow-covered plateau, partly hit by a blue shadow.

However remote the subject matter of Arnold Böcklin's (1827–1901) work may be from that of Segantini's, they certainly have in common the need to express themselves through allegory. But Böcklin went much further. Wagner and Nietzsche, Böcklin's contemporaries, tried to build a world of new myths, and, with their romantic excesses, they protested the rising danger of the Industrial Revolution. Böcklin created his own myth, new beings and plants, a landscape of symbols. He opposed those early years of modern mechanization with a stylized world of the beautiful and divine. This world of inner grace and brilliant colors was, unlike Wagner's, not tied to any folkloric roots; it arose from a deep-felt impression of nature, from a very personal, pantheistic belief.

Heinrich Wölfflin said about Böcklin that "what he creates is never the single case, but the result of many observations, the lucidly expressive image, as his imagination retained it." All of Böcklin's paintings have a focal point of view, a philosophical thought, and they pictorialize the painter's inner vision. Böcklin was foremost a landscape painter. Through his own mythological frame of reference he sought to find and express the soul of the landscape. He passionately believed in articulating his feelings through the intensity of the colors, and he admitted that colors were the propelling force in his creative process.

Böcklin was born in Basle, and the city's humanistic atmosphere contributed greatly to his interest in the classics. When he was twenty-three years old and beginning to find himself, Jacob Burckhardt had already recognized his potentialities, although he appreciated him only as a landscape painter. An ambivalent relationship developed between the two. Böcklin fought Burckhardt's influence on him as if it were an act of interference ("He made life impossible for me in my own home town"), but Romanticism and Burckhardt made him go to Italy, a journey that determined his future outlook. He also spent some time in Germany and made a great impact on the Munich school of painting at that time. For several years he lived in Italy, and for seven years in Zürich, where he became an intimate friend of Gottfried Keller, although he was spiritually closer to Conrad Ferdinand Meyer.

Böcklin's mythological frescoes in Basle are most representative of his creative will, but he is usually identified with such paintings as *The Island of the Dead* (which inspired Sergei Rachmaninoff's symphonic poem of the same title), or the *Great Pan*, which is at the Pinakothek in Munich. He was a visionary, and during the years of his later life he was obsessed by the idea of constructing a flying machine. ("I wouldn't give a hoot for all my paintings, if I could succeed in realizing this idea.") Böcklin died two years before the Wright Brothers took off the ground.

Johann Heinrich Füssli, also known as Henry Fuseli (1741–1825), was born in Zürich of a family in which painting and writing seemed hereditary and traditional. He studied theology but had strong leanings towards the arts, literature, and painting. Bodmer and Breitinger instilled in him a strong poetic feeling. Together with Lavater, Füssli attacked the "unjust prefect" of the district of Grünningen and accused him of several criminal acts and blackmail. Although all their accusations turned out to be justified, the two had to leave Zürich for a while. Lavater soon returned, but that turn of events became decisive for Füssli's life.

With important letters of recommendation he went to London, became tutor in the house of a noble family, and at that time translated Winckelmann's *Reflections on the Painting and Sculpture of the Greeks* into English. It was four years later that Sir Joshua Reynolds' influence made Füssli decide on a painter's career. Like most artists of the period for whom Italy was Mecca, Füssli journeyed to Rome and, with Michelangelo as his ideal, became a changed man. After an absence of sixteen years he returned to Zürich, where he created *The Oath on the Rütli*. The following year, 1779, he went back to London, where, with Reynolds and West, he was considered one of the great painters of his time and held many positions of honor. For six years he was professor of painting at the Royal Academy, and during this period he published his

Lectures on Painting, delivered at the Royal Academy, with additional observations and notes, which revealed his strongly subjective approach, his lasting admiration for Michelangelo and the heroic. He created many etchings and canvases, a series of paintings on Shakespearean characters and situations of the bard's plays, and about forty Milton pictures illustrating *The Lost Paradise.*

England has to be grateful to Füssli and if for no other reason than that he played a positive and helpful role in William Blake's life, recommending and helping Blake to his only commercial publisher, Joseph Johnson. Füssli felt a strong kinship to Blake's work and once said, "Blake is damned good to steal from." He, the celebrated master, did not have to steal from the struggling Blake, but, in their spiritual essence, some of Füssli's dreamlike paintings are near relatives to Blake's work. As a matter of fact, it was Füssli who influenced Blake. In the Swiss master's illustrations of some of the world's great books (Dante, Virgil, Shakespeare, and the *Nibelungenlied*), Füssli used distortions and elongations to express passion, anguish, and dramatic action. He helped to liberate Blake's imagination and issued for him a passport for freedom—to use whatever expression and form of his figures he felt was most dramatic and best suited for the pictorialization of his inner visions.

Whoever writes about Rodolphe Töpffer (1799–1846) cannot resist referring to Goethe who, when shown a little volume of caricatures by Töpffer, exclaimed: "This is terrific, this artist is full of scintillating wit and talent, certain passages show an inimitable perfection." When we see Töpffer's work today, we can only be surprised that Wilhelm Busch is known worldwide as the father of the cartoon, although he was preceded by Töpffer, who is little known. Neither Edward Lear nor Wilhelm Busch could have accomplished what they did without Rodolphe Töpffer, the creator of humorous drawings with explanatory text.

He was born in Geneva, the son of the painter Adam Töpffer. He was a very serious man with an exquisite sense of humor, a nineteenth-century James Thurber. He made his living as a teacher, ran his own school for some time, attracting boys from as far as America and England as well as other European countries. He was the first to introduce schoolboy hikes in the Alps, which afterwards he described in *Voyages en Zigzag,* with his own illustrations. He was appointed professor of belles-lettres at the University of

Geneva and delighted in writing humorous novels and short stories with his drawings, such as the masterpiece *La Bibliotheque de mon oncle.*

Töpffer is worth remembering for the adventure stories of *Mr Vieuxbois* and *Mr Cryptogame* in picture sequences, and for his picture novels *Master Paintbrush* and *The Journeys and Adventures of Dr. Festus*, which capture mood and movement with Daumier-like satiric intensity. In 1843, when describing a trip around Mont Blanc, he observed the many tourists who, already at that time, came to admire the scenic beauties. He learned to distinguish between four types of tourists. There is the serious-minded person, proud of his outfit, which demonstrates his earnestness; he smiles at everyone, ready to help, never disdainful or haughty. The loquacious tourist is accommodating and finds everything beautiful as long as he can talk about it, enumerating everything he sees, omitting nothing, whereupon he says: "Let's go!" The verifying tourist haunts galleries, museums, and monuments where, with the guidebook in his hand and seeing nothing, he verifies everything; finding everything as expected, he yawns; but when his itinerary disappoints him, he becomes furious. The perching tourist is a very rare specimen. Solitary and silent, he leaves early in the morning, a book under his arm; he walks a bit, then sits down on a rock or on the branch of a tree. There he perches for hours, devouring paragraphs and chapters. Finding no rock or tree, he would sit on the stony edge of the main road, enduring the mortification of his flesh.

With Töpffer one is reminded of Alice in Wonderland: one must see what he says so that one can know how he means it.

Perhaps I should have started this chapter with the beginning of the Swiss Federation or the Renaissance. It was then that the cities of Basle and Berne particularly had their share in the cultural explosion of Europe.

Niklaus Manuel, of whom I also speak as a dramatist in the chapter on the theatre, was *un uomo universale.* Born in Berne in 1484, where he died in 1530, he was one of those impressive Renaissance figures whose multiple creative urge expressed itself in many fields of activity. This brilliant man of many talents took advantage of Switzerland's link between the North and South, the Italian and German Renaissance, and the growing movement of the Reformation. The titans of Northern Italy and the imposing figure of Albrecht Dürer inspired him to a new freedom of expression, through which he liberated himself from the late medieval style, a Gothic-oriented world, and tried to achieve the Renaissance ideal of harmony and ease of form with a rather sensuous approach. Even though he did not completely free himself from the past (nor did Dürer), his mythological and Biblical paintings, his portraits and drawings reveal the new and experimental fervor of the time. Some of his paintings, such as *Pyramus and Thisbe* and *The Decapitation of John the Baptist,* are characteristic Renaissance products. His paintings included a dramatic series of the *Dance of Death,* which he designed for the Dominican monastery in Berne between 1516 and 1519.

About the same time—in 1515, to be exact—Hans Holbein the Younger (1497?–1543), son of the German painter of the same name, arrived in Basle where, together with his brother Ambrosius, he joined the workshop of the painter Hans Herbster as an apprentice. Hans Holbein's skill was soon talked about in the Swiss cantons, and in 1517 the magistrate Jacob von Hertenstein invited him to Lucerne.

After a short stay in Italy, Holbein returned to Basle, enriched by what he had seen, mainly by the works of Mantegna and Leonardo da Vinci. That very same year he was received as master into the painters' guild in Basle, which conferred citizenship on him a year later in 1520. Soon afterwards he had commissions from the municipality of Solothurn and then, being that far east on Swiss soil, he spent some time around Lake Constance.

Holbein made several portraits of Erasmus, with whom he was on friendly terms. With letters of recommendation from this famous humanist, Holbein set out on journeys which brought him to the Netherlands and England, where he became the court painter of Henry VIII. After two years, in the summer of 1528, Holbein was back in Switzerland and bought a house in St. Johann, a suburb of Basle; three years later he purchased another house in Basle. This only goes to show that in his mid-thirties he was an internationally recognized and well-to-do artist. The many commissions from his royal patron kept him in London, Germany, and Belgium for some time. The autumn of 1538 Holbein spent in Basle, on which occasion the city council offered him a pension. Five years later he died in London of the plague.

England and Switzerland share the honor of having been home to this painter and of having commissioned his major works. He was hardly more than thirty years old when he created one of the masterpieces of the age, the altar painting of the Virgin with the family of "Burgomaster" Meyer of Basle, an example of the most harmonious Renaissance composition. He added to it his attention to detail and his indifference to conventional beauty, characteristic of northern craftsmanship. His very personal artistic style was already noticeable in the highly imaginative work he did for Hans Baer in Zürich, and in the marginal drawings in a copy of Erasmus' *Laus Stultitiae* in 1515. In his façade paintings for the Hertenstein building in Lucerne, he achieved classic restraint and symmetrical balance which became even more strongly expressed in the eight scenes of a Basle Passion altarpiece and in his *Solothurn Madonna*.

In this first Basle period between 1515 and 1526, he was also very much interested in designing title pages and initials for books and working with woodcuts. Basle, at that time the center of Humanism, had many printers, and book illustrators were in great demand. In those years Holbein worked on the two series of woodcuts, his Old Testament illustrations and the *Dance of Death*.

The painting on the organ of the Basle cathedral and the interior frescoes he designed for the walls of the great council chamber in Basle show the sure touch of the master. Holbein interrupted his work on the frescoes when he left for London but tried to complete them during his third stay in Basle, when he also did a series of rather intimate portraits, to which belong the *Holbein Family* and the unfinished picture of a woman with loose hair.

A long road with many detours and side ways leads from Paul Klee (1879–1940) to Max Bill (1908–   ). It is a road which offers an astounding view of the many new forms of expression and often puzzling experiments of the visual artist in our century. Switzerland has brought forth far more than its goodly share in the artistic exploration of our existence and identity.

Owing to the country's neutrality, it could give birth to such a revolutionary movement in the arts as Dada. This movement came into being during the First World War as an automatic reflex to the beginning collapse of all old values, and as the true reflection of the twentieth century's trauma. It was a broad assault on the aesthetics and ethics of its time, and it could happen only at a place sheltered from the holocaust of man-made madness. A few artists who found refuge in Switzerland came together in Zürich and protested in the name of art against all art. Among them were the

German poets Hugo Ball and Richard Hülsenbeck, the Romanian poet Tristan Tzara, the Alsatian painter-poet Jean (Hans) Arp, and the Swiss painter Sophie Taeuber. Ball and Hülsenbeck claimed they accidentally found the word Dada in a German-French dictionary. Tzara maintained he discovered the word while sitting in the Terrace Café in Zürich one evening at 6 P.M. Ball owned a beer parlor in Zürich's Altstadt in the Spiegelgasse. It became the famous Cabaret Voltaire, meeting place for these unruly and free spirits, for exhibitions and lectures.

Primarily, Dada was a literary manifestation of natural emotions and everything irrational. Since Realpolitik, order, and logic led man to disaster, the Dadaists saw man's salvation in political and artistic anarchy. The strongest manifestations to emerge from the Zürich Dada movement were in literature.* Hugo Ball created his *Verses Without Words*, phonetic poems or sound paintings, the literary equivalent to the Dada collages which were introduced by Jean Arp (1887–1966).

The two most creative artists who grew beyond all anti-art slogans were Jean Arp and Sophie Taeuber, whom Arp later married ("She was always ready to accept the bright and the dark with silence . . . she had luminous skies descend upon this life," he said of her). Jean Arp grew up in an atmosphere of artistic tradition and training. When he discovered new ways of expression he could not immediately reconcile the past with the new forms and ideas which he felt alone valid. To find the truth and himself he sought solitude in the Swiss mountains where, in several villages, he spent the years between 1908 and 1910. He learned to converse with the silence of nature and to see his own abstractions in the very abstractions which nature reveals through its formations of stones and organic shapes.

When Arp and Taeuber joined the Dada movement in Zürich, they did it with the purpose of demolishing "the materialistic and rationalistic swindle in order to return man again humbly to nature as a part of nature." Once he said: "I love nature, but never nature's surrogate." As his poetry deflates logic and deforms meaning to evoke new images and sensations through utter simplicity, so he reduces man's haloed self-reflection by breaking up the unity of

---

* Later to emerge from this Zürich movement were Hans Richter's and Viking Eggeling's experiments with abstract and expressionist films. Furthermore, the Swiss, who have been leading in photography and particularly in typographic design, were at that time inspired to experiment with interesting, though sometimes playful, innovations.

objects into simple parts, avoiding "meaning or cerebral intention." He strongly believed that his works, "like nature, were ordered according to the laws of chance, chance being for me merely a limited part of an unfathomable *raison d'être,* of an order, inaccessible in its totality." The fourteenth-century fortress, Castello Visconti, in Locarno—Arp lived the last years of his life in a suburb of Locarno—was turned into an Arp museum.

Sophie Taeuber-Arp (1889–1943) was overshadowed by her husband's personality. One day art historians will correct this mistake and put her into her rightful place among the abstractionists. She was a unique person, modest about her own artistry, gentle but strong and knowing, seeing life with a ready smile and inmost gaiety. Jean Arp said that "Sophie opposed the loud, changing world with the steadiness of her inner heavens." And: "To wander with her was mere bliss. She greeted the world with silent jubilation. Every morning she approached her flowers like friends. She spoke with the stars and flowers." Kandinsky: ". . . she was without fear and reproach . . ."

Sophie Taeuber began to draw and paint geometric compositions, which she often filled with glowing colors. She also danced. (She took dancing classes with Rudolf Laban in his studio at the Seehofstrasse in Zürich.) She danced in the Cabaret Voltaire and in front of Kandinsky paintings, witty drolleries, in a grotesque as well as ecstatic manner. Although she gave up dancing to devote herself exclusively to drawing and painting, applied art and sculpture, movement and airiness continued to mark her work: circles with symmetric and asymmetric curves, rectangular and square forms, colors and silhouettelike dancing images. There, her concrete motifs seem to have so much rhythm that some of her pictures create a choreographic impact. Her world of perfect circles and lines and solid, uncluttered fields of colors breathes lightness. As Hilton Kramer pointed out in *The New York Times* when reviewing one of her rare New York exhibitions: "For Taeuber-Arp, even more than for Arp himself, the Dada ideology was a pretext for the purification of art itself. No artist I know exists at a greater distance from facile notions of 'anti-art.' "

Some critics maintain that certain aspects of Sophie Taeuber-Arp's work reveal traces leading into Paul Klee's world. Whatever may be reminiscent of Klee in her compositions, it never achieves Klee's poetic power and the cosmic significance of the gentlest gesture in his work.

Paul Klee was born in Münchenbuchsee near Berne in 1879 and

died in Muralto, a suburb of Locarno, in 1940. He crossed the paths of some of the art trends rampant early in this century, but his work developed in a highly individualistic way. He achieved reality in the tangible, a world of poetic images creating their own rationality for the irrational, their own logic for the illogical. His pictures have a dreamlike quality, but do not reflect a dream life in a vacuum. Klee teaches us to see the reality behind the unreal.

He was often reproached for his childlike attitude in theme, form, and execution. But he felt in Jungian fashion that "our pounding heart drives us down, deep down to the source of all." Carola Giedion-Welcker pointed out that for Klee any temporal and spatial limitation is merely coincidental, that he feels pulled back to what the source of all things may be, from final forms towards prototypes, "where primeval laws nurture all evolution . . . There, where the central organ of all temporal-spatial motion is." In going back to the very beginning he wanted to erase all knowledge of the past, to be as though newborn in order to create in an almost pristine state.

Of course, Klee knew only too well that no artist can sever all links with his past. There is a touch of the Oriental in his colorful, lyric fantasies and romantic abstractions. His intriguing use of letters interwoven in his paintings insinuate the beginning of the picture as it emerged from the letter. However unreal his paintings may appear, landscape as much as animals and plants dominate the visions of his very private reality. He searched for "an illumination of visions in the mind," as Antonin Artaud said, who, like Klee, searched for the hidden sense and a new myth in the magic of existence.

Klee is a solitary giant in the art field and among the Swiss painters. It is fascinating to think that the Bernese landscapes were the first impressions of Klee as well as Hodler. Klee was as close to nature as Hodler—we only have to consider what heightened symbolic meaning a tree had for Klee—but how different were the sensibilities of these two artists! Klee was Hodler's junior by only twenty-six years, but an entire world, not only a generation or a century, figuratively speaking, separated them from one another.

Switzerland produced many painters of repute whose activities fall between and around these two important figures, creating a logical continuity between yesterday and tomorrow. Cuno Amiet (1868–1961) was strongly influenced by the French school of paint-

ing, mainly by Gauguin and Van Gogh, and developed a very special sense of coloring. If there is such a thing as a specific Swiss
colorism, then Amiet applied it to his many canvases and favorite
themes, which were gardens, fruit harvests, and winter landscapes.
He spent four years in Paris, where he shared studio and living
quarters with Giovanni Giacometti, Alberto's father. But the most
productive period falls into the latter half of Amiet's life, and although he went through several phases in his development, color
remained his primary interest, and of whatever quality his paintings may have been, they emanated a tremendous joy of living. He
was the first Swiss artist to introduce the plein-air painting of
winter landscapes. This he practiced to the end of his long life.

The overpowering position France held in the art of painting
during the second half of the last century had its impact on many
Swiss painters. To go to Paris, at least for some time, was for the
French-speaking Swiss painters like going to their aesthetic home
town. Lausanne brought forth two painters of very different temperament and artistic inclination: Félix Valloton (1865–1925) and
René Auberjonois (1872–1957). Valloton immersed himself in
everything French, but kept aloof from the many experimentations
going on at that time in Paris. His paintings display a tendency
towards stylized realism. The Puritan rigidness and restraint in his
approach to his subject matter prevented him from fully unfolding
his capabilities, as he did so masterfully in his woodcuts. In that
graphic medium his imagination moved freely but with precision
and economy; it encompassed thematically everything from the
social scene to the portraits of luminaries. He revitalized this medium with an inventive mind and consistent strength. His artistry
was fulfilled in his woodcuts.

Auberjonois was a strange personality, combining an almost
sickish need for privacy with the attitudes of a sophisticated bohemian. His work is an annotation of life with the figurative element predominant: man in the landscape, in the theatre and circus atmosphere, and, above all, the female figure in the nude, as
dancer and acrobat. He had a strong feeling for the whimsical,
which he pictured as a caricaturist would. He made many portraits
of himself and such friends as Stravinsky and Ramuz. For quite
some time Auberjonois was in love with pointillism and applied
this technique for the many still life pictures, flowers, fruits, and
vegetable arrangements, but also for nudes and in his picturesque
landscape motifs, houses and streets in his beloved Valais.

Similarly, landscapes with houses, mostly in warm sunlight, are the subject matter of the watercolors created by Louis René Moilliet (1880–1962). He was an important stained glass painter and one of the best aquarellists of his time. In a way his work indicates that he is a relative—though a very remote cousin—of Paul Klee. As in Klee there is poetry in Moilliet's little squares, a rhythmic, almost architectonic, balance between bright and half-dark fields in his compositions. Later in his life he devoted much time to the creation of stained glass windows characterized by the same lyric transparency of motif and execution as his watercolors. His close friendship with Klee, Hesse, and many other artists of his time was of great benefit for all of them and brought about a state of mutual inspiration.

A word must be said about Ernst Morgenthaler (1887–1962). As a draughtsman and painter, he was a characteristic Swiss phenomenon—not only for continuing on the main traditional path chartered by Hodler and Amiet, but also for trying to bridge within himself the contrasts of two worlds: the world of peasantry (symbolized by his mother, who still lived in the tradition of Gotthelf) and the one of city sophistication (symbolized by many of his friends in Zürich). His early work shows great imaginativeness, but also his criticism of social conditions. And his entire later output vacillated between social awareness and mood paintings of the Swiss landscape, between conventional experiences and spontaneous, poetic expressions. In the main, most of his works impress with their improvised, sketchy quality which invites the spectator to go on dreaming Ernst Morgenthaler's dream. Two of his remarks made in 1954, after a longer sojourn in Paris, are characteristic for him and many Swiss artists: "Art is there from the very beginning. Its name is excitation of feeling. An artist tries to achieve the best that is in him to be able to express his excitation of feeling." And: "I don't believe in progress; I only believe in transformation."

Some contemporary Swiss artists try to overcome the twentieth-century chaos by creating playfully a measure of order through "concrete" art. Beyond the geometric solution of lines and squares, beyond the harmonious structure of basic simplicity, these artists seek a metaphysic perspective through the vocabulary of the most concrete reality. Piet Mondrian and Josef Albers are the archetypes of this school which, through Max Bill and Richard Paul Lohse (1902–   ), has received a new architectonic feeling, a new visual universality.

Lohse's contribution to the function of form in space is the musical element of a new optic language, accomplished with a fugue of shapes and colors. Color becomes a dynamic element in his harmonies of structural relationships. In demystifying the decorative figuration of verticals and horizontals, colored squares and rectangles, Lohse creates a new myth of cosmic harmony.

Max Bill, who also writes very well, said about the work of his compatriot:

> structure could be mere scheme
> but here it is aesthetic reality
>
> colors could be obliging
> but here they are characteristic of the type
>
> expression could be personal
> but here it is representative of our time

In principle, the clarity of line and the simplicity of design in Max Bill's work reflect his striving for mathematical order. His spiritual roots, as he told me, go back to Kandinsky; constructively he is closer to Klee; aesthetically he leans somewhat on Mondrian. Bill's paintings attempt to give space an intensified image through spatial fulfillment. He is also constantly experimenting with the interaction of colors upon one another. He emerged from the Bauhaus as one of its most individualistic artists, with a protean creative mind as a painter, sculptor, architect, graphic and industrial designer as well as a writer.

Max Bill believes that the aim in art as much as in life is to find means for a constructive harmony. The Bauhaus tried to accomplish a complete synthesis of art and science, which reaches in Bill's work final form. He sees in the constantly changing world a challenge and an opportunity to help re-create it through a total transformation of the environment with new and clean architectural and visual aspects foreshadowing the cultural climate of a future generation.

"I am of the opinion," Max Bill wrote, "that, with the help of concrete art, just those things can be expressed which really have symbolic meaning and which are not burdened with a literary or sentimental heritage. In this way I try to shape works with an innate direct and unambiguous symbolic power, like symbols for unity, infinity, freedom, human dignity." He thinks that concrete art is the visualization of an idea, and that an abstract idea can be

given a concrete *Gestalt* through the creative process. It is characteristic of his approach to creativity in the visual arts that he once
wrote an essay on mathematical thinking in contemporary art. To
him, circle and square are constant in the cosmic order; remoteness
and proximity in an inexplicable space can and ought to be measured and mastered by the artist whose task it is to create "order
from order-plus-disorder."

Some titles of Bill's paintings and sculptures reveal the mathematical thinking that prompted them—*Unbegrenzt and begrenzt*
(*Unlimited and Limited*) and *Energien der weissen Fläche* (*Energies
of the White Surface*)—and wrestle with the phenomenon of the
concrete in the abstract (or is it vice versa?). His sculptures *Kon-
tinuität* (*Continuity*) and *Unendliche Fläche in Form einer Säule*
(*Infinite Surface in the Form of a Column*)—the former to be seen
at the Zürich Lake, the latter in private possession in New York—
show how Max Bill reduces form to utter simplicity, how he disciplines himself to create the essence of an idea and the monumen-
tality of a concept, however emotional or cerebral, through a
minimum of material within the smallest possible space. All that
seems to matter is the drama of the visual experience. This is most
obvious in his design for the *Monument of the Unknown Political
Prisoner*, a sculpture of architectural shape, displaying a group of
three cubes of different sizes in a triangular space with a sharp-
edged, mirrorlike column in the centre.

Max Bill's sculptures are a far cry from the neo-classic style of
the nineteenth-century sculptors who accepted as their task the
creation of monuments, fountains, and figures in the historic tradition in order to give the public places and buildings a decorative
touch. The transition into the twentieth century proceeded step by
step. The three sculptors whose works can be seen in many Swiss
cities and who have hesitantly but gradually broken with the past
are Karl Stauffer (1857–1891), whose short life prevented him from
developing his potentialities; Carl Burckhardt (1878–1923), who
continued on Stauffer's path, trying to liberate himself from the
conventions of the past but shying away from any contemporary
search for new forms and concepts ("The uninhibited need to express one's own feelings at any price, to find in fury and haste an
incredibly new form for the 'mentally new experience' results in a
specificness that is more nerves and sensuality than soul"); and
Heinrich Haller (1880–1950), who was enamored with the young

and beautiful female figure, partly pictured restrained in movement and emotional expression, partly gay and strong in an almost athletic motion. Among his few male figures are the Negro boxer Jack Johnson, impressions after Karl Walser, and the recumbent figures of a boy and girl in front of the Zürich University.

Haller had a strong feeling for inner harmony but none for space and environment. This is why he composed so many of his figures with a frontal view in mind. The revitalized meaning of sculpture in space as much as its structural image separates the artists born in the nineteenth century from those of our time. Hans Aeschbacher (1906–   ), Bill's senior by two years, was still close to Haller when he began to work with figures, but he soon developed a very personal style while changing from portrait sculptures to pure abstractions. The designs of his architectural and monumental sculptures demand huge spaces. They need the landscape as much as the landscape seems to need them. Aeschbacher's works have clarity and structural logic without being motivated by a purely scientific approach. His abstract and yet dynamic stones, for instance, on the Zürich airport or at Lake Geneva and, particularly, in various gardens, are characterized by an elegant grace. His works never intrude on their environment, but give it a very specific meaning.

It may be a mere coincidence that Switzerland has produced some of the most fascinating artists of technical constructions or metamechanic sculptures. They are a logical outgrowth of Dadaism and could originate and flourish only in such highly technological countries as the United States and Switzerland. Alexander Calder's mobiles running amuck in a machine-made and machine-mad age had to lead to Jean Charles Tinguely's (1925–   ) metamechanics and metamatics which he created between 1954 and 1959, going from there to the construction of auto-destructive machines three years later, and finally arriving at sculptures with a built-in Sisyphus-content.

Tinguely is not the only Swiss artist to have gone the way of all technology. There is Oscar Wiggli (1927–   ) with his iron constructions and Bernhard Lüginbuhl (1929–   ) with his metal sculptures. All three were born when the Bauhaus began its experiments. Perhaps Laszlo Moholy-Nagy, one of the great Bauhaus innovators, pointed the way for these constructivists of the machine age with his *Light-Space Modulator* created in 1930. Tinguely, undoubtedly the most important of these sculptors, had to happen to us. His work is an apotheosis of the mechanized rhythm of our time, but, at the same time, the frightening writing on the wall.

He has admitted that he cannot paint or sculpt in any traditional manner. He chose motion as his point of departure to recreate artistically our mechanized age. From 1940 on, he produced highly complicated and eccentric machines, some of which symbolized waste and the expendability of man in being self-destructive as did his famous *Hommage to New York*, demonstrated in the garden of the Museum of Modern Art on March 17, 1960. He varied this idea with *Hommage to Dali* and *Etude for an End of the World*. The latter was produced in the Nevada desert in 1962.

This period in which Tinguely gave total expression to man's destructive genius was followed by what he called his "joyous period," in which his constructions of water-spraying tubes would playfully move around. But this seemed to go nowhere. After a year of indecision Tinguely received a commission to create something new for the Schweizer Landesausstellung in 1964. He represented his *Eureka*, a perpetually working machine, complete with wheels, arms, and levers, creating a constant movement of up and down and back and forth, working for no other purpose than to demonstrate the triumph of a modern-day *perpetuum mobile* in the form of rhythmic sculpture.

In 1953, Tinguely worked on a moving ballet décors with Daniel Spoerri (1930–   ), another Swiss representative of the daring art of dynamics and new ultrarealism, a Swiss Andy Warhol and Robert Rauschenberg rolled into one. Tinguely returned to the ballet in 1966 when he created the curtain for Roland Petit's *L'éloge de la folie*, a composition of wheels moved through pedals by a built-in dancer. Or how about the huge female figure colorfully painted which he called *Cathédrale* and which was seen in Stockholm? It was built in such dimensions that one could walk inside her. Among other surprises one found a bar. Mad? Probably. And painfully imaginative.

Of course, Tinguely expresses only a few aspects of our time, and, for all we know, later periods may say that these were its essential aspects. Since Tinguely is not alone in his raging experiments, these iconoclasts should shatter any stereotyped image we may have of what is Swiss.

Most of these artists were born in the second half of the 1920's.

So was Friedrich Kuhn (1926–   ). The world he re-creates in his paintings is a Kafkaesque and lost world in dissolution and decay. He throws together scurrilous shreds of ideas, and moments of distorted reality (as he remembers it), but almost all his canvases reveal a palm tree somewhere, which is to Kuhn a symbol for "a dream of recovery," as Paul Nizon described it. It is "in a certain way the broom used for the purification rite in a temple. However, it was also the signet of an independent advertising campaign. Finally, it was the sign of a new horizon, a flag promising new land . . ."

There is something morbid in Friedrich Kuhn's paintings, a vague hope pitted against a strong disbelief in life presented as a desperate outcry as well as the desire to escape the inescapable.

Meret Elisabeth Oppenheim (1913–   ) is one of the older pioneers of the younger generation. She became a surrealist after Alberto Giacometti had introduced her to André Breton. She brought an imaginative, ironic feeling to many colorful motifs of dreamlike reality, but moved later from the phantasies of romantic surrealism to paintings more strongly stressing abstractions. She is most famous for *Die Pelztasse (The Fur-Lined Teacup)* which falls into her early period and is in the possession of the Museum of Modern Art in New York. Ever trying to fulfill herself and to find new ways of expression, she turned to sculpture in 1958 and produced some stunning pieces, pure in form and strange in content, such as her *Einer, der zusieht, wie ein anderer stirbt (One who Watches How Someone Else Dies)*.

As the internationalism of art has constantly increased in the course of this century, an international style of the many isms has developed and may soon eclipse the importance of national tendencies characteristic of earlier centuries. Because of its essentially diverse cultures, Switzerland has never enjoyed a unified national trend in the arts, which may also account for the surprisingly lively variety among its twentieth-century artists.

The painter Willy Guggenheim (1900–   ), who hides behind the name Varlin, is a rare phenomenon. An outsider, he runs the gamut from the poseur with a cabaret joke to the satirist and caricaturist. He is a cross between the earlier George Grosz and Oskar Kokoschka, translated into Varlinese. In all his paintings the content matters a great deal but is presented as if with a disinterested gesture. This nonchalant stance is highly deceptive. His approach to his subjects is one of structural destructiveness. Life is caught on Varlin's canvases in its contrasting picturesqueness but always with sophisticated exaggeration whose final impact is the grotesque and scurrilous.

His paintings are full of city landscapes, portraits of buildings and people, of palaces and cemeteries, and of his own studio. The latter—in two versions, *Atelier I* and *II*, painted between 1964 and 1969—is a world in itself, reflecting the universal chaos in a private nutshell. These canvases are painted with Van Goghesque fury, as a triptych of life including everything from the painter's brush and colors—symbols of creativity—to a cemetery intruding the artist's studio. The space is frighteningly filled with the realities of life, an unlivable room crowded with memories and fearful antici-pations, somersaulting anxieties, hopelessly destructive—and yet one can almost hear Varlin's mocking laughter telling us that we should not take anything too seriously.

His human comedy is a clownish act of someone who cries tears over the lost bourgeois life. He seems to be, in good Swiss fashion, deeply attached to it. But he places himself outside this world he loves in order to gain the right perspective on it. Then he cannot help laughing about what he sees and loves and cannot help mock-ing it a bit. His imagination depends on reality, on streets, build-ings, rooms, people. He takes a good look at them and reports their stories as he sees them. What we call fate, he says, are our foolish pranks. In many ways he is the counterpart to his compatriot Friedrich Dürrenmatt.

Max Bill wrote the preface for the Swiss artists in the catalogue of the 34th Venice Biennale, 1968, which featured the work of Fritz Glarner. He said that Glarner "continues the work of Piet Mondrian in the same way in which Mondrian rationally followed the pictorial image of Paul Cezanne." Glarner, born in Zürich in 1899, emigrated to the United States in 1936. There he became a leading member of the American abstract artists and famous for such works as the huge mural for the Time Life Building in New York, a work completed in 1959.

Before his death Mondrian said that Glarner was giving a new dimension to his own work. Glarner's conceptions may be as lyric as those of Mondrian, but they have a far more dramatic rhythm cre-ated by an intense group relationship between his subtly structured rectangulars. He plays skillfully with a variety of dimensions and colors which evoke a balanced feeling of a strong expressive rhythm. Many of his relational paintings can be found in the museums of Basle and Boston, of Winterthur and Minneapolis, of Zürich and New York. Many private collectors have found pleasure in living with the lyric and dramatic playfulness of his decorative designs, among them Nelson Rockefeller, whose dining room in his New York town house has integrated décors by Fritz Glarner.

Switzerland is in no way isolated or different from the artistic trends of our time. Even though the country is the ideal nature-landscape, its artists have not escaped the pressures of modern technology and mass media, they have not denied "the logical consequences in the process of development and in the shifting of the political, social, and industrial energy centers from the area of nature-landscape to the city-landscape," as Richard Paul Lohse wrote. He introduced thirty-four young artists in an exhibition, "Ways and Experiments," in the Kunsthaus Zürich in 1968.

A smaller group combines logic and intuition in a systematic way, continuing the development of the Zürcher school in a purely individual manner. But, as Lohse pointed out, a larger group shows the influences coming from New York and London. "The means are expressive-decorative, there is a tendency toward symmetry, monumentalization and emblematicalness. The posterlike super-purism and the *trompe-l'oeil* as determining factor of the structural realization are other characteristics of this cold romanticism . . ."

The great number of entries to this exhibition made it necessary to exclude the Swiss Pop artists, among whom Peter Stämpfli (1937–   ) is the most expressive one. His meaningless, cold replicas of life are frightening in their total objectivity. The demystification of reality reaches on his canvases the other extreme of the nonobjective painting.

There is not one aspect of contemporary creative experimentation in which the Swiss artist would not wholeheartedly be involved. In the thirties, the Swiss people were slow in recognizing the new in the arts. This has essentially changed. One can see this readiness in the acceptance of the fashion and, however cautiously, of the mores of a world which rapidly changes. The responsibility of the artist has not diminished; it has grown. That the Swiss artist—whose community spirit has never left him, even when he has found himself in opposition to bourgeois society—has understood the meaning of his role is indicated by Richard Paul Lohse's final words in the catalogue of the exhibition "Ways and Experiments":

It may be easier for the generation of this exhibition to garner spontaneous recognition today, but, on the other end, just as easily hides the danger of being lonesome and quickly forgotten in the suction of change. It is one of the special characteristics of the present situation of Western culture to be more susceptible to quick reactions and changes of style. The decisive question is finally a personal one, that is a question of morality as we have faced it with the same immediacy and severity from the thirties until now, a question demanding from each generation a fundamental answer to the problem of how to overcome past paragons, to the value of inventiveness, of personality and intensity.

Max Gubler's (1898–   ) artistic awareness began at the age of twenty. With it began the tortures of the creative man, the compulsion to work, the despair of doubt. Faith in himself helped him over his many crises. He went to Germany and Italy, but his major journeys were those leading into his mindscape.

He was a man possessed. "There is nothing else but to work, to look neither right nor left," he wrote. "Every day spent in sadness is lost." There was the word "sadness" again, his insecurity, his need to express himself and to be understood. Criticism and advice came from his brothers, artists themselves, or from his friends, who realized the spark of genius in Max.

His work is the work of one who seeks. Fanatically opposed to naturalism, he looked for harmony through architectonic means. In most of his canvases the interplay of light and color takes on an important role in an often strangely balanced manner. The choice of color brightens his paintings and is a focal point, full of meaning, such as the red color which is of intense newness, "an affirmation of life, but just as much an affirmation of death" as the art historian Gotthard Jedlicka said. In one of Gubler's greatest works and largest canvases, *The Procession*, white is the dominant color within all colors, as if it would burn on all the faces, giving them a frightening expression of unreal reality.

Some of his early pictures reveal the lostness and aloneness of people on their way to doom. Even though his craft developed constantly, there remained a frightful questioning or a stubbornly absent look in all his faces. His landscapes, however, show a fullness and richness of color and design as if the painter wishes to say: Look, what nature does for me and what civilized man does to me!

Jedlicka called Gubler "the greatest painter in the realm of new Swiss painting; he is her only genius." It is difficult to categorize

Max Gubler because he kept remote from all isms of his time, standing apart as a man and artist. His work has signs of contemporariness and timelessness. It reveals the hand of the tortured creature man, with withdrawn intensity of soulfulness, with a touch of resignation and the flaming fire of man's will to overcome his being only human.

I have omitted a long list of twentieth-century Swiss artists who, singly and collectively, would complete Switzerland's contribution to the arts. It is impossible to discuss each of them. But this chapter must conclude with one towering figure, an artist of international stature: Alberto Giacometti (1901–1966).

He was very much of our time. He was light-years away from the impressionistic work of his father, Giovanni Giacometti, with whom he first studied. Alberto soon realized that "to render what the eye really sees is impossible." He was a draughtsman, painter, and, above all, a sculptor. Drawing was central to the vision of the painter, and as a painter he created with the eye of a sculptor. To him, the totality of the shape in space was the heart of the matter. He re-created the existentialist man, spiritual isolation through the reality of his unreal figures.

"Figures were never for me a compact mass but like a transparent construction," he said. His figures evoke feelings of *Angst*, loneliness and alienation. He struggled with each figure in space, trying to capture man surrounded by his void, establishing the relation of being to nothingness. He wrestled with each figure so long until no individuality was left, no psychological interpretation possible. (The longer a person sat for Giacometti, the less recognizable he became.) He erased the likeness of the features of face and body in order to reveal them. The closer one looks at his figures, the clearer it becomes that what we see is a tortured, yet vital, surface. But what a surface, full of the traces of volcanic outbursts, the tremors of dynamic pressures, and the sensation of motion! His figures have mystery, an anonymous quality of existence, the elusiveness of a silhouette walking into space.

"It was no longer a question of reproducing a lifelike figure but of living . . . ," Giacometti explained; and Jean Genet, his friend, had Giacometti's objects say: "I am alone, I am transfigured in a necessity which you cannot disturb. As I am what I am, I am indestructible. Being what I am and without reservation, my solitude knows about your solitude."

Alberto Giacometti began as a neo-impressionist. By the late 1920's he had joined the surrealists. At the end of the thirties he hardly painted any more. He was then completely absorbed by giving shape to many elongated figures existing in a state of uncertainty and eloquent in their anguish.

"The task of Giacometti," Jean-Paul Sartre once wrote, "is not to enrich the galleries with new work, but to prove that sculpture itself is still possible."

MUSIC TO SWISS EARS

IT is a historic fact that four of the five contemporary Swiss composers of international stature—Arthur Honegger (1892–1955), Ernest Bloch (1880–1959), Frank Martin (1890–   ) and Rolf Liebermann (1910–   )—have been active mainly outside the frontiers of their home country. Othmar Schoeck (1886–1957) was probably the most representative Swiss composer of our time, and he was preceded by many who played a very distinctive, and sometimes a very distinguished, part in the musical history of the world and of Switzerland in particular.

The Swiss people are mostly thought of as being *amusisch,* so much immersed in the pursuit of all practical aspects of life that they do not have the time or inclination for a more intimate relationship to any of the nine Muses. True, these somewhat more than five million people did not bring forth a Bach, Beethoven, or Mozart, a Verdi, Berlioz, or Debussy, a Chopin or Tchaikovsky. But how many nations did? Can powerful and literate England boast of more than a handful of composers (Purcell, Elgar, Britten, Vaughan, and the German Händel)? And who are the composers of Holland that gave us Hals, Rembrandt, and many more painting giants, down to our contemporary Mondrian? Or any of the Scandinavian countries (except the Norwegian Grieg and the Finn Sibelius)? Or can the Spaniards be proud of more than deFalla and their characteristic folk music?

Switzerland can at least maintain a symphony orchestra in most of its many small cities, besides having a number of great orchestras of international reputation. It is probably of less consequence that the famous singer Lisa Della Casa was born in Burgdorf, a small place in Switzerland, or that the Swiss-born conductors Rudolf Ganz and Walter Ducloux have established themselves in the New World. But the activities of the conductor-composer Ernest Ansermet (1883–1969), particularly his association with Igor Stravinsky and with Serge Diaghilev's Ballets Russes, had great significance. This conductor, whose authoritative interpretations of twentieth-century composers contributed a good deal to their understanding, also founded the Orchestra de la Suisse Romande in Geneva in 1918. As its conductor, or as guest conductor of other orchestras, he often introduced new works by Stravinsky, Prokofiev, Hindemith, and Bartok, and by his compatriots Honegger and Frank Martin.

Paul Sacher is a very unique appearance as a musicologist and conductor. As a conductor he divides his activity between Zürich (Collegium Musicum) and Basle (Basler Kammerorchester), but his greatest merits lie in two seemingly opposed directions. He has always been interested in the study and cultivation of pre-classic music and founded for this purpose the Schola Cantorum Basiliensis in 1933, whose guiding spirit and director he has remained to this day. On the other hand, as a man of means who is also vitally interested in modern music, he has been able to commission new works from young Swiss composers, but, by the same token, from Stravinsky and Bartok, from Krenek, Henze, and Britten.

It throws an interesting sidelight on the musical Swiss scene if we take into consideration that Ulrich Zwingli and John Calvin composed and had a strong feeling for music. Since medieval days the cloisters and cathedrals were musical centers; Sankt Gallen was leading in this respect, and in the days of the Reformation it was in Geneva, Basle, and Zürich where the reformed church songs were most advanced. The greatest influential composer of that period was the Swiss Ludwig Senfl (1488–c. 1543), who also was court composer of Emperor Maximilian I and of Duke Wilhelm IV of Bavaria. To serve the Church he composed motets and Masses, but he also composed for the schools, as well as songs and instrumental music for courtly entertainment.

The Reformation, no longer interested in elaborate church music, created a broader basis for the cultivation of secular music in the people's homes. This democratizing process undoubtedly led to some dilettantism, but also to the popular acceptance of a general musical education. The then constantly growing influence derived from Italian composers, particularly in the early eighteenth century from Vivaldi, and the stress on appealing to the layman's emotions brought about a new school of melodic composition. Swiss composers of the seventeenth century were slow in absorbing the Italian influence, but Johannes Benn consciously employed the *basso continuo* in his mass, *Non Turbetur Cor Meum* (1628), and Felician Suevus early leaned towards homophonic tunefulness and clear-cut sectional forms in his church music created between 1645 and 1655.

The Italian vogue of singers and composers during the Baroque period also exerted a strong influence on Jean Jacques Rousseau

(1712–1778), who, in turn, impressed Christoph Willibald Gluck, the great reformer of eighteenth-century opera, whose formula of the "grand simplicity" ushered in the classic era. Rousseau is less well known as a musicologist and composer than as the writer on social themes, as educator, and "inventor" of romanticism.

At the age of eighteen Rousseau had a scant knowledge of music, although he was deeply interested in it. When he came to Lausanne on one of his walking tours, he called himself a Paris musician. In the house of one of Lausanne's first citizens he played—probably for the first time in public—a small piece he had composed. It was not too well received. This, however, did not discourage him. At twenty-five he wrote the music to a piece of poetry, and it was published in the *Mercure de France*, then the most important periodical.

Rousseau became more and more interested in the history of music. He contributed articles on this art form for Denis Diderot's Encyclopedie and wrote a popular *Dictionnaire de musique*. At the very beginning, when he set out on a career as a musician, he invented a new system of musical notation. His idea was to substitute numeral signs, ordinary arithmetical numbers, for the conventional symbols representing musical notes. He went to Paris with his new system and the musical comedy, *Narcisse*, with text and music by himself. Nothing came of *Narcisse* and his new notation. But *Les Muses Galantes*, another opera in three acts, was presented, with Rousseau as conductor of his own work. It was an uneven creation, but it was heard in Paris and Versailles. Soon after, he was asked to improve the text and music of *La Princesse de Navarre*, which had music by Jean-Philippe Rameau and a hastily written libretto by Voltaire.

His great success as a composer and librettist came with his opera buffa, *Le devin du village*, written in Pergolesi's style in 1752. In the ensuing famous *Guerre des Bouffons*, fought between the adherents of the French and Italian type of opera, Rousseau sided with the Italians and was hanged in effigy by the artists of the Opéra. Eighteen years later he wrote the play *Pygmalion* and set it to music. What he mainly desired was to give his recitatives a natural expression. Therein lies his great merit as a composer because he became the paragon for Gluck, who wrote in the dedication of his *Orpheus*: "L'accent de la nature est la langue universelle: M. Rousseau l'a employé avec le plus grand succès dans le genre simple. Son *Devin du village* est un modèle qu'aucun auteur n'a encore imité." ("The accent of nature is the universal language:

M. Rousseau has employed it in a simple manner with great success. His *Devin du village* is a model that no author can help but imitate.")

With the beginning of the nineteenth century the Swiss became quite music conscious. Local organizations and societies began to stress music experience; the Swiss Society for Music was founded in 1808, and the Federal Organization of Singers in 1842. Pestalozzi's concept of a musical education for all people gained ground after he published his "Doctrine of Song-Education after Pestalozzian Principles" (*Gesang-Bildungslehre nach Pestalozzischen Grundsätzen*), which methodically tried to build a foundation for a new music pedagogy.

The cultivation of music broadened decisively in the early decades of the last century. Foreign, mainly German, composers and conductors made a strong impact on the new generation. Many young Swiss composers were heard; however, they achieved little more than local fame at that time. Hans Georg Nägeli (1773–1836) should be mentioned because he displayed individuality in his composition favoring vocal music and choral works.

In the latter part of the century the creative power of Swiss composers gained momentum. Friedrich Hegar became known beyond his country's borders for his oratorio *Menasse* (1885). At that time the composers may have realized that the growing trend of "festivals" worked in their favor, or perhaps this trend needed native composers for its realization. Whichever may have been first, and even though we may rightly suspect program music, a few works of interest were then created; above all, the inspiration of native motifs led to Eduard Munzinger's *Sinfonia suisse* and to Hans Huber's *Tell Symphony*. Mainly the form of the cantata and the concept of festive processions were utilized by the composers, and they are somehow reflected in Gustav Arnold's musical celebration of the victory at Sempach (1886), Karl Munzinger's contribution to the festival of Berne (1891), Hans Huber's work for the city of Basle (1892), and Emile Jaques-Dalcroze's composition occasioned by the great exhibition at his native Geneva in 1896.

The entire approach to festivals has changed in the twentieth century with the tremendous growth of tourism. Some Swiss places like Locarno or Lausanne, Lucerne or Gstaad have become a focal point of interest for music lovers during the summer festivals, in which anything characteristically Swiss has given way to an in-

ternational spirit with conductors, soloists, and sometimes orchestras coming from many different countries. But the orchestras
heard at these festivals are mostly from one or another part of
Switzerland.

The Zürich Chamber Orchestra, to cite only one example, is
always present at the Gstaad Festival. As a matter of fact, this
could also be called a Yehudi Menuhin Festival, because this internationally celebrated violinist put Gstaad on the festival map of
Europe in 1956. Menuhin had given a few concerts in Gstaad from
time to time when, in the mid-fifties, he was urged by Benjamin
Britten to start a music festival there.

Despite or because of its being quite different from the other
international music festivals in Switzerland, it has something
peculiarly native about it. First, Menuhin had to look for a suitable hall to play in, and he found only the church in Saanen, which
for a few weeks in the month of August is turned into a concert
hall. It proved to be acoustically perfect. To preserve the dignity
of the church the audience rises from their seats when Menuhin
and his artists walk through the center aisle to the altar-turned-
stage and, instead of applauding, silently rises again to express
its appreciation when the artists leave the stage. Before each concert the village pastor speaks a few introductory words.

"The audience is a mixture of international music lovers,"
Menuhin told me. "You will find Americans as well as many
people from England, Germany, France and the Scandinavian
countries. But the local people, the butchers, carpenters, candle-
stick-makers, the peasants and shepherds are the mainstay of the
audience and have been so through the years." A more than
eighty-year-old peasant woman, accompanied by her daughter,
said that she no longer came down into the valley except to hear
Menuhin play. Many years ago he had introduced her to classic
music which, as she could not mention often enough, she found
just as beautiful as the old country songs she knew.

Some of the musical titans came often to visit the country.
Johannes Brahms journeyed through it, and the young Mozart
deeply impressed the Swiss, particularly Solomon Gessner. Many
came to be heard, to conduct. During the years of World War I,
Switzerland offered refuge to Stravinsky—about whom I speak
in other chapters—and also to Ferrucio Busoni (1866–1924). He

came for briefer visits, but stayed in Zürich between 1915 and 1918, which was for him a creatively rich period.

The son of an Italian clarinetist and a pianist of German descent, he felt pulled between his Italian background and his love for German music. He became most conscious of this split in his make-up when Germany and Austria were at war with Italy. The city of Zürich then had symbolic meaning for him. During the war years he composed his two short operas, *Arlecchino* and *Turandot*, both endowed with a modern feeling of the *commedia dell'arte* style. Still in Zürich, Busoni completed the text for his opera *Doktor Faust*, based on the medieval legend of Faust, but he died before being able to finish this work.

On one of his concert tours Franz Liszt (1811–1886) came to Geneva, where in 1835 he was joined by the Contesse Marie d'Agoult, who had left her husband and family to join Liszt in Switzerland. He stayed with her for more than a year in Geneva, composing, working on the first versions of the Swiss and Italian books of the *Années de pèlerinage*, and teaching at the then newly founded Genevan Conservatory. He spent some time in Lugano with the Contesse in 1838, before their relations became strained. He returned to Switzerland in 1853 and 1856 only to see Richard Wagner, who was to become his son-in-law in 1870.

The case of Richard Wagner (1813–1883) merits special attention. If we subtract Wagner's rejection of an offer to become the conductor of Zürich's new theatre in 1833 at a time when he was an operatic coach in Würzburg, his attachment to Switzerland was an intense and dramatic one. It falls into two periods: Wagner as a refugee in Zürich from 1849 to 1858 (with a few interruptions only), and Wagner as the protégé of King Ludwig II of Bavaria, who set him up at Triebschen on the Lake of Lucerne where Wagner stayed from 1865 to 1872. Both periods can be characterized as the most formative and creative years of his genius, and both were dominated by his relationship to two married women: Mathilde Wesendonck and Cosima von Bülow, Liszt's daughter.

Wagner was involved in an abortive uprising and, as a refugee from Dresden with a price on his head, entered Switzerland at Rorschach in 1849. In the evening of the following day, the Sankt Gallen Express Coach brought him to Zürich, where he found asylum with the orchestra's conductor, Alexander Müller. On January 15, 1850, Wagner conducted his first concert in Zürich, Beethoven's *A-Major Symphony*, in the Kasinosaal. He had made the demand for more violinists. The request was granted. He wanted to perform sections from his *Flying Dutchman, Lohengrin,* and *Tannhäuser* the following year, but he asked for seventy musicians in the orchestra pit. The costs ran up to Fr. 12,000, a large sum even for prosperous Zürich in 1851. It was a successful evening. Wagner wrote his friend Franz Liszt: "What do you say, our burghers got the money together . . ."

Wagner also stimulated the progress of chamber music in Zürich. No doubt his presence in the country had a stupendous impact on Switzerland's musical life. He brought Hans von Bülow to the city, the greatest conductor of all times, who started the later vogue of the virtuoso conductor. But Bülow, even as a young man, was too headstrong to last long at the Zürcher Theater. After a fight with the theatre's *prima donna,* he left and went to Sankt Gallen. The theatre in Switzerland only profited from this temperamental outburst.

While conducting in Switzerland and briefly in London, Wagner found sufficient time to compose and to write. He always thought of himself as a poet-composer, a musical dramatist. The nine years spent in Zürich were a period of realization of the road he wanted to take and the first fulfillment of his great dream. Within three years he wrote the prose works in which his artistic and aesthetic principles were defined: *Die Kunst und die Revolution (Art and Revolution), Das Kunstwerk der Zukunft (The Work of Art of the Future), Eine Mittheilung an meine Freunde (A Communication to My Friends),* and *Oper und Drama (Opera and Drama).* While theorizing, he created. A new lyric type of the musical drama was in the offing. Wagner continued where Gluck left off and brought the music drama to new expressive heights.

In his prose works he was still the revolutionary, foreseeing a socialist state in which the people would appreciate the dramatic power of the opera, by then no longer an entertainment for the elite. He visualized the poet-composer, fashioned on his own model, of course, who would be able to advance and combine profound symbolism on stage, on a heroic level spiritually and on three indivisible planes technically: the verbal, the musical, and the dramatic.

These thoughts ripened in Zürich between 1849 and 1852. The dramatic poems for *Der Ring des Nibelungen (The Ring of the Nibelung)* were written. The scene was set. By 1857 the music for *The Rhinegold, The Valkyrie,* and a good part of *Siegfried* was finished. Then all of a sudden he stopped working on *The Ring.*

Did he see no possibility to mount this colossal work on any stage? Or was his creative mood channeled in another direction owing to a new life experience?

He had read Schopenhauer. Wagner's optimistic approach to the social realities gave way to a pessimistic philosophy in which he renounced the world and embraced metaphysics. He also embraced Mathilde Wesendonck, wife of one of his rich patrons. Beside the *Wesendonck Lieder,* the musical world was enriched by *Tristan and Isolde,* inspired by Wagner's dramatic and happy-unhappy liaison with Mathilde. It was an act of creative compulsion. He worked on *Tristan* between 1857 and 1859. There is a self-explanatory passage in a letter written by Wagner to his sister Klara, on August 20, 1858:

> Wesendonck in the face of his wife's unconcealed candor couldn't help but become increasingly jealous. Her greatness lay in the fact that she kept her husband always informed of her feelings and brought him gradually to the point of giving her up altogether. The sacrifices and struggles this entailed can be easily imagined. That she succeeded was due solely to the depth and nobility of her affection—entirely divorced from any self-interest—which gave her the strength to reveal herself to her husband in such greatness that the latter—when she finally threatened to take her life—had to step aside and thereby prove his steadfast love for her by supporting her even in her anxiety for me. After all, he wanted to keep the mother of his children, and for their sakes (it was they who proved the most invincible barrier between us) he accepted the renunciation. Though he was consumed by jealousy, she was still able to interest him in me to such an extent that he often assisted me financially. When at last it was a question of finding me a little house and garden after my own heart, it was she who persuaded him, after the most incredible battles, to buy for me the fine piece of property adjoining his own . . .

After a while life became uncomfortable and embarrassing in Zürich for Wagner. *Tristan* was completed in Venice and Lucerne. It goes without saying that Wagner must have been a fascinating personality, shrewd and ruthless in promoting himself, sure of his genius, self-adulating. He always lived beyond his means and courted financial disaster. Under the patronage of King Ludwig II he received a princely salary but still ran up debts. He was

quarrelsome and tried to interfere in the government of the king-
dom. Only posterity said amen to his liaison with Cosima von
Bülow, who bore him three children before he could marry her in
1870 and who fulfilled his life's dream by administering the Fest-
spielhaus in Bayreuth after Wagner's death.

In 1865 Wagner moved from Munich to Triebschen near Lucerne,
where he stayed about seven years. In this period he wrote his
essay on *Beethoven* and almost completed *The Ring*. It was the
time in which he worked feverishly on finding a suitable place for
his *Ring* cycle. In 1872 the foundation was laid in Bayreuth. And
Richard Wagner, with his family, left Switzerland.

In 1876 *The Ring* received its first triumphant performance in
Bayreuth, and in the same year another German-born composer
died in Hottingen, near Zürich. His name was Hermann Goetz, who,
born in 1840, had studied with Bülow. When he was twenty-three
years old he received an appointment as organist in Winterthur.
Seven years later he became the music critic of the *Neue Zürcher
Zeitung*, an office which did not keep him from composing chamber
and choral works, a piano concerto, and a symphony. He probably
was not a genius, but he had little time to create and develop. He
died in his thirty-sixth year, leaving one opera behind him, *Der
Widerspenstigen Zähmung* (*The Taming of the Shrew*), which
was an immediate success. A second opera, *Francesca da Rimini*,
was left incomplete. The Swiss like to think of Hermann Goetz—
who had come to live with them—as one of their composers.

It has often been said that contemporary Swiss music is a microcosmic reflection of the compositional trends of our time. This may
very well be. At about the turn of the century the ever-growing
interest in music brought about a prodigious climate for the young
composer. The intensity and variety of the creative will of the
generation growing up with the many divergent isms of our century are amazing, and so is the determination of the post-war
generation.

A great many Swiss composers, however, have worked along
predictable patterns: being influenced by Richard Strauss, like
Volkmar Andreae (1879–1962); or harking even to Johannes
Brahms, like Fritz Brun (1878–   ); or affected by the polyphonic
loftiness of Palestrina, like Paul Müller (1898–   ); or like Walter
Courvoisier (1875–1931), who wrote some excellent songs, even
though Hugo Wolf's heritage cannot be denied.

I think it may be difficult to define anything specifically Swiss
in the music of any composer I could mention, except that some

of their works may be essentially nourished by folkloric source material. The temperament more than anything else may betray a composer as a Swiss, but even there the French or German character may prevail, and the cultural influences from across the border have been decisive in most cases. As in Swiss literature, the frontiers of Swiss music are identical with the linguistic borders of the country. If Emile Jaques-Dalcroze referred to Hans Huber (1852–1921)—one of the most significant and prolific composers of the latter part of the last century—as "le véritable chef des musiciens suisse," this epithet must be taken as a compliment for his many-sided and impressive talent, and for nothing else. Dalcroze had great understanding for a multifaceted gift, since he himself had string quartets, violin concertos, and even operas to his credit, being a powerful writer of several volumes on *Art and Education* and mainly on *Eurhythmics* (about which more will be said in the chapter on the dance).

Whether some of the Swiss composers might have fared better and been more widely known if they had not been Swiss is a matter of conjecture. But, undoubtedly, some—and this may be said of composers of other countries, too—deserve to be more often heard on the concert stages all over the world. Thinking of Hermann Suter (1870–1926), I could cite his long oratorio, *Le Laudi di San Francesco d'Assisi*, written in 1924 and to this very day a most forceful hymnal work containing some of the finest choral passages. *The Face of Isaiah* is another impressive oratorio, by Willy Burkhard (1900–1955), who in this work combined the pulsebeat of our time with melodic memories of our medieval past. He also composed a great many pieces for orchestra and chamber groups. His *Violin Concerto*, dating back to 1943, should be called to the attention of the virtuosos, for it shows the composer's poetic power in an unusually structured work. *The Year*, a symphonic creation, has a unique quality with some of its movements achieving highlights of melodic beauty.

The strong inclination to write oratorios and cantatas, rhapsodic works with Biblical settings may be, from a generic point of view, a characteristic of Swiss composers. Such predilection would correspond with the predominantly didactic tone of the Swiss men of letters whose theological background is a recurring phenomenon. The musical counterpart to the important role of nature in literature would be a pastoral feeling, leading to the composition of *Lieder*.

Othmar Schoeck is one of the more significant contemporary

composers, even though he was not a pioneer. But whenever one speaks of great *Lieder* composers, Schoeck, who wrote about four hundred *Lieder*, is in the forefront. Or did his work simply set a final period behind Schumann, Schubert, Brahms, and Wolf? His principal song cycles were written to poems of Lenau, Eichendorff, Heine, Goethe, and Keller. Schoeck may be an afterthought of the romantic tradition. But with so many trends coming back full circle with frightening speed, it could easily be that he represented a new romantic beginning. Hermann Hesse spoke of Schoeck's "naive sensuous" sensibilities, "the parallels and conflicts" in his being, which were so attractive to Hesse, "his strength and ability to suffer . . . his sensual potency together with everything spiritual or in struggle with one another."

Schoeck also composed a "pastoral intermezzo for strings," which he called *Sommernacht (Summer Night)*, a work that transposes the essence of the *Lied* onto stringed instruments. He not only wrote orchestral and chamber works, but he was, as were so many Swiss composers, strongly drawn to the stage. He left us with eight operas which, however, did not stay in the opera repertories.

Heinrich Sutermeister (1910–   ), who was conductor at the Municipal Theater in Berne and now lives in Vaux-sur-Morges on the Lake of Geneva, has been more successful with his operas than Schoeck. Of all of them *Romeo und Julia* created a strong impression when it was premiered in 1940. His compatriot Hans Haug (1900–   ) came out with two Molière operas, *Tartuffe* and *Le Malade Imaginaire*, probably proving his talent best in his *Don Juan In der Fremde (Don Juan Abroad)*. Rudolf Kelterborn (1931–   ) wrote his own book for his three-act opera, *Die Errettung Thebens (Thebens Saved)*, with which he impressed some of the critics without, however, achieving an audience success. Kelterborn, being between the younger and youngest generation, is a serious artist whose roots are in the past but who tries to go his own way, as he proved with his *Meditationen (Meditations)* for six wind instruments.

As in Swiss literature, we find many young composers moving in various directions, echoing the immediate past of experimental music or trying to find new modes of expression. Jürg Wyttenbach (1935–   ) is a very sophisticated composer who, among other works, has written a one-act madrigal comedy, *Der Unfall (The Accident)*, and, in collaboration with Günter Grass, *Paraphrase*, for a narrator, flutist, and pianist. So far his most important work is

De' metalli, for baritone and orchestra, an impressive work in its complex structure, based on Leonardo da Vinci's *Profezie.* Wyttenbach is also known as an excellent interpreter of new piano music. Among those who experiment a great deal is Heinz Holliger (1939–   ), who, above all, composes song cycles, chamber music and solo works for piano, harp, and oboe, most of them in ultra-modern fashion. He often introduces improvisational elements so that the final sound effects are partly determined by the players.

Klaus Huber (1924–   ) and Armin Schibler (1920–   ) studied with Willy Burkhard, and some of the master's religious leanings influenced the basic approach to their compositions. Klaus Huber's oratorium *Soliloquia* (1959–1964) is a major work inspired by the prayers of Aurelius Augustinus, uniting invocation, praise, and solicitation. In order to achieve a cosmic feeling, the composer, as he said, tried to embrace the entire sound spectrum in structuring this oratorium in circling and spiraling sequences. All of Klaus Huber's works (of which the symphonic work *Tenebrae* is outstanding) are marked by the composer's sincerity and craftsmanlike abilities.

Armin Schibler has composed several works for the theatre, three operas, and quite a few ballets, the symphonic oratorium *Media in vita,* and a series of orchestral compositions. He found his way from Bach and Vivaldi to new forms of tonal expression. He is constantly seeking to find himself and therefore defies being categorized. In trying to explain his intentions he said, "I know about and visualize something total and new and I must come to terms with all the manifold movements of our time in order to mature and reach such synthesis." He admits he never tries to produce a "masterpiece" and feels compelled to use the tonal expression dictated by the theme regardless of whatever reaction the work may provoke. He asks for the same creative freedom which posterity granted a Klee or Kafka. "I accept the negative responses to my works because I realize how often a lack of resonance at first has been the fate of many a genuine message."

The compositions of most of the young Swiss composers are constantly featured by the European orchestras and have become recognized as a part of the new wave of experimental music. These composers live in Zürich, Basle, or Berne; they no longer feel isolated or frustrated by any "cultural narrowness." They no longer feel the need to create and achieve recognition outside their country as the generation preceding them did. Rolf Liebermann, the youngest of the older generation (1910–   ), achieved international recognition with his opera buffa, Moliere's *L'Ecole des Femmes*, which was heard from Salzburg to Louisville, Kentucky. Liebermann has always combined activity with creativity and established himself as an able opera *Direktor*. For several years he was *Intendant* of the famous Hamburg State Opera from which he was called to Paris to guide the Opera there. On the other hand, one has only to look at his output to notice that he has not neglected composing. He has written *Penelope*, an opera semiseria, several cantatas, a festive play for the city of Basle, and vocal and piano works. Although he went abroad, he paid homage to his country when he wrote his *Suite über schweizer Volkslieder (Suite on Swiss Folk Songs)*.

Liebermann was born in Zürich; his counterpart, Frank Martin (1890–   ), twenty years his senior, in Geneva. Liebermann turned to Germany, Martin first to Holland and then later also to Germany, where he accepted a professorship for composition at the Conservatory at Cologne, but where he stayed for only a few years. He is a dynamic personality, accepting challenges and looking for them. His opera, *Der Sturm (The Tempest)*, based on Shakespeare's play, went over many opera stages after its premiere in Vienna in 1956. Geneva saw the first production of his Moliere opera, *Monsieur de Pourceaugnac*, in 1963.

On the other hand, Martin has written symphonies and the music to several ballets, a *Mystère de la Nativité* which was first heard in Geneva and Salzburg in 1959 and 1960, respectively. He is unpredictable in the choice of his subject matter and style. In 1942 he rewrote the legend of Tristan and Isolde in *Le vin herbé* for twelve solo voices, seven string instruments, and piano.

At the age of eighty, Martin rewedded twelve-tone music to tonality when he composed a new piano concerto for orchestra. It was commissioned by the Viennese virtuoso Paul Badura-Skoda, who had asked for a complicated work. He received one. A rhythmic percussion section is followed by a long piano passage with an almost nonstop cadenza, then the orchestra humorously enters with the main theme, the saxophone conversing with the classic brass. A slow movement of dreamlike quality gives the pianist great opportunities to follow the composer's imagination. The final presto races through a climax of variations.

This piano concerto is characteristic for Frank Martin and may take a place in piano literature next to Bartok's and Ravel's works. Martin told an interviewer that he likes to busy himself. While he was setting François Villon poems to music, he toyed with the idea of letting an electric guitar and pop music inspire him for perhaps another concerto. I doubt that his temperament is typically Swiss.

Ernest Bloch was born in Geneva in 1880 and died in Portland, Oregon, in 1959. When he was thirty his opera *Macbeth* was produced at the Paris Opéra-Comique. Six years later he went to the United States where he held high positions at the Cleveland Institute of Music, the San Francisco Conservatory, and the University of California. As a teacher he had great influence on the development of serious music in America. As a composer he became more and more drawn to Jewish themes. He is mainly associated with his rhapsody *Schelòmo*, the symphony *Israel*, *Trois poèmes juifs*, or *Baal Shem*, but he never intended to reconstruct or resuscitate Jewish melodies. He wanted to re-create and paraphrase the dormant treasures of a people and give their aspirations powerful resonance in works of art.

Bloch also wrote many other works for which he will be remembered, a violin and piano concerto, five string quartets, a quintet, and symphonic music. His creative sensibility led to a very personal style, aided by a strong feeling for classic structure. He composed an *American Symphony*, reflecting the ambience of his adopted country, and a *fresque symphonique* he called *Helvétia*, into which he put his love for his native country and a kind of melodic apology for having left it.

What the opera *Macbeth* did for Bloch, the dramatic psalm *Le Roi David* did for Arthur Honegger (1892–1955). Its first production at the open-air Théâtre du Jorst in Mèziéres, near Lausanne, immediately brought him international recognition in 1921. He was the descendant of an old Zürich family, which could explain some of his rather Germanic leanings. He was born in Le Havre and studied at the Zürich and Paris conservatories, so that a great deal of his environmental influence was also French. One could not imagine a better or more profoundly Swiss background.

Honegger became first known as a member of *Les Six*, those famous French composers who banded together as a group after World War I. But Honegger was far more bound to them through ties of friendship than through any aesthetic principles. Before his success with *King David*—which, after the premiere, he rewrote into what could pass as a modern version of an oratorio—he composed a few stage works of which *Le Dit des Jeux du Monde* was the most promising. After the acceptance of his *King David* he turned his chief attention to the stage, from ballet to tragedy. He wrote the music to a Biblical drama, *Judith*, which was also first staged at the theatre in Mézières and was later turned into an opera. And, in a similar manner, his *Antigone* was created.

Honegger did not believe in the traditional form and style of opera with the singers carrying, more often than not, a nonsensical story. His stories are historical or mythological and always reveal a contemporary approach with psychological depth. In a way reminiscent of Gluck, he not only made the chorus an indispensable part of the dramatic action, he also elevated the chorus to the same important level held by the orchestra.

Of course he too composed chamber and symphonic music. To prove how contemporary a composer he was, we can cite *Pacific 231* in which he gave musical *Gestalt* to speed, to a locomotive in action. But he will always be remembered for his stage works, the greatest of which is *Jeanne d'Arc au bûcher (Joan of Arc at the Stake)*, with a libretto by Paul Claudel, first produced in Basle in 1938. Essentially, it is a dramatic oratorio with spoken words and movement or, as the composer thinks of it, a "mimodrama." Originally intended for concert performances, it has often been seen on two separate stages: on one we see Joan fastened to the stake throughout the performance, while the drama is acted on another. The most notable production of this oratorio—which has all the earmarks of a medieval mystery play—was done at the San Carlo Opera of Naples, with Roberto Rossellini as director and Ingrid Bergman in the speaking role. The scenic image of this Saint Joan is as full of novel ideas as its music.

Arthur Honegger wrote an autobiographical sketch, *I Am a Composer*, in which he said:

> Born in Le Havre of Swiss parents, I have lived the greater part of my life in France, pursued my studies there as if I had been French, yet carried deep within me a germ, a Swiss atavism, what Milhaud called "my Helvetian sensitiveness."
>
> What do I owe to Switzerland? No doubt, the Protestant tradition, great difficulty in deluding myself about the value of what I do, a naïve sense of integrity, a familiarity with the Bible—very disparate elements.

In looking into himself, Honegger somehow adumbrated some essential features of the Swiss composers.

THE THEATRE'S THE THING

IT has often been claimed that Switzerland's contribution to the theatre consists of only two dramatists of international stature, Friedrich Dürrenmatt and Max Frisch, who, moreover, seem to have no heirs. One usually overlooks another towering figure, Adolphe Appia (1862–1928), who was born in Geneva and can rightly be called prophet of the modern theatre. Even if Switzerland had not brought forth any luminaries of the theatrical world other than these three men, it would have done more than its good share in enriching the world that is a stage. But there is far more to it.

"Das Gute zu lehren, dem Bösen zu wehren" (to teach the good, to fend off the evil) it said at the entrance to the new Stadt-theatre in Zürich, opened with a festive play by Carl Spitteler in 1891. Conrad Ferdinand Meyer, who was supposed to have written the play, presented a prologue instead, closing with the lines:

> In days long passed a poet said in ancient Greece:
> Do send your tender youths to school!
> For you the stage is set to see the play!
> It is the poet's business to enlighten you.
> What noble word, what weighty duty!
> And now farewell and kindly pay attention!

Schiller's concept of the stage as a moral institution has always been a predominant feature in the Swiss theatre. It started with some of the earliest tropes, the Easter *Quem Quaeritis*, one of the Introit tropes which were discovered in a ninth-century manuscript at the Benedictine cloister of Sankt Gallen. Probably the earliest religious play in the German language was *Das Osterspiel von Muri (The Easter Play of Muri)*, dating back to the thirteenth century. Easter Passion Plays also took place in the wine market of Lucerne, dramatizing scenes from the Old and New Testament. They must have been recurring events, even though we only have a few documents referring to the year 1583.

At about the same time that the morality play *Everyman* was being produced outside the churches in England and Holland, Basle enjoyed a play of similar symbolic weightiness, an attempt to find an answer to man's ultimate question. It was Pamphilus

Gegenbach's *Spiel von den Zehn Altern (Play of the Ten Ages)*, done in 1515.

The trend of producing religious plays, or dramas with religious connotations, on certain occasions has been kept alive to this very day in the Wettinger plays and, every fifth year, in Einsiedeln. The nun Silja Walter writes impressive plays of a rare spiritual and poetic quality. Most of them have appeared in print. The spirit of reviving late medieval or Renaissance plays has also reached Einsiedeln. Its cathedral serves as a theatrical backdrop for Calderon's *Great World Theatre*, similarly as the cathedral in Salzburg does for Hofmannsthal's version of *Everyman*.

As if to simulate the atmosphere of medieval guilds, villagers of Einsiedeln study and enact such parts as the king, the rich man, the peasant, beauty, wisdom, and the beggar. A professional *régisseur*—for years it has been Erwin Kohlund—directs the play, using many people from the village as a Greek chorus to echo the words and action of the allegoric figures as well as to fill the huge square in front of the baroque church of the cloister for stress and counterpoint. All this makes the Calderon play in Einsiedeln a unique theatre experience. Its visual totality creates the impression of a ritual, reducing (or heightening) theatre to its origin, to a festive ceremonial. As if to stress this impression, the audience rises and joins the villagers onstage in the final hymn praising the Lord.

Switzerland should be justly famous for its *Fastnachtsspiele* (carnival plays) in which the serious tone of the morality play is kept alive but in which acting is most often intermingled with dancing and merrymaking. They are still going on today, and their history reaches far back into medieval days. Niklaus Manuel (1484–1530) would not have been the fascinating Renaissance figure he was (poet-painter-dramatist-soldier-statesman) had he not had his share in the early carnival plays, vigorously expressive and serving the ideas of the Reformation. He was preceded, however, by the historically interesting Zofinger carnival play, one of the earliest Swiss plays produced at Shrovetide, in the very same year that Manuel was born. This production was significant for its special use of costumes, sets, props, and detailed gesture.

One cannot very well omit mentioning the legend of Wilhelm Tell and its ever-recurring productions in Interlaken and particularly in Altdorf, the village where Tell faced the Austrian tyrant's hat which he refused to give its demanded reverence. Tell has become a symbol of man's passion for freedom, and this legendary figure seems to have had Nordic sources. Saxo Grammaticus (c. 1200) describes such a marksman. No one can say how this saga may have reached Switzerland. There is little historic evidence for or against his real existence, and he is, in all likelihood, an amalgam of various heroic deeds, filling the need for such a heroic figure. At a time when the growing national consciousness in Switzerland was in want of a unifying glamorous figure, Wilhelm Tell was a perfect hero and father image to polarize daring, strength, courage, and the will for liberation.

Tschudi, in his *Chronicon Helveticum*, turned the uncertainties of Tell's image into historic reality. On his journey to Switzerland, Goethe became impressed by the story and intended to write an epic about it, but with the tyrant Gessler pictured as a liberal despot. Fortunately, he left it to Friedrich Schiller to treat this subject. Schiller wrote an inflammatory drama of a suppressed people fighting for freedom (1804). It came at a time when the European liberals were in dire need of a guiding example for freedom-loving men, and Switzerland was in the forefront of fighting liberalism in the first half of the nineteenth century. But men have always been in need of such an idol. For fifteenth-century humanists, Tell gave greater meaning to the principles of moral freedom, while during the decades of feudalistic decay, he became a popular champion of the rights of man and a symbol of revolution in France. Wilhelm Tell has always been one of the two focal points of Swiss folklore, the other being the Rütli oath.

The dramatic figure of Tell has been a major staple of the Swiss stage, both popular and amateur, and one of the first versions was the *Urner Tellspiel (Uri Tell Play)* in 1512. Many Swiss writers succumbed to the temptation to write a Tell play, and the most interesting seems to be the one by Paul Schoeck (1882–   ) in Swiss dialect. He refrained from using the same folkloric scenes made immortal and, at the same time, threadbare by Schiller. Cleverly avoiding the pitfalls of all obvious clichés, Schoeck placed the entire action in the common room of an inn.

In our era of demystification of the arts we must expect that writers would try to dethrone certain myths. No one was more destined than Max Frisch to deglorify the Tell figure by reducing it to the realities of 1970 when he wrote his essay, *Wilhelm Tell für die Schule (Wilhelm Tell for the Schools)*. Bitter irony lies in the suggestion of its title that it was time to let the young grow up with a more realistic notion of this composite of a national hero.

Max Frisch retells the story in a calm, matter-of-fact manner but with an obvious tongue-in-cheek tone, making it clear that he had his fun with Tell and the Swiss as he sees them today. In order to divest his own story of its fictionalized elements and to build a logical bridge into our time, he interrupts his story with pseudo-scientific footnotes which have the same length as the story and whose literary function is to serve as a satiric platform. For instance, in these footnotes, he quotes Friedrich Engels' diatribe against the Swiss, an emotional outburst which Frisch also considers unjustifiable because undialectic; he quotes several sources and Tell historians to prove questionable certain assumptions which, through man's need for a heroic father image, have turned Tell into a haloed hero; he makes it clear that the reverential greeting of the Emperor's hat was an accepted custom, "a ritual of medieval legality," and not an arbitrary act of a tyrant; the Rütli oath had no revolutionary character; there was no fight for freedom of Swiss herdsmen, only the intent of the great landed proprietors to assure the guarantee of their old rights.

Tell's demystification (which had already begun in the nineteenth century) was Max Frisch's ruse for his *J'accuse* as a socio-political critic. He must have had his fun picturing the tyrant as a tired, bored, stout knight suffering from the *Föhn* and hepatitis, never wanting to hurt Tell, whose silent stubbornness he did not understand. There is purpose in characterizing Tell as a choleric with delayed reactions, a man—proud because he suffered from inferior feelings—who maneuvered himself into a situation where he had to prove himself in order not to lose face with his compatriots. And thus he became an assassin.

What Frisch—by taking the halo from his bearded hero—really wanted to say to his contemporary Swiss lies between two of his footnotes: "The belief in everything traditional, an essential part of the Ur-Swiss way of thinking whereby innovations are feared more than backwardness, has kept alive to this very day." And: "Also Tell's traditional word [that he would have killed the tyrant with his second arrow if the first had failed to hit the apple] has never become the measure of our freedom of speech."

Sometimes the most revolutionary ideas are uttered as asides and without the benefit of any publicity, falling on the deaf ears of time. About ten years before Bertolt Brecht and Erwin Piscator were old enough to think in theatrical terms, Charles Ferdinand Ramuz talked to Stravinsky about writing an epic theatre piece for him. They were about to discuss the fairy tale for grown-ups, *L'Histoire du Soldat*, which they wanted to do in a simple but new form, and Ramuz tells us that he suggested to the composer "to write a 'story' rather than a real play [Ramuz meant a traditional play] and pointed out to him that the theatre could be conceived in a far bigger dimension than usual and that, for instance, it would be perfectly suited to what one could call the epic style."

L'Histoire du Soldat narrates a story; it has moments of the broad epic sweep but never deviates sufficiently from the expected and traditional structure to achieve an epic impact. It seems that Stravinsky opposed too much looseness and freedom, and it is more than likely that Ramuz knew what he wanted without quite knowing what mechanics to apply. But this musical play which he wrote for Stravinsky is the forerunner of the story theatre of the sixties and seventies, while foreshadowing the narrative quality of the epic theatre. It succeeded best in the total integration of the spoken or half-sung word, music, and dance movement.

This concept undoubtedly reveals Ramuz as a man of vision. In our world of commercialized values we have come to believe too easily in outward success. The fact remains that more than a decade before the world was ripe for the idea of the epic theatre, Ramuz instinctively felt that there was another aspect to the stage not yet explored. I strongly believe that there are no isolated phenomena in history. Also, I am inclined to think that every century has its Napoleon, but not every Napoleon his century. In the arts and in our fast-paced time, we must substitute decade for century.

Some people are dreamers and not doers. In the art world this is more strongly pronounced than anywhere else in life, and it is also more fatal. To be anti-realistic to the core of one's being is not typically Swiss, but Adolphe Appia answered to this description. Without gross exaggeration one could say that he was a failure, but that his ideas triumphed. He became the prophet of the theatricalized theatre, with Gordon Craig his most articulate apostle. Appia's influence was seeded throughout Europe and America by the winds of the twentieth century. The men who cared about the fruits of these seeds have created the new theatre of our time. Appia's disciples, from Gordon Craig to Jacques Copeau, turned a dream into stage reality. His Swiss students, Jean Mercier and Oskar Wälterlin, became close associates in his endeavors. Mercier, before joining the theatre of Copeau, was Appia's assistant in Milan where, under Toscanini, he created a new stage image for *Tristan*. Wälterlin was instrumental in promoting Appia's ideas in Basle, and later, in other Swiss theatres, he gave Appia's message meaning for the ever-changing world.

It is significant that the theatre revolution for our time did not come about through the drama, but through the visual and physical image of the stage, through scenic design, lighting, and new concepts of production. The brutal, naked realism that followed nineteenth-century romanticism was opposed by Appia's poetic concepts of complete stylization of setting, lighting, and costumes. He wanted to create fluidity and suggestiveness, he wanted to paint a mood, an elusive and allusive feeling on the stage. All this he visualized as the "loftiest expression of the eternal in art" which, in the beginning, he saw fulfilled in music. Appia felt that light has the same potential power as music onstage, and can create a unifying mood and help convey the inner magic that is the deep-bedded, hidden, but very essential aspect of a play. Only light, he said, can express "the inner nature of all appearance," with its "infinite capacity for varying nuance." Light has the same emotionally suggestive power as music.

Some historians have wondered that the great theatre revolution at the turn of the century should have received its strongest impulses from music. Richard Wagner's groping towards a Gesamtkunstwerk (total theatre) and, later, Diaghilev's fusion of all theatre arts serving the dance were greatly instrumental in finding new means of theatrical expression. Even Antonin Artaud received his immediate impulses from the ritualistic feeling that emanates from Balinese dancers. Appia began as a student of music, but in his mid-twenties he felt the almost compulsive need to do something creative about the theatre. He had been in touch with Jaques-Dalcroze in Hellerau and with Richard Wagner in Bayreuth. At that time he was still doubtful as to how to change his role from the appreciation and critical analysis of the theatre arts into being a creative artist. He was, moreover, aware of his handicaps. He neither was brilliant in articulating his ideas, nor could he deliver an impressive drawing of his stage ideas. But his convictions were stronger than such realizations: "I began to practice a completely unknown art for which all the elements had yet to be discovered and organized. Still I was convinced that following my own vision I would find the truth."

He settled down in Brière, a village in the Canton de Vaud, where he lived until 1904. Sketches, stage designs, and verbal ideas were put on paper. In 1899 he published *Die Musik und die Inszenierung* (*Music and the Art of the Theatre*), which contains most of his basic concepts towards a rehabilitation of the stage space into a space stage. He declared that attention must be focused on the display of the actor's movements, on those of the soloists and the singing chorus. Appia visualized a plastic stage which would create spatial projection for the actor and, above all, mobile light with its inherent shades of color. This book was followed by a series of shorter studies.

In 1912 he worked in Hellerau on Dalcroze's *Echo and Narcissus*. On the same program was the scene in Hades from Gluck's *Orpheus and Eurydice*. Appia, who could never boast of having had good reviews, experienced a very positive reaction to his daring designs. Even such a critic as George Bernard Shaw, who was certainly hard to please, called the production "one of the best." Appia could note: "For the first time since the Greek era, a perfect fusion of all media of expression, in close mutual subordination, has been realized. . . ."

In the last decades of his life he devoted his attention more to stage problems of plays than of operas. In these years he became a prolific designer and writer, as if feeling he would soon lose his race with time. The days were gone when he loved to wander through woods and fields, to meditate and dream before writing down thoughts or putting stage visualizations onto paper. There was fear of death in his haste and urgency. In 1925 and 1926 he began to suffer from heart trouble. Two years later he died while in a nursing home near Nyon, whose surrounding landscape was dear to him.

As long as we are conjuring up the creative spirit emanating from the French part of Switzerland, we must not forget Robert Pinget, born in Geneva in 1919. He is one of those Swiss writers who, early in life, was attracted by the magnetic power of Paris and the latest trend of the *nouveau roman*, à la Alain Robbe-Grillet. In 1959 Pinget wrote a novel which he called *Fiston*, a modern version of The Prodigal Son seen from the abandoned father's viewpoint. This unique novel, written in the form of a never-ending letter that can't be sent since the father does not know where his son has gone, was turned into a play, *Lettre Morte* (*Dead Letter*). The old man: "I started to write to him . . . The letter where I say I'm writing to him, I don't know what else to do . . ." It is a play about the gap between the young and the old, two different worlds with different meanings. All the old man can think of, in a thousand variations, is what has he done to deserve such a lot? He speaks to the barman and the post-office clerk, whose roles are played by one actor because essentially they are stand-ins for another Godot. Godot, the great unfathomable, who, when asked: "What did you say?" answers "without looking up from the paper: Nothing." The clerk is urged to look somewhere for a letter from the old man's son. The official impersonality per se replies: "What does it matter to me whether people write letters or wait for replies . . ."

There is a light counterpoint to this message of despair and futility in an intermezzo between the two scenes. Itinerant actors enter the bar. They have just played a boulevard comedy, called "The Prodigal Son," and they reenact the scenes of a father imploringly writing to his son, who does return and brings his newly-wed wife along. This vaudeville experience sandwiched between tragic numbness hits the spectator like a flippant joke made about his naked existence. He knows that Pinget's prodigal son will not return, nor will his son. If Samuel Beckett had not written *Waiting for Godot* a few years previously, Robert Pinget's *Dead Letter* would have become the classic play of the Theatre of the Absurd.

Beckett, Pinget's close friend, translated another of his plays, *La Manivelle (The Old Tune),* a brilliant radio play which can stand the test on any stage. It questions whether our past is not just an illusion with which we live or need to live. The empty prattle of two men reminiscing about their past is an absurd battle of challenges, one man contradicting the truth of any statement made by the other, so that finally the pasts of both men become illusory. A barrel organ introduces the play with an old tune, but then jams while the two men talk on the street in the midst of the traffic noises. At the end the tune is heard again and rises with the street noises to a crescendo. "Tune finally rises above them triumphant."

"When you think when you think . . ." are the last words of the play. Perhaps we can only endure the cruel noisy absurdity of our existence because we can think of our past the way we wish.

Friedrich Dürrenmatt (1921–   ) and Max Frisch (1911–   ) have appeared on the cyclorama of the world stage like two incandescent meteors. They have more than enriched Swiss literature and drama. They have created such an impact on Swiss letters that men of learning and literary historians, when speaking of Swiss literature, are apt to refer to a pre- and post-Dürrenmatt-Frisch period. No greater compliment could ever be paid to any writer.

They are both writing in German, but they are not German writers. In their way of thinking and expressing themselves, in their entire spiritual being, they are Swiss, even though—or because—they display the peculiarly ambivalent to negative attitude towards their own kind. Frisch has more consciously denied and more stubbornly decried Swiss attitudes than has Dürrenmatt, and this difference reflects their different temperaments and intellectual outlook. But I cannot imagine that any other German-speaking region could ever have produced such men of letters, so distinctly marked: Made in Switzerland.

When Dürrenmatt was asked by a Swiss critic what his attitude towards the "Swiss problem" was, he said: "You're mistaken, Doctor, I'm sorry to say so but Switzerland is no problem for me, it is just a wonderful place where I can work." In Frisch's attitude towards Switzerland, the humanly problematic aspects are more clearly pronounced. Frisch seems to think in broader terms and sees in many writers the type of intellectual refugees who are nowhere at home. Their residences, wherever they settle or how often they move, do not carry the identification of roots; they are temporary, even if temporary for a lifetime, as in Dürrenmatt's and Frisch's case. "I am a Swiss," Frisch exclaimed, "and do not want to be anything else, but my commitment as a writer is not directed towards Switzerland." However, Frisch realizes that you cannot run away from yourself and the things (landscape and people) that shaped you, and be able to do creative work in such a state of flight from yourself and your kind. It basically is a question of acceptance, which Dürrenmatt acknowledged in a more facetious way and Frisch fully recognized when he wrote:

> Satire does not leave us without a fatherland . . . If being without a fatherland is considered as something that concerns our commitment, then I certainly do not mean the repudiation of one's own compatriots, but, on the contrary, the freedom towards them so that we can accept them in their reality once and for all.

An entry in his diary of 1949 gives us a still broader aspect of what Frisch means: "To have a home is indispensable, but it is not bound to a country. Home is the man whose being we perceive

and reach. In this respect it may be tied to the language. Perhaps:
because home is not in the language alone. Words only connect
where our wave lengths coincide . . ." In summing up his thoughts,
he says: "We are not necessarily without a home, if we are without a fatherland."

Whenever Frisch feels himself confronted by his native surroundings, he reacts to it like a son to his father: in a mood of
challenge and self-denial. Rationalizing his reaction, he sees the
writer rather as a supranational being, claiming "a free freedom—
across all borders of countries, languages, and races, united in
the affirmation of the individual . . . and in our productively and
tacitly silent refutation of all fatherlands."

If the argument of who was greater, Goethe or Schiller, could
be reconciled by the German people with an Olympian pride in
having two such fellows, the same solution could be applied to
any quarrels and qualms among the Swiss as to who is the more
important writer: Dürrenmatt or Frisch. They are very different,
but similar at the same time. Using the Jungian terms of extrovert
and introvert makes the typing rather easy. Dürrenmatt answers to
the former, Frisch to the latter. There is far more intellectual
brooding, an intense probing within and a need to speak from
personal experience in Frisch than in Dürrenmatt. Frisch strongly
identifies with his own characters. Dürrenmatt creates from the
safe distance of the observer, gaining perspective on his characters
without ever becoming aloof, often acting like the benign father
figure who cannot help explaining to his children the dangers embedded in the follies, foibles, cruelties, and frightening compulsions
of man. Dürrenmatt is *concerned*. Frisch is *involved*.

Like the intellectual he is, Frisch charges the writer with spiritual leadership, demanding man's involvement in man's doings and
destiny, taking issue with the burning issues of the times. Dürrenmatt, who claims to have no biography, once wrote: "As far as
Frisch is concerned one is struck by his inclination . . . that he does
not drop his very personal, private experiences in his art, that he
cannot forget himself, that his problem is at stake, not a problem.
He is enmeshed in his art." When I asked Max Frisch about it, he
retorted: "We both have reason to envy each other. I admit it
might be easier to allow myself a wider and more impersonal
scope. But I think it is dangerous for any writer not to create out
of his own experiences, otherwise his work might tend to become
too thin and pat—while I only run the risk of being too private."

Both began writing prose and only afterwards came to the

theatre. Dürrenmatt first expressed himself as a graphic artist,* Frisch started as an architect. Did this project two different roads that had to be taken by them, two different approaches? Perhaps. We can detect something visually playful or playfully visual in Dürrenmatt. (For instance, the people of Güllen becoming trees in *The Visit* is not a dramatist's but a painter's idea.) Frisch's dramatic designs take place in a geometric pattern, with a definite perspective in mind. There is something inevitable about his characters, their motions and foredoomed schemes. Frisch's sketches in his diaries have the quality of first drafts for edifices to be built. Dürrenmatt is visual in his purposefulness; Frisch is purposeful in his visualizations.

Dürrenmatt and Frisch began writing plays with serious intent and an enjoyment of theatricalizing ideas that demand the reality of the make-believe world as a necessary outlet. This came at a crucial point in history. The dropping of the bomb was like a second-act curtain, and there was doom and despair drawn on the faces in the lobbies of the world theatre: some were fumbling for perhaps a last cigarette, others escaped into the hysteria of grotesque laughter about the absurdity and futility of waiting for the bell to ring for the next and, no doubt, final act.

The two great intellectual events of the forties and fifties, existentialism and, in the wake of it, the Theatre of the Absurd, hardly touched Dürrenmatt or Frisch. It may have been due to their linguistic ties with Germany that Bertolt Brecht was much closer to them. Thornton Wilder's influence came mainly on the detour of Wilder's acceptance of certain Brechtian ideas. Bernard Shaw's presence—he always used the stage as a pulpit—has been more noticeable in Dürrenmatt's case than in Frisch's, who has the Shavian didactic intent but without the lightness with which Shaw manipulated scenes and characters. Dürrenmatt finds it much easier to watch his characters go their own way and to laugh about, and with, them. ("Literature," he said, "must become so light again that it no longer counts on the scale of today's literary criticism. Only then will it be weighty again.") Frisch can develop the so-

---

* In her all-embracing and penetrating biography of Friedrich Dürrenmatt, Elisabeth Brock-Sulzer touches upon his talent as a draughtsman and sees in his "drawing an exercise leading to his writing." Even his handwriting seems to be revealing: "Peter Schifferli once said, Dürrenmatt hardly ever writes, he always draws, he has no handwriting. In fact, he mostly writes in block letters, in private letters, too, as well as in his signature in which only the last three letters run into each other."

phisticated humor of the intellectual, the spirit of biting irony. Dürrenmatt displays a grotesque laughter, seeing life as God's joke, albeit the best of all His possible jokes.

Neither of our two men denies Bertolt Brecht's influence on him. But while Dürrenmatt says, "The writer cannot devote himself to politics. He belongs to the whole man," Frisch claims that the writer must be fully conscious of his duty towards his community, towards his polis. Both of them attended Brecht's classes. But Dürrenmatt was not as attentive as Frisch and even dropped out before the final exam. "My plays," he said, "should be staged as one stages folk plays, one should treat me as a kind of conscious Nestroy and will then fare best. One should stick to my ideas and forget the depth of their meaning." This is an un-Brechtian thought. Brecht wants the spectator to be metamorphosed into judge and juror, so that he can come up with a verdict which Brecht expects to be a death sentence for the bourgeois establishment. Frisch expresses the same thought with different words in *The Chinese Wall:* "As everywhere you have the choice: to be witness to those who have no voice, or to fall silent yourself."

When he met Brecht in Zürich in 1947, Frisch felt that an hour with Brecht was more enlightening than a whole semester of theatre studies. He considers Brecht a classic because he opened up a new field and created a new style. Where flaws can be found in Frisch's plays, they are mainly due to the disciple's inability to cut the umbilical cord tying him to the master. *Andorra,* a play of great emotional power in the traditional Aristotelean manner, is marred by its introduction of Brecht's shock-into-awareness theory. The symbolic image of the Mute in *The Chinese Wall* plays a similar part of epic distance and pivotal importance as the mute girl Katryn in Brecht's *Mother Courage.*

Both playwrights try to avoid preaching, but Frisch, being intense and often in a fighting mood for the good of mankind, can fall into the intonation of an editorial, whereas Dürrenmatt, seeing in front of him the pastor's spectre of didacticism in good Swiss fashion, flees rather into a tragi-grotesque comedy style. He said in his essay on the problems of the theatre:

> Tragedy presupposes guilt, despair, moderation, vision, a sense of responsibility. In the muddle of our century . . . there are no more guilty and also no men responsible. No one wants to take the blame and no one wanted anything to happen . . . We are all collectively guilty, embedded collectively in the sins of our

fathers and forefathers. We are the offspring of children. That is our misfortune, but not our guilt. Comedy alone fits our measures. Our world has led to the grotesque as well as the atom bomb . . . The world (thus the stage representing this world) is for me something monstrous, an enigma of misfortune which must be accepted, but to which one must not surrender.

With the innate need of turning the stage into a platform, both use sometimes a *conférencier,* or master of ceremony, figure in disguise. The most obvious examples are the Contemporary in Frisch's *The Chinese Wall* and the figure of the Monk in Dürrenmatt's first play, *It Is Written,* who says:

I appear only a few times in this play, two or three times perhaps. Why, it even happens once in a while that I don't have to appear at all, because the director has cut me out to shorten the play or because he is one actor shy. Even now, as I am talking to you, I am not much more than a silence filler. To be sure the curtain has gone up and all eyes are on the stage, but no one quite knows how it goes from here.

In whatever they write, Dürrenmatt and Frisch are compelled by the ethos of their convictions, and both occasionally slip into pathos because of the weightiness of their themes. The stage is to them a heightened background and poetic place for verbal and visual symbols. Two examples may show how the painter-dramatist and the architect-dramatist have tried to serve their urge to communicate in stage terms and how they recognize each other's contributions. An excerpt from the *Diaries* of Max Frisch:

In the second play of Friedrich Dürrenmatt [a greatly underrated play and misunderstood when first performed: *The Blind*] . . . there exists the following scene: a blind man, who does not perceive the destruction of his duchy, believes that he is still living in his secure fortress. In his belief, in his imagination, he rules over an unscathed and spared land. Thus he sits in the midst of ruins, which he, of course, being blind, cannot see, surrounded by all kinds of the dissolute rabble of war, mercenaries, prostitutes, robbers, pimps, who in wanting to make a fool of the blind duke now deride his belief while allowing themselves to be received as dukes and generals, the prostitute, however, as a persecuted abbess. The blind duke addresses them in such a way as he imagines they deserve. We, however, see the repulsive individual whose blessing as abbess he believingly begs for—on his knees . . . Model example of a theatrical situation: the statement resides wholly in the opposition between perception and imagination. Here the theatre can play alone.

In *Problems of the Theatre*, Dürrenmatt speaks of the dematerialization of the stage set and the realization of the theatrical poetic image:

> . . . In *The Marriage of Milord Mississippi* . . . I expressed the indefiniteness of the local (in order to give it spirit of wit, of comedy) by having the right window of a room look out upon a northern landscape with its Gothic cathedral and apple tree, while the left window of the same room opens on a southern scene with an ancient ruin, a touch of the Mediterranean and a cypress. The really decisive point in all this is that, to quote Max Frisch, the playwright is making poetry with the stage, a possibility which has always entertained and occupied me and which is one of the reasons, if not the main one, why I write plays. But then—and I am thinking of the comedies of Aristophanes and the comic plays of Nestroy—in every age poetry has been written not only *for*, but *with* the stage.

It is often said that someone was "discovered." I incline to the opinion that a creative person can be discovered only by himself and that, strangely enough, in the process of self-discovery someone passes by and, struck by the emanations of self-discovery, does something about it. Such a coincidental event quite often—and not so strangely at all—happens with creative men possessed by genius. Talents must often wait for such an occasion, and sometimes a long time.

At the age of twenty-six, leaving painting, philosophy, and his first sketches in prose, Dürrenmatt wrote his first play, *It Is Written*. Kurt Horwitz passed by and staged it at the Zürcher Schauspielhaus. It was a scandal and a failure. This was in 1947, and ever since Dürrenmatt has produced play after play and divided his feeling of belonging between the theatre in Basle and Zürich. Three years previously Kurt Hirschfeld, the *Dramaturg* of the Schauspielhaus, had urged the novelist Max Frisch to try his hand and pen at a play. *Santa Cruz* was the title of Frisch's first play. It cannot be called a convincing stage realization, as little as *It Is*

Written, but both plays were strong dramatic experiences and awoke the latent feeling for the theatrical in both writers.

For more than a decade the German dramatists had been dispersed all over the world, imprisoned or killed, and a whole generation of dramatists was wiped out by Hitler and the German nation. Some of the best German-speaking actors fled to Switzerland. There was a tremendous need for playwrights. Dürrenmatt and Frisch stepped into the void.

The Nazi period and the war years were a cultural windfall for Switzerland. There has never been better theatre in Zürich, Basle, and many smaller cities before or after that time. The Zürcher Schauspielhaus, in particular, fulfilled a historic mission* in these years, but it must be said that no other European theatre ever had such a chance. The directors, actors, and designers recognized the enormous task forced upon them by history, to preserve the spirit of the German theatre and to remain a symbol of the dignity of man.

The Schauspielhaus had an enviable series of firsts. It premiered the four most important Brecht plays, while their author fled from Sweden via Siberia to Los Angeles: *Mother Courage* in 1941, *Galileo* in 1943, and in the same year, *The Good Woman of Sezuan*; five years later came *Puntila*. Carl Zuckmayer's *The Devil's General*, written in the United States, had its first production in Zürich, and so had John Steinbeck's *The Moon Is Down* which, staged in 1943, was one of the great successes of that weighty season. Thornton Wilder saw his play *Alcestiade*, still waiting to be produced in his native country, on the stage of the Schauspielhaus.

The political events of these years turned the Swiss theatre into a sanctuary, a place of refuge for the writer, into a platform of discussion in which playwrights of all languages were heard. Even in the years of Switzerland's total isolation and fear of invasion from the north and south, many playwrights or their plays found their way across the Swiss borders. This was a histrionic moment of historic greatness. And after the war, the spirit of the Zürcher Schauspielhaus gave birth to two major playwrights, Friedrich Dürrenmatt and Max Frisch.

Dürrenmatt once said: "A play is never finished. A play is becoming." One can never close a chapter on a writer of some magni-

---

* Friedrich Dürrenmatt: "Just because of its imperfections, the Zürcher Schauspielhaus is a perfect theatre, and therefore I love it more than any other theatre."

tude with any apodictic statements. One can never finish such a chapter. As long as the writer is alive, he is in a state of becoming. After his death, history sees to it that its needs remain related to the writer's work, which may continue to live a thousand lives or die a thousand deaths.

DANCE: INFLUENCES AND EFFECTS

THERE is not a single nation in the world which has not had its folkloric dances and shared in the popular dances of the time, but there have been only a few nations endowed at one time or another with the creative spirit in the dance. America and England took to the ballet rather late, Germany only recently, but both America and Germany, as little tradition-bound as they were, embraced the rebels of the free dance early in this century. Switzerland, where the European version of the modern dance was born, has never been a particularly dance-hungry country, probably as little as the Germans. The dance geniuses it produced can be counted on the fingers. But the Swiss have learned to play host to dance and dancers with an endearing, though nonchalant, enthusiasm.

Historically seen, the theatre dance was born in Italy. But the French created what is known as ballet essentially with the help of the Italian Renaissance and Baroque geniuses. In the nineteenth century the Russians became leaders in the field mainly with French, but also some Italian and Swedish dancers, choreographers, and teachers. In turn, the Russians—Michel Fokine, Mikhail Mordkin, and George Balanchine—had a great share in making America a creatively leading nation in the dance field. Despite the fact that all the arts have the stamp of their local origin and historic period, they have international scope and significance. The dance, with its legible language of movement, is readily understood by all nations and civilizations.

Switzerland, as indicated, does not have a famous dance history of its own, even though the country is very strong in its colorful folkoric dances and carnival mummeries. However, three of her great cities imitated the example of other metropolises by having their ballet companies led to new heights by Russian choreographers in mid-century: Nicholas Beriozoff in Zürich, and Waszlaw Orlikowsky in Basle. Geneva has played host to George Balanchine. Early in 1970 he became artistic consultant at the Geneva Grand Theatre, where the opera ballet is guided by Alfonso Cata, who could be considered a South-American Swiss.

But Switzerland's great contributions to the dance lie in the fact that it was in Ascona where the seeds were sown for the German *Ausdruckstanz;* that it was in Geneva where Emile Jaques-Dalcroze, a native Swiss, devised his eurhythmic theories, having a decisive influence on ballet and on modern dancers; and that finally, some very capable dancers and choreographers have come from this country. Two Swiss artists should be added, or rather singled out, whose activities lie on the periphery of the dance world. They are comedians in their fashion whose humor made the world laugh, something for which the world is always grateful: Trudi Schoop and Grock, the clown.

The Opera Ballet Companies, particularly the one in Zürich, have their own *Theatertanzschulen*, essential as a potential pool for future dancers. As in most other opera houses, the ballet not only contributes to opera and operetta productions, but also features its own ballet programs, sometimes coupled with short operas. For many years Zürich had in its ballet masters, Hans Macke and Jaroslav Berger, skillful though not exciting choreographers. Later Nicholas Beriozoff achieved a high standard in the individual accomplishments of his ensemble and created a balanced repertory of classic, semi-classic, and new ballets. A man of taste with a sense for the theatrical, he can remain rather faithful to an original as he did in his revival of *Petrouchka*, or he can be daring as proved in his revival of *The Nutcracker* in which, besides other things, Herr Drosselmeyer became a newly conceived character. He was no longer the old wizard with a patch on his eye but was metamorphosed into a charming *bon vivant* with top hat and twirling cane.

Beriozoff had his counterpart in Orlikowsky in Basle, where he was preceded at the Stadttheater by the Viennese Rosalie Chladek and the German Heinz Rosen. In 1955, Waszlaw Orlikowsky came to the Basle Stadttheater, saw, and conquered the situation. With theatre blood in his veins, his passionate search for precision and perfection made it possible for him to give new life to the opera ballet in that city. He opened with the staging of *Swan Lake* which successfully proved that he was able to adjust classic works to the taste of our time without changing basic choreographic concepts. The famed German dance critic, Horst Koegler, said he knew of no other unabridged version of *Swan Lake* in our Western world which could compete with Orlikowsky's as to style and dramatic impact. Orlikowsky also created several new ballets, of which *Dorian Gray Today* (1966), to the music of the Swiss composer Max Lang, was one of the more memorable ones.

Switzerland has several smaller "big" cities, such as Berne, whose theatre dance has been pleasantly noticed from time to time without demanding too much attention; Lausanne with its hopeful

Association du Ballet de la Jeunesse Romande; or St. Gallen, which mainly is associated with the name of Mara Jovanovits. Even though her name may not have the right Swiss sound—she had a Serbian father and a Bulgarian mother—this dancer-choreographer was born and reared in St. Gallen. After having studied with Gert Palucca in Dresden and Kurt Jooss in Dartington-Hall in England, she became ballet mistress and choreographer of the small theatre in St. Gallen. She could not help but develop dancers out of amateurs and actors. Facing what I would call a God-given smallness, she decided on doing the right thing: she avoided staging such classic ballets as *Giselle* or *Swan Lake* in a pitiful manner and took the risk of failing as a choreographer of new short ballets of her own invention with the limited means at her disposal. Mara Jovanovits developed a simple style, clear in structure, with expressive power and intensity in what she desired to convey.

The calibre of most of the ballerinas and premiers danseurs in the various companies runs the gamut from outstanding to acceptable. Some have come from abroad to join one or the other group; some Swiss-born dancers have proved their mettle and stayed. But a few felt the need to be recognized outside their native land. One who left and became internationally known is Hans Meister.

He grew up in Schaffhausen and, at the age of eleven, enrolled in classes at the Zürich Opera Ballet School. Five years later, when his family moved to Zürich, he became determined to embark on a dance career. His taste was still eclectic. During a visit to Paris he was enchanted by the Paris Opera Ballet, as well as by the companies of Roland Petit and Janine Charrat. His impressions hardened his determination to make the dance his profession. While he was studying at Teacher's College, the music lessons intrigued him most. He soon played in the school orchestra—he chose the cello —and danced in concerts at the theatre in St. Gallen.

His talent unfolded when he joined the Royal Ballet School in London. In 1957 Celia Franca, director of the National Ballet of Canada, saw him dance in a class and engaged him for her company. From there he came to the Metropolitan Opera Ballet in New York, where the ballet mistress, Dame Alicia Markova, gave him leading parts for several seasons. His ambitions led him as far as Russia. In 1968 he arrived in Leningrad, and six weeks later he danced the *Sleeping Beauty pas de deux* in the Maryinsky Theatre with the Kirov Ballet. After a smaller, then larger part in *The Fountain of Bakhchisarai*, he was permitted to take the part of the Prince in *Swan Lake*. In one season he appeared with the Kirov in twenty-four performances, an enviable record for any Russian dancer. And how did his dancing improve? he was asked by an interviewer: "We all dance with our legs and feet, the Russians dance with the whole body . . . Training under these great teachers, becoming part of the way of life of the Kirov, is a tremendous honor and experience. I shall not only benefit from this now while I am dancing, it will be of great help to me when my dancing days are over and I will turn to teaching."

———————————

True to Switzerland's destiny, it has played host to some of the great names in dance history. Switzerland meant a great deal to Igor Stravinsky who, as one of the most important composers of our century, meant a great deal to the dance world. He often came to Switzerland, whether it was to work there or to care for his sick wife. ". . . Diaghilev came to visit me in Clarens, where I was staying," he wrote in his autobiography. "I played him the piece I had just composed and which later became the second scene of *Petrouchka*. He was so much pleased with it that he would not leave it alone and began persuading me to develop the theme of the puppet's sufferings and make it into a whole ballet."

At the beginning of World War I, Stravinsky took up residence in the French part of the country. Herbert Read wrote about it in *Stravinsky and the Muses*:

> Very significant in Stravinsky's life must have been those years of forced seclusion which he spent in the canton of Vaud, Switzerland—they began with the outbreak of war in 1914 and were prolonged to 1920. Here a circle of poets, musicians, and painters was formed—it included Stravinsky, Ernest Ansermet who was so often to conduct his work, Ramuz, a great poetic writer not sufficiently appreciated in the English-speaking world, who was to provide the texts for *L'Histoire du Soldat* and some of the songs, the brothers Alexandre and Charles-Albert Cingria, and René Auberjonois who was to paint the décor for *Soldat*. It was a time of joyful collaboration and of the development of mutual understanding between poets, musicians and painters— Ramuz has devoted a volume of reminiscences to the period, which Stravinsky, in his *Chroniques de ma Vie*, recommends as a faithful record of the deep mutual affection and comprehension, the response of one sensibility to another, which developed in this atmosphere of amity and contentment.

Diaghilev's Ballets Russes were inactive during the last year of the First World War. The theatres were closed as much as the frontiers. Stravinsky felt restless, isolated as he was, cut off from the world which was then bleeding.

His friend the Swiss poet and novelist C. F. Ramuz suggested that they create something simple. They thought of something that would not need a regular stage, something reminiscent of the strolling players. Stravinsky's thoughts quite naturally turned to Russian folklore, and he came up with the story of a soldier who sells his violin to the Devil, wins it back at a game of cards, marries a princess, and finally loses his soul again. The premiere of *L'Histoire du Soldat*, for seven musicians, two dancers, a narrator, and a mime, took place in Lausanne in 1918. Décor and costumes were designed by the Swiss René Auberjonois.

Ramuz collaborated once more with Stravinsky when, in 1922, they concocted a little play to be acted by clowns, dancers, and acrobats. It concerned a cock who is fooled by a fox, *Le Renard*, but is rescued by a cat and a goat. The score was originally composed for a private performance for the Princess Edmond de Polignac, who later gave Diaghilev permission to use it. The scenario of this ballet burlesque with singing was again based on a Russian folktale, apparently gallicized by Ramuz. Stravinsky was delighted with Bronislava Nijinska's choreography and with her interpretation of the title role.

Nijinska's name evokes the memory of her brother, Vaslav Nijinsky, who, on return from his American tour in December 1917, settled at St. Moritz. It was the last winter of work and hope before twilight embraced him. He wanted to found a school, and there could be no sadder relic from those days than Nijinsky's notebook, on the first page of which he had written: *Dancing School of V. Nijinsky, San Moritz, Switzerland, 22 March 1918*. It was then that the moments of lucidity became threateningly shorter. On January 19th he danced for the last time when he agreed to appear at a charity performance at the Hotel Souvretta. It was in those days that Nijinsky began to write his *Diary*, draw and paint, days in which he spoke of his "marriage to God."

It was God, above all, but then it was Nature, spelled with an immense capital N, to which his relationship assumed an aspect of a growingly intensified personalization.

Once in the mountains I came to a road which led up to a peak, I climbed up and stopped. I wanted to make a speech on the mountain; I felt a wish to do so, but I did not because I thought that everyone would say that I was mad. I was not . . . I wanted to shout from the top of the mountain into the village of St. Moritz. I did not . . . I went on and came to a tree. The tree told me that one could not talk here, because human beings do not understand feelings. I went on. I was sorry to part with the tree, because the tree understood me. I walked. I climbed up 2,000 meters—stood there a long time. I felt a voice and shouted in French: "Parole!" I wanted to speak, but my voice was so strong that I could only shout: "I love everyone! I want happiness! I love everyone! I want everyone!" I want to love everyone and be understood, and therefore want to speak all languages but cannot, therefore I write, and my writings will be translated.

At the end of the *Diary* he wrote:

I ask the Swiss people to take care of me. I want to publish this book in Switzerland because I live here. I like Switzerland . . .

                    Signed: God and Nijinsky
                    Saint Moritz-Dorf
                    Villa Guardamunt
                    February 27, 1919

In March of that year, in Zürich, Professor Bleuler diagnosed his case as incurable schizophrenia. It was the beginning of a long end, lasting for somewhat over thirty years.

It was in the year 1913 that Diaghilev had asked Emile Jaques-Dalcroze for one of his assistants to give his company a better feeling for and understanding of rhythm. Dalcroze, a Swiss, happened to have been born in Vienna in 1865, but at the age of eight he came to his native country and later studied music at the conservatory in Geneva. His searching mind was fascinated by all the arts, particularly the arts of the theatre, and, as a matter of fact, he became director of a theatre in Algiers at the age of twenty. But his essential interest was in music. After having been Professor of Harmony at Geneva for several years, he was invited to Hellerau, a garden city and suburb of Dresden, where an institute was built for him and put at his disposal for the instruction of his method.

It was there that Diaghilev observed his work. Dalcroze chose Miriam Rambach, one of his disciples, to work with the Russian dancers who, even though they admitted that their sense of timing, their rhythmic feeling, might be faulty, rebelled and called Rambach *Rythmitchka*. Only Nijinsky, a Pole like Miriam Rambach, worked intensely with her and was appreciative of what he could learn about Dalcroze through her.

At the turn of the century Dalcroze had begun to compose, to write music criticism, and to practice teaching. It was as a teacher that he wrote his name in the book of history. Dalcroze reached maturity as an artist and vision as a teacher at a time when the creative minds of the nineteenth century had had their say and a paralyzing feeling of stagnation demanded revolutionary thoughts and action. Dalcroze was deeply disturbed by a generally mechanical and false approach to the appreciation of music and its artistic expression.

He realized that you could not teach playing an instrument or singing a song "without any thought of such work becoming a means of self-expression." He felt that the simplest rhythmic problems were misunderstood and that the mere memorization of a musical piece remains meaningless if it cannot be related to one's thoughts and feelings. He compared such artists and students to people "who possess the vocabulary of a language and are able to read what others have written, yet are unable to put their own simple thoughts and impressions into words."

Dalcroze became convinced that rhythm was basic to creating harmonies on an artistic level, as much as to hearing music on a general one. His pioneering theories, known under the generic name of *Eurhythmics* (good rhythm), evolved when he began to realize the innate link between rhythm in hearing and moving as well as seeing. He made use of his concept of the indivisibility of rhythm in man by setting up a system of bodily exercises designed to develop mastery of musical rhythm which, as he saw it, depended on our motor consciousness for its fullest expression. He divided the body into three zones, with the upper part being the spiritual and intellectual center, the emotional sphere being located in the middle of the body, and, quite logically, the animal in man, or his physical center, being identified with the lower parts, the abdomen and hips. In using the body as the interpreter of musical rhythm, he achieved an artistic music visualization with his rhythmic movement chorus.

Originally, Dalcroze's aim was to help his music students to a wider scope of musical understanding. This he achieved. But from about 1905, his theories were generally recognized as progressive steps in a new direction, and they reoriented the teaching and understanding of music. Dalcroze's great importance, however, lies in the influence he exerted on the theatre dance and twentieth-century choreography. Some of the most important dancers profited from his concepts, from Ruth St. Denis to Kurt Jooss, from Mary Wigman and Hanya Holm to Uday Shankar. Miriam Rambach, one of Dalcroze's most outstanding disciples, became Dame Marie Rambert and a great inspiration in the development of the English ballet.

It may be difficult to pinpoint how much Dalcroze's ideas helped Nijinsky in creating his choreography for *The Rite of Spring,* in which he had to battle with Stravinsky's then startling sense of rhythmic and harmonic structure. Nijinsky translated this difficult score into a nonacademic movement language with a touch of the archaic and a strong rhythmic pulsebeat. The contemporary and rather conservative dance critic André Levinson described the effect Dalcroze's eurhythmics had on Nijinsky:

> It is interesting to see what Nijinsky made of this music, defying as it does all attempts at plastic transcriptions. The sole aim of the dance movements he originated for the production was the realization of the rhythm. He thought of this rhythm as a gigantic force, the only thing capable of dominating the primitive soul of man. The dancers, by very simple means, became an incarnation of the various elements of the music, the respective duration and force of the sound, its quality and quantity, the speeding up and slowing down of the pace.

And Lincoln Kirstein, in his *Book of the Dance,* refers to Stravinsky's score as having "precipitated a revolution in the field of music as important as Nijinsky's in the field of dance" and that it "was for its time (and still is) of the utmost rhythmic subtlety."

John Martin, the American dance critic, once said that Isadora Duncan gave the modern dance its spirit, and Mary Wigman its body. This *body* woke up to the reality of its artistic life in Ascona in the year of 1913, when Mary Wigman "walked up to that beautiful hill called Monte Verità," as she told me. "I did not know that this walk should decide my life. I only knew that I was supposed to meet a man there of whom the painter Emil Nolde had told me, he moves as I do and he dances as I dance—without music. That was Rudolf von Laban. He became my teacher."

At that time Mary Wigman happened to stay in the Ticino. She had a contract in her hands, due to be signed, which would have doomed the modern dance and her, as a teacher of glorified calisthenics based on the Dalcroze method. Fortunately, during those summer months she was possessed with dancing and intoxicated with aimless improvisations. When she told Laban of her contract to be signed, he only said to her: "Congratulations. This is a beautiful and secure position for lifetime. But," and he paused, "actually you are a dancer who ought to be on stage." This remark changed Mary Wigman's life. She did not sign the contract. "I decided to remain free, even though I faced a frightening nothing. But this nothingness was tempting and promising, full of artistic adventure. Luckily, the torrents of my dancing dreams were forced into a disciplined direction, giving my artistic dream its final *Gestalt*."

Ascona and Laban became a focal point for the modern dance, which then was in its growing pains. Each summer Laban came to Ascona to preside over his summer sessions. Students came from everywhere, but mainly from Germany. Among them were such visitors as Else Lasker-Schüler, the poetess from Wuppertal who continued to dream her Oriental dreams in the italianate environment of Ascona.

But beyond the fact that Laban inspired Mary Wigman and unleashed the creative daimon in her, he himself began to work at that time on his now world-famous notation system. Mary Wigman said that every morning he knocked at the door of her room with the beautiful view at the Lago Maggiore. He would enter with the words: "Here comes the choreographer!" and was always armed with an old-fashioned travel bag full of notes and drawings which he would spread out on table and floor.

There was also something of a magic healer in Laban. This modern shaman acquired such a reputation by making an arthritic lady move and by dispelling the somatic part of many a psychosomatic disease. His circle in Ascona grew from year to year not only because of his personal magic, but because, above all, he could make the dancers "see," as Mary Wigman put it, because he could create a poetic awareness in them which had all the potentialities of artistic greatness. Some fulfilled them, particularly Mary Wigman, who has felt drawn back to Ascona summer after summer, as if she wanted to say thanks to Monte Verità, where she gave birth to her own genius.

Mary Wigman became a focal point* in the new expressionistic dance for which the Germans had the highly descriptive word *Ausdruckstanz* and which found its counterpart in the United States as modern dance. From all over the world young people made their pilgrimage to Dresden, where Wigman had opened her school in the twenties. With relentless dedication to find the final artistic expression through the human body in terms of the twentieth century, Wigman and her circle of dancers challenged themselves, their audiences, and time.

Among Mary Wigman's students was a young man who had a very specific gift for self-expression and an irrespressible urge to move. His name was Harald Kreutzberg, born in Reichenberg, Czechoslovakia, in 1902, of an Austrian mother and a father whose native town was Philadelphia. One day Max Terpis, a Swiss dancer who had become ballet master at the Opera House in Hannover, noticed Kreutzberg in Wigman's class of beginners. He engaged him and gave him small parts in his theatre in Hannover where, in turn, Max Reinhardt discovered Kreutzberg. He became a member of the famous Reinhardt theatres, appearing first in *Turandot* and then as Puck in *A Midsummer Night's Dream*, in which part he also made a deep impression on the American public when Reinhardt showed his famous production of the Shakespearean play in the United States in 1927.

Although this first acting part convinced Kreutzberg he could not only dance but also act, the dance remained the one self-expressive art form to which he knew he could give his most and utmost. While in America he gave a dance recital with Tilly Losch. Later, with his partner Yvonne Georgi, who had studied with Dalcroze and Wigman, he toured the world for several years.

Kreutzberg combined theatricality with a taste for the bizarre and fantastic. He had an impressive way of establishing a situation

---

* During the dictatorship of Fascism in Germany and for many years afterwards, Mary Wigman came to Zürich each summer for the courses she gave in modern dance, assisted by Kurt Jooss, Harald Kreutzberg, Victor Gsovsky, and many others. These Zürich courses were the continental counterpart to the dance courses and festivals in Bennington, New London, and Colorado Springs in America. In the last few years of these summer courses Mary Wigman also invited some American luminaries to participate in them, to teach and demonstrate their techniques in Zürich.

and creating a character with a few poses and gestures, a very personal way, even though he was strongest where he used Mary Wigman's technique. He said about himself:

> I am not a leader nor a creator of any school of dancing. I dance to express myself. I dance from my heart, blood and imagination. As an actor uses words to tell the story of the drama, as a composer narrates his themes in bars of music, I express my mood, my poesy, my inner feeling with movement, with my body.

In 1959 Harald Kreutzberg gave his farewell recital in Frankfurt, but he continued to choreograph for other performers and companies. He founded his own school in Berne, where he lived and taught for many more years. Every country in the world would have welcomed him, but he chose Switzerland. There was certainly more than one motivation that prompted this decision. Among other reasons he may have wanted to show his gratitude towards Max Terpis, the Swiss ballet master who was the first to issue a passport into the world of the arts for Harald Kreutzberg.

Rarely is a Swiss girl associated with flamenco dancing and the sensitive playing of castanets, but Susana (whose surname is Audeoud and who is now settled in Berne as a dance teacher) is that strange phenomenon of a Swiss Spanish dancer. And why not, if José Greco was a boy from Brooklyn, and Inesita hailed from California.

Susana was a classic ballerina who had studied in Paris. But then she became convinced that a twentieth-century dancer must know as well the modern expressive dance, with which she became familiar in her native Switzerland. In 1947 Susana journeyed to Spain. While taking classes in a Barcelona studio she met José Udaeta, then ballet master at the Madrid Opera, who engaged her as prima ballerina.

Both found pleasure in the native rhythms of Spain and with great intensity turned to the Spanish dance, developing a program of astounding variety over the years. Their first tour, in May 1948, took them through Switzerland. Probably out of sentimental reasons it was there that Susana wanted to start her career as a Spanish dancer. She was an immediate success. It was said that one could not help recognizing that she spoke a movement language of her choice as if it were a language she had invented. As so often happens with languages which one adopts and into which one grows, one brings to the new idiom an innocent freshness that gives even the stereotype a new feeling.

This is what Susana was generally praised for and what one could observe, whether she danced the traditional Jota or the Bolero, which she took with her from the village of Torrent in Valencia. For more than twenty years she was partnered by José with whom she also created a variety of stylized dances inspired by impressions gathered in Spain, such as the Escorial, or by figures of history and the arts.

In all her dances Susana not only showed her technical proficiency, but also gave each creation an artistic life of its own and a bigger dimension through her acting ability, which found particular expression in such dances as her gypsy dance or in the storytelling ballets. Another accomplishments of hers was to grasp the nuances of the *flamenco,* which she studied with Estampio and La Quica in Madrid, two of the great teachers of the old *flamenco* school. Susana became possessed by what the Spaniards call *duende,* "the demon," in the ancient sense of inspiration. The intensity and passion which sang in her *flamenco* movements were as astounding as the verve and humorous lightness which she brought to some regional and rustic dances.

To the many generalizations about the Swiss belongs the stigma of a people without humor. The impression of a certain heaviness or gravity and, oftentimes, of soberness is thrown in as evidence for such indictment. But is not gravity a presupposition to humor? Did not even Mark Twain allude to the tragic significance of humor when he wrote: "Everything human is pathetic. The secret source of humor itself is not joy but sorrow. There is no humor in heaven." Soberness, diligence, and serious intent do not necessarily preclude any phase of the entire humorous scale from sensible fun to biting satire. They may, however, color a person's sense of humor. These and similar qualities often combine forces to suppress quantitatively the feeling for fun.

Humor may have different hues. It may be dry, wry, prankish, clever, smart, sarcastic, naïve, and even soulful. It is, no doubt, indicative of a person's psyche. On the other hand, it is questionable whether an entire nation can be without humor, even though its folklore background mostly predetermines the type of humor which, of necessity, is then varied by each individual. It has been my observation that the Swiss love humor; only they are somehow embarrassed when caught in the act of laughing by strangers, particularly when they are foreigners. Switzerland is the country of the "in" jokes, and this is another reason why the Swiss may appear to be without humor to the outsider. One finds most Swiss, especially the intellectuals, usually in a mood of self-criticism. This may be related to their smallness, which may be cause and reason for certain peculiarities about which, in turn, they are oversensitive. This alone is an endless source for humor on a small scale. The only thing that may be said against Swiss humor with a certain amount of descriptive accuracy is its lack of finesse or sophistication. If there is another idiosyncratic characteristic about their humor, then it is the fact that humor changes in each canton. Some observers maintain that the laugh muscles of the Swiss are sometimes a bit slow in their response. But this too differs from language to language, from canton to canton, from city to city, from Swiss to Swiss.

Even if humor is a matter of cantonal temperament, it has not prevented Zürich from having had some of the best cabarets, or Geneva from having given birth to Rodolphe Töpffer, humorist and creator of the cartoon. The satirical weekly, *Der Nebelspalter*, is written for German consumption, but "splits the fog"—as its title says—for all Swiss. Bits of humor and satire can be found everywhere in Swiss literature and the arts, and when it comes to having real fun, the Swiss gave the world one of its greatest clowns and one of its finest dance humorists. The clown I mention was a great musician to boot: his name was Charles Adrien Wettach, better known to the world as Grock.

He was born at Moulin de Loveresse, so small a place that all encyclopedias add: "near Reconvillier," which is not too big a town itself. The year of his birth was 1880. Grock died in 1959, but his memory is still very much alive, fixed by the image of the clown who moved the piano closer to the stool, instead of the stool to the piano. His father learned the trade of a watchmaker, but at heart he was an acrobat and appeared as an amateur acrobat in circuses around the country. His son spent each summer with a circus and soon became an expert tumbler while playing the violin, piano, and xylophone. Grock discovered the musical clown in himself, and his physical and mental somersaults with instruments gained in scope and hilarity with the years. He began to clown in a café when he was nineteen years old, and from 1911 on he broke all records of world fame as the simpleton with instruments. There was laughter in each of his movements and gestures, in each moment of his clownish ideas.*

The Swiss dance humorist who made a name for herself was Trudi Schoop. Thomas Mann spoke of her great art and "the phenomenon of her soulful and humorous talent." Some critics spoke of her side-splitting comic effects; others found her clever, but too obvious and naïve. And probably both were right.

Trudi came from an artistic family in Zürich, began as an actress, studied dancing in Vienna. At the international competition in Paris, in 1932, her comic ballet, *Fridolin on the Road*, won fourth prize and started her on her career. Her style was that of gentle humor in the form of vignettes or serials of a comic strip. There was her Fridolin, a simple lad who left home to see the world, only to get himself into and out of scrapes, including an unhappy marriage. In *Want Ads* she pictured all that really lies behind the advertisements in the classified section of a newspaper. In *All For Love* were seven tragicomic episodes showing fortunate and unfortunate aspects of love, scenes in which she appeared as a child, nightclub dancer, fortuneteller, a mother stealing for her children, and a clown. Displaying a quick change in her comic and sometimes tragicomic versatility was her forte. There was always a touch of the clown in whatever she did.

Her most ambitious and best work was the *Blonde Marie*, "a silly symphony in the flesh," to music composed by Paul Schoop, her brother. Marie, a servant girl, attracts the attention of a tenor in a tavern; as a chorus girl she has her lucky break when she can replace the sick soubrette; as the wife of a rich man she has an affair with an artist and shoots her husband; finally, she tells her life's story to the gentlemen of the press, then suddenly wakes up, realizing she is still the servant girl who cannot help spilling the tea.

Perhaps the way in which Trudi Schoop became a dancing comedienne may explain some of the complexities of Swiss humor—or of humor per se. "I began to dance in serious things," she once told reporters, "but in my first recital people insisted on laughing at the wrong places, so I said, 'All right, if they want to laugh, I'll give them a chance to do it in the right places.' And I began

*Today Switzerland's best known clown is Dimitri, who was born in the Ticino. After having studied mime with Marcel Marceau and Étienne Decroux, Dimitri was introduced to circus clowning by Grock's partner, Maïsse. Dimitri is known as "The Clown of Ascona," and has his own theatre in the Ticino.

to make these places stand out. But that isn't the whole story," she continued. "To me comedy is life as it appears to us in moments of escape, while tragedy is life as it is at heart. Naturally, the two are sometimes identical."

Trudi Schoop was only funny in her comedy ballets because she knew how tragic was what she did. Grock once remarked: "It is said that Miss Schoop is the only woman comic in the world. I am proud she is Swiss, too."

The world revered Grock and Trudi Schoop because they made thousands of people laugh who would have laughed at the suggestion that these two comedians were born in Switzerland.

ARCHITECTURE AND LANDSCAPE

ARCHITECTURE is about more than just how people live. It reveals man's sensibilities, aesthetic feelings, and philosophy of life. Architecture mirrors a nation's socio-cultural past and present, its economics and, last but not least, its geography. Morality may be a matter of geography, as the saying goes, but housing certainly is—and, in the final analysis, morality has a great deal to do with housing.

Seen from an historic viewpoint, one can easily divide Swiss architecture into two major phases. The first phase has grown geographically and ethnically through the centuries, patterned by the needs and conditions of each region and canton, whereas the second phase, the contemporary international style, was introduced in the late 1920's and crystallized in the mid-1930's into the now accepted form of building. The latter period coincided with the emergence of a generation of very able architects—as Alfred Roth, one of its representative exponents, explained to me—pushing forward on a broad front, being essentially progressive. At that time Switzerland brought forth the greatest architect of the twentieth century, Le Corbusier (a pseudonym for Charles-Edouard Jeanneret, 1887–1965), who, together with Frank Lloyd Wright and Walter Gropius, gave our time its new architectural face.

Le Corbusier exerted strong influence on the first gathering of the International Congresses for Modern Architecture (CIAM) which took place in La Sarraz, north of Lausanne, in 1928. It was not mere chance that this congress was held in Switzerland, but because in the second half of the 1920's the country was very active in publishing material on city planning and architectural designs. Siegfried Giedion (1888–1968), a Swiss art historian and disciple of Heinrich Wölfflin, was chosen to be the first secretary-general of the CIAM. Giedion became a most important spokesman for, and scholar of, twentieth-century architecture, analyzing and clarifying its potentialities and aims, defining and detailing the origins and directions it has been taking. With unconventional insight, Giedion related the past to the present, weighing the consequences of industrialization and trying to find the roots of such basic concepts as symbolism and abstraction, constancy and change, in archaic cultures. In his later years he divided his teaching career between the Federal Institute of Technology in Zürich and Harvard University.

He wrote a penetrating book, *Space, Time and Architecture*, in 1941, important for an understanding of contemporary architecture.

While traveling through Switzerland, one cannot help being surprised and impressed by the variety of architectural styles. Each canton, and often certain districts within each canton, varies from all others in its distinct building patterns, crystallized over the centuries through the climatic needs and folkloric background peculiar to the region. The developed style has most often been dictated by the physical condition of the territory and the means of construction available—the wood, stone, and harnessable water-power which are the country's main natural resources. The art of building in Switzerland has always been essentially functional. In the steep and narrow valleys of the many mountainous terrains, we usually find wooden constructions, ingeniously held together as if by nature itself. To safeguard the kitchen area from fire, they are usually encased by masonry. In certain mountain regions, as in the Grisons, wood is reinforced by stone corners and stone roofs. The tourists may find the narrow streets in the mountain villages romantic and quaint, but their narrowness provides a functional protection for the village against the storms and hardships of long winters.

The three linguistically different parts of Switzerland display unmistakably their cultural affinity to their three great neighbors in their architectural styles, as well. This is as noticeable in the small villages as in the larger cities. Geneva, Basle, Berne, Zürich, and Lugano have preserved—in spite of their cosmopolitan atmosphere —their individualistic characteristics and made the most of their historic past. One of the most unique cities in the world from an architectural viewpoint is Berne, famous for its arcades, which have an Oriental touch.

Some places in Central Switzerland, such as Schwyz and Zug, still show traces of a medieval character. Many cities, from Biel in the west to Schaffhausen in the east, are built around medieval walls and fortifications, with churches, monasteries, and towers in Gothic and Romanesque style. The majority of architectural gems, however, go back to the seventeenth and eighteenth centuries, with very personalized and beautifully detailed decorations and stunning ornamental devices. The city of Appenzell best exemplifies how structural refinements can develop to the point of elegance and sophistication.

Italian influence in the sunny Ticino is to be expected and is quite remarkable in its artistic expression. Even the buildings in the mountainous regions evoke a warm, southern mood. The larger and richer towns are most often built with stuccoed stone, while in the villages uncovered stone prevails. The Ticino has always been the land of the finest stone-carvers, and their art is highlighted by its many churches, of which the Madonna del Sasso in Locarno and Santa Maria degli Angioli in Lugano are, in their way, masterpieces of fifteenth-century Italian architecture.

The Ticinese people have brought forth some of the finest architects. It began with Carlo Maderno (1556–1629), who was appointed *stuccatore* by the Pope and helped to rebuild the church of St. Peter but who mainly left his mark as a hydraulic engineer and architect of some of the impressive fountains in Rome, such as the one on St. Peter's Square. Maderno's nephew, Francesco Borromini (1599–1667), was undoubtedly overshadowed by Bernini, with whom he worked, but art historians acknowledged Borromini's merits, next to Bernini's, for having crowned the victory of the Catholic Church with the dome of St. Peter. Borromini was the first among the Baroque architects to use plants, garlands, wreaths, and palm branches as ornamentation. Some of his ideas were daring and extended the formal embellishments of the Baroque. Kenneth Clark said in *Civilisation* that "Rules didn't exist for Borromini, and to this day he shocks the academically minded. And then I suppose one must say that the restless convolutions of Borromini's High Baroque often come very close to the swirls and twirls of late Gothic." One more name of the early Ticinese builders and engineers should not be forgotten. Domenico Fontana (1543–1607), who was also attracted by the many possibilities in Rome at that time, became famous for having devised a way to move the huge obelisk from the southern part of St. Peter's Square to its center. He was highly praised and decorated for this engineering feat, since the Romans of the late Renaissance wondered how their forefathers in ancient days could have brought the obelisk from Egypt to Rome so easily, while it took them years and years to figure out methods and means of moving the stone only a few meters. Fontana also had many fine architectural designs to his credit and was known as a skilled city planner.

Today the Ticinese, as have the Swiss of all other regions, embrace the simplified and scientifically logic style of the international school, with its emphasis on comfort and airiness. It is amazing how the Swiss cities, as highly industrialized as they are, have kept their characteristics intact while integrating the twentieth-century monolithic style. All the more regrettable is the fact that the countryside faces the invasion of real estate speculators who operate primarily with the money of international investors.

The danger became real in the 1960's. The rapidly growing tourism invites the building of more and more hotels and condominiums at lakesides and in mountain resorts, at the very places people come to enjoy. Very soon the landscape will be dotted with buildings, and Switzerland, famous and admired for its scenic beauty, will have the most marvelous facilities—without the scene to marvel at.

Uniformity is an inherent weakness of modern architecture. Despite or just because of the growing need for new buildings everywhere in our era, it is imperative to think less in terms of investment than in aesthetics. Every design has a spatial obligation, a fact constantly to be borne in mind in a country whose livelihood partly depends on its scenic beauty. Professor Alfred Roth assured me that no public building, be it a school, hospital, or post office, is permitted to rise without free and fair competition. The jurors, who are architects, are supervised by the organization of architects. But in the area of private building there are no competitions and only a few regulations in existence. The competition of the free market reigns supreme, and every investor-builder tries to save expenses.

The *Neue Zürcher Zeitung* featured an informative article on "The Hard Pressed and Overtaxed Architect" on July 12, 1970, in which the architect as an artist is pitted against the architect as a total entrepreneur. The dangers are obvious. Wherever buildings are mushrooming, the architect as an artist will lose ground, the very ground which an artistic design might have saved.

In the beginning of Switzerland's awakening to the new architecture, one of its leading men, Werner Moser, pleaded for a more human and less monumental way of building. His logic dictated that, because of the intimate character of their country, the Swiss should avoid falling victim to the craze of bigness, of towering heights and staggering dimensions. The measure of man, his vision of himself, became the guiding concept for most architects. Here, too, Le Corbusier's influence was noticeable, for he was strongly opposed to the accepted measure of the meter and defended the use of the human "foot" scale.

Generally, the Swiss architects have adhered to the principles of their innovators. After Le Corbusier built his revolutionary little villa for his mother on Lake Geneva and published his book, *Vers une Architecture (Towards an Architecture)*, in the early 1920's, a new spirit began to assert itself. A few basic concepts became more and more evident in the new buildings that went up between the mid-thirties and seventies. Above all, a careful regard for outdoor living developed, based on one of Le Corbusier's favorite ideas: only air, light, and sun can bring about a renewed feeling for life. He said verbatim: "To live man needs sun—space—green. His activity is rhythmically arranged by the rising and setting of the sun. The planning of cities must follow this principle."

Other features stressing outdoor living are flat roofs with roof gardens—today this has become a routine thought for builders—or sliding doors and big windows, in order to erase the feeling of separation between the interior and exterior. Le Corbusier's genius envisioned a totally new and integrated form of building in which space and light, material and color respond to the emotional needs of man. Being also a painter, sculptor, and poet, Le Corbusier gave his space conceptions an aesthetic feeling, whether he designed a one-family house or a model for a contemporary city of 3,000,000 inhabitants. He felt that purposefulness could achieve its purpose only if it was supported by artistic form.

He believed that the greatest architectural ideas are those that are basically simple, and he proved it, for instance, by creating bigger space through movable walls. The trend towards giving relatively small homes the appearance of spaciousness, creating simple and functional forms while taking the surrounding nature into account, has continued. Carefully designed residential houses based on Le Corbusier's principles can now be found in all cities of the country.

Since their largest cities are rather small and their economic standard high, the Swiss have never had to cope with the greatest problem for most countries: the rebuilding of slum areas. The tenement buildings in the poorer districts of Zürich—Switzerland's largest city, with somewhat over a million inhabitants—represent good middle-class housing by the standards of any other metropolis. The only problem the entire country faces is the universal problem of our mechanized time: to remain master over the traffic on the roads leading to the cities and in their streets.

It is not surprising that a country geared to industry and technological accomplishment, as Switzerland is, should have produced engineers of distinction. The Federal Institute of Technology in Zürich can pride itself on having had students of such calibre as Robert Maillart (1872–1940) and Othmar Hermann Ammann (1879–1965). Both proved that the aesthetics of a bridge need not be secondary to its engineering.

Maillart's bridges, built in various parts of Switzerland, as for instance his elegant Schwandbach Bridge in the canton of Berne, are stunning works of art. This bridge grows into its surroundings as if it were a part of nature, and the sweep of its construction has besides its factual and visual power what could be described as aesthetic rhythm. Max Bill said about Maillart: "If the aesthetic aspect of his work seems to outweigh the technical, it is because we regard his constructions as aesthetic achievements in space and not so much as technical masterpieces which of course they equally well are."

What makes him so important is the fact that Maillart combined artistic sensibility with technical know-how. His technical innovations changed the building method. He eschewed the old principle of "bearing and loading," and in his so-called mushroom construction, columns, beams, and floors are no longer differentiated as in any wood or steel construction, but, as Max Bill emphasizes, "the columns continue merging into the beamless floor slab in an organic manner." Maillart's approach was one of total integration, in which each part had to serve its constructive function.

Othmar Hermann Ammann was even bolder than Maillart in certain aspects. He became the incontestable master of the suspension bridge. The impressive dimensions of his designs, their simplicity and clarity, the floating lightness and elegance of his steel constructions have not yet been surpassed. He certainly made an art of building bridges, and proof of it is in some of the famous bridges in the United States.

After a short practice as an engineer in Switzerland and Germany, Ammann became convinced that his genius could best unfold in the New World. It was here that in the beginning of this century the greatest opportunities waited for him. In 1916 he collaborated on the building of the Hellgate Bridge across the East River in New York City. For this design he received the "Thomas Fitch Knowland Prize."

From then on commissions and challenges followed one another. The New Yorkers who daily use the George Washington Bridge, the Triborough and Whitestone bridges are hardly aware that they were built by a Swiss; nor do the Californians give much thought to the fact that Ammann had a goodly share in the design and execution of the Golden Gate Bridge, probably one of the world's finest bridges. People may admire the architectural beauty and engineering skill while driving through the Lincoln Tunnel connecting New York with New Jersey or while riding across the Delaware Memorial Bridge in Wilmington, without ever having heard the name of Othmar H. Ammann. Even those sitting in the MIT Auditorium in Cambridge, Massachusetts, may not know the name of its architect. Many designs came from the offices of Engineer Ammann, including designs for American highways with complex overpasses and road bridges. Perhaps it is the lot of architects and engineers in general to remain rather anonymous.

Those who knew of Ammann's importance honored him. He received an honorary doctorate from the Federal Institute of Technology in Zürich, from Yale, and the universities of New York, Columbia, and Pennsylvania. These, of course, are only tokens of appreciation. Ammann built his own monuments, suspended between states and across rivers. These memorials may appear light and lofty, but the steely will of a purposeful and practical mind has put them there. And probably there is a great deal of Swissness about all that.

PART TWO

THE CREATIVE ATMOSPHERE OF SWITZERLAND

SOME CAME TO STAY

NECROPOLIS

THERE is a variety of reasons for poets and writers to wish to live in Switzerland—and many, indeed, came to stay only for a while, and never left. They came from many lands, though mostly from Germany. It is as if, symbolically speaking, they wanted to be buried in the heart of Europe.

It may seem odd that so many creative minds should desire to exile themselves on Swiss soil, especially in their last years, in spite of man's instinct to return to his birthplace for his eternal rest. But the desire of an all-embracing peace with himself, his past, and the world arises from a man's contemplation and acceptance of his last hours. And Switzerland seems to offer this, that intangible something that one seeks in an atmosphere of silence and tranquillity, even though the seemingly symphonic harmony may be the result of great contrasts in nature and man.

In the canton Valais, where the German and French tongues imperceptibly cast and mingle their shadows, we find the grave of Rainer Maria Rilke, who, as Rodin's secretary and an admirer of French culture, embraced the French spirit with the dreamy, probing heaviness of the German. Not far from where Rilke is buried, in the churchyard of the enchanting village Raron, rises the Simplon, beyond which lies the "land where the lemon trees bloom, where the gold orange glows in the deep thicket's gloom," as Goethe ecstatically sang of Italy. The dramatist Georg Kaiser lies buried on top of Morcote, and the poet Stefan George, another refugee from the Third Reich, is interred near Locarno. Alfred Polgar, the Austrian critic and elegantly sarcastic feuilletonist, came to spend his last days in Zürich after a long exile in America. Thomas Mann also sought his final refuge in Zürich and closed his eyes in this city which has sheltered many literary men. And we should not forget Robert Musil, who, more eccentrically, willed that his ashes be strewn to the wind in the woods near Geneva. One could go on, listing name after name.

The Swiss poet and essayist Max Rychner once said:

> . . . Our helvetic soil has the characteristics of a Necropolis: here are the tombs of Rilke, George, Thomas Mann, Joyce, Klages, Musil, Georg Kaiser, Derleth, Mombert, Wiechert.

There must be something wrong with the world if so many of its most sensitive and conscious men come to our land in order to die here in their flight, fear, or disgust. The mentioned names belong to one generation. A great many things were also wrong with Switzerland during the lifetime of that generation of poets, but one thing that was right was that those men were able to live and write freely within our frontiers. This is only to be expected, at least for a small state whose best justification for existence it is to realize the greatest possible freedom for each individual.

A plaque on the building in Spiegelgasse 12 in Zürich says:

Here lived and died in the winter of
1836–37 the 23-year-old poet and scientist
Georg Büchner

It is mere coincidence that, in the same little street in Zürich's Altstadt, Goethe was Lavater's guest on his first journey to Switzerland, in 1775, and that Lenin lived there from February 1916 to April 1917. But if it is coincidence, then it is one of symbolic significance, for both Goethe and Lenin are meaningfully polarized in Büchner. He was the dramatic poet that he was because he was a revolutionary, and the kind of revolutionary that he was because he was a poetic dramatist.

Büchner's work and ideas were prophetic. In the romantic age he could write his realistic and expressionistic play *Wozzeck*, a brutal drama of mental aberration and obsession. With his *Danton's Death*, the first passive, existentialist hero was born. As a revolutionary, Lenin's spirit was foreshadowed by Büchner by almost an entire century. Büchner did not believe in the intelligentsia as successful rebels and wrote to Karl Gutzkow in 1835: ". . . The relationship between the poor and rich is the only revolutionary element in the world; hunger alone can become the goddess of liberty . . . Feed the peasants, and the revolution will suffer from apoplexy . . ."

To escape the reactionary claws of Metternich's police, Georg Büchner fled into exile and came via Strasbourg to Zürich, where he tried to be accepted as a lecturer (*Privatdozent*) at the University of Zürich, then only three years old. In September 1836 he received his doctorate there, based on his investigation "About the Nervous System of the Barbels." Two months later he became a faculty member after his trial lecture on the head nerves of fishes met with everyone's approval. But he could lecture only during the fall semester of 1836–37, for he fell sick and became a victim of typhoid fever. On the 21st of February, Büchner was buried where today Zürich's Kunsthaus stands. The town bought this area in 1875 and Büchner's remains were reinterred in the Zürichberg cemetery.

For quite some time he was forgotten. *Wozzeck* was published for the first time in 1879. It was in the late 1880's that Büchner's genius was rediscovered. When Gerhart Hauptmann lived in Zürich in 1888, he and a circle of German writers to whom Frank Wedekind also belonged were deeply impressed by Büchner's "poetic spirit ejaculated like burning lava from infernal depths," to use Hauptmann's description. He and Wedekind often visited Büchner's grave and they knew "every word and every letter he had written," as Wedekind declared.

During the short time Büchner stayed in Zürich, he was enthusiastic about life in this city. On November 20, 1836, he wrote to his family:

As far as the political events are concerned you may be quite calm. Don't get disturbed about the old wives' tales in our newspapers. Switzerland is a republic, and since the people usually do not know better but to say that any republic is an impossibility they tell the good Germans about anarchy, murder and homicide day after day. You will be surprised when you'll visit me; already on your way you will find friendly villages with beautiful houses, and then the closer you'll get to Zürich, and certainly along the lake, everywhere prosperity; nobody in Germany has any notion of what these villages and towns look like. The streets here are not full of idle and petty officials, one does not risk to be run over by an aristocratic carriage; on the other hand, everywhere a healthy, strong people, and for a little money a simple, good, clean republican government supported by a property tax, a sort of tax which would be decried as the height of anarchy everywhere with us . . .

A letter to his family a few weeks previously proves Büchner's ability to telescope a political situation with a descriptive image: "How the struggle between Switzerland and France will end, the heavens only know. But the other day I heard someone say:

'Switzerland will drop a little curtsy and France will say it was a deep one.' I think he is right."

Büchner lived in the house of Mayor Dr. Ulrich Zehnder, together with a Hessian refugee couple by the name of Schulz. (Wilhelm Friedrich Schulz was sentenced to five years' imprisonment in Germany for his anti-militaristic activities and was liberated in a most adventurous and romantic manner, with the help of files smuggled into his cell by his wife Caroline; both then found refuge in Switzerland.) Caroline acted like a mother when Büchner fell sick, and she kept a diary of the poet's last days. Thus, she records the arrival of Büchner's bride Minna, who came from Strasbourg two days before his death. Only three weeks earlier Büchner had written her that he had rented "an elegant large room in a wonderfull house at the outskirts of the city . . . The house is not far from the lake, in front of my windows are the waters of the lake and on all sides the Alps like clouds glistening in the sun. Will you come soon? . . . Addio, piccola mia!"

When she came, Frau Schulz recorded in her diary, "he still recognized her which was a painful joy for her." And on Sunday, the 19th: ". . . . Minna and I sat alone in my cosy little room. We knew that a few steps away from us a man was dying, and what a man! . . . We read a few poems, we spoke of him until Wilhelm entered to call in Minna so that she could close her beloved's eyes. She did it with great calm, but then she broke out in loud pain. I took her in my arms and cried with her . . . The evening passed while we talked of the deceased . . . Almost anything that was around us reminded us of one or another clever remark he had made about it. Now our tears were running and now we had to laugh when we recalled his biting satire, his witty ideas and humorous jokes."

———————————————

Rainer Maria Rilke spent the years of World War I in Munich and later in Vienna, where he worked in the archives of the Ministry of War. Although he escaped the horror of fighting at the fronts, he was repulsed by the patriotic propaganda he was expected to produce, which he considered to be "slanted and irresponsible misuse of the pen." A Munich reporter once burst in to see Rilke without an appointment, to ask him about his political views. "You are at the wrong door," the poet replied. "I'm not engaged in any kind of politics."

Even though he refused to be drawn into the daily political

reversals and cares of a war-torn world, at the end of 1923 he foresaw new storms threatening, new wars and catastrophes. As far as he himself was concerned, sheltered as he was, the poet blessed those years which he could spend in Switzerland—good years, as he said, which insulated him from the darkness and difficulty of life and brought him indestructible gains.

In May 1919, shortly after the armistice, he was invited by the Countess Dobrzensky to spend some time in her chalet at Lake Geneva. He was glad to be able to leave Munich, which reminded him too much of the war years. His trip to Switzerland seemed like a journey to a new freedom, a step outside his yesterday. Switzerland, he wrote, "was in former years only a transit country" and he always mistrusted "its famous beauty," which impressed him as being "too obvious, too pretentious." He had felt that everything there was to be found in a luxury edition, "nature with its depths and heights, full of abundance, where everything was doubled and full of underlined things." He thought the Swiss landscape was too "eclectic." It has often been said that Rilke never searched for an inspiring environment, that his creative urge was propelled by a dynamic power from within which denied any outside influences, visual or otherwise. But this is only half the truth, as his own reactions during his stay in this country prove.

As a matter of fact, his attitude towards the Swiss landscape and people quickly changed. From his very first walks in Zürich ("I must be allowed to begin life everywhere") he felt a growing interest in the topography and history of each neighboring village and town he saw. Rilke often returned to Zürich, where he found a great deal of stimulation and saw many friends, most often among them the composer Ferruccio Busoni. But Zürich was too big a town for Rilke; he did not take to its modernity, its rapid pulse. He felt most comfortable in the French part of Switzerland, in Geneva and some smaller places in the Valais. He also found great satisfaction in his stay in Soglio, a picturesque town in the Bergell valley, with its Italian sky and a fascinating library where he could find books dating from the time of Napoleon to the present. He did some of his most concentrated work there. By then he was determined to "stay in Switzerland as long as it will be possible."

Unfortunately, he had to leave Soglio after a few months ("It was not easy to take leave from Soglio. Much within-ness was interrupted again . . ."). He only reluctantly embarked on a lecture tour. Formally attired, white-gloved, he read his poems to packed houses in Zürich, Sankt Gallen, Basle, Berne, and Winterthur. He had six hundred listeners in Zürich alone, where he had to repeat his lecture.

Even though his books were best-sellers in Switzerland at the time, he did not trust "the often dry Swiss, difficult to penetrate" and introduced each lecture with an extemporaneous talk, to adjust to local ambience, so that "even very personally shaped and 'difficult' poems were received with unusual intensity." It was the last lecture tour of his life. In Lucerne, where he admired the city's old bridges with their gable-framed pictures, he felt disappointed that "none of the native patrician families" came to his lecture, apparently unaware that Lucerne was one of the more conservative towns in the country, with a latent and often open dislike for anything foreign.

On the other hand, his reception in Basle was most gratifying. After his lecture "one of the most beautiful and oldest houses [belonging to the Burckhardt family] opened in a hospitable and friendly manner. . . . Unexpectedly a few intensely rich hours followed in which even the known Swiss handicaps were no longer felt."

Rilke lived in his own world, outwardly disciplined and composed, inwardly haunted and tortured. He always maintained an aesthetic distance from daily living. But, strangely enough, wherever he went he tried to attach himself to those whom he envied for having roots, to what was native and reached far back into the past, as J. R. von Salis also underlined in his book, *Rainer Maria Rilke's Swiss Years*. In Winterthur he was received with open arms by the family Reinhart, the great art patrons and collectors; in Meilen on Lake Zürich, he found a great admirer and friend in Nanny Wunderly-Volkart, whom Rilke appointed as executress of his last will.

After many months of tiring journeys within Switzerland, followed by a trip to Venice and Paris, and then back to Geneva and Berne; and after months of indecision about whether to settle in Germany or Czechoslovakia, he finally found in 1920 what he had sought, and he found it in Switzerland. ("I wonder,—and that it should be really readied for me, at the last moment, when so to speak I stood at the Swiss border beyond which only the trouble of new uncertainties could press upon me. And Switzerland had spoiled me for more than a good year with so many good friends and welcoming places—, I really had no right any longer to ask more and more again from her: But lo! she reserved for me the very best, something completely fulfilling, this place of total refuge which on the maps of my life will always be marked as a central point. . . .")

His life, however, was not yet settled, and his happy period at the castle Berg was only a prelude to what later became his final retreat. He was aware of the feeling that no place where he could rest was the right soil in which to root himself. He hungered for that inner peace which, fortified by a benign environment, would give him the power to concentrate. He desperately sought continuity and, above all, to return to the point where his life and work were interrupted in 1914 by the war.

Rilke stayed at many places in this country. About Locarno he wrote: "Spring in Locarno behaves like the teacher's favorite student who sits in the first row and has always learned everything that Our Dear Lord assigned for next Monday." Geneva was an important point of arrival and departure during Rilke's last journeys. Once he postponed his departure from this city day after day ("Geneva was never before so beautiful . . ."). On the Lake between Geneva and Lausanne lies the little town of Saint-Prex. Rilke fell in love with it and preferred it to all other places of that neighborhood. At the sight of it he felt a deep calm and, after a rhapsodic description of "an old cloister-like building and a row of houses with expansive gardens which open towards a beautiful beach at the end," he tells us how he loved to sit "there in front of this wall emotionally stirred . . ."

Even before Rilke visited Berg, he had traveled through the mountainous Valais, which reminded him of Spain and Provence. He said about the Rhone Valley: "My image of Switzerland has been immensely enriched since I have known *this* landscape: the vastness of this valley absorbing an entire flatland, the remoteness of its mountain slopes which are quite open despite their mass and steepness, the beautifully picturesque gradation of the hills in front of the mountains and the inimitable loveliness of their settlements leading up to the towers of their castles—all this is organized in a way which nowhere denies its large scale—beautiful like a pure talent and all the time at all places wonderfully executed."

It was there, in Muzot, that Rilke discovered a medieval-looking tower offered for sale. Werner Reinhart, the patron of literature and art, bought this little castle for Rilke and installed him there permanently. A few pieces were added to the seventeenth-century furniture on the two floors which the poet used. There he stayed to the end of his life. There he returned from each short trip. And there he wrote some of his most mature works. (Did writing by candlelight give some of his lines a touch of obscurity?) This medieval ivory tower surrounded by the momentous landscape of the Valais was the inspiring background for his cycles of *Sonnets to Orpheus*. There he completed *The Dionysian Elegies* and gave Paul Valéry's poems their Rilkean imprint in German. And as if the many-tongued country had permeated the poet's mind—or his mind the country—he briefly abandoned his mother tongue to write French poems, the *Quatrains Valaisans*, a paean to his new environment. These poems ecstatically expressed how much the experience of the landscape meant to him. "After all," he wrote, "no one is obliged to know (isn't it so?) what importance the great Swiss hospitality would gradually assume for the continuation of my life and work after those years of deepest bewilderment and interruption . . ." While living in Muzot, Rilke wished to apply for Swiss citizenship and to use the *Quatrains Valaisans* as evidence of his feelings for the country ("I cannot prove better that I have this country in *my blood*, and I hope that this will be sufficiently convincing for the authorities who will have to decide on my application").

In the last stages of his constantly deteriorating health, Rilke became aware of a cancer condition. Two Zürich physicians he consulted tried to reassure him, but when he returned to his retreat in Muzot he made his last will in which, among other things, he asked:

> . . . I prefer to be buried in the high situated churchyard next to the old church of Raron. Its enclosure belongs to the first places where I received wind and light of this landscape together with all the promises which later it helped to realize for me with and in Muzot.

On February 28, 1927, Rainer Maria Rilke died, a victim of leukemia. As he desired, he was buried in the churchyard of Raron.

Another literary giant of this century, James Joyce, came to Switzerland on his long and tiring odyssey with the outbreak of hostilities of the First World War. He had been living in Trieste for some time, and the Austrian government gave him permission to leave this city under the condition that he settle in a neutral country and give his word of honor to take no sides in the conflict.

Joyce came to Zürich on June 21, 1915. "I have just arrived here from Trieste after a rather adventurous time," he wrote a few days later from the Gasthof Hoffnung, Reitergasse 16, his very first address in Zürich. The lines were addressed to Harriet Shaw Weaver, who played a major part in Joyce's career. "The Austrian authorities were kind enough to give me a permit to the Swiss frontier when the partial evacuation of the city [Trieste] was ordered by the military command. I stopped here as it is the first big city after the frontier. I do not know where I shall live in Switzerland. Possibly here . . ."

By then Joyce had started on his monumental work, *Ulysses*, and the greatest part of this landmark book was written in Switzerland. At that time—as much as during World War II—Switzerland was the cultural storehouse for all of Europe, but it was also a center of espionage and a battlefield of international intrigue. Preoccupied with his work and with his first attack of glaucoma about a year after his arrival, Joyce kept his promise of total neutrality, which was also manifest by his obvious disinterest in politics. He made the acquaintance of some of the leading literary people in Zürich, among them Stefan Zweig, but he met neither Lenin nor Romain Rolland, who were both politically active in Switzerland during the war years—Rolland searching for ways to peace, Lenin biding his time before leading the second greatest revolution in memory. But undoubtedly Joyce was at Hugo Ball's Cabaret Voltaire, and of course it is interesting to speculate that the creator of Leopold Bloom was present at the birth of Dadaism. Essentially, he devoted his time in Zürich to his writing. Through a delicate manipulation of Miss Weaver, Rockefeller's daughter was instrumental in making it possible for Joyce to finish his work.

However, the going was slow. Difficulties with his sight complicated his already slow working habits. Early in 1917 he wrote to Miss Weaver: ". . . I am still under doctor's care and rather depressed that the eye attack—possibly on account of the infamous weather—is lasting so long . . . I can read and write however and am continuing my book at the usual snail's pace . . ." And in August of the same year, Mrs. Joyce reported to Miss Weaver that her husband was recovering slowly after the difficult operation. Joyce went to Locarno to convalesce, where he stayed at the Pension Villa Rossa and later at the Pension Daheim. In spite of his condition he continued to work and sent the first part of *Ulysses* to Ezra Pound from Locarno.

Joyce traveled very little while in Switzerland. As soon as his condition permitted, he went back to Zürich, where he wrote to Mademoiselle Guillermet on February 28, 1919: ". . . Perhaps one day I shall go to Geneva. I never go anywhere, it seems, unless somebody fetches me to a train and locks me into a compartment with a ticket . . ."

At the end of hostilities he went immediately back to Trieste because, as he said in one of his letters, "Life is cheaper here than in Switzerland . . .". In October 1934 he returned to Zürich for a very short visit, but it was only then that he first drove around the lake to Rapperswil where he had tea, as if he were a tourist. He also took the time to renew contact with some of his Zürich friends. This brief stay later bore fruit. While in Paris he wrote in a letter on March 8, 1938: ". . . I sent you an article by Mrs. Giedion in the Zürich Weltwoche. It seems they are going to print four others on me and Zürich and on me and music etc. and some people told me I am going to be made *Ehrenbürger* . . . (honorary citizen)."

In September 1938 he was in Lausanne and wrote to his Italian collaborator Paul Ruggiero: "We shall be in Zürich by the end of October . . . ," but he went to Paris instead, where the outbreak of war surprised him. With many others he fled to Southern France and wrote to Ruggiero from near Vichy in August 1940: "We are planning to go to Zürich all of us together. I have written to the Swiss legation asking for our permits. Are there many people staying in Zürich? Is it possible to get a flat and what is life like there? Another question: Is there a French school where German is also taught? As you see, history repeats itself."

Paul Ruggiero made strenuous efforts to help Joyce and his family to settle in Switzerland, but "the Swiss authorities," as Joyce wrote to James Johnson Sweeney, "when considering the application would require a guarantee in Switzerland amounting for me and my family to Fr. Swiss 50,000. . . ." On November 23, 1940, after his situation became more desperate, Joyce wrote to Louis Gillet: "Here is the situation. The Swiss, having finally discovered that I am not a jew from Judea, but an aryan of Erin, have requested a bank deposit and guarantee of 500,000 FF. This was done. They put 200,000 F in my name in a Zürich bank and they guaranteed a collateral of 300,000 F. The Swiss next demanded a detailed declaration of my personal fortune. This was done also, and we are waiting . . .".

On December 1, 1940, Joyce could finally write to Ruggiero: "The visas arrived in Vichy yesterday . . .". Soon afterwards Joyce left for Zürich, and on December 20 he wrote to the Mayor of the city in his best German: "Upon my arrival here a few days ago I learned that you were kind enough to add the weight of your influential recommendation to my request to the authorities for an entry permit, with the result that permission to reside in Zürich has now been granted to me and my family. The connection between me and your hospitable city extends over a period of nearly forty years and in these painful times I feel highly honored that I should owe my presence here in large part to the personal guaranty of Zürich's first citizen."

When Joyce arrived in Zürich, he was a very sick man. He had to undergo surgery for an intestinal ulcer and died about a month after his arrival, on January 13, 1941. He was buried in the Flünntern cemetery in Zürich.

Many intellectuals of this century have learned to live between nations and hemispheres, to have several passports of countries that wished to claim them as their own or which they desired to claim as theirs. Home and home country lost significance as symbols for roots and gained the notion of something abstract in the frightful shifting caused by cataclysmic events. Early in his life Hermann Hesse chose to detach himself from the doubtful connotations of what is considered Germanic, and Thomas Mann was taught a historic lesson the hard way. Both, using the German idiom, grew beyond all boundaries into the creative sphere of a supra-nationality. Both, in their ways, felt strongly attached to Switzerland.

Thomas Mann spent the summer of 1947 in Europe. On his return to the United States, the passport official asked him: "Are you *the* Thomas Mann? Welcome home!" Mann wrote about this incident to Hesse and added: "Well, yes—home. One can say so. Actually what 'home' is I no longer really know, after all, I have never known it." But hardly two months had passed between the writing of this letter and his European sojourn, and Mann wrote: "Europe lies so far back already. Like a dream to which I often and lovingly hold on to in my thoughts, particularly to the renewed contact with Switzerland, to meeting you again."

1933 was the year in which Hitler seized power, a year that separated men with convictions and a touch of humanity from their "home." After a short trip to France, Thomas Mann and his family moved to Zürich, where they stayed until September 1938. Mann, whose maternal grandparents were Swiss, wrote to Hesse in July 1933 that they ought "to look for something definite at once and to turn to Zürich. Since I am going to lose my German citizenship, I will become a Swiss, I suppose . . .".

The next letter addressed to Hesse came from Küsnacht near Zürich, speaking in the main of the tremendous success his daughter Erika had had with her literary Cabaret, *Die Pfeffermühle*, in the Altstadt of Zürich, not far from where the Cabaret Voltaire once introduced Dadaism to the world. In contrast to the World War I atmosphere, the actors of *Die Pfeffermühle* clearly spelled out their satires and political barbs. In Mann's words, dated Küsnacht 3.1.34: ". . . The main fun is the colossal success with which Erika reopened her literary cabaret here the day before yesterday. I enjoy it more than the aproval which my novel may find, a sign of growingly friendly abdication in favor of the young . . .".

Mann was then working on his monumental work of the Biblical legend of Joseph. In the summer of 1937 an attack of gout brought him to the Swiss spa Ragaz. "I've never been sick and try very hard not to be insulted too much," he wrote on a postcard to Hesse, who celebrated his 60th birthday that year on July 2. To Hesse's surprise the *Neue Zürcher Zeitung* carried a congratulatory article by Thomas Mann that day, saying among other things:

> I also love the man and the human being in him, his serenely contemplative, roguish-kind way, the deep beautiful look of his unfortunately sick eyes whose blue lights up the lean and sharply profiled face of an old Swabian peasant. I came to know him personally much closer only four years ago when, under the first shock after the loss of country, home and hearth, I was often in his lovely Ticino house and garden. How I envied him then!—not only for his safety in freedom, but mainly for all the advantage he had over me in having gained mental freedom so much earlier, in his absolute philosophic distantiation from all German politics . . . There was nothing more comforting and wholesome in those confused days than speaking to him.

In September 1938, Thomas Mann and his family moved to the United States, stayed at Princeton first, then fell in love with the climate and landscape of Southern California, which reminded them of the Ticino. Even though they built a beautiful home in the Pacific Palisades, the European in Mann was stronger than any attempt on his part to adjust to the American way of being.

It was at that time that I met him in California, and I still remember how in our conversaions his thoughts returned to Europe and the past time and again, how the growing political darkness made him fear for everyone and everything he left behind. "I fear— if fear is the right word—that this will be a long, dragged-out process now set in motion and that when the waters will have receded there will be a Europe changed to the point of unrecognizability so that there will hardly be a question of returning home, even if physically possible," he wrote Hesse in 1941. How strong were his ties to Europe and particularly to Switzerland is revealed in another passage in that same letter: "I wish these lines of thanks may be in your hands at any possible time to tell you how often our thoughts are with you and Switzerland in general which had bound us up so cordially for five years."

How often does it happen that we realize flaws in someone's features which, however, do not detract from our feelings for the person. It only proves the onlooker to be as human as the beloved object. We cannot help loving because of something as much as in spite of it. In July 1941, Thomas Mann wrote another letter to Hesse, from the Pacific Palisades in California:

> Dear Mr. Hesse, a letter from Switzerland and from you gives me much joy. You can't imagine with which intensity I pull out such a letter with the Helvetia stamp from among those stupid, long American envelopes and give it preference over all other things. Strangely enough, the *Schwyzers* have not at all behaved particularly nice towards all of us who were without a fatherland and not on good terms with our government. Yet the five years of my life spent there have made me feel so heartily attached to the country that thinking of it looks to me like homesickness.

In 1947 Thomas Mann decided not to return to Germany for good. ("That I won't go back there is a foregone conclusion for some time now. I told the gentlemen in Munich that inner and outer reasons prevent me from doing so.") It was a complicated problem for him, fraught with ambivalent feelings. The awareness that he and the Germans had gone different ways weighed heavily. But the outside pressures on him were strong, receiving, as he did, invitations from Frankfurt and Munich. ("My confusion is great since these possibilities opened up. I have not yet assented, but I will probably have to do it, and my quietude is gone. I suppose I should not take it so difficult, but I cannot help feeling this *Wiedersehen* after sixteen years of estrangement as a ghostlike adventure and a real trial.")

Almost year after year Thomas Mann journeyed to Europe, often lecturing here and there, and always spending some time in Zürich. He became visibly tired of crossing the Atlantic so often. "I'll be glad to be on board ship and I have my secret doubts whether I'll give in again and renew the dance next May (which would be in eight months only). Switzerland of course I would miss," he wrote Hesse and, remembering one of his last and lasting impressions: "Well, it is a charming country, and the other day crossing the Alps when we drove in the car to Stresa made a deep impression on me." And, alluding to Hannibal's crossing of the Alps during the Second Punic War in 218 B.C.: "How did they manage it with the elephants at that time?" And his next thought jumped to his lectures in Switzerland: "If one comes from far away and not too often, one also receives many *Fränkli.*"

On July 1, 1949, he told Hesse: "Next May, life and good health provided, we will be back again because I wish to spend my 75th birthday in Zürich . . .". And again in the spring of the following year, a letter reached Hesse from America: "I will or am supposed to fly to Paris in the beginning of May on the occasion of the French edition of *Doctor Faustus,* however I yield to the pressure only because I long for a few months in Switzerland. Before the middle of May we will then be in the Ticino and visit you." But he arrived a few days later:

> Baur au Lac   17.V.1950
> Dear Hermann Hesse, ... Last night we arrived in our little car from Paris, and I cannot tell you how sheltered I feel in this former home of mine which somehow remained to be a home . . ."

Two years later the decision was made, and Thomas Mann moved with his family from California to Zürich. They arrived in Erlenbach on Christmas Eve, 1952. In January of the following year, Hesse wrote him: "I wish you would soon again have the feeling of being sheltered and at home! My thoughts about you are gayer since I know you in Erlenbach." In March 1954, Hesse received a note from Mann:

.... I don't write you from Erlenbach. I am in the Waldhaus Dolder whereto I escaped from the horrors of our moving to Kilchberg which in the main is directed by Erika. We bought there quite a nice reasonable house: Alte Landstrasse 39—my final address, so I hope. In my later years there was a bit too much wandering about.

The following year, 1955, started as a year of celebration. It was the eightieth birthday of Thomas Mann. He went to Stuttgart and Weimar in May, to celebrate the 150th anniversary of Friedrich Schiller's death, and in both cities he was guest of honor and delivered the key address. A few days later he traveled to his native town Lübeck, which bestowed upon him honorary citizenship. On June 10 he wrote to Hesse:

The dear world and, above all, dear Switzerland have done everything to turn my head but there are quite a few healthy forces of resistance. I had most *fun* with the "doctorate of the natural sciences" which the E.T.H. awarded me in imaginative way. That at least is something new and original. Between you and me, I'll also be a Swiss citizen very soon via the Kilchberg community. The Federal Council seems to be willing to have it take place outside all routine which was also indicated by the fact that Petitpierre [at that time President] joined our celebration in Conrad Ferdinand Meyer's house and delivered a speech in German with the most charming French accent.

Soon after these celebrations, Thomas Mann fell ill and had to be brought to the Kantonsspital in Zürich, where he died from a thrombosis on August 12. Hesse, at that time staying at Sils Maria, wrote a farewell note published in the *Neue Zürcher Zeitung:*

In deep mourning I take leave of Thomas Mann, the dear friend and great colleague, the master of German prose, who was not enough appreciated despite all honors and success. What stood behind his irony and virtuosity, a heart, a faithfulness, responsibility and the ability to love, for decades not at all perceived by

the huge German public, all this, his work and the memory of
him, will keep alive long beyond our confused times.

CASTALIA

SWITZERLAND happened to Hermann Hesse (1877–1962) as
much as Hesse happened to Switzerland. Relationships usually come
about through a thousand and one coincidences. One can rarely
say that they were destined to happen and to grow as an organic
part of our lives. One can say it about Hesse's relationship to
Switzerland.

"If there would be more people who have such deep contempt
for boundaries of countries as I have, then there would no longer
be wars or blockades. There is nothing more spiteful than frontiers,
nothing more stupid." These are some of the opening sentences
with which Hesse's book *Wanderung (Wanderings)* begins. He
tried to present himself as "a nomad, not a peasant. I am an admirer of unfaithfulness, of the change, of fantasy." He realized
that one cannot be poet and burgher, searcher and keeper at the
same time.

But in many ways he was both poet and searcher as well as
keeper of the past. Burgher he never was. However, hidden in his
deepest "within," his relationship to the soil, his desire to belong
was as strong as his need to live close to nature and to feed his
soul with its beauty. When he almost simultaneously discovered
the painter in himself and the landscape of the Ticino—he was
then about forty years old—he wrote: "When I draw or paint the
Ticino landscape I always have a feeling of gratitude and joy as
if painting would be an attempt at expressing something of my
love and gratitude for this lovely land."

In 1919 Hesse moved from Berne, where he had lived for seven
years, to Montagnola near Lugano. For some time he stayed at the
Casa Camuzzi where many pictures were painted and some of his
greatest works were written: *Klingsor's Last Summer, Siddhartha,
The Steppenwolf,* and *Narciss and Goldmund.* In 1931 his friend
and patron Hans C. Bodmer built a house for him overlooking
Lake Lugano. It was a gift for lifetime.

Was it the peasant or the poet in Hesse who not only felt the
need of replenishing his enthusiasm with the sight and fragrance
of the landscape but also desired to grow with the seasons and
touch the soil on which he lived? Hesse then wrote:

To be at home somewhere, to love a piece of land and to till it, not only to look at it and paint it, but to participate in the modest happiness of peasants and herdsmen, in the Virgilian rhythm of the rustic calendar, unchanged through two thousand years, that seemed to me to be a beautiful, enviable lot, even though I had once tasted of it and experienced that it does not suffice to make me happy.

And lo, this sweet lot should once more happen to me. It fell into my lap like a ripe chestnut would fall on the hat of the wanderer. He only has to open and eat it. Against all my expectations I have become settled once more and own a piece of land, not as my possession but as a lifelong tenancy! Just now we had our house built on this land and moved in, and now began for me once more a stretch of peasant life, known to me from many remembrances . . .

Through Hesse's romantic simplicity, behind which hides weighty meaning, runs an important keyword: Nature. It already plays a great part in his first novel, *Peter Camenzind*, which, written in Basle in 1904, made him famous. This story is as autobiographical as most of the other stories of Hesse. Camenzind expresses the wish to write a great work, "in order to bring today's man closer to the magnificence of silent nature and to make him love it."

Three years later, in 1907, Hesse got to know the Italian part of Switzerland more thoroughly, and from then on he longed to live there, as if he had found his predestined home country or a desired asylum, as he said. He felt the Ticinese landscape, with its vineyards and churches, to be like the touch of a gentle hand reminding him of maternal proximity and warmth, of a more childlike, simpler, gayer state of being.

Hermann Hesse was born in Calw, a small place in Württemberg. At that time his father was still a Russian subject. When Hermann was four, his family settled in Basle for five years, and they all became Swiss citizens. When they returned to Calw, young Hesse applied for German citizenship in order to be able to attend the Gymnasium. In 1899 he returned to Basle and worked as an apprentice in a bookstore. There he also married Maria Bernoulli of the famous Swiss family of mathematicians.

His success with *Peter Camenzind* enabled Hesse to live on his writings. He moved to Gaienhofen with his family, near the Swiss border on Lake Constance, but then settled in Berne in 1912, from where he went to the Ticino seven years later. Moving back and

forth, thinking nothing of opting for German citizenship in order
to be admitted at a school, only proves that it meant little to him
to which country he belonged. As a German writer he felt allegiance to the language rather than to the country, and he stayed
in the region to which he was then attached and which he proudly
describes as Alemannic.

When he asked for Swiss citizenship in 1923, it was a very
conscious act, expressing his disillusionment with Germany's political maturity. Moreover, he thought that "here in Helvetia we have
a wonderful, exemplary constitution." In a letter written on November 3, 1945, he said: ". . . When in the years after the first World
War, I saw how almost unanimously the whole of Germany sabo-
taged its republic and showed that it had not learned the least, it
was easy for me to become a Swiss citizen. This I felt I could not
have done during the war, despite my condemnation of German
power policy. In one of my books [The Steppenwolf] I have then
projected fearfully my warning of the coming of a second World
War, but I was only sneered at with a friendly laugh . . ."

In many of his works Hesse made it abundantly clear that the
world was his home, and that his only interest was in man. His
protagonists run amuck through the various layers of their sub-
conscious in longing to free themselves from their inner chaos and
find oneness with fate, a oneness of all being. Throughout his entire work we encounter the struggle of lonely man with the problems of existence and the yearning for new meaningfulness in an
age that has lost its bearings. Hesse always counteracted the
exuberant and puerile facets of romanticism with knowing rationality and an overactive consciousness.

There was something of an idyllist and a great deal of an ascetic
in him. But although he carried his own monastery with him
wherever he went, he never left the world of reality. Hesse the
belligerent nonconformist, the fighter for a just cause, is less well
known. In 1915 when Romain Rolland moved to Switzerland to
write and work for a "union sacrée de l'esprit européen," Hesse—
whose letters to Rolland belong to the best documents expressing
his political viewpoint—was with him in this fight. Hesse was
convinced of the necessity of such a union of the European spirit
which, as he wrote, "would soon grow mightily." In August of that
year the two men met in Switzerland. They fought together with
little chance for the immediate realization of a great dream.

Hesse literally suffered from the thought that senseless hatred
dominates the world. He even rebuked his friend Rolland in a

letter dated January 15, 1932, for using the expression "huns" with regard to the Germans in one of Rolland's essays on the war: "The expression 'huns' is not worthy of you, my revered friend, and it would fit just as well a few excesses committed by your own countrymen. Men are beasts if no star watches over them, but we must not reproach a single people for having a monopoly on beastliness." In 1933, when the Nazis seized power, Hesse's books were not burnt, but he was publicly vilified and branded as a traitor. He protested against the "brutal, bloodthirsty stupidity of the people," and all of a sudden there was no longer any paper to be had in Germany to print his books. His *opus magnum, Das Glasperlenspiel (The Glass Bead Game,* mistakenly translated as *Magister Ludi),* had to be published in Switzerland.

In 1938, at a time when the country was threatened to be overrun and divided, Hesse addressed his Swiss countrymen admonishingly:

> The federation has come about under the pressure of necessities, and through centuries it withstood many menaces from without and within. Those from within always were the more dangerous ones, and so it is today. Misguided by foreign fashions, some of our fellow citizens call the form of our democracy outmoded and our ideals dead . . . The rejuvenation which Switzerland needs, is, above all, a rejuvenation of the hearts, even more an awakening to reality, an opening of the eyes for the abysses which surround us . . .

Despite his despair, he never gave up his belief in man. In a letter written in that very same year, he said: "I believe in man as a wonderful possibility which even in the deepest mire does not perish and which permits him to re-emerge from the greatest dehumanization, and I think this possibility is so strong and so tempting that, time and again, it makes itself felt as hope and challenge . . ." Hesse remained a man of principle, deaf to the noise of the world, never deviating from his path of aloneness and meditation, untouched by the vanity of vanities. When, in 1954, a Chinese asked for permission to translate his books, he replied: "Today's China has forbidden Confucius and Lao Tse, or at least stigmatized them as undesirable, and in a country that at this moment of its history cannot bear its own classics I would not like to see any of my books translated."

However, he owed much to the Chinese. They taught him the

secret art of expressing morsels of wisdom with deceptively simple, but poetic, means. In many ways his *Weltanschauung* was closer to the East than to the Western world. He was attuned to the Zen spirit of Eternal Loneliness as no other European writer. He stood aloof with the need of someone who knew he could only grow in his magnificent aloneness.

Switzerland, in its sheltered isolation, offered a seemingly ready-made framework for Hesse's desire to live a life in its most private, mystic fashion. But beyond feeding his own needs, he came to see in Switzerland the country closest to his utopian conception of what he described in *The Glass Bead Game* as Castalia, whose inhabitants are an elite of cognoscenti, of knowing people combining Western and Eastern wisdom. Their lives running along a mystic-aesthetic path enable them to achieve a mellowed philosophy, detached from the irrelevances of daily living, and reconciling man's probing mind and most humane soul. This great work containing Hesse's final thoughts was written at a time when Switzerland seemed to have been the last and almost lost island in a power-drunk and war-mad world. It cannot be maintained that Hesse's Castalia is the mirror reflection, however blurred, of Switzerland. Hesse criticized the one-sidedness of a sheltered, esoteric life ("No noble and exalted life exists . . . without knowledge of devils and demons, and without continual struggle against them."). On the other hand, the flowering beauty of Castalian existence—the utopia of a relatively humane republic, enviously protected by the elite of its order, a world in which music and mysticism, Mozart and Lao Tse dominate rules and rulers—has certain features of that Switzerland which, as a heightened dream image, Hesse partly saw and partly wished it to be.

If Switzerland has been destined to be home for the spiritually homeless, then we can easily understand and accept that a higher destiny willed it to have men such as Rainer Maria Rilke and Friedrich Nietzsche (1844–1900) find their homes there. Through the humanistic atmosphere of Basle or in the valleys and on the heights of the Engadin moved the haunting image of *Zarathustra*, the growing silhouette of a lonesome wanderer through a tortured life. In his happiest moments, Nietzsche liked to refer to himself as "the hermit of Sils Maria."

Erich Heller pointed out in *The Disinherited Mind* that there were "as many striking differences between Rilke and Nietzsche as definite similarities. They were both uprooted and homeless. *'Wer jetzt kein Haus hat, baut sich keines mehr'* [He who has no house now will no longer build one], writes the one, and the other: *'Weh dem, der keine Heimat hat!'* [Woe to him who has no home!]" If both were uprooted and lonely men, they seem to have needed the freedom of a vacuum in order to re-create out of their own denials of the reality around them a higher reality in which the Nietzschean "will to illusion" could triumph; to re-create out of their private agonies an impersonal world of universal meaning in an almost compulsive need to triumph over themselves.

Nietzsche studied at the universities of Bonn and Leipzig. Wilhelm Vischer, member of a well-known academic dynasty in Basle, read a few essays Nietzsche had written at that time. He liked them and offered the twenty-four-year-old Nietzsche a professorship. His own *alma mater* sent a letter of recommendation which underlined the fortes of the young Nietzsche and closed with the words: "He can do anything he wants to." He was appointed professor of classic philology at the University of Basle and soon afterwards became a Swiss citizen. When the Franco-German War broke out in 1870, he wanted to be a part of the Prussian army. As a Swiss subject, he could serve only as a medical orderly. He took a leave of absence from the University but fell sick accompanying the first transport of wounded soldiers and returned to Basle.

Nietzsche came to the city of Jacob Burckhardt, the great historian, and Franz Overbeck (1837–1905), an agnostic in a church-historian's clothes. Overbeck was a great Biblical scholar, regarded by Karl Barth as the forerunner of dialectical theology. With his unorthodox beliefs, he was Nietzsche's brother in spirit, and they became close friends. Nietzsche often longed for a word of understanding that would give comfort to his mind. He found it with Overbeck, but rarely with Burckhardt, who usually reacted to the fiery spirit of Nietzsche's work with cautiousness and a touch of irony. Only *Beyond Good and Evil* seems to have found favor in his eyes.

The early 1870's were the years of Nietzsche's Wagner admiration. At that time Richard Wagner lived with his family at Triebschen, near Lucerne. He appreciated Nietzsche's rhapsodic enthusiasm for his ideas and works, as expressed in Nietzsche's first book, *Die Geburt der Tragödie aus dem Geiste der Musik (The Birth of Tragedy From the Spirit of Music,* 1872), and his

Unzeitgemässe Betrachtungen (Untimely Meditations, 1873–76). Of these essays Wagner particularly liked the last one: "Richard Wagner in Bayreuth."

By mere chance Nietzsche was a guest in the composer's house the night his only son Siegfried was born. Nietzsche's sister was also invited to witness the close relationship between the poet-philosopher and the poet-composer. She stayed with them in Triebschen at one time, on "the island of the blessed," and described one of the many walks they all took together in the evenings:

> The aim of our walk was the hermitage, a house built of bark, situated on the highest point of the estate and offering in bright moonlight a precious view far across the lake and its surrounding chain of mountains . . . Gradually the spell of silence was broken; Wagner, Cosima and my brother began to talk of the tragedy of human life, of the Greeks, the Germans, of plans and wishes. Never, neither before nor after, have I found the same wonderful harmony in the conversation of three so different human beings; each of them had his own note, his own theme, and stressed them with all vigor, and yet what perfect harmony! Each of these individual natures was at its height, shone in its own splendor and yet none darkened the other.

As long as Nietzsche was of use to Wagner as his apostle and literary errand boy, everything went smoothly. He trusted Nietzsche and gave him the manuscript of his autobiography to read, which at first was scheduled to be printed in twelve copies only. But whenever Nietzsche deviated from Wagner's concepts, he showed little patience and sympathy. When Wagner left Switzerland to exchange the role of the lonely genius of Triebschen with that of the master of Beyreuth, their break was inevitable. Nietzsche came to detest Wagner's chauvinism, anti-Semitism, and his obeisance to Christianity, which found its apotheosis in *Parsifal.* Nietzsche considered it an insincere idealization of "pure foolishness." On the other hand, Nietzsche's *Menschliches, Allzumenschliches (Human, All-Too-Human,* 1878), with a motto by Voltaire, was rejected by the composer.

A year later Nietzsche fell severely ill. Attack after attack set in; he was plagued by headaches, eye pains, and vomiting. He had to give up teaching, but thanks to the generosity of the University of Basle, his pension sufficed to help him make ends meet.

His sister took him to the Engadin. In Sils Maria he found the landscape and climate that "returned me to life," he said. He was happy "in this constantly sunny October air, this waggish playfulness of the wind wafting from morning into night, this pure light and moderate coolness, the utterly lovely, serene character of hills, lakes and woods on this plateau." He needed a comforting and inspiring environment and recognized his very being in the reflection of this landscape.

The next ten years were years of restlessness, sickness, and incredible productivity, as if his entire system had been alerted and made aware of the deadline of his existence. Whether he left Sils Maria for a sojourn to Italy or to Germany, he always returned to the Engadin, to an environment that had hidden healing and creative powers for him. On August 14, 1881, he wrote his friend, the musician Peter Gast: ". . . I accepted as a reward that this year gave me two things which belong and are very close to me: Your music and this landscape."

A heightened sensibility and receptivity towards nature, towards a certain environment and climate, played a great part in his life. He discovered the ability to "absorb and retain landscape images deep within him. The representation of historic pictures, the human being in motion remains eternally remote from me." Human beings were of little interest to him, they were inconstant, fleeting realizations, but a landscape was the expression of nature's will, it inspired him to make it the scene of *his* creative will. In 1884 he wrote to Overbeck: "Indeed, who can feel with me what it means to feel with every shred of one's being that the weight of all things must be defined anew."

However, during these ten years in which he redefined many things, he tried desperately to break through the walls of his solitude. He admitted in a letter addressed to Overbeck: "I need a young person in my proximity who is intelligent and sufficiently learned to be able to work with me. I would not mind concluding a two-year-marriage pact for this purpose." The young lady he had in mind was Lou Salomé, who later became Rilke's beloved and, still later, one of Freud's devoted disciples and friends. Lou had studied philosophy and art history at the University of Zürich. Nietzsche had met her in Rome, and when he realized that she did not want to live with him in any illicit or legalized relationship, he tried to give their friendship a purely spiritual feeling.

Nietzsche, who wrote that "A married philosopher belongs to a comedy," proposed marriage to a number of women he hardly knew and was always relieved when rejected. But he saw in Lou a person of kindred spirit and a potential disciple. He even wrote his sister: "Could you not come to Switzerland and invite this young lady?" But nothing materialized. In Lucerne, where she said no to Nietzsche, he insisted on being photographed with her and his friend Paul Rée. Nietzsche staged the scene: Lou on top of a cart pulled by the two men. He intended to show how the two philosophers would put their strength into the service of the young lady driving them on with inspiration. The poet-philosopher who once wrote that man should not forget his whip when going to the woman, requested a whip for Lou which she might crack over his head. He was desperate in his loneliness.

"Truth is ugly . . . We have Art in order not to perish of Truth." And he continued to write one work after the other. He remained alone in his ecstasy as well as in his despair. After ten years, in 1889, he suffered a total breakdown and remained insane until he died.

It may be difficult for us to associate Frank Wedekind (1864–1918) with Switzerland, but here are some facts and figures.

When Benjamin Franklin Wedekind attended the Gymnasium in Aarau, he was known as the boy from San Francisco. His schoolmates took him for someone who had come from the Wild West and not for the German boy who was born in Hannover. And when he went to Lausanne for further studies four years later, he still traveled on an American passport.

His father had left Germany after the lost revolution in 1848 to practice medicine in California. There he met a young girl who had grown up in Riesbach near Zürich. She was then only twenty years old and had four years of an insecure life as a singer behind her. Dr. Wedekind treated her when she came to San Francisco. Both felt shipwrecked, and they subsequently married and returned to Europe. They settled in Hannover, but Dr. Wedekind, an ardent democrat and admirer of George Washington and Benjamin Franklin, felt very unhappy in Bismarck's prussianized Germany. While on vacation in Switzerland, he found the castle Lenzburg near Aarau for sale and bought it. In the fall of 1872, when Frank was eight years of age, the Wedekind family settled there.

Thus, Frank Wedekind grew up in Switzerland, and it was here that he received his first recognition and encouragement by the Zürich circle of poet friends to which Gerhart and Carl Hauptmann belonged. It was in Zürich that his very first play was published, *Der Schnellmaler* (*The Blitz Painter*), followed by his then sensational drama, *Frühlingserwachen* (*Spring's Awakening*), written in 1890 and one year later issued by the Zürich publisher Jean Gross.

Frank seemed to have accepted his family's residence in Aarau as his own headquarters, from where he strayed away as early as he could. His entire outlook on life was, in every aspect, diametrically opposed to any rustic or bourgeois existence. His parents wanted him to study law, so he went to Munich where he found the bohemian atmosphere without which he could not live. He studied life and literature far more intensely than law and was determined to become a writer.

His parents first learned about their son's literary ambitions when the *Neue Zürcher Zeitung* reported on a celebration of the Swiss colony in Munich, occasioned by the commemoration of the five-hundredth anniversary of the battle of Sempach. Wedekind wrote and spoke an apparently rhymed, patriotic prologue for this festivity—a work that was lost—about which the *Neue Zürcher Zeitung* said: "The law student Wedekind harvested roaring applause for the fiery recitation of the prologue from his own pen and thus earned a well-deserved recognition of his eminently poetic talent."

In the same year, 1886, his father withdrew his support when he learned that Frank had wasted a whole year of his studies. The young poet moved to Zürich, where he worked as an advertising manager for the Maggi concern for some time, and wrote for newspapers, but a reconciliation with his father enabled him to pursue his writing career while dividing his stay between Lenzburg and Zürich. It was an important period of inner growth and outside stimulation for Wedekind, who also continued his studies at the Zürich University.

When his father died in 1888, his share in the family fortune made it possible for him to devote all his time to writing. By then Wedekind was well known in the literary circles in Zürich, and it was here that the first productions of this controversial dramatist took place. In September 1900, the year in which Wedekind decided to move to Munich, the Pfauentheater in Zürich premiered his *Liebestrank* (*Love Potion*), and the Stadttheater, during its twenty-year-long Alfred Reucker era, made Wedekind acceptable to the Zürich audience.

Basically, Wedekind's attitude towards life was that of a revolutionary who, in his plays, tried to reveal bourgeois morality in its extreme hypocrisy and absurdity, as an evil poisoning the hearts of the young people. Accusing society of being insensitive to the natural instincts in man, he painted dramatic pictures of a condemned and brutalized humanity. Thus, he preceded D. H. Lawrence in the struggle for sex liberation. But what is usually overlooked is Wedekind's pathos of moral conviction, the ethic and didactic basis from which this crusader proceeded to hold the proverbial mirror up to man's nature. It is this, and this alone, that Wedekind has in common with many Swiss writers.

Most of his mature years he spent in Munich, even though he returned to Switzerland time and again. The year before he died he stayed several months in the country, mainly in Basle, Davos, and Zürich, reading from his last play *Heracles* and acting, together with his wife Tilly, in some of his established plays. By then he had lost much of his physical vigor but nothing of his mental intensity.

As if he had known that he had only a few more months to live, he returned to the places where he began his life and career. In retrospect, this unconscious act appears like the sentimental gesture of a highly unsentimental writer.

The reasons for some of the greatest writers, painters, and actors to have settled in Switzerland and found their Castalia there are as manifold as their individual needs and concerns.

Vladimir Nabokov (1899–   ) established temporary residence in Montreux in 1959 in order to be near several members of his family, including his son Dmitri, who is pursuing an opera career in Italy. So the legend reads. Nabokov is a brilliant writer in several languages, which he masters to perfection. He has also lived temporarily in those countries whose languages he knows to the very roots of their etymology. It may be a matter of his private history that he left Russia to live in England, Germany, France, and the United States, but his journey to the West and finally to the Western hemisphere was compelled by the mood of world history rather than by his personal desires. It was due to the popular success of his novels that he could give up teaching at American colleges and devote all his time to literary work. As he once remarked facetiously, he is now kept by a little girl by the name of *Lolita*. That he chose Switzerland as his temporary residence has, as was said, geographic reasons. But this appears as too simple a reason for such a sophisticated mind as his. There seems to be something final about his temporary residence in Montreux.

The inner or spiritual reason—if there is such a thing—for Georges Simenon (1903–   ) to have finally settled near Lausanne was to find guaranteed seclusion in a land known for its internationally guaranteed seclusion. Now that he is getting older, he may need solitude in a larger dose in order to keep up his record of turning out three or four novels a year. While writing at such a rapid pace he has traveled a great deal, living for more than a decade in the United States and later in France. He once lived on a cutter, making long journeys of an exploring nature around the coasts of Northern Europe. Is living on a cutter not a symbolic gesture of desiring total isolation?

In the beginning of his writing career, Simenon published about 1,500 short stories. By now he has piled up close to 200 novels, a great many belonging to the Inspector Maigret series, all issued under his name. But since he also used seventeen pseudonyms in order to have his novels accepted by different publishers at the same time, the statistics may be all wrong. And so may be any attempt at trying to find out why Simenon settled in Switzerland. It cannot be because, as I have read somewhere, he enjoys swimming and golf. Only Inspector Maigret could help us there. But he is too busy working on more important cases.

Or is it as simple as Charlie Chaplin's (1889–   ) case? When he left the United States in 1952, angered by politicians and newspaper columnists who linked him with "subversive" causes, and pressed by the United States government for back taxes, he was not sure where to turn to. Then "a friend suggested Switzerland . . . with a tinge of melancholy we picked up our belongings and with the four children arrived in Switzerland." They found a suitable place near Vevey.

In *My Autobiography* Chaplin vividly pictures the estate into which he moved, with its five-acre lawn and tall trees "which frame the mountains and the lake in the distance . . ."

> Thus we came to live in the village of Corsier, which has a population of 1,350 . . . If we were not so preoccupied with our family, we could have quite a social life in Switzerland, for we live relatively near the Queen of Spain and the Count and Countess Chevreau d-Antraignes, who have been most cordial to us, and there are a number of film stars and writers who live near. We often see George and Benita Sanders, and Noel Coward is also

a neighbor. In the spring many of our American and English friends visit us. Truman Capote, who occasionally works in Switzerland, often drops by . . . Often on the spur of the moment we decide to go to London and Paris, sometimes to Venice or Rome—all within easy reach in a couple of hours.

Cutting his last ties from the United States was a particularly sad moment in his life, if for no other reason than that his phenomenal career as the world's greatest and most tragic clown was closely connected with the rise of the film industry in Hollywood. Dissolving all assets and obligations in the United States included dissolving their household and dismissing maid and butler. His former butler, who is a Swiss, wrote a farewell letter to the Chaplins in which he said among other things:

I have not written you for a long time as I have an awful time expressing myself correctly with my Swiss-English . . . I am happy to hear the children like Switzerland. Of course, for grown-up people it takes more time to get used to any foreign country. I do say Switzerland is one of the better ones. The best schools on the globe. Also the oldest republic on the globe . . . 1st of August is the 4th of July there. Independence Day. Not a holiday, but you will see the fires on all mountain tops. As a whole, one of the few conservative and prosperous countries. I left there in 1918 for South America. Have been back twice since. I also served two terms in the Swiss Army. Born in St. Gallen, eastern part of Switzerland. I have one younger brother in Berne and one in St. Gallen.

The very best wishes to all of you.

Respectfully yours,
Henry

At the end of his autobiography, Charlie Chaplin is no longer uncertain about his fortuitous choice of Switzerland as the place to be in and to observe, with a gratifying feeling of contentment, the approaching twilight hours.

I realize that time and circumstances have favoured me . . . Yes, the world has given me its best and little of its worst . . . I have no design for living, no philosophy—whether sage or fool, we must all struggle with life . . . Schopenhauer said happiness is a negative state—but I disagree . . . I sometimes sit out on our terrace at sunset and look over a vast green lawn to the lake in the distance, and beyond the lake to the reassuring mountains, and in this mood think of nothing, but enjoy their magnificent serenity.

Everyone seems to find his own Castalia in Switzerland. Oskar Kokoschka has his house in Villeneuve, not far from where Chaplin lives. He settled there when he was an older man who had established a world reputation in painting. More than practical reasons brought Noel Coward or Oskar Kokoschka there, even though the practical aspects may have weighed heavily in favor of it. In Kokoschka's case, remembrances of the past may have played a major part in his decision to live on the shore of the Lake of Geneva.

When Kokoschka was still a struggling artist defying convention and tradition, he was the protégé of the well-known Viennese architect Adolf Loos. Between 1908 and 1910 Kokoschka made several trips to the French part of Switzerland, where he was sent by Loos, and Kokoschka's greatest experience was the discovery of the mountain landscape. One of his famous early paintings, *Winter Landscape*, was done then and there. In 1909 Kokoschka went to Leysin to work there, but after a few months Loos forgot to send the money for his rent. Kokoschka then left for Montreux where Loos's friends gave him shelter and the opportunity to continue his feverish work on landscapes. But Loos did not forget to further this young artist in whom he strongly believed before anyone else recognized his great gift.

A year later, in 1910, he sent Kokoschka to Auguste Forel, the great Swiss psychiatrist and entomologist, who wrote about *The Ants of Switzerland* and made important contributions to *Hypnotism and Psychotherapy* and *The Sexual Problem*. This scientist whose study of the ants influenced his approach to psychiatry and who, as director of the cantonal asylum at Burghölzli, instituted humane methods of treatment and the use of occupational therapy, wrote years later in his autobiography, *Out of My Life and Work*, about his meeting with Kokoschka:

In January 1910 the modernistic painter, Kokoschka, then little known, came to me and asked if he might paint me. I told him that he could do so on condition that I did not have to buy the picture, and if I could work at my table as I pleased while he was painting me. This modern painter, who looked at me especially from behind and from the side, cared nothing for likeness, but only for the expression of moods! In point of fact, as the picture turned out, only one eye and the left disabled hand were particularly good and expressive . . . I did not buy the picture, but since the artist has achieved a very considerable success! *Mundus vult decipi, ergo decipiatur.* (The world wants to be deceived, so it may be deceived.)

Adolf Loos had introduced Kokoschka to Forel, who then lived in the Rhone Valley, in a letter, describing him as "the greatest artist of the future." Loos offered the Forel portrait, which has since become a classical example of the modern psychological approach to portrait painting, to the Museum in Berne for 200 francs. The offer was rejected.

The Lake of Geneva and Kokoschka are no strangers. A strong predilection for landscape painting characterizes Kokoschka's work, and this longing brought him back in 1924 for a few months, to a place near Vevey. He painted several pictures of the majestic mountains, seen from tower-perspective, with the vision of a twentieth-century man who sought to express the soul of the landscape and not its eye-fooling photographic image.

The number of those minor and major writers who have found the Italian part of Switzerland to be the most ideal Castalia is endless. Hermann Hesse's prose gave this dream its most articulate and colorful expression. Climate and landscape conspire to compose an atmosphere conducive to creativity, and many creative minds cannot escape the feeling of an almost mythological Arcadia. From Ludwig Berleth to Hugo Ball, from Walter Mehring to Hans Habe, they all have been attracted either by the inexpressible magic and the ideational concept of a realistic paradise, by possibly the best kind of isolation, or a *dolce far niente* existence.

Erich Maria Remarque (1898–1970) came to Porto Ronco near Ascona at a time when it was still a sleepy fishing village. It was shortly after his world success with *All Quiet on the Western Front*, published in 1929, that Remarque bought a house on the Lago Maggiore, to escape the growing threat and constantly swelling clamor of Nazism. He became an exile in 1938 when Hitler deprived him of his German citizenship. During World War II he lived in New York and became an American citizen. After the war he spent most of his years again on the Swiss shore of the Lago Maggiore, where he died in September 1970. He was buried in the village cemetery on top of the hills of Ronco overlooking the lake and landscape to which he had been attracted and attuned for forty years.

His house in Porto Ronco, built below the road and reaching from its terrace down to the lake, was a little museum. One Oriental rug was lying on top of another (Remarque was a great connoisseur of rugs), the walls were covered with paintings, mostly French impressionists, and the furniture was Venetian eighteenth century, a period in which he delighted. His Swiss villa was also a small select library and the place where he wrote most of his novels. He was a slow, painstaking writer. He often had a phonograph running while working; he loved music and had wanted to become a composer in his youth. Music stimulated and inspired him as much as the landscape.

From his first outcry against the brutality and stupidity of warfare, with his first novel, he never ceased to be alarmed by mankind's follies and madness. I came to know him while translating his *Arch of Triumph* and sat with him on many a summer day on his terrace in Porto Ronco.

Remarque was very much of our century, and yet he never lost his cavalierlike gesture reminiscent of former times. He brought to his German prose a breathless Hemingwayesque style, but reclaimed the old broad canvas of narration. He saw the twentieth century involved in a crucial conflict between technological progress and cultural regression. He was frightened by the possibility that an Orwellian future, with science triumphant over man's heartbeat, might be unavoidable. In his writings he desperately pitted the vitality of man to endure and to overcome against the cruelty of reality. He had an old-fashioned faith in the real values of existence, an almost romantic feeling for love and faith and understanding. Time and again he turned to the tortured creature, man, to the refugees without papers in a world without heart. And time and again he tried to hold on to that spark of humanity which, he was sure, no wars and holocausts, no stupidities and treacheries could ever extinguish.

There he sat in his Castalia looking out into the landscape which his eyes could not passionately enough embrace, looking at the mountain beyond which there is another lake. "The people," he

said one afternoon, "probably know why they call that lake the
eye of God."

SANCTUARY

DUE to its historic role and geographic position, Switzerland has
always been a place of refuge for those whose native country was
no longer safe for them. That these refugees should come mostly
from Switzerland's neighbors, Germany, Austria, France, and Italy,
is obvious. And that the *Fremdenpolizei*, the department of the
Swiss police force in charge of aliens, has not always treated all
those refugees with kid gloves is as understandable as an act of
self-defense as it is inexcusable in a country which traditionally
stands for freedom and tolerance. On the other hand, Switzerland,
a tiny island, was surrounded in 1939 by powerful armies whose
ruthless leaders had a fifth column in the land and were apt to
strike at a whim's notice. The number of refugees from neighboring countries was constantly growing, and thousands of deserters
mingled among them.

There may have been reasons of a pressing political nature
whenever the police resorted to an unyielding or harassing attitude.
In 1939, when a great many German writers found asylum here,
they were prevented from publishing in order to prevent Hitler
from finding a pretext too easily to intervene militarily in Switzerland. But no doubt self-preservation, caution, and fear were often
excuses for arbitrary acts in individual cases.

Ignazio Silone (1900–   ) referred to the case of the Austrian
writer Robert Musil, who found asylum in Switzerland during
the Hitlerian holocaust but who found little understanding of his
case with the police. However, Silone underlines that "fortunately,
there have always been magnanimous people in Switzerland who,
with their own means, have made up for the failures of public officials." Silone himself lived at that time as a refugee in Zürich.
After having taken part in illegal work against Mussolini's Fascists,
he fled to Switzerland in 1930 where he stayed for fourteen fertile
years, writing his most important works, *Fontamara*, *Bread and
Wine*, and *The Seed Beneath the Snow*. In 1944, Silone disguised
himself as a priest, like his hero in *Bread and Wine*, and, crossing
the German lines, sought contact with the American army.

While the well-known Musil had to be helped by Pastor Robert
Lejeune in order to overcome his personal difficulties, a yet rather

unknown Austrian dramatist, Fritz Hochwälder (1911–   ), lived in one of the Swiss refugee camps from which he emerged as a dramatist of renown. He was officially permitted to establish residence in Switzerland where he has lived and written plays ever since. Although his drama *Das heilige Experiment (The Strong Are Lonely)*, produced in 1947, brought him international recognition—it ran in Paris for two years and traveled the stages of most European theatres—the Swiss stages have rather avoided paying tribute to his dramatic talents. The world premieres of his later plays, such as the Huguenot drama, *Donadieu*, took place at the Viennese Burgtheater. A bitter remark made by Musil, and retold by Silone, "Today they don't know us, but as soon as we will be dead they will claim having granted us asylum," may be found in different moods and tenses and is, in the last analysis, a scurrilous variation of the old theme of the prophet in his own country.

Despite all difficulties, Switzerland has remained a symbol of the right of man to find refuge if need be. How else can we explain Max Frisch's remark in his eulogy on the dead Bertolt Brecht: "A year ago when I saw Brecht the last time he did not create the impression of a sick man, but he seemed exhausted, ate carefully and confined himself to questions concerning a quiet house on Lake Geneva . . ." Even Brecht, then living in East Berlin as a celebrity but having his money in the West, must have flirted with the thought of finding refuge in this country and a few peaceful years in the twilight of his life.

Among the innumerable refugees who settled in or passed through Switzerland, the name of Voltaire (1694–1778) shines the brightest of all luminaries. The man who gave the eighteenth century his profile fled from Frederick the Great in 1753 and, after a short adventure of being thrown into jail in Frankfurt, first found refuge at the Abbey of Senones near Colmar for a few weeks. Since he was persona non grata both in France and in Germany, he headed for Switzerland. At the end of 1754 he arrived in Geneva. He was then sixty and hoping to be shielded from persecution.

Being a Catholic, he could not buy any property in Geneva, so a house was bought for him with his own money. The day he moved into this house, which he called "Les Délices," he began to sign his letters "Voltaire the Swiss." Eighteen years after his arrival in Geneva he would still begin one of his letters (Ferney, February 12, 1772), addressed to the Russian Empress Catherine

II, with the words: "Madame, I'm afraid that Your Imperial Majesty may well be weary of letters from an old Swiss arguer . . ." Voltaire often remarked about his joy in being in the republic of rebels and reformers.

By then he had amassed a little fortune and wanted to live like a *grand seigneur*. He rebuilt and redecorated the house, owned four carriages, postilions, lackeys, and kept open house. He delighted in the view from his new home, which he thought was more beautiful than anything in Constantinople, "a palace of a philosopher with gardens of an Epicure, a delicious retreat." He could not resist building his own theatre, where he arranged a performance of his play *Zaïre*, attended by the best known Genevese families. This angered the authorities, who saw a potential threat in theatrical diversions, and the Calvinists preached many a sermon against Voltaire.

In his article on Geneva, written for Diderot's *Encyclopaedia*, he aroused the anger of his Genevan hosts even more by saying that Calvin had "cruelty in his soul" and that the Protestant ministers believed neither in the Bible nor in Hell, but were simply deists, like Voltaire himself. Such left-handed compliments were to no one's liking in Geneva, and Voltaire's protests that his manuscript was misread by the printer—that he had written "austerity" and not "cruelty"—was not believed. To remain master over his fate and master in his own house, he purchased two châteaux on French territory, Tourney and Ferney. They were a few steps from the Swiss frontier and guaranteed him an inexpugnable position. "I lean my left flank on the Jura," he wrote in a mock-strategic manner, "my right on the Alps, and I have the Lake of Geneva in front of my camp. A handsome château on the confines of France, the hermitage of Les Délices on Genevan territory, a fine house at Lausanne: in this way I creep from den to den, escaping from Kings and from armies."

He lived in Ferney for twenty more years and wrote some of his greatest works there. Like his *Candide*, who retired to the shores of the Propontis and discovered that the secret of happiness was to cultivate one's garden, Voltaire turned Ferney into his garden. He rebuilt his mansion and built many houses for the workers he attracted and with whom he set up workshops for silk stockings, lacemaking, and a small watch industry. He cleared land, turned to agricultural reforms, renovated the Church, and had *Deo erexit Voltaire* (Voltaire erected this to God) carved on the façade. He could truly brag that he had established a working paradise at

Ferney—now called Ferney-Voltaire—where people were happy because they were tolerant (". . . . in my hamlet where I have made more than a hundred Genevese and their families at home, nobody notices that there are two religions") and because they loved their work as he loved his. ("The greatest gift God gave man is the necessity to work" was a thought he expressed in many variations in his letters in the later years of his life: "I realize daily that work is the life of man . . . work mobilizes the forces of the soul and gives it great pleasure.")

Today when it is more questionable than ever that this is the best of all possible worlds, Voltaire has remained the symbol he has always been, the rebellious spirit who can think and express his thoughts clearly. In the mid-twentieth century the house in Geneva, which he baptized Les Délices and in which this egregious hermit lived for several years, has become a Voltaire Institute, with the huge terra cotta statue of the seated, aged Voltaire by his contemporary, the famous sculptor Houdon; it contains 12,000 volumes of Voltaire's works, manuscripts, letters, and notebooks, as well as photographs and microfilms of original Voltairiana dispersed throughout the world.

Voltaire, of course, is an odd example, when we speak of Switzerland as a sanctuary. He may have been a refugee in the technical sense, since he was persecuted in his own country and in Germany, but he was so rich that his money could have bought whatever there was for sale. And he was a person of such world renown that his witty pen could challenge the very government that offered him asylum.

Very few refugees who at any later date sought shelter and protection in Switzerland were in such an enviable position as Voltaire. In the late eighteenth century, the political situation—with Napoleon pitted against the rest of Europe—created unease, rebellions, and shifting allegiances in Switzerland. The republic went through many changing phases, but, in comparison to its neighboring countries, it was still a place of relative freedom. At that time the Swiss could still afford being generous in welcoming refugees from foreign countries.

A good example of such a refugee is Heinrich Zschokke (1771–1848), whose works were as popular as the writings of Mme. de Staël, his contemporary. He was an incredibly prolific writer whose far-reaching acclaim during his lifetime finds faint echo a century later. His name has been relegated to history books on literature, his volumes have become collectors' items, and his writings material for Ph.D. dissertations.

Zschokke wrote a series of historical novels in the manner of Sir Walter Scott, and the educational story, *Das Goldmacherdorf*, translated under the title of *Goldenthal*. His style was fluent and he always found a way of touching the heart of the average reader. He saw the highest goal of the writer in "inspiring the most human feelings in man, in a sense for truth, the rights of man and the ennobling of the mind of my contemporaries." In this he was strongly attuned to the basic tenets of most Swiss writers.

In love with his adopted country, he wrote a popular history of Switzerland in 1822, closing it with these prophetic words:

> Not from Germany, not from abroad comes the enemy before whom the Swiss heart should quail. The most formidable adversary of our freedom and independence, when he comes, will appear in our midst. But he must bear a mark by which everyone may know him: it is he who prefers the honor of his own canton to the everlasting glory of the whole Confederacy, his own personal or family advantage to the public good . . . So shall the holy cause of the fatherland be the holy cause of every cabin and a God-like public spirit, like a celestial fire, consume all personal and cantonal selfishness.

His *Schweizerbote (Swiss Messenger)* was a much read periodical in its time, "which in its way tells in a simple manner all that happens in the dear home country and, moreover, what the clever people and fools do in the world." There is a Benjamin Franklin touch in some of his writings, and Benjamin Franklin's influence may have been stronger on Zschokke than has ever been pointed out. He also admired America's rise, writing in an article: "From now on America shall be the home of human culture and the beacon of the globe, towards which the sages of all countries will look with longing in grateful blessings." Zschokke also wrote a book of verses, *Stunden der Andacht (Hours of Devotion)*, characterized by the seriously religious feeling of a free-thinking poet. It was criticized by all zealots but became a best-seller which enabled Zschokke to build a beautiful home in Aarau for himself and his family.

Zschokke was born in Magdeburg and spent the early years of his life in Germany as a teacher and dramatist, and as a student of philosophy and theology he became a professor of Church history, aesthetics, and *Moralphilosophie*. But he could never adjust to the prevailing Prussian spirit and never learned to kowtow to men in power. One day he decided to take his inherited fortune with him to Switzerland. When, on September 3, 1795, he entered the republic near Schaffhausen, he knelt down and kissed the ground.

However, he little enjoyed his immediate stay. He soon received honorary citizenship in Graubünden, but he had to leave this part of Switzerland, then under the protection of the Austrian crown. He feared for his security and fled to what was then the Swiss federation under the protection of Napoleon. Zschokke's eloquence and gift of political mediation helped him, the foreigner, to important political positions. As commissar of the government, he finally moved from Basle—where his work for peace and unification of the country was greatly appreciated—to Berne, from where he intended to find a suitable place to live with nature and for literature. He was then thirty years of age and wanted to throw overboard a successful diplomatic career in the ever-shifting political situation which was, to say the least, precarious in Napoleon's era.

In a letter from Berne, in 1802, Zschokke said:

France keeps Switzerland constantly in a state of dependency and rebellious agony . . . I'm not rich enough to view with indifference to be eclipsed at a later date by a state-wide revolution. This is why I remove myself at the right moment, accompanied by the love of the people and respect of the government . . . I'm longing to own some property . . . and want to marry . . . I negotiate about an estate at different places . . . Some time ago Malens in Graubünden gave me the right of citizenship, to prove its gratitude. Swiss citizenship in one town is different from being a citizen of the Swiss federation. The former enabled me and my descendants to have a share in the woods, community pastures and Alps in one of the most prosperous communities in Bünden. According to the utterances of a few important men, also the city of Basle seemingly wants to bestow upon me such citizenship. But this is not half as lucrative and useful because Basle owns little common property and no Alps . . .

He settled in the canton Aargau, where he married a pastor's daughter and raised a large family. As forestry commissioner, he had sufficient time to devote himself to literature. And his many volumes grew faster than the trees in his woods.

When Zschokke wrote that "The liberal state should not be forced upon the people, it should emanate from the people itself," it was a statement of exhortation addressed to the Swiss of 1802. It still held true in 1848 as well as in 1939. In 1848 the German revolutionaries lost their cause against Metternich's police state, and many Germans fled to America (Carl Schurz and confrères, among whom was Frank Wedekind's father) as well as to Switzerland. Friedrich Engels remarked in his remembrances of the rebellious days of 1848–49 that "Switzerland showed the exiles its rough side at that time."

But there have always been exceptions. One of them was the born rebel and "poet to boot," Georg Herwegh (1817–1875). He first was expelled from the theological college at Tübingen and became a journalist. When he was enrolled for military service, his rebellious spirit made him commit an act of insubordination, and he had to flee to Switzerland. There he lived for several years. In 1841 he brought out his first volume of poems, *Gedichte eines Lebendigen (Poems of One Who Is Alive)*. They were political poems which expressed the mood and feelings of the majority of the young people in Germany, their hopes and aspirations. Despite the fact that the book was confiscated, its underground distribution made several editions of it possible.

Herwegh returned to Germany a year later. He was then received by the people like a hero, and even by Frederick William IV, with the historic words: *"Ich liebe eine gesinnungsvolle Opposition"* ("I love an opposition that has convictions"). In Herwegh's case, history repeated itself. He lived in Paris when the second volume of his poems under the same title was published and again confiscated. In the rebellious year of 1848, Herwegh organized a troop of German workers and led them in an uprising in southern Germany, where they were defeated at Schopfheim in the province of Baden. Herwegh managed for a second time to escape to Switzerland where he then lived for eighteen years. It was not before 1866 that he was permitted to return to Germany.

Very few difficulties were encountered by those who, during World War I, fled to Switzerland, then a meeting place for many revolutionaries. Lenin, of course, comes first to mind. But Trotzki and, going back in history, Krapotkin, must also figure prominently in the files of the Swiss *Fremdenpolizei*, as well as Bakunin, who died in his Swiss exile, in Berne, in 1876. Such a militant pacifist as Romain Rolland was offered asylum at the beginning of the First World War, in spite of the fact that, in his famous series of articles, he urged Germany and France to respect truth and humanity, and both warring countries vehemently protested these "inflammatory" essays. In 1922 Rolland settled in Villeneuve in the canton Vaud, where he lived until 1938. During all that time he kept up his correspondence with great men all over the world from his residence in neutral Switzerland. He entertained contact with pacifists, socialists, and communists, and went to Soviet Russia in 1935. He was a spiritual leader of the "left" without belonging to any party or espousing any doctrine except the one of truth and being human.

The schizophrenic condition in which Switzerland found itself at the end of the thirties, facing the gigantic initial success and methodical persecution with which Hitler terrorized the world into a state of panic, boded ill for those who sought refuge then. That many people should have wanted to escape and many more had to leave Austria and Germany after March 1938 was obvious. Switzerland was the most logical place to which to flee. Among the many who came was Carl Zuckmayer, who wrote about his experiences in his autobiography, *A Part of Myself*:

> I shall not forget how I was greeted by the *Fremdenpolizei* . . . when I first went to report my presence as a political refugee. Switzerland has a long tradition of offering political asylum. Nevertheless, I was snarled at in dialect and treated as if I were a potential embezzler, swindler, forger of checks, possibly even a Communist. How much money did I have? Could I prove that I had a bank account . . . Indigents were not welcome here; why hadn't I stayed where I belonged? What crime had I committed (this is literal) that I had been forced to take flight?
>
> . . . .
>
> The behavior of a number of eminent individuals was entirely different. For example, the Swiss writer Caesar von Arx, whom I did not know personally, at once offered me all the aid and support that his prestige and influence in the country afforded. Robert Faesi, the Swiss professor of literature, likewise threw

his full energies into helping the German and Austrian writers who were seeking refuge in Switzerland. Then there was the group around Zürich Schauspielhaus . . . .

It would have been logical for Zuckmayer or Franz Werfel, whom he met in Zürich, to secure immediately a visa for the United States. But there was the fear of the language barrier and the deceptive feeling of being Europeans who had better stay in Europe. Even so, though only at the last moment, Zuckmayer, Werfel, Thomas Mann, Walter Mehring, and many others escaped across the Atlantic.

As a citizen of the United States and on an official errand, Zuckmayer returned to Germany. He walked through the rubble of cities which he had known so well, and he saw his parents and some of his friends again. But in his autobiography he tells us that it was the city of Zürich that "held a special place" and gave him a feeling of home. It was here, watching "the swans by the lakeside," looking "into the window of Oprecht's bookshop on Rämistrasse," and then facing the Schauspielhaus: "it was like passing through the stages of gestation, and I should have taken nine months to do it . . . For here, right now, I was reborn. I felt as if I ought to utter a prayer as I walked from Zeltweg across the courtyard to the stage entrance . . . I was home."

This happened immediately after the war. Years passed in which Zuckmayer crossed the ocean back and forth. He was only one of the many uprooted intellectuals and artists who learned to live between languages and hemispheres, between yesterday and tomorrow, whose today has been questionable. Zuckmayer admitted, "I did not belong to one of the victor nations, but neither did I belong to the defeated. Now, after returning home, I had really become homeless, and I did not know how I would ever find a homeland again."

He found it in 1958 when he settled in Saas-Fee, "God grant— the last house of our lives." In 1961 the community of Saas-Fee gave him honorary citizenship. At the end of his autobiography, Zuckmayer quotes the first sentence of his certificate of citizenship:

Eternal rights and eternal friendship should be confirmed and fixed in writing, since in the course of time past things are soon forgotten.

And Zuckmayer concludes: "The meaning of my story is to be found in this sentence." I shall close this chapter with a variation on this theme: The meaning of Switzerland as a sanctuary can be found in Carl Zuckmayer's account of his life, and the fate of those who lost their home and national identity only to find it again in a land that seems remote from the maelstrom of twentieth-century life, in the best of possible worlds. For many—to speak with *Candide*—this is one of the few gardens left which man can cultivate in order to find happiness without having to pursue it.

SOME CAME TO SEE

FROM CELLINI TO KLEIST

SWITZERLAND'S scenic beauty has attracted visitors from everywhere during the last 350 years. One of the first travelers was Benvenuto Cellini (1500–1571), who crossed the Wallenstädter Lake in a most adventurous manner. Of course, according to his autobiography, Cellini hardly did anything without having his adventures. He came to a town "which is called Zürich . . . a wonderful town, as neat as a gem; there we rested a whole day. Next morning we continued our journey early and hit upon another beautiful town, called Solothurn . . ."

However, I do not intend to speak of adventurous journeys through Switzerland, nor of tourism in general. I wish to devote this chapter to some literary luminaries whose attraction and reaction to Switzerland had considerable meaning to them and to world literature.

Aside from its scenery it has been Switzerland the republic that has made people curious to see for themselves how democracy works. I only know of isolated cases in which the latter was a deterrent factor. A classical example of a man looking backwards rather than forwards was Sebastian Brant (1458–1521). He was born at Strasbourg and by chance came to Basle, where he studied and received his doctorate of law in 1489. For ten years he enjoyed Basle's humanistic atmosphere and the beauty of its environment. But when Basle joined the Swiss confederation in 1499, Brant turned his back on the city he loved and returned to his native town.

In the meantime he had written in Basle one of the great works of world literature, and one that was immediately translated into several languages: *Das Narrenschiff (The Ship of Fools)*. In idiomatic and vigorous language, Brant satirized unsparingly the follies and weaknesses, the serious crimes and trivial shortcomings of his contemporaries. In the wake of its impact this work found many imitators, among them even Erasmus and Hans Sachs.

Brant's thoughts and beliefs were still of medieval concepts. Even though he aimed at improving the conditions of church and monarchic empires, he believed in them as holy institutions and shied away from any revolutionary movement. The Reformation was anathema to him, and so was the idea of people ruling themselves in a democratic republic. Since the Swiss confederation took a prominent position in both directions, Sebastian Brant preferred to serve Maximilian I as imperial councilor and count palatine.

Johann Wolfgang von Goethe's (1749–1832) stature in the world of letters is unique as one of the last universal geniuses, and the word *unique* describes best his relationship to Switzerland. He has often been reproached for having become the captive of his own role and ambition at the court of Weimar, as the reigning servant of Duke Charles Augustus; it has also been said that from then on the mastery of life was his chief concern and helped him wear his Olympian halo with dignity and grace in his later years. On the other hand, when Napoleon, after meeting Goethe in Erfurt, uttered his famous "Voilà un homme!" his reaction to him was more than an exclamation of admiration; Bonaparte seemingly wanted to refer to a superior being, combining ordinary humanness with the most extraordinary accomplishments of man's sensibilities and intellect.

Goethe could be a skeptic and disbeliever, but he was totally involved in life, exploring all its possibilities on all levels of existence. For him, truth was everywhere, but certainly nowhere in compromise; he saw it in the embrace of all opposites. In his poetic and dramatic writings he touched upon and probed the universality of feelings and thoughts, as a romantic or a classicist, and even more so did he try to penetrate them in his conversations with Eckermann and in his *Maxims*. There was no problem left untouched by him, no stone of wisdom unturned.

Perhaps this is why we can also find his reactions to Switzerland moving in different directions. Goethe came to this country three times, and three times, as if he had been a different human being, his journey's purpose, ambience, and result were of another nature. It was in 1774, after his betrothal to Lili Schönemann, daughter of a rich banker—we would now call her a flirtatious society girl— that he took refuge in nature and, so to speak, escaped to Switzerland to test his ambivalent feelings.

Goethe's enthusiasm for the scenic beauty of the country is reflected in many incidental exclamations. He said of Berne that it was the loveliest town he had ever seen, and in Zürich, gliding with his boat "On the Lake," he was provoked to write some thoughtful lines, beginning with: "Fresh food, new blood/Do I absorb from this free world:/How lovely and how good is nature/

holding me at her breast!" But Lili was mainly on his mind when he wrote the four-line poem *From the Mountain:*

> If I, dear Lili, would not love you,
> O what delight would offer me this view!
> And yet if, Lili, I wouldn't love you,
> Could I find here and there my happiness?

Still, a year later, when he had broken his engagement to Lili Schönemann, he wrote, recalling the Swiss scene, a poem whose first lines say: "In lovely dales, on snow-covered heights,/Your image always was with me . . ."

Among the manuscript papers relating to Goethe's *The Sorrows of Young Werther* were letters written from Switzerland in which he tells of a sexual adventure in Geneva and often refers to the landscape: "Yes, I have climbed up the Furka, the Gotthard! These sublime, incomparable scenes of nature will always linger in my mind . . ." From his third journey to Switzerland, Goethe wrote: "Culture around Lake Zürich has really reached the highest point, and the time of vintage makes everything very lively." But there is one passage in which Goethe is quite critical of the Swiss and their attitude towards freedom, a statement which seems to shed some light on his then torn emotions and aspirations in following a career at the court, which started immediately after this incident:

> Are the Swiss really free? Free those well-to-do burghers in their walled-in cities? Free those poor devils on their cliffs and rocks? . . . They once freed themselves from a tyrant and could believe themselves free for a short time. Now the dear sun created out of the suppressor's carrion a swarm of little tyrants through a strange rebirth; now they continue to tell the old fairy tale which one hears to the point of nausea: they once liberated themselves and had remained free; and now they sit behind their walls, captives of their customs and laws, their gossiping and philistinism, and out there on the rocks it's worth their while to talk about liberty if half the year they are kept prisoners by the snow like marmots.

Even though the original letters were not found, one cannot dismiss these comments as of a spurious nature. Some scholars maintain that these letters must have been written at a time before Goethe met Lotte. This would indicate a trip to Switzerland at an earlier period, which is doubtful. It is more plausible that these notes date from Goethe's journey of 1774 and were written during his first impressions after his flight from Lili.

During this first trip, Goethe wrote in Oberried at the Lake of Zürich a few succinct verses addressed to Johann Kaspar Lavater (1741–1801), who had corresponded and visited with the poet in Frankfurt. The Zürich pastor Lavater, then at the height of his fame, had captivated Goethe with his genial personality and religious fervor, with which he tried to return to an apostolic Christianity. Lavater's fame rests with his four-volume work, *Physiognomic Fragments*. Goethe was so intrigued by this study that he also wrote a series of physiognomic fragments, deducing a person's characteristics from his features. Goethe called his studies *Contributions to Lavater's Physiognomic Fragments*.

Goethe's second journey to Switzerland, which he undertook with the Duke of Weimar in September 1779, was crowned by the poet's repeated meetings with Lavater in Zürich, of which Goethe said that it was "Seal and climax of the whole journey and a pasture of heavenly manna." It was only some years afterwards, when Lavater began to play the part of a prophet and believed in Cagliostro's miracles, that Goethe turned away from him. And then the long and intimate friendship came to a sudden end.

His third trip to Switzerland is biographically of little interest. It happened in July 1797, the year in which Goethe wrote many ballads in competition with Schiller. The most accomplished of Goethe's poems, *Hermann and Dorothea*, was then finished. At that time Goethe also worked intermittently on *Faust* and wrote his essay of *Laokoön*. From Switzerland he brought with him a poem entitled *Swiss Alp*, one of his short poems in which a seeming simplicity radiates a simile of significance. In this case, the poet compares the silver-gray snowcap of the mountains quickly following the summer mountain colors with youth being so close to old age, like a "fleeting dream tying together yesterday and today."

Moreover, Goethe's third visit was characterized by his plan to write an epic on *Wilhelm Tell*. For this purpose he studied the history of this legendary incident, its environment, and the salient features of the Swiss people. This plan was abandoned and left to Friedrich Schiller, whom Goethe instructed about the Swiss and with whom he left a vivid image of the landscape.

Visits of German poets in Switzerland were no rarity, and many preceded those of Goethe. At the early stages of dramatic literature in Germany, Johann Christoph Gottsched (1700–1766) was the foremost literary theorist and critic, a dictator of taste who forced upon the fledgling writers of a slowly awakening German literature the pseudo-classic fashion of the French. It was Johann Jakob Bodmer (1698–1783), born at Greifensee near Zürich, who challenged Gottsched and contributed decisively to the development of German literature when, in 1741, he published his *Critical Observations on the Poetic Images of Writers*. In this essay he attacked the spiritual enslavement of German literature and theatre through the artificially imposed imitation of French pseudo-classicism. Bodmer's ensuing controversy with Gottsched ended with the latter's views being finally eclipsed. Bodmer was the first to have made English literature accessible to the Germans, translating Milton and Shakespeare, and pleading for descriptive poetry.

He had great influence on Friedrich Gottlieb Klopstock (1724–1803) with his translation of Milton's *Paradise Lost*. As a matter of fact, it gave the young German poet's thoughts and impulses a new direction. His original idea of writing a historic and national epic was discarded, and Klopstock mapped out a religious theme, *Der Messias (The Messiah)*. He worked many years on it and combined baroque passages of moving pathos with a sincerely felt pietism which was, at that time, a strong movement in Europe.

Bodmer felt that he had a great share in the discovery of this religious-oriented poetic genius and invited Klopstock to visit him in Zürich in 1750. Klopstock accepted the invitation. German literature profited from it, since Klopstock brought home with him one of his most beautiful odes in which he extolled *The Lake of Zürich (Der Zürichersee)*. The visit was less successful with regard to the friendship between Bodmer and Klopstock; Bodmer thought the young man much too passionately interested in worldly pleasures, too easily falling in and out of love.

However, Bodmer was not too greatly discouraged by his experience with Klopstock, for two years later his invitation was extended to Christoph Martin Wieland (1733–1813) who, in the year of 1752, published a few Pietistic poems, *Twelve Moral Letters in Verses (Zwölf moralische Briefe in Versen)*, and his *Anti-Ovid*.

Bodmer was out of luck with his German poet friends even though their religious and didactic fervor matched their poetic power, an ideal combination in Bodmer's eyes. After a few months, Wieland and Bodmer also parted. Yet Wieland remained in Switzerland another eight years. He continued to write under the spell of Bodmer and Klopstock for some time. While still in Switzerland, in 1758 and 1760, two of his tragedies showed a marked change in his attitude, which Lessing expressed succinctly when he said that Wieland "foresook the ethereal spheres to wander again among the sons of men." 1760 was the year in which he finally returned to Germany and a more lighthearted philosophy of life and love.

If there ever was a classical example of a creative mind finding peace and inspiration in the idyll of a landscape, then it was Heinrich von Kleist (1777–1811), whose only happy moments in life were those in Berne and on the Thun Lake.

He loathed the time he spent in military service in Germany, forced upon him by family tradition. During the years of his studies he was tormented by ambivalent feelings, unable to decide whether to devote his life to science or to literature. He never was at peace with himself, but about the months spent in Switzerland he could say, they were full of "quiet, silent, serene delight," a fertile period in which his genius found itself, even though his greatest works were done later. It was here that his first poetic dreams were fulfilled and some of his dramatic ideas ripened.

Wanderlust may have been one of the romantic traits of the Germans. But Kleist's restlessness and need to move from place to place had all the earmarks of a compulsion during a mental crisis. He falsely associated his longing for inner peace with simplicity. From Paris he wrote to his bride Wilhelmine: "I still have some money left which will suffice to purchase a farm in Switzerland which should enable me to support myself if I will do the work . . ." But Wilhelmine rejected the idea of being the wife of a peasant.

At Basle he entered Switzerland, which he called his "new fatherland." He moved on to Berne, where he met with Heinrich Zschokke and other writers. The poets often met and read from their own writings, discussing and inspiring one another. In those days Kleist felt reassured of his own creative power and reconciled with the world and himself. He then wrote his satiric comedy, *Der Zerbrochene Krug (The Broken Jug).*

The desire for a simple life in the country, however, was still with him. He wrote to his sister Ulrike: "I have been deadly serious about buying some property in Switzerland . . . Zschokke, too, wants to buy land, even in my proximity, and he also speaks sometimes of Swiss citizenship which he could procure for me . . ."

In 1802 Kleist settled in Thun, a town favored by Napoleon, who, for some time, kept the country in a state of uncertainty and restlessness, with fighting going on in various places, with peasants revolting, with the Russian and Austrian armies battling the French on Swiss soil. "It looks as if Switzerland would become a part of France, and I loathe the mere thought of it," he wrote his sister, and he postponed buying a farm. He first stayed in the city of Thun. Above the door of his living quarters, a few inscribed lines, found on many houses in the German part of Switzerland, intrigued Kleist. He seems to have been fond of these lines, which he probably found descriptive of his own life:

> I come, I do not know from where.
> I am, I do not know what.
> I go, I do not know whereto.
> I wonder that I am so gay.

In the spring of 1802 Kleist rented an isolated cottage on an island in the river Aare, where it flows into the lake. From his window Kleist could see the gigantic panorama of snowcapped mountains, among them the Jungfrau. It was an ideal place for him to work, but after a short while he took sick and had to go to Berne to recover. The quickly changing political events in those days forced him to leave this city. But during those months his play *Die Familie Schroffenstein (The Family Schroffenstein)* and the first draft of *Robert Guiskard* were finished.

In July 1803 a second trip to Switzerland found Kleist in a state of heightened anxiety, mainly hiking through the country, trying to empty his sick mind. His will for self-destruction found its first manifestations; he burnt his manuscripts. Not able to die alone, unconsciously seeking the drama of it, he invited his friends to die with him. Their refusal only delayed the seemingly inevitable.

The time Kleist spent in Geneva, Berne, and Thun was a futile attempt to recapture the joys experienced at these places once before, but the trip remained uninspiring. The signs of darkness during this journey were the first harbingers of his suicide, which occurred several years later.

A ROMANTIC VICTORIAN TREND

The majesty and beauty of the scenery of Switzerland, as you know, have made it a thoroughfare of travelling Europe, and especially of the English, who swarm in it to the most outrageous extent. And yet so vast and varied, so savage in some regions and so lovely in others, is the country we have been through, that the steamboats on the lakes, and the great hotels and the splendid roads which one meets with from time to time, leave too slight traces on the face of Nature to take away the sense of freshness and wildness that characterize it.

OLIVER Wendell Holmes (1809–1894), the American poet-physician whose firecracker wit delighted the readers of *The Autocrat of the Breakfast-Table*, wrote the preceding lines. It is no longer true that the majority of all visitors come from the British Isles, although the English discovered the scenic beauty of Switzerland in the latter half of the eighteenth century. John Ruskin (1819–1900), who saw the Alps for the first time when he was fourteen years old and spent eleven summers and two winters in the mountains, was more responsible than anyone else for the wave of English tourism to Switzerland in the last century. His enthusiasm made him write some of the most brilliant and moving passages: ". . . mountains seem to have been created to show us the perfection of beauty" and "The best image the world can give of Paradise is in the slope of the meadows, orchards, and corn-fields on the sides of a great Alp, with its purple rocks and eternal snows above. . . ."

In Ruskin's well-known essays on painting and painters he gave some good, though nowadays obvious-sounding, advice: "We do not want châlets and three-legged stools, cow-bells and butter-milk. We want the pure and holy hills, treated as a link between heaven and earth." To this very day his investigations of the effects of the mountains on religion, art and literature, war and social economy are still absorbing reading, and there is some lasting truth in the Victorian way he saw the Swiss mountain dwellers:

> . . . . They do not understand so much as the name of beauty, or of knowledge. They understand dimly that of virtue. Love, patience, hospitality, faith—these things they know. To glean their meadows, side by side, so happier; to bear the burden up the breathless mountain flank, unmurmuringly; to bid the stranger drink from their vessel of milk; to see at the foot of their low deathbeds a pale figure upon a cross, dying, also patiently . . . .

Ruskin the aesthete was also interested in mountaineering. Fascinated by the idea that man so often feels compelled to accept the challenge of the mountains, he gave some thought to its psychological aspects: ". . . . if you go through with the danger, though it may have been apparently wrong and foolish to encounter it, you come out of the encounter a stronger and better man, fitter for every sort of work and trial, and nothing but danger produces this effect."

Ruskin's contemporary, Matthew Arnold (1822–1888), was often referred to as the Victorian Wordsworth. But he was a better critic than poet, who believed that "it is not enough that the Poet should add to the knowledge of man, it is required of him also that he should add to their happiness." He also found rhyme and reason in the Swiss landscape, to which he often referred in his poems. He also wrote a cycle of seven poems entitled *Switzerland,* which, however, in the main are emotional manifestations of his love for nature and a certain Marguerite. In the *Stanzas in Memory of the Author of "Obermann"* we read:

> Lake Léman's waters far below!
> And watch'd the rosy light
> Fade from the distant peaks of snow;
> And on the air of night
>
> Heard accents of the eternal tongue
> Through the pine branches play!

Although the English were among the most daring mountaineers for some time and are said to have popularized skiing in Switzerland,* not all Englishmen took to the mountains. Joseph Addison (1672–1719), who was among the Britishers in Central Switzerland in 1701, had an ambivalent feeling about the mountains, which he always viewed from a safe distance (". . . the prospects of the Alps . . . fill the mind with an agreeable kind of horror"). However, Addison was fond of the Swiss cities, especially of Berne, and the ambience of the entire country ("I have often considered, with a great deal of pleasure, the profound peace and tranquility that reigns in Switzerland . . .").

There is, of course something frightening and forbidding about high mountains, as well as some magic and emotional appeal. Hilaire Belloc (1870–1953), French-born English poet, essayist, and historian, wrote powerful prose with a great felicity in the descrip-

---

* A group of indigenous pioneers in the Glarus introduced skiing in Switzerland.

tion of landscape. He was known for his wit and was not easily forced into a defensive position. But when facing Switzerland's mountains, he reported in *The Vision of the Alps:* "I saw between the branches of the trees in front of me a sight in the sky that made me stop breathing, just as great danger at sea, or great surprise in love, or a great deliverance will make a man stop breathing."

It is undoubtedly the inexplicable element of surprise and, moreover, a feeling of our own insignificance which these giants of merciless calm and serene beauty make us sense and with which they seem to belittle us, taking no notice of our fear or exhilaration. Nature often makes us painfully aware of the fragile fabric of our psyche. The Swiss claim that a sudden warm wind can easily unnerve them and disturb their equilibrium. Robert Louis Stevenson (1856–1894), the Scottish novelist, essayist, and poet, made himself immortal with *The Strange Case of Dr. Jekyll and Mr. Hyde* and *Treasure Island*. He also wrote first-rate journalism, with a deep awareness of atmosphere and landscape. In 1880 the doctors discovered a touch of tuberculosis in him and sent him to Davos. He stayed there for almost two years, and it was in Davos that he wrote *Treasure Island*. He gave an interesting account of that warm wind that "cunningly winds about the mountains and breaks, warm and unclean, upon our mountain valley. Every nerve is set ajar; the conscience recognizes, at a gust, a load of sins and negligencies hitherto unknown; and the whole invalid world huddles into its private chambers, and silently recognizes the empire of the *Föhn*."

It was always the Swiss landscape and its atmospheric secret to which the English poets were mysteriously drawn. Rarely is the Swiss himself the center of attraction, and if so, then mainly in the glorified role of a fighter for freedom. In this respect, he was often the hero of many poems, particularly in the enghteenth century when, for instance, William Collins (1721–1759) wrote among his *Odes on Several Descriptive and Allegorical Subjects* one entitled *Ode to Liberty*, or George Keate (1729–1797) his *Helvetiad*. William Wordsworth (1770–1850) sang in his sonnet, *England and Switzerland, 1802:*

> Two Voices are there; one is of the Sea,
> One of the Mountains; each a mighty voice:
> In both from age to age thou didst rejoice,
> They were thy chosen music, Liberty!

In Oliver Goldsmith's (c. 1730–1774) *Traveller*, we can read:

> ......
> Where rougher climes a nobler race display,
> Where the bleak Swiss their stormy mansions tread
> And force a churlish soil for scanty bread.
> ......
> So the loud torrent, and the whirlwind's roar,
> But bind him to his native mountains more.

When, in 1798, Switzerland was invaded by the French, Wordsworth wrote his moving sonnet, *Thoughts of a Briton on the Subjugation of Switzerland*. He was one of the English poets whose names are closely associated with Switzerland. He came to this country twice, in 1790 and 1820, with his sister Dorothy (1771–1855). Poems such as *The Simplon Pass* express the subtle sensations Wordsworth felt in the mountains, but his sister's alpine descriptions are even more powerful. We may choose any passage at random, for instance the one about Grindelwald:

> The sunshine had long deserted the valley and was quitting the summits of the mountains behind the village; but red hues, dark as the red of rubies, settled in the clouds and lingered there after the mountains had lost all but their cold whiteness and the black hue of the crags. The gloomy grandeur of this spectacle harmonised with the melancholy of the vale; yet it was *heavenly* glory that hung over those cold mountains.

Dorothy Wordsworth was an excellent diarist, and much of her descriptive prose became basic material for her brother's poems. Her spontaneous and unsophisticated communication of the mood of a landscape remains unsurpassed and exhibits all the elements of poetic expressiveness. Such a line as "The moonlight lay upon the hills of snow" sounds like the first line of one of her brother's poems.

The poet and his sister encountered yodeling by a group of peasant women for the first time, and an imaginative description of it tells us that it was "a song not of articulate sounds but in which the voice was used as a mere instrument of music more flexible than any instrument—sweet, powerful, thrilling beyond description."

When Percy Bysshe Shelley (1792–1822) eloped with Mary Godwin (1797–1851) to the continent in 1814 (first to Paris, then to Lucerne and Brunnen, via Neuchâtel), it was in keeping with the romantic *Zeitgeist* and Shelley's realization of a dream image: the Woman-Symbol of Intellectual Beauty. Claire Clairmont, Mary's stepsister, accompanied the couple, making up the domestic triangle. It was a gay party which, after two months in Switzerland, ran into financial difficulties, and the travelers headed back for England.

The same gay trio returned to Geneva in May 1816, where they stayed into the autumn months. It was a wonderful, wanton, and productive period for everyone concerned. Shelley and Mary traced the scenes of Rousseau's lovers of *La Nouvelle Héloise*. Shelley wrote such poems as the "Hymn to Intellectual Beauty" and "Mont Blanc," but his inmost experience with the mountainous landscape remained purely self-reflective:

> . . . and when I gaze on thee
> I seem as in a trance sublime and strange
> To muse on my own separate fantasy . . .

Mary was inspired to write the novel *Frankenstein*, the first and now widely known science fiction. Claire inspired Lord Byron (1788–1824), while literally throwing herself into his arms, to compose the third canto of *Childe Harold*:

> It is the hush of night, and all between
> Thy margin and the mountains, dusk, yet clear,
> Mellow'd and mingling, yet distinctly seen,
> Save darken'd Jura . . .

Claire eagerly copied Byron's poem at the Villa Diodati near Geneva, where all four lived together. She became pregnant and, in January of the following year, gave birth to Byron's daughter, whom he called Allegra.

Byron undertook a tour of the Bernese Oberland, the scenery of which is reflected in his poetic drama, *Manfred*, an apotheosis of the romantic spirit, and Byron's *Faust*. "Half dust, half deity, alike unfit to sink or soar," expresses Byron's sense of guilt and feeling of remorse, man's doomed spirit as romantic *Weltschmerz*. While staying at Lauterbrunnen, he visited the waterfalls of Staubbach.

He described in poetic prose what he used as background inspiration for *Manfred*:

> The torrent is in shape curving over the rock, like the tail of a white horse streaming in the wind, such as it might be conceived would be that of the 'pale horse' on which death is mounted in the Apocalypse. It is neither mist nor water, but a something between both . . .

Byron is, of course, most closely associated with Switzerland through his poem, "The Prisoner of Chillon," which was the result of a boat trip which he made in Shelley's company. Byron also wrote a lesser known sonnet, "On the Castle of Chillon," whose first stanza says:

> Eternal Spirit of the chainless Mind!
> Brightest in dungeons, Liberty! thou art,
> For there thy habitation is the heart—
> The heart which love of Thee alone can bind . . .

In his travel book, *Adventures in Switzerland*, Alexandre Dumas père* (1802–1870) described the ancient state prison of Chillon as it was used by the Duke of Savoy: ". . . The captivity of Bonivard within its walls so dominates the memory that the name of a prisoner who, in 1798, escaped from the fortress in a manner almost miraculous, is all but forgotten. This unhappy wretch managed to make a hole in the wall with a nail wrenched from the sole of his shoe only to find himself in another larger cell. By sheer strength of wrist he then pulled away an iron bar . . . The print of his foot on the side of the loophole testifies to the prodigious efforts he made . . . the prison of the martyr had become a temple and his pillar an altar . . . One night—it was in 1816 . . . a boat approached silently . . . from it stepped a pale-faced man . . .

* Dumas would have denied that he came to Switzerland as a refugee; perhaps he was only a quasi-refugee after he had been implicated in the disturbances during the funeral of General Lamarque in June 1832. The truth is that the Orléans government suggested to Dumas that his absence from France was more than desirable. Dumas' impressions of Switzerland became the background material for the first of several amusing books of travel. As a quasi-refugee, Dumas was preceded by Alphonse de Lamartine (1790–1869), who, for a short while, also escaped to Switzerland during Napoleon's Hundred Days, in 1815.

He requested to be shown Bonivard's cell. There he remained alone for a long time. When he had gone, another name was inscribed on the martyr's pillar—Byron."

The list of literary luminaries "who came to see" and whose visual experiences enriched the world is endless. From Alfred, Lord Tennyson (1850–1892) to the Austrian satirist Karl Kraus (1874–1936)—whose poems about Sils Maria and Vallorbe belong to some of the best poetry written in German—they all took away from some part of the country impressions which ignited a verbal flame of ecstatic imagery. Even Mark Twain (1835–1916), when arriving at Lucerne on the Vierwaldstädter Lake, could not help saying, "The first discovery I made was that the beauty of the lake had not been exaggerated."

Somerset Maugham (1874–1965), who spent the last year of World War I in a sanatorium in Switzerland in order to cure his tuberculosis, reacted to the monumental loveliness of the Swiss landscape with his gentle cynicism. In trying to eschew the rapturous flow of praise, Maugham escaped into ironical whimsy in describing the environment of Lucerne in his story, The Traitor: ". . . it was true that the lake was absurd, the water was too blue, the mountains too showy, and its beauty, hitting you in the face, exasperated rather than thrilled, but all the same, there was something pleasing in the prospect, an artless candor . . ."

STRINDBERG AND TOLSTOI

THERE are a few tangential points which Frank Wedekind, of whom we have spoken, and August Strindberg had in common. They were both periodically and late in life seemingly naturalistic writers (Wedekind foreshadowing the volcanic verbalization of the expressionists; Strindberg adding to his naturalism, psychological depth and then mysticism). They were both symbolists, preoccupied with the female sex, and saw in the woman a destructive force (while Strindberg believed that women could not help acting the way they did, out of hostility and a predilection for intrigues, Wedekind saw women acting out of a primary, irrepressible urge to devour the male). Moreover, these two writers were successively attached to one and the same woman. The young Viennese journalist, Frieda Uhl, Strindberg's second wife, joined Wedekind in Munich after having asked for a divorce from Strindberg. She was an inspiring force in Wedekind's career and presented him with a

son who bore the name of Friedrich Strindberg and whom Wedekind loved dearly. But too many points of difference, of which they
were painfully aware from the very beginning, made Frieda Strindberg and Wedekind soon go different ways.

In 1894, two years before Wedekind was joined by Frieda, the
writers had met in Paris without taking a great liking to each other.
As a matter of fact, after a couple of months they avoided one
another's company. But they must also have met in Switzerland
in 1886, the year when Strindberg decided to live in Lenzburg for
a while. Wedekind returned that summer from Munich to be with
his family in the Aargau, and the town of Lenzburg is much too
small for the two not to have met. Wedekind, of course, was then
at the very beginning of his writing career, while Strindberg had
already made a name for himself and was well known in all literary
circles.

Of the six years of Strindberg's aimless wandering on the continent as a voluntary exile, he spent two in Switzerland. Most of
1884 was spent at the Lake of Geneva at Ouchy, and in the summer months at Chexbres (where his only son Hans was born); in
1886 he was in Lenzburg and Othmarsingen. Both were significant
years in his life and accomplishments.

While he was living in the French part of Switzerland on the soil
hallowed by the name of Rousseau, Strindberg's philosophy of life
came closest to Rousseau's doctrines. In many essays published
in 1884 Strindberg sharply criticized a society which, in his view,
not only tolerates unproductive professions but permits them to
profit the most. To cultivate the soil is the most wholesome occu-
pation. The call back to nature can be heard when Strindberg
condemned city life. The cities are doomed to die, he said in a
letter written on May 24, 1884, but first they must fulfill their
destiny: "the artificial culture must disappear, but the genuine
culture will go on living." (Seen from the vantage point of the
latter half of the twentieth century and of our urban problems,
we cannot easily disagree.)

It was the time in which Strindberg turned from Christianity
by way of deism to atheism. His stay in Switzerland was briefly
interrupted when he went back to Stockholm to stand trial for
blasphemous remarks in the first volume of his collected stories,
Married, which was issued in the early autumn of 1884. He first
hesitated to leave his wife, Siri von Essen, and the children. He
also hesitated to endanger his freedom. But his publisher, Karl Otto
Bonnier, met him in Geneva and persuaded him to go back to

Sweden with him. At the trial Strindberg defended himself. He was greeted with an ovation when he arrived in Stockholm and was loudly acclaimed after the "Not Guilty" verdict. It gave him the conviction of having been on the right path, however radical his clarion calls against Christianity, aristocracy, and false romanticism may have sounded.

But these events were accompanied by great excitement and taxing tensions. By then his mental condition was not the best. According to Karl Jaspers' investigations in *Strindberg and Van Gogh*, schizophrenic symptoms had already been noticeable two years previously. His wife Siri could still thank Strindberg in public for seven years of a wonderful marriage. But his second volume of *Married*, on which he worked that year, was even more radically anti-feminist than the first that had led to the trial. His marriage began to be poisoned by his suspicions and self-torturing complaints. Most of his works showed his growing mental anguish. Aware of all this, he may have tried to rid himself of his innermost torment by writing these stories with cathartic intention.

However, socio-political questions were not subjugated by his concern with marital problems. In an essay, *Nationality and the Swedes,* he sided with the Finns against his compatriots in Finland and expressed his hope that the Russian people would soon be able to liberate themselves from the rule of the Czars. The most important point made in this article is couched in the form of an exhortation that the Swedes should become Europeans and work towards the realization of a pan-Europe, a European federation based on the image of little Switzerland. Strindberg first embraced internationalism before he turned socialist.

In the spring of that year he also wrote a short novel, *Agonies of Conscience*, in which he dealt with the problem of peace, extolling arbitration in all international controversies. During the summer of 1884, another story was written, "The Island of the Blessed." It is a satire on society. First Strindberg pictures an ideal island on which people do not have to work for food and shelter, because everything that man needs is there in abundance. On this island are no laws, no police, no kings, and no church. The scene changes; the same people on another island must work hard for a living. Immediately, laws and police become necessary, a king is crowned, a state church inaugurated, and officials live off the hardworking people. Undoubtedly, Rousseau and Voltaire godfathered this story.

During the year 1886, which Strindberg spent in the German

part of Switzerland, his productivity was immense and of great importance. It did not take him more than nine months to write the four volumes of his autobiography. *The Son of a Servant* and *The Time of Ferment* were published late that spring and early that fall, respectively. *The Red Room* was held over until the following year. The fourth one, *The Author*, first rejected by his publisher, was issued in 1909. With these books Strindberg continued the series of confessions and self-revelations that have ever flowered on Swiss soil.

In the same year he found sufficient time to engage in research in France for his study, *Among French Peasants*. He had a plan of designing a huge canvas of contemporary European peasantry. But when the first installment was published in 1889, he was no longer interested in the problems of agricultural socialism. What was far more important in 1886 was Strindberg's renewed interest in writing for the stage, and this was of the greatest consequence for dramatic world literature. He finished the first version of *Comrades*, which then had the title *Marauders*. He also began to write *The Father*, finishing it the following year, one of his more important plays and one of the most gripping psychological dramas of the modern theatre.

Is it mere coincidence that these two years which Strindberg spent in Switzerland have been of paramount importance to him and to the world of letters? Many penetrating minds have tried to describe and define the creative spark in man, and none of these attempts have ever been satisfactory. An environment can enchant, inspire, confine, frighten, isolate, uplift, and terrorize. It can become a catalyst. Perhaps there is such a thing as a creative climate. And in this context, I must add Tolstoi's story in Lucerne to the one of Strindberg.

In the first half of the year 1857, Leo Tolstoi made his first journey to the West, through France, Italy, Germany, and Switzerland. He stayed at the Hotel Schweizerhof in Lucerne, from where he intended to enjoy the beauty of the Alps.

His stay in Lucerne would have been of little consequence had he not written the story he called *Lucerne*, which reflects, for the first time in his writings, Tolstoi's sudden awareness of man's betrayal of man. The story, probably based on a real experience, tells of a crippled man who makes his living by singing and begging. This tale conjures up the cruelty of reality, the contrasts of poor and rich, turning into the contrasts of good and evil. Tolstoi the storyteller loses control over his pen and slips into the role of social philosopher. The entire *Weltanschauung* of the mature Tolstoi is telescoped in this story, the signal turning point in his career.

He came to admire the beauty of nature, and these majestic impressions paled against the background of a seemingly everyday experience. An insignificant event—listening to a begging troubadour from the Aargau—became a point of departure for the juxtaposition of fundamental principles of life, and for the image of the monster that he came to see in social evil. From then on Tolstoi was no longer the same.

Disgusted by the rich guests of the Schweizerhof, mainly Englishmen, proverbially withdrawn and stiff, Tolstoi walks through Lucerne's streets. Returning to the hotel, he is attracted by the street singer who accompanies himself on a guitar. Tolstoi is appalled by the callousness of "those hundreds of beautifully dressed people who had come to listen to him" yet who did not throw a penny into the man's hat. The awkwardness with which that little cripple is begging and the unconcerned response of the gaily laughing crowd creates in Tolstoi "a feeling of pain, of bitterness and, above all, of shame for the little man, for the crowd, for myself as if I had asked for money and had harvested nothing but sarcastic laughter."

The scene is set for the confrontation of good and evil. Tolstoi runs through the streets until he finds the little man, whom he takes with him to the Hotel Schweizerhof, demanding to sit with this begging troubadour in the midst of all the pretentious riches, and ordering a bottle of champagne. This is all there is to Tolstoi's story. But the writer reveals the entire scale of social ugliness through the reactions of the guests and waiters who, in their way, display disdain for the crippled street singer, as much as for Tolstoi's eccentricity. In contrast to pride, prejudice, and humiliation, the figure of the begging singer appears in a halo of modesty, humbleness, and forgiveness (". . . in his soul is no reproach, no anger, no regret . . .").

Tolstoi, losing track of the story as story, talks himself into a fury of philosophical thoughts on the harm materialistic society inflicts on the natural, unspoiled man (". . . ask men what is the highest ideal on earth, and they all will tell you: money"), on the poetry of life without which no one can live and to which everyone is blind and deaf ("All love it, they all search for it . . . and no one recognizes its power . . . no one knows how to honor and thank those who give poetry to mankind").

Tolstoi began to question the very basis of civilization with this story and was later led to question organized religion and government, as well as private property. Finally, he gave up all he possessed in order to live the life of extreme simplicity. He also realized that his anger against the rich and such poor wretches as the waiters and doormen was evil, that anger and all resistance of evil are wrong. ("Endless is the kindness and wisdom of Him who permits all these contradictions to be . . .")

Has it any significance that this turn of events and thoughts in Tolstoi's life occurred on Swiss soil and in Lucerne? Hardly. It could have happened at any other place. But these contradictions which, at the same time, seemed frightening and liberating to Tolstoi, occurred in the then most progressive republic, whose laws tolerate and sanction the contrasts of modern civilization, a fact that stirred the poet and compelled the philosopher in Tolsoi to meditate.

But then, looking from the balcony of the Hotel Schweizerhof at the beauty of nature surrounding the city, he cannot help thinking that all those people being now sheltered in their rooms and warm beds do not feel the same "carefree, gentle joy of life," not as much "inner harmony as is in the soul of this little man" who will now rest "on foul straw" or sit somewhere "on a dirty threshold." Probably only the sight of the serene majesty of nature could have made Tolstoi close his story with such thoughts of reconciliation, addressed more to himself than to his readers: "In your pride you thought you could tear yourself away from the law of universality. No, you too, with your despicable mean anger against the servants—you too answered to the need of harmony of the eternal and infinite."

CODA

BEFORE writing this book, I tried to travel through Switzerland with open eyes, but not with the eyes of the tourist who walks in surprise and, with the feeling of paid-for enjoyment, through a museum. I have never seen Switzerland as the toy country often pictured. I spoke to the "unknown citizen" on the street as much as I debated the country's problems with its well-known leaders in the arts, sciences, business, and politics. I spoke to the old and young, the reactionaries and revolutionaries.

I had a talk with Max Frisch in which his last words of advice were: "Don't try to write too nice a book about us." I found this self-critical attitude symptomatic of the intellectuals in Switzerland, particularly among the younger people. Whenever I said I intended to paint a panoramic picture of Switzerland's cultural contribution to our civilization, I found, more often than not, a facetious and, at best, an embarrassed smile accompanying the reply: "What cultural contribution?"

None of these doubters of their country's culture were without culture. Most of them were creative artists and well-known professionals who readily admitted that Switzerland has brought forth a few great men in past centuries, but that the Swiss are now living on the glory of their past, not only ignoring anything that is new, but also stifling it as best as they can.

The Swiss suffer from *"narrow*-itis." Their intellectuals and creative people especially look with claustrophobic eyes around them. Their blessings seem to them curses. They take their lot so seriously that they discuss themselves in many publications, exploring, explaining, attacking, and negating themselves. I like Jean Rudolph von Salis' image of "difficult Switzerland."

Essentially, its difficulty lies in the fact that it must continue to live its own legend, its own uniqueness as a state, and its own beauty. There is no people or country that cannot proudly refer to some legendary beginning which is being taught in school and extolled by patriotic poets from time to time. Most nations overcome their legends and manage to live the ever-changing actuality of their lives happily ever after. Not so the Swiss, as Max Frisch proved when, as late as 1970, he tried to dim Wilhelm Tell's halo with his attack on Switzerland's hero image in his little book, *Wilhelm Tell for the Schools.*

Another myth believed everywhere by everyone is the glorification of Switzerland as a peaceful country, or a country living in peace for four hundred years. The Swiss strove for collective security for that long. But the fact is that peace has been theirs only since 1848, that their last civil war took place in 1847, and that they were the greatest warriors in Europe, fighting the mighty powers surrounding them but also fighting among one another the bloodiest battles imaginable. The image of Switzerland as we know it now is about 120 years old.

To this very day every Swiss carries a gun and is called up regularly to serve in the Swiss militia. In a country in which every citizen has his guns at home, ready at a minute's notice to defend his freedom and neutrality, the legend of Wilhelm Tell and the glorified reality of the Rütli oath cannot easily die.

The reputation of Swiss soldiery was established in the fourteenth and fifteenth centuries, when the Swiss defeated Austria and Burgundy. The victory of the Swiss confederacy over the Duke of Burgundy changed the balance of power in Europe, since Burgundy was a formidable rival of the King of France and a dangerous enemy of Emperor Maximilian. At that time the Swiss made a decisive contribution to the tactical change of warfare (which must be underlined, even though it is far from being a cultural contribution). A people's army, foot-soldiers of brutal determination, defeated the armies of the knights on horseback. The significance of what later became the infantry was then proved by the Swiss soldiers.

At that time the confederacy of Swiss cantons was still in an aggressive mood, encouraged by their strength and major victories. The Swiss were out for more land and, during their Italian campaign, they suffered their first defeat, at Marignano in North Italy in 1515. In spite of it, they still gained command of the territory known as the Ticino, which they treated as a subjugated territory for a long time. The Ticino was not raised to the status of an autonomous canton before the Napoleon era.

As if Switzerland wanted to give the world an example, it had learned its lesson from its first defeat and decided on a policy of perpetual neutrality. This did not mean peace for the Swiss who continued to fight among themselves. But the neutrality of the country was honored by all great powers, princes, and popes because they all respected the Swiss as a soldier—and needed him. It was not until 1859 that service in foreign wars by Swiss citizens was forbidden by law, and thus the end of the Swiss mercenaries fighting for other rulers was reached. The last vestige of Swiss soldiery can still be found at the Vatican, with its famous Swiss Guard. But rumors have it that the Vatican has a difficult time nowadays recruiting enough Swiss for this job.

The soldiers were as solid and reliable as their country has become, and the stories of their heroic feats are legends and legendary by now. At the beginning of the French Revolution in 1792, for example, history tells us that one of its first victims was the Swiss Guard defending the gates of the Tuileries Palace.* So many centuries of bloody heroism must have left some mental residue. Small wonder that the Swiss man is proud of his militia and proud of going regularly to his military exercises. Its militia has become a part of Switzerland's folklore.

The Swiss constitution went through several rewrites. Some of the more difficult days experienced by the Swiss were during the French invasion. Napoleon, however, was much too clever to dismember the famous confederation from which he expected substantial military support. He gave Switzerland a new constitution in 1803 which he called "Mediation Act," and in handing in the new law to a confederate delegation, Bonaparte used the historic words: "Nature created your country as a federalistic one." Nine years later he sacrificed, among others, not less than 8,000 Swiss mercenaries during his famous Russian campaign.

The more or less final version of the Swiss constitution was written in 1848, the true beginning of today's Switzerland. It was the result of the great liberal movement during the earlier half of the nineteenth century. The people voted for the new constitution and its liberal image with 169,000 *Yeses*, against 71,000 *Noes* from the so-called Ur-cantons (Uri- Schwyz, Ob- and Nidwalden, as well as Appenzell), whose people said: "We detest this new union as an unbearable yoke of the free men of the Ur-cantons." But Gottfried Keller referred with pride to those men of 1848 and wrote that he "owed them a great deal of gratitude in all secrecy. From a vague revolutionary and irregular partisan *à tout prix*, I educated myself, looking to them for inspiration, to become a conscious and level-headed person." Taking the cue from Gottfried Keller, one can state in all fairness that the constitution of 1848

---

* But most history books neglect to say that one of the great men of the French Revolution, Jean Paul Marat, was born in Switzerland and that Etienne Dumont, a native of Geneva, wrote the most important speeches for Mirabeau.

bore all the signs of judicial prudence and expressed the wishes of a vast majority of the populace.

One of the young contemporary rebels, the writer Peter Bichsel, points out in his essay, *The Switzerland of the Swiss*, that the liberals of the early nineteenth century are the real fathers of Switzerland ("I must thank them for my personal freedom"), but "their descendants would consider the people of 1848 as indecent because the liberals were the opposition, the renewers, the 'left.' The constitution is their work. But they have no descendants. Nobody refers to 1848. One still conjures up the spirit of 1291. We still hold on to Tell. He obliges us hardly to anything except our independence."

Since the late 1950's, the Swiss youth are just as restless as youth everywhere, particularly because a rebellious spirit has emerged from the well-to-do middle class, that which constitutes the core and majority of the Swiss. For almost an entire century the bourgeois, somewhat right of center, has been the true image of the Swiss. He is so strong that he has been able to absorb all revolutionary movements, integrating socialism into his huge industrial program, paralyzing all communistic trends, and assimilating the fascistic fronts in the late thirties. This "bourgeois" shows resilience and the inner strength of his stubborn and level-headed forefathers, herdsmen and peasants of whom he never ceases to be proud. This incarnation of the "establishment" can perhaps best be tagged as an arch-conservative liberal. He is a guardian of the past with the mission of a liberal, forced upon him by history and geography as much as by the world which dreams of keeping a peep-hole open into its lost paradise.

All this must have cultural consequences. And it has. Pastor, essayist, and poet Kurt Marti wrote very perceptively and convincingly about this topic in his book, *Switzerland and Its Writers —the Writers and Their Switzerland.* Speaking of the strong bourgeois establishment, he refers to its decisive influence on the writer who "feels this establishment as stagnation, as intellectual narrowness, as latent non-freedom," and Marti sees the writer's position as "much weaker than, for instance, the one of his German colleagues who criticize another—in the past never so successful— bourgeoisie which for this reason did not remain intact. The contempt for the writer who does not represent the establishment but keeps a critical attitude towards it coincides with a disdain for the writer's profession. This may historically go back to the fact that the poet, in contrast to the visual artist, never belonged to a guild; therefore his work was never considered honest labor in the bourgeois sense . . ."

Paul Nizon took up Marti's thought in his book, *Discourse in Narrowness*, and went one step further. He calls our attention to the fact that

> the legendary values of the original confederates, let us call them urge for independence and undaunted courage, were developed in the struggle against the aristocracy, and aristocracy at that time meant, above all, also a sophisticated way of living and mainly educational privileges. It stands to reason that from this position of opposition something like a cultural animosity was kept alive; that everything intellectual (in its critical-creative, not in its glorified interpretation of the term) took on the color of a negative, bombastic and arrogant quality in the understanding of our self. The assumption that the *old Swiss* within the Swiss rejects cultural claims in this sense as something alien to his native kind, cannot so easily be refuted.

No doubt, this is a psychologically interesting explanation with which Paul Nizon tries to harden his argument that the Swiss artist, and particularly the writer, faces a cultural vacuum at home. He may even be on safer ground when he refers to the fact that the "city" as a cultural image is strongly pushed into the background in contrast to the native emotions tied up with the image of the "landscape." Nizon also feels that the Swiss is inclined to type himself as a democrat, considering democracy as an emotionally colored concept fraught with Rütli-oath-like, heroic remembrances, equating it with upright-brave simplicity which excludes and looks with disdain at anything different from the average, viewing intellectualism with great suspicion.

Paul Nizon's arguments may sound convincing as long as he concentrates on describing the Swiss, and he is mainly concerned with his contemporaries. The moment he compares the artist's position in other nations with that in Switzerland he weakens his point. He claims that the best creative sons of his home country had to escape their narrowness and look for inspiration and recognition in other countries, that they had to become exiles in order to find themselves (such as the novelists Albin Zollinger and Robert Walser). Or he refers to Max Frisch's protagonist Stiller who, after returning home from the "world," is arrested and incarcerated; he is a man actually swallowed by the narrowness of his home; in self-defense Stiller denies his identity and shouts into the unreality of his reality: "I am not Stiller!" The feeling of narrowness is followed by flight, escape. Narrowness is felt as absence from the "world." Another point made is that the writer, cut off from the world, suffers from lack of material. It is said how very difficult it is to fashion "world literature in the sense of contemporary literature out of Swiss everyday material, out of Swiss destinies and characters against the background of Switzerland. Certainly not in that self-evident, vital sense as [the writer] would love to do and as he knows it from other literatures—(again to give a great example, mainly for the purpose of contrast) as he knows it from the American literature."

True, such works as John Steinbeck's *The Grapes of Wrath,* Dos Passos' *Manhattan Transfer,* Arthur Miller's *Death of a Salesman,* or Thornton Wilder's *Our Town* emerged from the American atmosphere—even though Wilder wrote his by now classic play in Switzerland. But Paul Nizon and his confrères are concerned mainly with the post-war conditions of today and tomorrow, conjuring up the past as proof of the present and future. The arts and particularly literature, the novel and theatre, are in a state of crisis everywhere. During most of this century the creative artist has searched for his identity and for the meaning of life, which is best proved by his frantic groping from -ism to -ism. Frisch's Stiller is not a Swiss phenomenon alone. Saul Bellow's Herzog and a dozen other protagonists are in the same or similar shoes.

In Marshall McLuhan's world, which is shrinking to an electronic village at a rapid pace, all intellectuals and creative minds are facing or will shortly face the same Swiss problem of narrowness. In former times it took decades for an artistic movement to unfold. It now takes hardly a year or two. It was most often localized in one country for a long time before spreading and finding its epigones somewhere else. Today from abstract to pop art, from concrete to minimal art, it is more or less the same in New York, Paris, London, and Zürich at about the same time. The restlessness of the rebellious youth belongs with the *Zeitgeist* everywhere.

Because of the tremendous anxieties caused by the tremendous experiences in our time—in science and technology as much as in all the arts—man has become more of a conformist than ever before. If we continue to use America as a prime example, then there is hardly any other country in which the conformist is more at home. America has never been known for being physically or geographically small. But it has always been known for its suspicion of the intellectual, "the egghead" (for its "if you are so smart, why aren't you rich" attitude), for its notorious neglect of its artists, who had to prove their artistic mettle in Europe first in order to be accepted and recognized at home. And do the Swiss writers and visual artists alone feel like leaving their native country because its atmosphere is not sufficiently stimulating? Since America was cited as example let us stay with it.

When Zollinger and Walser left Switzerland, Henry James, T. S. Eliot, and Ezra Pound went to Europe, to England in particular. Later, in the twenties and thirties, the greatest American writers escaped to Paris and Spain. Do we have to enumerate the many luminaries of the pen like Ernest Hemingway, F. Scott Fitzgerald, Gertrude Stein, and Thornton Wilder? The latter probably spent more years of his life in Germany, Switzerland, and Italy than in America. And if the Swiss-born Angelika Kaufmann lived in Italy and England all her life, did not the American-born Mary Cassatt go to Paris, where alone she could flower? Is it not said of the greatest architect of our time, Le Corbusier, that he had to leave Switzerland, and that he built almost everywhere in the world, but received not one assignment in his home country? And did not, for instance, the American, Jacob Epstein, one of the great sculptors of our time, move to England, where he became his self and was knighted? The Swiss artist is apparently not alone in feeling compelled to escape the very atmosphere into which he was born.

Ezra Pound once remarked arrogantly that culture is created by twelve people. The process of democratization has multiplied this figure, but the figure of those who are the culture-makers in a country is still a very modest one in relation to the population as a whole. No one can deny that Austria, and its capital Vienna, brought forth the largest number of musical geniuses. But Haydn and Mozart were treated like servants by their aristocratic patrons, nor did the contemporary Viennese take Alban Berg and Anton von Webern to his bosom. The masses of the Viennese liked their Johann Strauss, and the *Schrammelmusik* in Grinzing at the *Heurigen* with wine, woman, and song. It has always been a relatively thin layer of Viennese society that appreciated a Gustav Mahler or Hugo Wolf.

The broad masses of man—the ever more frightening majority of people everywhere, the glorified Mr. Average—are insensitive to the poetry of life. This is a truism to which the Swiss are no exception, even though they may have their peculiarities, derived from too much tradition-bound existence and mentality, which the Swiss historian Herbert Lüthy pinpointed in his book, *Switzerland as Antithesis:*

> There is a certain Swiss pettiness, a cult of the immediate useful and profitable, a social conformism inimical to everything imaginative which have made this country inhospitable to the arts and the graces.

When one considers the great number of giants and luminaries in almost all spheres of scientific, humanistic, and artistic endeavor brought forth by the Swiss, one can only wonder whether this obtuse resistance of the majority of people to the higher things in life, after all, does not have the effect of an incentive and challenge—for how else can we explain all the accomplishments on record? Has mutation become so common that we can no longer speak of mutation as such? Or is resistance to the arts and graces so very much obvious because of the proverbial narrowness in space?

However, not every creative mind in Switzerland suffers from narrow-itis. For example, the discomfort arising from narrowness of existence is denied by painter-sculptor-writer-architect Max Bill. When he received the *Kunstpreis* of the city of Zürich, he delivered a speech which he called "Comfort in a Small State." He praised the governmental form of the small state which may often make detours but, avoiding any major catastrophes, progresses, however slowly, and creates a feeling of political and economic security which, in turn, creates a feeling of comfort. "Comfort *(Behagen)* is what makes life worth living," he said. "It concerns that balanced equanimity which man needs to be able to function effectively in his activities. To make this feeling of comfort possible for everyone, one has looked for new ways and means time and again. It can be said without exaggeration that all modern religions, including Christianity and Communism, have striven for this comfort as a general condition for man at least theoretically." Revolutions, Max Bill maintains, have brought about more reactionary movements than a quietly developing democracy. To preserve this type of democracy, to preserve comfort, the justification of existence in Switzerland, it is necessary to think of new things, to plunge into intellectual adventures all the time. Max Bill suggests that the feeling of comfort can only exist if man's basic form of life continues to develop and if his possibilities are not wasted but properly used.

If nothing else, Max Bill proves that "narrowness" is a mental attitude which can be turned to full advantage. Bill's gesture may point to another quality observable among the Swiss, to which Friedrich Dürrenmatt also referred in 1956 when the magazine *Die Weltwoche* asked him which, in his opinion, is the most negative quality of the Swiss. Dürrenmatt replied to this question: "That he believes to be so positive." But if he is so positive, it is only because of his inferior feelings, for in reality he is so negative and doubtful of himself.

On the occasion of another questionnaire, this time about the Swiss film and its potentialities, Dürrenmatt replied to *Die Weltwoche*: "The legend of our virtue stifles the possibilities which may still lie hidden in our vices." Is it really true that the Swiss "knows neither good nor evil, only the accepted and prescribed virtues of his fathers . . .?" as another Swiss rebel, the little known writer Hans Morgenthaler (1890-1928), an outsider and self-destructive genius, once said. In his fury and disappointment in himself, Morgenthaler wrote in his novel, *Woly. Summer in the South:* "Every Swiss is well off and therefore badly off." This is exactly what Max Bill denies. He does not believe in the romanticized and operatic nineteenth-century myth that great works can only be written in dirty garrets by starving artists. In his eyes, the Swiss can, if not psychologically handicapped, create because he lives in an atmosphere of "being well-off," and can fully turn his energies to the unfolding of his talents. In the last analysis, Max Bill, denying the self-torturing image of narrowness, somehow echoes a thought of Leonardo da Vinci, who said that "Small rooms discipline the mind; large ones distract it."

Because of their unique position among the nations of the world, the Swiss are very much concerned about their image. They seem to be more dependent on it than other peoples, and oversensitive to anyone's reactions to them. Their own self-styled myth is intricately interrelated with their image abroad. Peter Bichsel's opinion is that "We have become accustomed to seeing Switzerland with the eyes of our tourists . . . Our image of our country is a foreign product. We live with the legend which was made around us . . . We have become used to being a museum. We have fun to be admired by foreigners . . .".

Jean Rudolph von Salis, in his essay *Switzerland Censured*, blames his own people for having created a distorted picture of themselves. "Switzerland has not penetrated the awareness of the foreigners as a historic-cultural entity . . . What counts are the spiritual accomplishments of a people, of their thinkers, artists, poets, composers, scientists; but it seems that exactly these things of which, by the way, there is no lack in our country, are never claimed by our people as the great accomplishments of their home country. This is why foreign eyes do not see us as a nation that, above all, has always contributed its share to human culture, and still does."

This is an essential point. It is most essential for this book, which in the main deals with Switzerland's culture, past and present. Moreover, this book received its strongest impetus through my reaction to the ignorant generalizations with which most of the people I have met identify Switzerland as a country and the Swiss as a people. I realize if I wished to correct the historic and cultural misconceptions that haunt the world I would in all fairness have to write many books about many nations. As long as man exists, prejudice will exist.

However, it seems to me that the Swiss are a most unique example of a people who have become the favorites of destiny because geography, history, and the needs of the world have conspired to shape the fate of this nation which to this day has remained a nation of many nations. Switzerland is a perfect window display, for all the world to see how different people—as a matter of fact, differing from canton to canton and village to village— manage to live together in the spirit of a workable federal union. A recent poll taken among leading men everywhere showed Switzerland at first place of all countries in the world, as to skill in self-government.

But such a universal accolade does not presume that all people love the Swiss. On the contrary, one does not love one's classmate who is the favorite of the gods and teachers; one is suspicious and envious of the ways and means by which he maintains his status of efficiency and excellence. One looks for his weaknesses and is inclined to magnify them. It is comforting to know that, after all, he is not perfect. And the Swiss, as a people, are not perfect. By no means. Even though the French Swiss in the west are different from the Italians in the Ticino, and both are quite different from the German-speaking Swiss in the north (among whom, in turn, are great differences), there are nevertheless certain common characteristics noticeable. Famous and less famous guests have not only admitted the inspiration and enjoyment they derived from their stay in Switzerland, but they also were neither blind to nor inarticulate about the flaws they saw in the people's character.

Voltaire, champion of tolerance, justice, and reason, had nothing nice to say about the Genevans, and the French statesman and historian Adolphe Thiers, who lived in Vevey for some time, spoke of the Swiss as a little stingy people. Clichés can contain as much truth as truisms sometimes do. All otherwise positive features, such as efficiency and quality, punctuality and friendliness are seen in the Swiss from the angle of an acquisitive, avaricious, and businesslike drive of the people—an attitude which, to a great extent, may be justified. But as an exercise in logic let me ask: Would we find fewer faults with the Swiss businessman whose product is less reliable and whose service less efficient? If the hoteliers were neither clean, punctual, nor friendly, and would offer us their lovely landscape for the same amount of money and less pleasant service, would we then love the Swiss more for it—only because we no longer see the smile studied at the Lausanne School-for-Hoteliers and no longer notice the routine behind the things that work?

The Swiss are often called boring, a people with a narrow horizon, and reserved. These epithets were underlined in a survey by *Die Weltwoche*, which recently published the findings of its correspondents from ten countries in a booklet, *Switzerland with Foreign Eyes*. The above mentioned qualities were, for instance, stressed by the Dutch people, who certainly know from their own experience how it feels to be boring and reserved or to have to struggle with one's narrow horizon. The cleanliness and solidity of the Swiss are set off by the people's self-complacency; their insistence on tradition and their money-mindedness have stamped the well-fed bourgeois as a Swiss symbol of triumphant averageness.

Some kinder eyes see them as a cultured people who, however, have not produced any creative minds. Their humanitarian and missionary works—who still today associates the Red Cross, a worldwide organization, with Switzerland?—their role as mediator, and their country as the place of international conferences, all this is clouded by the suspicion of materialistic motives. Jean Rudolph von Salis rightly said that it is difficult to make the foreigner believe that the country's riches are a consequence of its neutrality, but that Switzerland did not stay out of all armed conflicts in Europe in the last hundred and fifty years in order to enrich itself. A few Swiss, among them such writers as Max Frisch and Walter Gross, have rightly reproached Switzerland for doing too little with its neutrality in order "to do justice to a now rare freedom," as Frisch said. Both writers pleaded for an "engaged neutrality" of an activized ethos, and Frisch asked his country to become "a spiritual Geneva."

Since World War II, materialism has become rampant all over the world. Through the rapidly growing process of democratization more people of different nationalities have been able to prove that acquisitiveness and avariciousness are common human qualities. In these decades Switzerland has suffered from the fact that more and more people were hiding black money in this country. There is more foreign than Swiss money in the construction of new buildings which, now mushrooming in valleys and on mountain slopes, endanger the beauty of Switzerland's landscape. It has become fashionable to own at least an apartment in one of the many condominiums and for the world's richest and most famous people to move into towers which in their beautiful and powerful majesty compete with their neighboring mountains. These edifices and the roads leading to them have to be built with the help of foreign labor whose presence on Swiss soil has created social problems. That the Swiss profit from this flight of foreign money into their country is—to express it euphemistically—unavoidable.

We cannot blame anyone who wishes to bask in the sun of Switzerland's security or to feel protected in the shadow of its armed neutrality, which, by the way, is often belittled and satirized, and correctly so, because it only exists through the will and by the grace of the mighty powers that are. Its armed neutrality has been called anachronistic, since man's next excursion into self-destruction will be unable to distinguish boundaries, not even those of continents, and may take place high above and over the snow-capped heights of a Matterhorn or Mont Blanc. But as long as mankind is teasing itself with minor Armageddons, Switzerland's neutrality will preserve its value because of some of the ugliest qualities of the rich and powerful in the world.

There are no larger and smaller communities in the world which are not characterized by certain easily identifiable habits and features, shaped by climate, geography, and history. The Swiss are no exception. That their women could be judges and teachers, but had no right of self-determination in the oldest of all "direct" democracies until very recently, was a natural target of a good-humored amusement and bitter mockery at the Swiss system of modern patriarchy. The people's slowness and pettiness—reproaches most often heard—can generally be observed. On the other hand, out of the people's obsession with the smallness and narrowness of their existence, they have developed an almost frantic missionary drive—which is, as I have tried to point out in another chapter, only the other extreme of their former militant strength and prowess as the best warriors anywhere. For the same reason, they developed their now legendary and mocked-at efficiency, which is best il-luminated by an anecdote. An American firm produced the thinnest wire imaginable and proudly sent a sample of it to its Swiss part-ner, who congratulated the American on his accomplishment, adding that they were able to pierce a small hole through it.

Such abilities and neurotic drives to excel have created a feeling of smugness and self-complacency. The Swiss are also reproached for not easily taking criticism. In this context, Max Frisch's Doctor in the play *Andorra* comes to mind. Frisch, one of the most con-cerned writers of our era, referred symbolically to the Swiss and Switzerland, when he makes his character say:

> You can believe one thing: There is no nation in the whole world which, in the whole world, is as much beloved as we are. Beloved is not the word for it. I've met people who have no idea where Andorra lies, but every child in the world knows that Andorra is a bulwark, a bulwark of peace and freedom and the human rights.

Beyond all smugness and self-mockery the Swiss cannot help being fully aware of the beauty of his country. We could let the noted figure from Andorra continue: "Every child in the world knows that Andorra is beautiful. To mention the name Andorra is to awaken the most colorful images of the most beautiful beauty in everyone." Switzerland's varied beauty has attracted and pleased many thousands of travelers and vacationers year after year. This may mean much for the individual, yet little for the world. But what has enriched the world were the many creative minds which were enriched by the country's beauty. Of those many inspired artists, some were mentioned in this book. Various centers or colonies of creative spirits were formed at different times in and around Zürich, which has always attracted the artist, but also in the Valais and around Lake Geneva.

Probably the strongest attraction has been exerted by the Ticino, whose valleys and mountains, whose shores on its lakes have played the role of inspiring host with great success. Hermann Hesse, living on the hills of Montagnola near Lugano, dreamt of

a utopia in his novel, *Glasperlenspiel or Ludi Magister*, in which
men of knowledge lived in the beauty of aesthetic mysticism,
combining the wisdom of East and West. This utopia was an ideal
reflection of the peaceful island called Switzerland. In fact, in the
Ticino and particularly in Ascona, many artists, writers, scientists,
and dreamers gathered, wanting to improve the world, or rather
create a colony of the spirit and mind in its most ideal form. In
1905, a group of reformers of life banded together on what is
now Monte Verità, the mount of truth, today overrun by tourists.

Once it was just another hill rising up from the Lago Maggiore,
a hill that dreamt of becoming a mountain. There, around the turn
of the century, a group of people settled who dreamt of being able
to turn against technology and the social order by giving mankind
an example of how to live. With their hatred of all conventions,
they also threw overboard their conventional clothes. They were
the first hippies, foreshadowing most everything that was then
unheard-of and that later in the century became an accepted part
of our new ways of life. They were dreamers trying to free themselves from the fetters of mechanized life and its many taboos, and
they were carried aloft by the flaming ideas common to all world
reformers. Their community was conceived of as an ethic-social-
vegetarian-communistic society, but, as with all such attempts to
give reality to a half-baked dream, it went the way of all ideals.

But other dreamers and doers followed; for instance, a group
of theosophists and mystics. Its driving force was Mrs. O. Fröbe-
Kapteyn who, inspired by Ludwig Derleth, Carl Gustav Jung, and
Karl Kerényi, arranged the famous Eranos discussions held annually in the early autumn in Ascona since 1933. Long after Mrs.
Fröbe's death the Eranos meetings are still taking place in Ascona
each year. Some of the greatest European minds gather there—men
who feel the inner strength to speak of what moves and tortures
them and who wish to exchange their thoughts with others, men
who feel the need to listen and to be enlightened.

The mount of truth and its environment have been a focal point
of meditation, being witness to many creative thoughts, to new
ideas and movements. Some of the best minds came as if they were
anticipating a spa for rejuvenation; some of them stayed. Hugo
Ball, co-founder of Dadaism in Zürich, settled in the Ticino and
wrote in his diary on August 15, 1917:

> The idea of the natural paradise—it could have been born in
> Switzerland only. The most remote virgin world met here with

the loveliest idyll, the icy air of snow-covered summits with the gentlest chimes of the south. Switzerland is the refuge of all those who bear a new blueprint in their hands. It was and is now, during the war, the preservation of natural beauty, the national park in which the nations keep their last reserve. Here stood the cradle of that law-giver in whose rejuvenating imagination mingled the world of the artist and reformer, aesthetic and political enthusiasm: the cradle of Jean-Jacques Rousseau. All those who wreck or wrecked their brains over the question of how to get mankind back on its feet, how to guarantee a new mankind, live or once lived in this country.

A detailed enumeration of all the works created on Swiss soil by non-Swiss artists, inspired by the atmosphere and landscape of Switzerland, must be left to the mind of a statistician, but it would surprise the innocent as much as the cognoscente. The intangible something inherent in the beauty of the Swiss landscape, the indefinite fragrance of its atmosphere, and the magic of its clearly defined image have made sensitive souls sing and see in flowering colors.

There are many other mountains and lakes and wonders of nature all over the world. There are many more cities that hold secrets of surprise. It was said of Naples, for instance, that one must see it, and then can die. It can be said of Switzerland that one must see it and then cannot help but create.

All this makes life difficult for the Swiss, who must go through all the feelings of a beautiful woman (of which I know little but which I can surmise). Early in the morning a look into the mirror reassures her of her beauty. Wherever she goes, enthusiastic, penetrating eyes accompany her, as well as loving and envious looks; wherever she appears, she is an object of attention and desire, she is wanted by too many and rejected by those who are afraid and suspicious of so much beauty; she cannot help being generous with herself, but only she knows how miserly she really is with her beauty. She knows the weaknesses of man as much as she knows her own value. Her beauty complicates her life and character. She knows too well what she is worth because everyone tells her how beautiful she is. And very few can forgive her that she is not only beautiful but also rich, and rich not only because she is beautiful. To complete and complicate matters, she does not mind and secretly supports the rumors that she is virtuous.

It is sad that so very few people see beyond her shape and fea-

tures the beauty within her, visualize the people she has given birth
to, the poety she has evoked in man, the thoughts she has kindled,
the deeds she has done. She is so used to being stared at and admired
that she herself, more often than not, forgets or even denies that she
is anything else but beautiful and rich.

That is why this book was written.

BIBLIOGRAPHY

If not stated otherwise, all translations from the German and French are by the author.

GENESIS AND SOME REVELATIONS

Lüthy, Herbert. *Die Schweiz als Antithese.* Zürich: Verlag Die Arche, 1969.

RELIGION: From Zwingli to Barth

Barth, Karl. *The Humanity of God.* London: Collins, 1960.
   Church Dogmatics. Edinburgh: T. & T. Clark, 1958.
Brunner, Emil. *Theology of Crisis.* New York: Charles Scribner's Sons, 1930.
Burckhardt, Jacob. *Briefe.* Band I. Basel-Stuttgart: Benno Schwabe & Co., 1963.
Burckhardt-Biedermann, Th. *Bonifacius Amerbach und die Reformation.* Basel: R. Reich vormals C. Detloffs Buchhandlung, 1894.
Cox, Harvey. *The Secular City.* New York: The Macmillan Co., 1965.
Dürrenmatt, Friedrich. *Theaterprobleme.* Zürich: Verlag Die Arche, 1955.
Ebeling, Gerhard. *The Nature of Faith.* Translated by Ronald Gregor Smith. Philadelphia: Muhlenberg Press, 1961.
   Wort und Glaube. Tübingen: J. C. B. Mohr, 1960.
Erasmus, Desiderius. *Lugduni Batavorum,* the Leiden Edition of the works of Erasmus, edited by J. LeClerc, 1703–1706.
Farner, Konrad. *Revisionismus.* Frankfurt a/M.: Stimme Verlag, no date.
Küng, Hans. Articles on Hans Küng in *Newsweek,* January 25, 1971, and in the *Manchester Guardian,* June 30, 1971.
Reston, James. *On the Nobility of Old Age.* In *The New York Times,* September 23, 1970.
Zweig, Stefan. *Triumph und Tragik des Erasmus von Rotterdam.* Wien: Herbert Reichner Verlag, 1935.

EDUCATION, or The Belief in Love

Bachofen, Johann Jakob. *Das Mutterrecht.* Erster Band. Mit Unterstützung von Harald Fuchs, Gustav Meyer und Karl Schefold. Herausgegeben von Karl Meuli. Basel: Benno Schwabe & Co., 1948.

Burckhardt, Carl J. *Erinnerungen an Hofmannsthal und Briefe des Dichters*. Basel: Benno Schwabe & Co., 1944.

Briefwechsel Hugo von Hofmannsthal—Carl J. Burckhardt. Frankfurt a/M.: S. Fischer Verlag, 1956.

Burckhardt, Jacob. *Briefe*. Band I, II, III, and V. Basel: Benno Schwabe & Co., 1963.

Weltgeschichtliche Betrachtungen. Basel: Benno Schwabe & Co., 1956.

Die Kultur der Renaissance in Italien. Ein Versuch. Stuttgart: Alfred Kröner Verlag, 1952.

Egger, Eugen. *Die Schule der Schweiz*. Berlin-Basel: Verlag Julius Beltz. No date.

Ernst, Fritz. *Europäische Schweiz*. Eine geistesgeschichtliche Studie. Zürich: Artemis Verlag, 1961.

Das Wunder Pestalozzis. In Eduard Korrodi: *Geisteserbe der Schweiz*. Erlenbach-Zürich: Eugen Rentsch Verlag, 1943.

Häberlin, Paul. *Bestimmungen des Menschen und Sinn der Erziehung*. Genf: Unesco-Kommission, 1951.

Hesse, Hermann. *Hermann Hesse. Eine Chronik in Bildern*. Bearbeitet und mit einer Einleitung versehen von Bernhard Zeller. Frankfurt a/M.: Suhrkamp Verlag, 1960.

Korrodi, Eduard (ed.). *Geisteserbe der Schweiz*. Erlenbach-Zürich: Eugen Rentsch Verlag, 1943.

Marti, Kurt. *Die Schweiz und ihre Schriftsteller—die Schriftsteller und ihre Schweiz*. Zürich: Evangelische Zeitbuchreihe, 1966.

Müller, Otto (ed.). *Die Stimme Pestalozzis*. Basel und Olten: Urs Graf Verlag G.M.B.H., 1941.

Pestalozzi, Heinrich. *Schriften*. In Eduard Korrodi: *Geisteserbe der Schweiz*. Erlenbach-Zürich: Eugen Rentsch Verlag, 1943.

Rousseau, Jean Jacques. *Oeuvres complètes*. Par V. D. Musset-Pathay. Paris: Chez P. Dupont, 1824.

Troxler, Ignaz Paul Vital. *Schriften*. In *Die Menschenschule*. Allgemeine Monatsschrift für Erziehungskunst und Lehrerbildung im Sinne Rudolf Steiners. Herausgeber C. Englert-Faye. Basel: Jahrgang 11, Heft 4/5, April/Mai, 1937.

In *Die Schweizer Rundschau*. Zürich: Verlag der Buchdruckerei H. Börsigs Erben A.G. Jahrgang 57, Heft 1, April, 1957.

Wölfflin, Heinrich. *Kunstgeschichtliche Grundbegriffe*. München: H. Bruckmann Verlag, 1921.

Gedanken zur Kunstgeschichte. In Eduard Korrodi: *Geisteserbe der Schweiz*. Erlenbach-Zürich: Eugen Rentsch Verlag, 1943.

Zuckmayer, Carl. *Ein Weg zu Carl J. Burckhardt.* In *Dauer im Wandel.* Festschrift zum 70. Geburtstag von Carl J. Burckhardt. Herausgegeben von Hermann Rinn und Max Rychner. München: Georg D. Callwey, 1961.

SCIENCE + A Few Random Remarks

Carol, Hans. *Aus einem Gespräch mit C. G. Jung.* In *Neue Zürcher Zeitung,* June 2, 1963.

Einstein, Albert. *Mein Weltbild.* Herausgegeben von Carl Seelig. Zürich-Stuttgart-Wien: Europa Verlag, 1953.

(The quotation used was published in the *Berliner Tageblatt,* November 11, 1930, for the first time.)

Jacobi, Jolande. *Die Psychologie von C. G. Jung.* Eine Einführung in das Gesamtwerk von Jung. Zürich: Rascher Verlag, 1945.
Ein Leben—von innen gesehen. Zu C. G. Jungs Buch "Erinnerungen, Träume, Gedanken." in *Neue Zürcher Zeitung,* June 2, 1963.

Jung, Carl Gustav. *Erinnerungen, Träume, Gedanken.* Aufgezeichnet und herausgegeben von Aniela Jaffé. Zürich: Rascher Verlag, 1962.

Marti, Kurt. *Die Schweiz und ihre Schriftsteller—die Schriftsteller und ihre Schweiz.* Zürich: Evangelische Zeitbuchreihe, 1966.

Piaget, Jean. *Genetic Epistemology.* From an essay adapted from the first and third of the Woodbridge Lectures delivered by Dr. Piaget at Columbia University in 1968. The essay was published by *Columbia Forum,* Fall 1969.

Whitrow, G. J. *Einstein. The Man and His Achievement.* Published by the British Broadcasting Corporation, London, 1967.

THE LITERARY LINGUAE OF THE SWISS

FRENCH

Amiel, Henri-Frédéric. *Fragments d'un Journal intime.* Augmentée de fragments inédits et précédée d'une introduction par Bernard Bouvier. Tome Premier.
Collection Helvetique. Genève: Editions Georg et Cie., 1922.
Philine: Fragments inédits du Journal intime. Publiés par Bernard Bouvier. Paris: J. Schiffrin, 1927.

Andrews, Wayne. *Germaine. A Portrait of Mme de Staël.* New York: Atheneum, 1963.

Arnold, Matthew. *Amiel.* In *Essays in Criticism.* Second Series. London, New York: The Macmillan Company, 1889.

Constant, Benjamin. *Journaux intimes.* Paris: Gallimard, 1952.

Cordey, Pierre. *Mme de Staël et Benjamin Constant sur les bords du Léman.* Paris: Éditions Payot, 1966.

Gibbon, Edward. *Autobiography.* London: J. M. Dent & Sons Ltd. New York: E. P. Dutton & Co., 1911.

Goncourt de, Edmond and Jules. *The Goncourt Journals 1851–1870.* Edited, translated, and with an introduction by Lewis Galantière. New York: Doubleday & Co., 1937.

Ramuz, Charles-Ferdinand. *When the Mountain Fell.* Translated by Sarah Fisher Scott. New York: Pantheon Books Inc., 1947.

Aimé Pache. Ein Waadtländischer Maler. Zürich: Humanitas Verlag, 1941.

Souvenir sur Igor Stravinsky. Translated by Dollie Pierre Chareau. Lausanne: Mermod, 1946.

Rousseau, Jean Jacques. *Correspondance.* Tome Troisième. *Oeuvres complètes de J. J. Rousseau.* Paris: Chez P. Dupont, 1824.

Staël, Germaine de. *Lettres à Ribbing.* Paris: Gallimard, 1960. *Mme de Staël, ses amis, ses correspondants.* Choix de lettres 1778–1817. Paris: Édition Klincksieck, 1970.

THE LITERARY LINGUAE OF THE SWISS

ITALIAN

Vollenweider, Alice (ed.). *Neue Erzähler aus dem Tessin.* Bern: Benziger Verlag, 1968.

Wermelinger, Max. *Die Italienische Schweiz heute.* In *Neue Zürcher Zeitung*—Schriften zur Zeit. No. 21, 1971.

Francesco Chiesa und die Bewusstwerdung der Tessiner Italianität. In *Neue Zürcher Zeitung*, July 4, 1971.

THE LITERARY LINGUAE OF THE SWISS

GERMAN

Brock-Sulzer, Elisabeth. *Friedrich Dürrenmatt. Lebensbild und Werkanalyse.* Zürich: Verlag Die Arche, 1970.

Burkart, Erika. *Moräne.* Der Roman von Lilith und Laurin. Olten und Freiburg im Breisgau: Walter Verlag, 1970.

Dürrenmatt, Friedrich. *Theaterschriften und Reden.* Herausgegeben von Elisabeth Brock-Sulzer. Zürich: Verlag Die Arche, 1970.

Frisch, Max. *Tagebücher.* Frankfurt a/M.: Suhrkamp Verlag, 1950.

Gotthelf, Jeremias. *Werke in 20 Bänden.* Herausgegeben von Walter Muschg. Basel: Verlag Birkhäuser, 1948.

Hohl, Ludwig. *Nächtlicher Weg.* Erzählungen. Zürich: Artemis Verlag, 1934.

Keller, Gottfried. *Sämtliche Werke.* München-Zürich: Droemersche Verlagsanstalt Th. Knaur Nachf., 1954.

Korrodi, Eduard. *Geisteserbe der Schweiz.* Erlenbach-Zürich: Eugen Rentsch Verlag, 1943.

Leber, Hugo (ed.). *Texte. Prosa junger Schweizer Autoren.* Einsiedeln, Zürich, Köln: Benzinger Verlag, 1946.

Mann, Thomas. *Die Entstehung des Doktor Faustus. Roman eines Romanes.* Frankfurt a/M.: Bermann-Fischer Verlag, 1949.

Marti, Kurt. *Die Schweiz und ihre Schriftsteller—die Schriftsteller und ihre Schweiz.* Zürich: Evangelische Zeitbuchreihe, 1966.

Meyer, Conrad Ferdinand. *Sämtliche Werke.* München-Zürich: Droemersche Verlagsanstalt Th. Knaur Nachf., 1959.

Muschg, Walter. *Tragische Literaturgeschichte.* Wien: Francke Verlag, 1958.

Natan, Alex (ed.). *Swiss Men of Letters.* Twelve Literary Essays. London: Oswald Wolff, 1970.

Schmid, Karl. *Unbehagen im Kleinstaat.* Zürich und Stuttgart: Artemis Verlag, 1963.

Schweizer Schriftsteller im Gespräch. Band I and II. Basel: Friedrich Reinhardt Verlag, 1970.

Walser, Robert. *Das Gesamtwerk.* Genf: Verlag Helmut Kossodo, 1969.

Weber, Werner. *Tagebuch eines Lesers.* Bemerkungen und Aufsätze zur Literatur. Olten und Freiburg im Breisgau: Walter Verlag, 1966.

Forderungen. Bemerkungen und Aufsätze zur Literatur. Zürich: Artemis Verlag, 1970.

THE VISUAL IMAGE BEYOND HODLER

Arp, Jean (Hans). *On My Way.* Poetry and essays. New York: Wittenborn, Schultz, Inc., 1948.

Zweiklang. Zürich: Verlag Die Arche, 1960.

Artaud, Antonin. *Bilboquet.* In *Oeuvres complètes.* Tome I. Paris: Gallimard, 1956.

Bense, Max. *Max Bill.* Translated by George W. Staempfli. London: Hanover Gallery, 1966.

Bill, Max. *Die Komposition I/1925 von Piet Mondrian.* Jahresbericht 1956 der Zürcher Kunstgesellschaft.

Ein Denkmal. In *Werk,* Heft 7, 44. Jahrgang, Juli 1957.

Catalogue of the Max Bill Ausstellung Kunsthaus Zürich, November 23, 1968,–January 5, 1969.

Catalogue Venezia 34 Biennale 1968. Internazionale d'Arte, Venezia, 22 Giugno–20 Ottobre, 1968.

Burckhardt, Carl. *Zeus und Eros.* Briefe und Aufzeichnungen des Bildhauers Carl Burckhardt. Herausgeber Titus Burckhardt. Olten und Lausanne: Urs Graf Verlag, 1956.

Genet, Jean. *L'Atelier d'Alberto Giacometti.* In *Derrière le miroir,* No. 89, June 1957.

Giacometti, Alberto. *New York Museum of Modern Art: Alberto Giacometti.* New York: Museum of Modern Art, 1965.

Giedion-Welcker, Carola. *Bildinhalte und Ausdrucksmittel bei Paul Klee.* In *Werk,* Heft 3, 35. Jahrgang, März 1948.

Hodler, Ferdinand. *Leben, Werk und Nachlass.* Herausgegeben von C. A. Loosli. Bern: Verlag von R. Suter & Cie., 1921.

Jedlicka, Gotthard. *Max Gubler.* Frauenfeld: Verlag Huber & Co., 1970.

Klee, Paul. *Über die moderne Kunst.* Bern: Verlag Benteli, 1945.

Loetscher, Hugo (ed.). *Varlin.* Zürich: Verlag Die Arche, 1969.

Montandon, Marcel. *Segantini.* Bielefeld & Leipzig: Verlag von Velhagen & Klasing, 1904.

Morgenthaler, Ernst. *Ein Maler erzählt.* Aufsätze, Reiseberichte, Briefe. Zürich: Diogenes Verlag, 1957.

Neuburg, Hans, und Lohse, Ida Alis (ed.). *Richard P. Lohse.* Teufen: Verlag Arthur Niggli, 1962.

Nizon, Paul. *Friedrich Kuhn.* Zürich: Verlag "Um die Ecke" Silvio Riccardo Baviera, no date.

Selz, Peter. *Introductory Note.* In *New York Museum of Modern Art: Alberto Giacometti.* New York: Museum of Modern Art, 1965.

Töpffer, Rodolphe. *Die merkwürdigen Abenteuer des Malers Pencil.* Vorwort von Adolf Guggenbühl. Zürich: Schweizer Spiegel Verlag, 1935.

Wege und Experimente. 30 Junge Schweizer Künstler im Kunsthaus, Zürich, Januar 17–März 17, 1968.

Wölfflin, Heinrich. *Kleine Schriften.* Herausgeber Joseph Gantner. Basel: Benno Schwabe & Co., 1946.

Wyss, Bernhard. *Erinnerungen an Böcklin.* Nach gedruckten und ungedruckten Aufzeichnungen von Angela und Carlo Böcklin, Gottfried Keller, Albert Welty, Adolf Frey, u.a. Basel: Rhein-Verlag, 1921.

MUSIC TO SWISS EARS

Honegger, Arthur. *I Am a Composer.* Translated by Wilson Clough and Allan Arthur Willman. New York: St. Martin's Press, 1966.

Pahlen, Kurt. *Music of the World.* Translated by James Galston. New York: Crown Publishers Inc., 1949.

Schoeck, Othmar. *Festgabe der Freunde.* Herausgegeben von Willi Schuh. Erlenbach-Zürich: Eugen Rentsch Verlag, 1936.

Wagner, Richard. *Sein Leben in Briefen.* Leipzig: Breitkopf & Härtel, 1913.

Briefwechsel zwischen Wagner und Liszt. Leipzig: Breitkopf & Härtel, 1887.

THE THEATRE'S THE THING

Brock-Sulzer, Elisabeth. *Friedrich Dürrenmatt.* Lebensbild und Werkanalyse. Zürich: Verlag Die Arche, 1970.

Dürrenmatt, Friedrich. *Theaterschriften und Reden.* Herausgegeben von Elisabeth Brock-Sulzer. Zürich: Verlag Die Arche, 1966.

Theaterprobleme. Zürich: Verlag Die Arche, 1955.

Schiller. Eine Rede. Zürich: Verlag Die Arche, 1960.

Es steht geschrieben. Basel: Benno Schwabe & Co., 1947.

Frisch, Max. *Stücke.* Frankfurt a/M., Wien und Zürich: Büchergilde Gutenberg, 1962.

Tagebuch 1946–1949. Frankfurt a/M.: Suhrkamp Verlag, 1960.

Emigranten. In *Schauspielhaus Zürich* 1938/39–1958/59. Herausgeber: Kurt Hirschfeld und Peter Löffler. Zürich: Schauspielhaus Zürich, no date.

Wilhelm Tell für die Schule. Frankfurt a/M.: Suhrkamp Verlag, 1971.

Müller, Eugen. *Schweizer Theatergeschichte.* Ein Beitrag zur schweizer Kulturgeschichte. Zürich-New York: Verlag Oprecht, 1944.

Pinget, Robert. *Lettre Morte.* Paris: Les Éditions de Minuit, 1959.

La Manivelle. Paris: Les Éditions de Minuit, 1960.

Ramuz, Charles-Ferdinand. *Souvenir sur Igor Stravinsky.* Translated by Dollie Pierre Chareau. Lausanne: Mermod, 1946.

Volbach, Walther R. *Adolphe Appia. Prophet of the Modern Theatre.* Middletown, Conn.: Wesleyan University Press, 1968.

DANCE: Influences and Effects

Ingham, Percy B. *The Jacques-Dalcroze Method.* In *The Eurhythmics of Jaques-Dalcroze.* London: Constable & Co., 1912.

Kirstein, Lincoln. *The Book of the Dance.* New York: Garden City Publishing Co., 1942.

Nijinsky, Vaslav. *Diary.* Edited by Romola Nijinsky. Translated from the Russian by Romola Nijinsky, assisted by Jennifer Mattingly. New York: Simon and Schuster, 1936.

Pirchan, Emil. *Das Kreutzberg-Buch.* Stuttgart-Wien-Zürich: Wilhelm Frick Verlag, 1956.

Stravinsky, Igor. *Chronicle of My Life*. London: Victor Gollancz, 1936.

Susana Y José. *Spanischer Geist im Tanz*. Text Gerhard Zacharias. Gestaltung Haimo Lauth. Wien: Frick Verlag & Co., 1970.

ARCHITECTURE AND LANDSCAPE

Bill, Max. *Robert Maillart*. Translated by W. P. M. Keatinge Clay. New York: Frederick Praeger, 1969.

Clark, Kenneth. *Civilisation. A Personal View*. New York: Harper & Row, 1969.

Le Corbusier (Jeanneret-Gris, Charles Edouard). *Oeuvres complètes*. Zürich: Dr. H. Grisberger, 1939.

Neue Zürcher Zeitung. *Der bedrängte und überforderte Architekt*. July 12, 1970.

Smith, G. E. Kidder. *Switzerland Builds—Its Native and Modern Architecture*. New York and Stockholm: Albert Bonnier, 1950.

SOME CAME TO STAY
NECROPOLIS

Büchner, Georg. *Gesammelte Werke*. Zürich: Artemis Verlag, 1944.

Gheerbrant, Bernard. *James Joyce. Sa vie, son oeuvre, son rayonnement*. Paris: La Hune, 1949.

Gilbert, Stuart. *Letters of James Joyce*. London: Faber and Faber, no date.

Goethe, Johann Wolfgang von. *Gesammelte Werke*. Berlin: Verlag Ullstein, no date.

Mann, Thomas. *Thomas Mann-Hermann Hesse Briefwechsel*. Herausgegeben von Anni Carlsson. Frankfurt a/M.: Suhrkamp Verlag, 1968.

Rilke, Rainer Maria. *Briefe*. Wiesbaden: Insel Verlag, 1950.

Briefe an seinen Verleger, 1906–1926. Leipzig: Insel Verlag, 1934.

Rychner, Max. *Bedachte und bezeugte Welt*. Agora. Eine humanistische Schriftenreihe, Band 16. Hamburg: Marion von Schroeder, 1962.

Salis, J. R. von. *Rainer Maria Rilkes Schweizer Jahre*. Frauenfeld-Leipzig: Verlag von Huber & Co., 1936.

SOME CAME TO STAY
CASTALIA

Chaplin, Charlie. *My Autobiography*. London: William Clowes & Sons, Ltd., 1964.

Forel, Auguste. *Out of My Life and Work*. Translated by Bernard Miall. London: George Allen & Unwin, 1937.

Förster-Nietzsche, Elisabeth. *Das Leben Friedrich Nietzsches.* Leipzig: C. G. Naumann, 1897.

Heller, Erich. *The Disinherited Mind.* New York: Farrar, Straus and Cudahy, 1957.

Hesse, Hermann. *Wanderung.* Berlin: S. Fischer Verlag, 1922.

Die Eidgenossenschaft. In *Civitas Nova,* Lugano, 1938.

Briefe. Frankfurt a/M.: Suhrkamp Verlag, 1965.

Politische Betrachtungen. Ausgewählt von Siegfried Unseld. Frankfurt a/M.: Suhrkamp Verlag, 1970.

Gesammelte Werke. Frankfurt a/M.: Suhrkamp Verlag, 1970.

Hoffmann, Edith. *Kokoschka. Life and Work.* London: Faber and Faber, Ltd., 1947.

Kutscher, Artur. *Wedekind. Leben und Werk.* München: List Verlag, 1964.

Nietzsche, Friedrich. *Briefe an Peter Gast.* Herausgegeben von Peter Gast. Leipzig: Insel Verlag, 1924.

Nietzsches Briefwechsel mit Franz Overbeck. Leipzig: Insel Verlag, 1916.

Friedrich Nietzsche Werke. Herausgeben von Georgio Colli und Mazzino Montinari. Berlin: Walter de Gruyter & Co., 1958.

Aus dem Nachlass der Achtzigerjahre. München: Carl Hanser Verlag, 1956.

Podach, Erich. *Friedrich Nietzsche und Lou Salomé. Ihre Begegnung 1882.* Zürich und Leipzig: Max Niehaus Verlag, no date.

Simenon, Georges. *Pedigree.* Translated by Robert Baldick. London: Hamish Hamilton, 1962.

Würzbach, Friedrich. *Nietzsche.* Sein Leben in Selbstzeugnissen, Briefen und Berichten. Berlin: Propyläen Verlag, 1942.

SOME CAME TO STAY

SANCTUARY

Frisch, Max. *Brecht ist tot.* In *Die Weltwoche,* August 24, 1956.

Kohn, Hans. *Nationalism and Liberty.* London: George Allen & Unwin, 1956.

Leithäuser, Joachim G. *Er nannte sich Voltaire.* Stuttgart: Cotta Verlag, 1961.

Schaffroth, Paul. *Heinrich Zschokke als Politiker und Publizist während der Restauration und Regeneration.* In Argovia, Jahresschrift der historischen Gesellschaft des Kantons Aargau, vol. 61. Aarau: Sauerländer, 1949.

Silone, Ignazio. *Begegnungen mit Musil.* In *Forum,* Wien, Februar 1965.

Voltaire. *Oeuvres complètes de Voltaire.* Paris: Garnier Frères, 1880.

Zschokke, Heinrich. *Des Schweizerlands Geschichten für das Schweizer Volk.* Wien und Prag: In der Carl Haas'schen Buchhandlung, 1823. *Ausgenwählte Schriften.* Aargau: Reangus, 1830.

Zolling, Theophil. *Heinrich v. Kleist in der Schweiz.* Stuttgart: W. Spemann, 1882.

Zuckmayer, Carl. *A Part of Myself. Portrait of an Epoch.* Translated by Richard und Clara Winston. New York: A Helen und Kurt Wolff Book. Harcourt Brace Jovanovich, 1970.

SOME CAME TO SEE
FROM CELLINI TO KLEIST

Cellini, Benvenuto. *Autobiography.* Translated by Ann Macdonell. London: J. M. Dent & Sons, Ltd., 1907.

Goethe, Johann Wolfgang von. *Gesammelte Werke.* Berlin: Verlag Ullstein. No date.

Lessing, Gotthold Ephraim. *Litteraturbriefe.* In *Saemtliche Werke.* Stuttgart: J. G. Cotta'sche Buchhandlung und Gebrüder Kröner Verlagshandlung. No date.

Zolling, Theophil. *Heinrich v. Kleist in der Schweiz.* Stuttgart: W. Spemann, 1882.

SOME CAME TO SEE
A ROMANTIC VICTORIAN TREND

Addison, Joseph. *The Works of Joseph Addison.* London: George Bell and Sons, 1890.

Arnold, Matthew. *Poetical Works of Matthew Arnold.* London: New York: The Macmillan Company, 1929.

Belloc, Hilaire. *The Path to Rome.* London: George Allen, 1902.

Byron, Lord. *The Works of Lord Byron.* New York: Charles Scribner's Sons, 1905.

Dumas, Alexandre Père. *Adventures in Switzerland.* Translated by R. W. Pummer and A. Craig Bell. Philadelphia: Chilton Company, no date.

Goldsmith, Oliver. *The Works of Oliver Goldsmith.* London, New York: Harper & Brothers, 1900.

Maugham, Somerset W. *The Complete Short Stories.* New York: Doubleday & Co. Garden City, 1932.

Morse, John T. *Life and Letters of Oliver Wendell Holmes.* Boston and New York: Houghton, Mifflin and Company, 1896.

Ruskin, John. *The Works of John Ruskin.* Edited by E. T. Cook and Alexander Wedderburn. London: George Allen, 1904.

Shelley, Percy Bysshe. *The Complete Works of Percy Bysshe Shelley.* London: Oxford University Press, 1961.

Stevenson, Robert Louis. *Essays of Travel.* New York: Charles Scribner's Sons, 1907.

Twain, Mark. *A Tramp Abroad.* New York and London: Harper & Brothers, 1879.

Wordsworth, Dorothy. *Journals of Dorothy Wordsworth.* Edited by E. de Selincourt. New York: The Macmillan Company, 1941.

SOME CAME TO SEE

STRINDBERG AND TOLSTOI

Erdman, Nils. *August Strindberg.* Berechtigte Übertragung von Heinrich Goebel. Leipzig: H. Haessel Verlag, 1924.

Tolstoi, Leo N. *Sämtliche Erzählungen.* Frankfurt a/M.: Insel Verlag, 1961.

CODA

Ball, Hugo. *Die Flucht aus der Zeit.* München-Leipzig: Duncker & Humblot, 1927.

Bichsel, Peter. *Des Schweizers Schweiz.* Zürich: Verlag Die Arche, 1969.

Bill, Max. *Das Behagen im Kleinstaat.* In *Erneuern und beharren.* Bern: Jahrbuch der Neuen Helvetischen Gesellschaft, 1970.

Frisch, Max. *Andorra.* Frankfurt a/M.: Suhrkamp Verlag, 1961.

Lüthy, Herbert. *Die Schweiz als Antithese.* Zürich: Verlag Die Arche, 1969.

Marti, Kurt. *Die Schweiz und ihre Schriftsteller—die Schriftsteller und ihre Schweiz.* Zürich: Evangelische Zeitbuchreihe, 1966.

Nizon, Paul. *Diskurs in der Enge.* Bern: Kandelaber Verlag, 1970.

Salis, J. R. von. *Schwierige Schweiz.* Zürich: Orell Füssli Verlag, 1968. *Switzerland and Europe. Essays and Reflections.* Selected essays from *Schwierige Schweiz* and *Im Laufe der Jahre.* Translated by Alexander and Elizabeth Henderson. London: Oswald Wolff, 1971.

INDEX

Aarau Gymnasium, 49, 228
Addison, Joseph, 254
Adler, Alfred, 68
Adlischweiler, Anna, 9
Adolphe, 84-85
Aeschbacher, Hans, 142
Aim of Education, The, 40
Aimé Pache, 90
Albers, Josef, 125, 139
Alice in Wonderland, 99, 132
All Quiet on the Western Front, 234
Alpen, Die, 102
Alps, 128, 131, 135, 238, 253
Amerbach, Boniface, 4-5
Amiel, Henri-Frédéric, 84-89, 113
Amiet, Cuno, 137, 139
Ammann, Othmar Hermann, 201-202
Anabaptists, 7-8, 11, 12
Andorra, 176, 277
Andreae, Volkmar, 158
Annalen der Physik, 50
Ansermet, Ernest, 150, 184
Anshelm, Valerius, 59
Anthroposophy, 42
Apollinaire, Guillaume, 125
Appenzell, 14, 47, 197, 267
Appia, Adolphe, 165, 169-171
Aquinas, Thomas, 22
Arch of Triumph, 235
Arnold, Gustav, 153
Arnold, Matthew, 88, 254
Arp, Jean (Hans), 135-136
Art and Revolution, 156
Artaud, Antonin, 137, 170

Arx, Caesar von, 243
Ascona, 181, 188-190, 234, 278
Association du Ballet de la Jeunesse Romande, 183
Attention: Switzerland, 120
Auberjonois, René, 138, 184, 185
Augusta Rauracorum, xv
Ausdruckstanz, 181, 190-191

Bachofen, Johann Jakob, 44-45
Bakunin, Mikhail, 243
Balanchine, George, 181
Ball, Hugo, 135, 213, 234, 278-279
Balthasar, Hans von, 15-16
Baroque, 37-39
Barrès, Auguste Maurice, 85
Barth, Karl, 3, 16, 19, 20-22, 225
Basle, xiv, 3, 4, 6, 8, 10, 11, 20, 22, 31, 32, 33, 36, 38, 39, 42, 43, 51, 56, 61, 64, 66, 67, 129, 132-134, 151, 161, 170, 178, 182, 197, 210, 225, 226, 230, 241, 246, 251
Bauhaus, 140
Beauty, xv, 16, 31, 56, 95, 129, 199, 200, 221, 247-248, 252-259, 276, 277, 279, 280
Beckett, Samuel, 172
Beethoven, Ludwig van, 43, 158
Bellinzona, 94
Belloc, Hilaire, 254-255
Bellow, Saul, 270
Benn, Johannes, 151
Berger, Jaroslav, 182
Bergman, Ingrid, 164
Beriozoff, Nicholas, 181, 182
Berleth, Ludwig, 234

Berne, xiii, xiv, 3, 4, 6, 8, 10, 11, 24, 50, 51, 57, 59, 72, 103, 127, 128, 132, 161, 192, 191, 197, 210, 220, 221, 234, 251, 252, 254
Berner Chronik, 59
Bernoulli, Daniel, 53
Bernoulli, Jakob, 53
Bernoulli, Jean, 51, 53
Bernoulli, Maria, 221
Bernoulli, Nicolas, 53
Beromünster, 43
Bianconi, Piero, 93
Bibliotheca universalis, 60
Bibliotheque de mon oncle, La, 132
Bichsel, Peter, 116-117, 268, 273
Bildungsroman, 106
Bill, Max, vii, 125, 134, 140-141, 145, 201, 272-273
Billeter, Erika, vii
Binswanger, Ludwig, 76
Bismarck, Otto Prince von, 32, 228
Blake, William, 131
Blaurock, Georg, 7
Bleuler, Eugen, 67-68, 74-75, 186
Bloch, Ernest, 150, 163
Böcklin, Arnold, 129-130
Bodmer, Hans C., 220
Bodmer, Johann Georg, 57
Bodmer, Johann Jakob, 103, 130, 250
Body and Soul, 40
Bonhoeffer, Dietrich, 19
Borromini, Francesco, 198
Boss, Medard, 76
Brahms, Johannes, 154, 158, 160
Brant, Sebastian, 246
Bread and Wine, 236
Brecht, Bertolt, 122, 168-169, 175, 176, 179, 237, 241, 243
Breitinger, J. J., 103, 130
Brock-Sulzer, Elisabeth, vii, 101, 175
Brun, Fritz, 158
Brunner, Emil, 20
Brunner, Johann Conrad, 59
Buber, Martin, 16

Büchner, Georg, 206-208
Bullinger, Heinrich, 3, 8-9
Bülow, Cosima von, 155, 158
Bülow, Hans von, 156, 158
Burckhardt, Carl, 141
Burckhardt, Carl Jacob, 45-47
Burckhardt, Jacob, 3, 23, 31-39, 113, 129-130, 210, 225
Burckhardt, Johann Ludwig, 64-65
Burckhardt, Louise, 32
Burckhardt, Lucius, 120
Bure, Idelette de, 11
Burgdorf, 26, 150
Bürgi, Joost, 53-54
Burkart, Erika, 123-126
Burkhard, Willy, 159, 161
Busch, Wilhelm, 131
Busoni, Ferrucio, 154-155
Byron, Lord, George Gordon, 82, 257-258

Cabaret Voltaire, 135-136, 213, 216
Calder, Alexander, 142
Calderon, Pedro de la Barca, 15, 166
Calvin, John, 9-13
Calvinism, 5, 9-13, 21, 30, 86, 238
Camus, Albert, 98, 113
Candide, 238, 245
Canto, 118-119
Capote, Truman, 232
Carol, Hans, 70
Carroll, Lewis, 99
Cassat, Mary, 271
Castalia, 220-236
Castelli, Carlo, 97
Cata, Alfonso, 181
Catherine I, Empress of Russia, 52
Catherine II, Empress of Russia, 237-238
Catholicism, 3, 4, 12, 13-17
Cellini, Benvenuto, 246
Cendrars, Blaise, 89
CERN, 58
Cezanne, Paul, 90, 145
Challenges, 112
Chaplin, Charles, 231-233

Charles Augustus, Duke, 247
Chasen, Alexander, vii
Chiesa, Francesco, 94-95
Child's Conception of Time, The, 76
Chillon, 258
China, 223
Chinese Wall, The, 176, 177
Chladek, Rosalia, 182
Chresthomatie, 17
Christianity, xiv, 3, 35, 39, 260, 272
Chronicon Helveticum, 41
Church Dogmatics, 20, 22
Cingria, Charles-Albert, 89, 184
Civilisation, 198
Civilization of the Renaissance in Italy, The, 33
Clairmont, Claire, 257
Clarity and Certainty of the Word of God, The, 6
Clark, Kenneth, 198
Claudel, Paul, 16
Cocteau, Jean, 91, 115
Codex Manesse, 107
Collins, William, 255
Commander, Pastor, 15
Commentary on the Psalms, 10
Commentary on Romans, 20, 21
Commercialism, 13, 35
Communism, 72, 73, 268, 272, 278
Confession, A, 88
Conservatism, xiii, 3, 4, 32
Constant, Benjamin, 79, 82-85, 88
Constellations, 125
Contacts, 46
Cop, Michel, 10
Cop, Nicholas, 10
Copeau, Jacques, 169
Coppet, 81-84
Corbusier, Le, 196, 199-201, 271
Corinne, 81
Corti, Walter Robert, 48
Cosmic Liturgy, 16
Courvoisier, Walter, 158
Coward, Noel, 233
Cox, Harvey, 20

Craig, Gordon, 169
Curchod, Suzanne, 79-81

Dadaism, 125, 134-136, 142, 213, 216, 278
Dalcroze, Emile Jacques-, 153, 159, 170, 181, 186-188, 189, 190
Danzig, 46
De L'Allemagne, 81, 84
Dead Letter, 171-172
Decurtius, Caspar, 17
Della Casa, Lisa, 150
Delphine, 81
Derleth, Ludwig, 205, 278
Devin du village, Le, 152, 153
Deyverdun, Georges, 79
Diaghilev, Serge, 150, 170, 184, 185
Diaries (Frisch), 177
Diary of a Reader, 112
Diderot, Denis, 152, 238
Difficulties with the Arts, 112
Diggelmann, Walter Matthias, 18, 117-118
Dimitri, 194
Diocletian, Emperor, 15
Discomfort in a Small State, 112
Disinherited Mind, The, 224-225
Doctor Faustus, 104, 218
Dornach, 42
Dos Passos, John, 270
Du, 47
Ducloux, Walter, 150
Dumas, Alexandre Père, 258-259
Dumont, Etienne, 267
Dunant, Jean Henry, 65-66
Dürer, Albrecht, 133
Dürrenmatt, Friedrich, 3, 23, 96, 100-102, 114, 145, 165, 172-180, 273

Ebeling, Gerhard, 19-20
Eggeling, Viking, 135
Einsiedeln, 6, 15, 60, 166
Einstein, Albert, 49-51, 53
Eliot, T.S., 271
Elizabeth I, Queen, 9

Émile, 28, 29, 30
Engelberg, 14, 15
Engels, Friedrich, 168, 242
Enlightenment, Age of, 29
Epstein, Jacob, 271
Eranos, 278
Erasmus, Desiderius, 4-5, 39, 133, 134, 246
Erastus, Thomas. *See* Lüber
Ernst, Fritz, 26
Euler, Leonhard, 51-53
Eurhythmics, 42, 186-188
Evening Hour of a Hermit, The, 26
Existentialism, 87, 96, 175, 206
Existenzphilosophie, 39

Faesi, Robert, 243
Farel, Guillaume, 11, 12
Farner, Konrad, 18-19
Fastnachtsspiele, 166
Fichte, Johann Gottlieb, 28
Figaro, Le, 108
Filippini, Enrico, 97-99
Filippini, Fellici, 93
Fitzgerald, F. Scott, 271
Florence, 34
Föhn, 70, 168, 255
Fokine, Michel, 181
Fontana, Domenico, 198
Forel, Auguste, 233-234
Forge, Étienne de la, 10
Franklin, Benjamin, 228, 240
Frau Blum Wants to Meet the Milkman, 116
Frederick the Great, 53, 237
Frederick William IV, 242
Freiligrath, Ferdinand, 105
Fremdenpolizei, 236, 243
Frémont, General John C., 63
French Revolution, 80, 81, 267
Freud, Sigmund, 66, 68, 69, 71, 74, 75, 108
Fribourg, 56
Frisch, Max, vii, xiv, 23, 56, 89, 97, 100-102, 113, 114, 120, 165, 167-

Frisch, Max—(*cont.*)
168, 172-180, 237, 265, 269, 275-276, 277
Fröbe-Kapteyn, Mrs. O., 278
from the diary, 126
Frühlingserwachen, 229
Füssli, Johann Heinrich (Fuseli, Henry), 130-131

Gaienhofen, 221
Galen, Claudius, 61
Gallia comata, 41
Ganz, Rudolf, 150
Gast, Peter, 227
Gauguin, Paul, 138
Gautier, Théophile, 87
Gegenbach, Pamphilus, 165-166
Genet, Jean, 148
Geneva, xiv, 10, 11, 12, 30, 46, 57, 58, 64, 65, 66, 77, 80, 131, 132, 142, 150, 151, 162, 165, 171, 181, 186, 197, 205, 209, 210, 233, 234, 237, 238, 239, 252, 260, 267, 275, 276, 277
George, Stefan, 205
Geschichtslosigkeit, xiv
Gessner, Conrad, 60
Gessner, Solomon, 103, 154
Giacometti, Alberto, 138, 148-149
Giacometti, Giovanni, 138, 148
Gibbon, Edward, 79-80
Giedion, Siegfried, 196
Giedion-Welcker, Carola, 137, 214
Gilliard, Edmond, 89
Giono, Jean, 93
Girolano, Aleandro, 5
Glances into the Being of Man, 43
Glarner, Fritz, 145-146
Glasperlenspiel, Das, 223, 278
Gluck, Christoph Willibald, 152, 156
Godwin, Mary, 257
Goethe, Johann Wolfgang von, 41, 43, 103, 108, 127, 131, 160, 174, 205, 206, 247-249

Goethe's Conception of the World, 42

Goetz, Hermann, 158

Goldsmith, Oliver, 256

Gomringer, Eugen, 123, 125-126

Goncourt Journals, The, 87

Gotthelf, Jeremias, 23, 100, 102-105, 107, 139

Gottsched, Johann Christoph, 249-250

Grass, Günter, 97, 160

Great World Theatre, The, 15

Grebel, Conrad, 7

Green Henry, 106, 113

Grisons, xiv, 197

Grock, 182, 193-195

Gropius, Walter, 196

Gross, Jean, 229

Gross, Walter, 275

Grosz, George, 144

Gstaad, 153-154

Guardian of the Center, The, 71

Gubler, Max, 147-148

Guerre des Bouffons, 152, 156

Guggenheim, Willy, 144-145

Guisan, Henri, 72, 73

Günther, Werner, 109

Gutzkow, Karl, 206

Habe, Hans, 234

Häberlin, Paul, 27, 40

Haller, Albrecht von, 102

Haller, Heinrich, 141-142

Haug, Hans, 160

Hauptmann, Carl, 228-289

Hauptmann, Gerhart, 207, 228-229

Hauser, Arnold, 37

Hegar, Friedrich, 153

Heidegger, Martin, 39, 76

Heidi, 99-100

Heller, Erich, 224-225

Hemingway, Ernest, 235, 271

Herrmann, Wilhelm, 20

Herwegh, Georg, 105, 242

Hesse, Heiner, vii

Hesse, Hermann, 39, 139, 160, 215-219, 220-224, 234, 277

Hirschfeld, Kurt, 178

Hirschi, Samuel, vii

Histoire du Soldat, L', 169, 185

History of the Decline and Fall of the Roman Empire, The, 79-80

History of Religion, 84

Hitler, Adolf, 72, 113, 179, 215, 234, 236, 243

Hochwälder, Fritz, 237

Hodler, Ferdinand, 127-128, 137, 139

Hofmannsthal, Hugo von, 46, 166

Hohl, Ludwig, 114-115

Holbein, Hans, 133-134

Holmes, Oliver Wendell, 252-253

Honegger, Arthur, 150, 151, 163-164

Horwitz, Kurt, 178

How Gertrude Teaches Her Children, 27

Huber, Hans, 153, 159

Huber, Klaus, 161

Hugo, Victor, 29

Huguenots, 57

Huizinga, Johann, 33

Hülsenbeck, Richard, 135

Humanism, 3, 4, 5, 35

Humboldt, Alexander von, 67

Hume, David, 31

Humor, 192-195

I Am a Composer, 164

Identity, xiii, 100, 245, 270

Imago, 108

Industrial Revolution, 17, 36

Infallible? An Inquiry, 16

Inglin, Meinrad, 111

Inhelder, B., 76

Institutes of the Christian Religion, 10, 11

Institutiones calculi differentialis, 52

Institutiones calculi integralis, 52

Instruction in Faith, 11

Introductio in analysin infinitorum, 52

Isolation, xiii, xv, 119, 210, 224, 231, 234

Italian Switzerland Today, 93

Jacobi, Jolande, vii, 69, 73, 74

Jahrbuch für psychologische und psychopathologische Forschungen, 68

Jakob von Gunten, 110

James, Henry, 105, 271

Janet, Pierre, 67

Jaspers, Karl, 39, 261

Jean-Richard, Daniel, 57

Jedlicka, Gotthard, 147

Jenatsch, Jörg, 15

Jenni, Adolfo, 95, 96

Jesus of Nazareth, 21

John XXIII, Pope, 22

Johnson, Uwe, 97

Jooss, Kurt, 190

Journal intime, 84, 86, 88, 113

Journey in Minor Asia, 45

Jovanovits, Mara, 183

Joyce, James, 117, 205, 212-215

Jung, Carl Gustav, 58, 66-71, 73-74, 174, 278

Jura, xiii, 238

Kafka, Franz, 110, 117, 144, 161

Kaiser, Georg, 205

Kamer, Paul, vii

Kandinsky, Vassily, 136, 140

Kappel, 8

Kaufmann, Angelika, 271

Keate, George, 255

Keller, Gottfried, 23, 71, 100, 105-107, 109, 113, 130, 160, 267

Kelterborn, Rudolf, 160

Kepler, Johannes, 53

Kerényi, Karl, 278

Kierkegaard, Sören, 21

Kinderdorf Pestalozzi. *See* Pestalozzi Village

Kinkel, Gottfried, 33

Kirstein, Lincoln, 188

Klee, Paul, 134, 136-137, 139, 140, 161

Kleist, Heinrich von, 251-252

Klimt, Gustav, 127

Klopstock, Friedrich Gottlieb, 103, 250

Knox, John, 13

Kocher, Theodor, 58

Koegler, Horst, 182

Kohlund, Erwin, 166

Kokoschka, Oskar, 144, 233-234

Korrodi, Eduard, 111

Kramer, Hilton, 136

Kraus, Karl, 259

Kreutzberg, Harald, 190-191

Kuhn, Friedrich, 144

Kultur der Renaissance in Italien, Die, 33

Küng, Hans, 16-17

Küsnacht, 69, 216

Kutter, Markus, 120-121

Laban, Rudolf, 136, 189-190

Lagrange, J. L., 51

Lamartine, Alphonse de, 259

Lang, Max, 182

Lausanne, xiv, 30, 77, 79, 82, 152, 153, 185, 196, 211, 214, 228, 238

Lavater, Johann Kaspar, 130, 206

Lawrence, D. H., 230

Le Figaro, 108

Le Locle, 57

Lear, Edward, 131

Lectures on Painting, 131

Legacy, The, 18, 117

Leibnitz, Gottfried Wilhelm von, 53

Lejeune, Robert, 236

Lenin, Vladimir Ilyich, 72, 206, 213, 242

Lenzburg, 228, 260

Leo XIII, Pope, 17

Leonard and Gertrude, 26

Lessing, Ephraim Gotthold, 103, 251

Let My Name Be Gantenbein, 100

Lettres à une Princesse d'Alle-magne, 52
Levinson, André, 188
Liebermann, Rolf, 150, 161-162
Liehburg, Max Eduard, 71
Liszt, Franz, 155
Locarno, 56, 94, 99, 136, 137, 153, 198, 205, 211, 213
Loetscher, Hugo, vii, 120, 121-123
Lohse, Richard Paul, 139-140, 146-147
Lolita, 230
Lonesome Dialogue, 16
Loos, Adolf, 233, 234
Losch, Tilly, 190
Loyola, Ignatius, 16
Lüber, Thomas, 5, 6
Lucerne, 43, 134, 153, 155, 210, 225, 228, 257, 259, 262-264
Lucian, 8
Ludwig II, King of Bavaria, 155
Lugano, 94, 220, 277
Lüginbuhl, Bernhard, 142
Luther, Martin, 4-5, 9, 13, 19
Lüthy, Herbert, xi, 272

Macke, Hans, 182
McLuhan, Marshall, 270
McLure, William, 28
Maderno, Carlo, 198
Maeder, A., 68
Magnificence, 16
Maillart, Robert, 201
Malraux, André, 113
Manesse, Rüdiger, 107
Mann, Erika, 216
Mann, Thomas, 104, 194, 205, 215-220, 244
Manuel, Niklaus, 59, 132-133, 166
Manz, Felix, 7
Marat, Jean Paul, 267
Marceau, Marcel, 194
Marti, Kurt, 18, 116-117, 268
Martin, Frank, 150, 151, 162-163
Martin, John, 188
Martini, Plinio, 97

Maternal Right, The, 44
Maugham, Somerset, 259
Maximilian I, 247, 266
Mechanism of Perception, The, 76
Mehring, Walter, 234, 244
Meier, Herbert, 119-120
Meister, Hans, 183-184
Memories, Dreams and Reflections, 74
Menuhin, Yehudi, 154
Mercier, Fanny, 86, 87, 88
Mercier, Jean, 169
Mercure de France, 152
Meyer, Conrad Ferdinand, 107-108, 112-113, 130, 165
Middle Ages, 34, 41, 55, 56, 60, 65
Miller, Arthur, 270
Milton, John, 131, 250
Minkowski, Hermann, 50
Moholy-Nagy, Laszlo, 142
Moilliet, Louis René, 139
Mondrian, Piet, 139, 140, 145, 150
Mont Blanc, 64, 132, 257, 276
Moraine, 123-125
Moréas, Jean, 108
Morgenthaler, Ernst, 139
Morgenthaler, Hans, 273
Moser, Werner, 199
Mozart, Wolfgang Amadeus, 16, 154, 271
Müller, Johannes von, 41
Müller, Paul, 158
Muschg, Walter, 112
Musil, Robert, 205, 236, 237
Mussolini, Benito, 72, 236
Muzot, 210-212
My Autobiography (Chaplin), 231

Nabokov, Vladimir, 230-231
Napoleon, 15, 81, 82, 94, 169, 239, 241, 247, 251, 258, 267
Narrow-itis, 114, 119, 161, 265, 268-273
Natural History of Switzerland, 60
Nazism, 22, 39, 51, 53, 71, 72, 73, 113, 179, 205, 223, 234

Nebelspalter, Der, 193
Necker, Jacques, 80, 84
Nessi, Angelo, 93
Neuburg, Hans, vii
Neuchâtel, 11, 30, 31, 77, 109, 257
Neue Wege, 17
Neue Zürcher Zeitung, 71, 95, 111, 158, 199, 216, 219, 229
New Story-Tellers from the Ticino, 93-100
Newton, Sir Isaac, 49
New York, 146, 202, 270
New York Times, The, 13, 136
Nietzsche, Friedrich, 33, 109, 129, 224-228
Nijinska, Bronislava, 185
Nijinsky, Vaslav, 185-188
Nizon, Paul, 118-119, 144, 269, 270
Nobel Prize, 58, 66, 108
Noces, Les, 92
Nolde, Emil, 189

Oecolampadius, John, 4
Olympian Spring, 109
On Life and Its Problem, 43
On the Psychology and Pathology of So-called Occult Phenomena, 67
Opera and Drama, 156
Oppenheim, Meret Elisabeth, 144
Orelli, Giorgio, 97
Orlikowsky, Waszlaw, 181, 182
Orwell, George, 32, 235
Out of My Life and Work, 233-234
Overbeck, Franz, 225, 227

Pahlen, Kurt, vii
Panne, Die, 101, 102
Paracelsus (Theophrastus Bombastus von Hohenheim), 43, 58, 60-62
Parents and Children, 40
Paris, 77, 80, 89, 127, 138, 139, 152, 163, 183, 210, 237, 242, 251, 260, 270, 271
Part of Myself, A, 243

Péguy, Charles, 16
People of Seldwyla, The, 106
Pestalozzi, Heinrich, 3, 23, 25-28, 29, 40, 43, 47, 78, 153
Pestalozzi Village, 48
Philosophy of Spiritual Activity, The, 42
Physiognomic Fragments, 249
Piaget, Jean, 76-78
Picasso, Pablo, xiv
Pinget, Robert, 171-172
Piscator, Erwin, 168
Poetry as a Means in Shaping the Environment, 126
Polgar, Alfred, 205
Portnoy's Complaint, 84
Porto Ronco, 234-236
Pound, Ezra, 113, 213, 271
Prague, 51, 53
Preen, Friedrich von, 32
Principles of Art History, 37-39
Prisoner of Chillon, 258
Prometheus and Epimetheus, 109
Promise, The, 102
Psychologie der Weltanschauungen, 39
Psychology of Intelligence, The, 76
Punitive Work, 119

Quatrains Valaisans, 212

Rachmaninoff, Sergei, 130
Ragaz, Leonhard, 17
Rambach, Miriam (Dame Marie Rambert), 186-188
Ramuz, Charles-Ferdinand, 89-93, 168-169, 184, 185
Rauschenbach, Emma, 69
Rauschenberg, Robert, 143
Read, Herbert, 184
Recherches chimiques sur la végétation, 64
Red Cross, 46, 72, 275
Rée, Paul, 228
Reflections and Nuances, 115
Reformation, 3-6, 8-10, 12-14, 132, 151, 246

Refuge, xiv, xv, 155, 179, 184-186, 205-220, 230-235, 236-245
Reign of the Evil One, The, 91
Reinhard, Anna, 7
Reinhardt, Max, 190
Reinhart, Werner, 211
Remarque, Erich Maria, 234-236
Renaissance, xiii, 3, 13, 33-39, 41, 53, 56, 58, 60, 102, 108, 113, 132, 134, 181, 198
Renaissance and Baroque, 37
Reston, James, 13
Reucker, Alfred, 229
Reynolds, Sir Joshua, 130
Richelieu, 46
Richter, Hans, 135
Rilke, Rainer Maria, 45, 47, 128, 205, 208-212, 224, 225, 227
Ring of the Nibelung, The, 156-158
Robbe-Grillet, Alain, 171
Rodin, Auguste, 205
Rolland, Romain, 108, 213, 222, 223, 243
Romans, xiv, xv, 15, 34, 45, 198
Romansh, xiv, 93
Romanticism, 29, 31, 32, 41, 43, 81, 82, 130, 222, 252-259, 273
Romeo and Juliet in the Village, 106
Rorschach, Hermann, 75-76
Rosen, Heinz, 182
Roth, Alfred, vii, 196, 199
Roth, Daniel, vii
Roth, Philip, 84
Rousseau, Didier, 30
Rousseau, Jean-Jacques, 23, 28-31, 80, 103, 127, 151-153, 257, 260, 261, 279
Ruggiero, Paul, 214
Ruskin, John, 37, 253-254
Rütli, 73, 130, 167-168, 266, 268, 269
Rychner, Max, 111, 205

Saas-Fee, 244-245
Sacher, Paul, 151
Sachs, Hans, 246

Sachs, Dr. Hanns, 108
Sacramento, 63
Saint-Exupéry, Antoine, 113
Salis, Jean Rudolph von, 210, 265, 273-274, 275
Salomé, Lou, 227-228
Salzburg, 61, 162, 166
Samson, Bernhard, 6
Sankt Gallen, 7, 8, 14, 56, 151, 156, 165, 210, 232
Sankt Moritz, 128, 185-186
Sartre, Jean-Paul, 98, 149
Sattler, Michael, 8
Saussure, Horace-Bénédict de, 64
Saussure, Nicolas-Theodore, 64
Scenery, xv, 31, 197, 199-201, 247-248, 250, 252-259, 276, 277
Schaffner, Jakob, 113
Schäppi, Max, vii
Schérer, Edmond, 87-88
Scheuchzer, Johann Jakob, 59-60
Schibler, Armin, 161
Schifferli, Peter, vii, 175
Schiller, Friedrich, 103, 165, 167, 174, 219, 249
Schleiermacher, Friedrich, 19, 20
Schmid, Karl, 112-113
Schoeck, Othmar, 150, 159-160
Schoeck, Paul, 167
Schönemann, Lili, 247-248
Schoop, Paul, 194
Schoop, Trudi, 182, 194-195
Schopenhauer, Arthur, 157, 232
Schulz, Caroline, 208
Schulz, Wilhelm Friedrich, 208
Schwarzenbach, James, 56
Schwyz, 8, 197, 267
Secular City, The, 20
Segantini, Giovanni, 128-129
Self-criticism, 193, 265, 277
Senfl, Ludwig, 151
Servetus, Michael, 12-13
Seven Legends, 107
Shaw, George Bernard, 171, 175
Shelley, Percy Bysshe, 257
Ship of Fools, The, 246

Silone, Ignazio, 236-237
Sils Maria, 224, 227
Simenon, Georges, 231
Sixty-Seven Articles, 7
Social Contract, 29
Social History of Art, The, 37
Solferino, 65
Sonnets to Orpheus, 212
Souvenir de Solférino, Un, 65
Souvenirs sur Igor Stravinsky, 91
Space, Time and Architecture, 197
Spiritual Heritage of Switzerland, 111
Spitteler, Carl, 72, 108-109, 165
Spoerri, Daniel, 143
Spyri, Johanna, 99-100
Stadler, Edmund, vii
Staël-Holstein, Baron Eric de, 82
Staël, Mme. Germaine de, 79, 81-84, 239
Stämpfli, Peter, 146
Stauffer, Karl, 141
Steiger, Robert, 59
Steinbeck, John, 179, 270
Steiner, Jörg, 119
Steiner, Rudolf, 39, 41-42, 44
Steppenwolf, The, 220, 222
Stevenson, Robert Louis, 255
Strasbourg, 11
Stravinsky, Igor, 91-92, 150-151, 154, 168-169, 184-185
Strindberg, August, 259-262
Strindberg and Van Gogh, 261
Studies in Word-Association, 67-68
Susana, 191-192
Suter, Hermann, 159-160
Sutermeister, Heinrich, 160
Sutter, John Augustus, 62-63
Swan Song, 28
Sweeney, James Johnson, 214
Swiss Alp, 249
Swiss Literary Letters, 111
Switzerdütsch, xiv
Switzerland as Antithesis, xi, 272
Switzerland Censured, 273

Szeminska, A., 76
Szondi, Leopold, 76

Taeuber, Sophie, 135-136
Tell, Wilhelm, 71, 127, 166-168, 249, 265, 268
Temps, Le, 87
Tennyson, Alfred Lord, 259
Terpis, Max, 190
Theology of Crisis, 20
Thiers, Adolphe, 275
Three Old Women in a Mountain Village, The, 115
Thun, 251-252
Thurber, James, 131
Ticino, 93-99, 189, 194, 198, 216, 220-221, 224, 266, 274, 277, 278, 279
Tinguely, Charles, 142-143
Tolstoi, Leo, 88, 262-264
Töpffer, Rodolphe, 131, 193
Topi, Guilio, 94
Tourism, 55, 199
Towards an Architecture, 200
Trial of Harry Wind, The, 118
Triebschen, 155-158, 225, 226
Trieste, 212, 214
Tristan and Isolde, 157
Trogen, 47-48
Trotzky, Leon, 242
Troxler, Ignaz Paul Vital, 43-44
Truthfulness, 16
Tschudy, Aegidius, 41, 167
Tudor, Mary, 9
Twain, Mark, 192, 259
Tzara, Tristan, 135

Udaeta, José, 191
Uhl, Frieda, 259, 260
Uli, the Farmhand, 104
Ulm, 49
Ulysses, 213
Unterwalden, 8
Uri, 8
Usteri, Paul, 59

Vadian, Joachim, 14
Valéry, Paul, 212
Valle, Martino della, 97
Valloton, Félix, 138
Van Gogh, Vincent, 138, 145, 261
Varlin. *See* Willy Guggenheim
Venice, 35, 56-57
Vienna, 43, 46
Vinci, Leonardo da, 133, 161, 273
Vindonissa, xv
Vischer, Wilhelm, 225
Visit, The, 175
Vogel, Traugott, 111
Völkerwanderung, xiv
Vollenweider, Alice, 93
Voltaire, François Marie Arouet, 29, 152, 226, 237-239, 261, 275
Vuilleumier, Jean-Pierre, vii
Vuilleumier, Ruth, vii

Wagner, Richard, 129, 155-158, 170, 225-226
Waiting for Godot, 172
Waldshut, 8
Walser, Karl, 110, 142
Walser, Robert, 109-111, 117, 269, 271
Walter, Silja, 166
Wälterlin, Oskar, 169, 170
Wanderung, 220
Warhol, Andy, 142
Waste Water, 121-122
Weaver, Harriet Shaw, 213
Weber, Heinrich, 50
Weber, Werner, vii, 96, 111-112
Wedekind, Frank, 207, 228-230, 242, 259-260
Wedekind, Tilly, 230
Weltwoche, Die, 273, 275
Werfel, Franz, 244
Wermelinger, Max, 93, 95
Wesendonck, Mathilde, 155, 157
West, Penny, vii
When the Mountain Fell, 90
Whitehead, Robert, 49

Wieland, Christoph Martin, 103, 250-251
Wiggli, Oscar, 142
Wigman, Mary, 188-191
Wilder, Thorton, 121, 175, 179, 270, 271
Winckelmann, Johann Joachim, 130
Winterthur, 36, 50, 210
Wölfflin, Heinrich, 36-39, 129, 196
Wölflin, Heinrich, 6
Word and Faith, 19
Wordsworth, Dorothy, 256
Wordsworth, William, 255-256
Wreath Winder, The, 122-123
Wright, Frank Lloyd, 196
Wunderly-Volkart, Nanny, 210
Wundt, Wilhelm, 74, 75
Wydler-Roth, Irene, vii

Yverdon, 26, 28

Zarathustra, 224
Zehnder, Dr. Ulrich, Mayor, 208
Zen, 224
Zentralblatt für Psychotherapie, 71
Zollikon, 7
Zschokke, Heinrich, 239-242, 251-252
Zuckmayer, Carl, 46-47, 179, 243-245
Zug, 8, 197
Zürcher Schauspielhaus, 179
Zürich, 7-9, 25-26, 36, 38, 46, 50, 56-57, 59, 67, 72, 74, 102, 107, 130, 134, 135, 141-142, 146, 151, 155, 158, 161, 165, 178, 179, 186, 190, 194, 197, 200, 202, 205-209, 213-215, 218, 228-230, 244, 246, 247, 270, 277
Zürich Carolinum, 26
Züricher Novellen, 106-107
Zweig, Stefan, 213
Zwingli, Huldrych, 3-5, 5-9, 12, 14, 15, 151